ON AND OFF BROADWAY

A Theater/Dining/Lodging Guide To

New York City

**OTHER TRAVEL GUIDES FOR THEATER ENTHUSIASTS
BY SHARON WATSON:**

■   Dining in London's Theatreland: A Theatre/Dining Guide to London

■   Ontario for Theatre Lovers: A Theatre/Dining/Lodging Guide to Toronto, Niagara-on-the-Lake, and Stratford

MONTHLY NEWSLETTER BY SHARON WATSON:

■   On and Off Broadway: A Monthly Theater/Dining Guide to New York City

For further information, contact

Britain Books
P.O. Box 66005
Washington, DC 20035-6005

301/858-6213

ON AND OFF BROADWAY

A Theater/Dining/Lodging Guide To

New York City

by

Sharon Watson

BRITAIN BOOKS

ON AND OFF BROADWAY
A Theater/Dining/Lodging Guide to New York City

Published by Britain Books
6719 Tomlinson Terrace
Cabin John, MD 20818

Editor
Harlan L. Watson, Ph.D.

Research Assistant
Shelley A. Morin

Restaurant Research
Marsha Rinkus

Cover
Jands, Inc., Silver Spring, MD
Tom Kiddy, Art Director
Doug Harman, Designer
Carolyn Hobson, Account Executive

Map Artwork
Jands, Inc., Silver Spring, MD
Christy O'Connell
Shawn Batts

Manufactured in the United States of America.
Library of Congress Catalog Card Number: 97-93212
ISBN 1-882310-03-9

In memory of my grandmother, Tracey Righi,
a five-star angel,
whose great cooking and warm heart
made her kitchen the finest place on earth

ACKNOWLEDGMENTS

I want to thank all the friends, friends-of-friends, hotel concierges and managers, strangers in elevators, and readers of my other travel guides who shared their favorite New York restaurant experiences with me. They helped pave my way to the great culinary orchard that exists on and off Broadway. I also appreciate their insight into the best (and worst) places to stay. And a special thanks to my sister, Marsha Rinkus, who, like me, never let a blizzard or two get in the way of tracking down a good restaurant. Her enthusiasm and great company made a pleasant job all the more pleasant.

I would also like to thank Bennett Boskey, who was unfailingly available for editorial advice when needed; Shelley Morin for her patience and skill on various editorial tasks and fact-checking; and the talented people at Jands—Carolyn Hobson, Tom Kiddy, Doug Harman, Christy O'Connell, and Shawn Batts—who produced the maps and worked on the cover design.

Last, but never least, thanks to my husband, Harlan Watson, for his editorial skill and moral support, and for once more minding the cats and keeping the home fires burning while I explored the many pleasures for theater lovers on and off Broadway. His presence over the years has also brightened many excursions to New York, even as he struggled to keep my good-value-side alert by constantly reminding me that people really want big portions and small prices, not the reverse.

CONTENTS

CONTENTS

INTRODUCTION

On and Off Broadway is not a typical travel guide. Instead, it is a special-interest guide written for those who feel that of all the many rich experiences New York City has to offer, its vibrant theater life is its greatest gift to the world. These theater enthusiasts also feel that the best complement to a stimulating evening of theater is dining well. And when they return to their hotel, they want more than just a place to hang their hat with none of the charms of home. If this describes you, then you are the person I've had in mind each and every time I've checked into a hotel, popped into a restaurant, or settled into my theater seat. Whether your budget is great or small, this book is for you.

I'm a theater enthusiast who wants to experience all the best. But I've often been staggered by how much all the best costs in New York City. However, over the course of time and much research, I've learned how to get the very best value for every dollar spent on hotels, restaurants, and theater.

On and Off Broadway will help you find the best places to stay—whether you prefer a world class hotel with every possible amenity, a tiny B&B, a loft apartment, or a small, stylish boutique hotel. And it will tell you how to never, ever, pay the published rack rate.

On and Off Broadway will help you find your favorite kind of dining experience, whether it's a sidewalk table at a bistro reminiscent of Paris, a fantasy garden in the most famous park in the world, an old-world cafe where you can still get three courses for under a tenner, or a quintessentially romantic restaurant where some say the ghost of a controversial vice president still roams. It also highlights many before- and after-theater menus that allow you to sample the artistry of some of the best chefs in the city at a fraction of the usual cost. Many great brunch specials and prix fixe menus are also detailed.

Finally, *On and Off Broadway* will help set your theater-going course by showing you how to get tickets before leaving home, on arrival, or half-price on the day of performance. And it highlights Manhattan's many unique neighborhoods where you'll find the Off-Broadway theaters that contribute so much artistic energy to the city and make this dynamic crazy quilt of an island so stimulating.

Not just for visitors, *On and Off Broadway* will also point the native New Yorker to some of the best restaurant values in town, encourage exploration of the nooks and crannies of other neighborhoods, and remind the jaded why they fell in love with this splendid city in the first place.

MANHATTAN

Manhattan

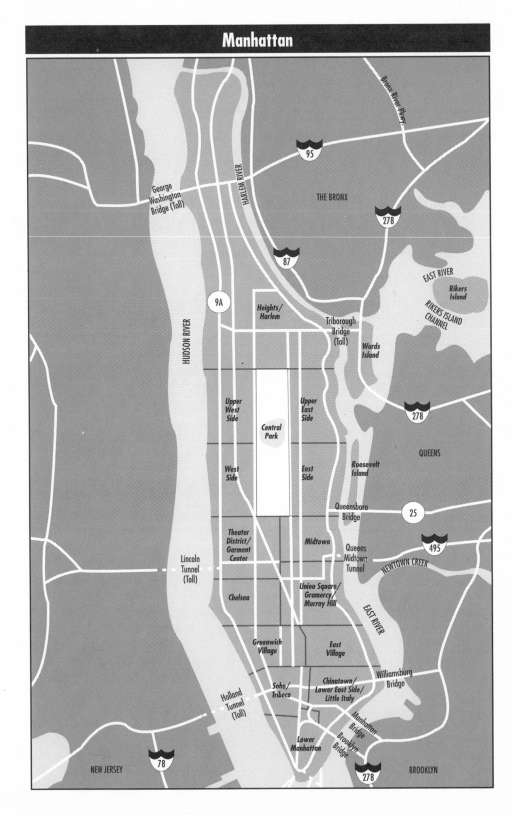

NEW YORK CITY'S MANY FACES

***

The Neighborhoods

Over the years, countless writers have tried to capture the essence of this eclectic and fascinating stretch of real estate. Cosmopolitan and gauche, exhilarating and daunting, charismatic and frightening, beautiful and unsightly, New York City wears many faces.

Of the five separate boroughs that comprise New York City, Manhattan is the smallest. A concrete jungle surrounded by water, it is undeniably unique. Measuring just 13.4 miles long by 2.3 miles wide, this compact expanse encompasses some of the world's most famous sights and exclusive addresses, as well as spectacular restaurants, world-class art exhibitions, and the most diverse theater to be found anywhere in the world. It is above all a city of great contrasts, shifting from rags to riches. From its smooth patina of glamour, power, and wealth to wrenching poverty painful to see, this is *the* city of all cities and the cultural center of the United States. From the mansions along Fifth Avenue to the slums of the Lower East Side, both millionaires and paupers call it home. Tourists think of it as the Big Apple, eager to bite into its many pleasures.

While it can be enormously expensive, Manhattan also offers simple pleasures that cost little, or nothing. Take time to explore this complex island and you'll find many such unique pleasures along the way. It might be catching sight of the Statue of Liberty from an esplanade on the Hudson River, seeing the spectacular city skyscape from the observation deck of the Empire State Building, walking across the Brooklyn Bridge at sunset, watching the twinkling lights of the city and the harbor from a moonlit ride on the Staten Island Ferry, skating on the ice at Rockefeller Center in the shadow of the massive Christmas tree, chilling out with an Italian ice on the steps of the New York Public Library on a warm summer day, having a brown bag lunch in Bryant Park's 19th Century-style garden, enjoying a free performance of Shakespeare in Central Park, or experiencing the heartfelt emotion of Ellis Island where so many of our ancestors arrived to pursue their American Dream. These are some of the silk threads that make up the tapestry and the golden moments of a day in this greatest of all cities.

Manhattan is so full of possibilities, no matter how many times you visit, there's always the chance of turning a corner and finding something completely unexpected. Delightful surprises seem to occur when you least expect them—you might wander by a movie or music video shoot, or find your favorite film star sitting next to you in the theater, or discover that the Broadway star you just saw in a performance is dining at the table next to yours.

Like other great cities such as London and Paris, Manhattan is a place best explored on foot to truly appreciate its diversity and ethnic character. Patrician Fifth Avenue divides the city into eastern and western sectors. Facing north, all that is right of Fifth Avenue is the East Side and all that is to the left is the West Side. It's that simple, mostly. Its grid layout, with avenues running north-south and numbered streets running east-west (with the numbers increasing as you head north), makes it easier to navigate than most cities. That is, until you hit Greenwich Village and on down where the jumble of named streets is confusing and you'll need a map to find your way around.

While Manhattan is full of instantly recognizable landmarks that are part of its architectural, scenic, and historic legacy, we each view it from our own personal perspective, so that it can be a totally different experience from person to person. For architectural buffs, art lovers, and lovers of the arts, it has so much to offer, its appeal is obvious. Many of us enjoy New York because it is the culinary capital of the world. Its restaurants reflect the diversification of cultures that make up the city and allow culinary adventurers to sample food from any country in the world.

For others, it is a shopper's paradise. There are the Fifth Avenue designer shops that carry the most prestigious names in the fashion world, the chic boutiques of SoHo, and the funky East Village hole-in-the-walls where you can find unique, offbeat, and sometimes even spectacular prizes. The area from East 60th to East 90th Streets on and off Madison Avenue is rife with shops specializing in quality vintage furnishings and collectibles, from glassware, china, and porcelain to prints, carpets, and maps. And for serious book lovers, rare, antique, and out-of-print dealers abound throughout the city. Bauman's Rare Books in the Waldorf Astoria Hotel is a landmark. For used volumes, the legendary Strand Book Store at Broadway and 12th Street is the largest.

And to some, New York City is primarily a sports town. It certainly has some of the most avid and vocal sports fans anywhere. They cheer for the Knicks and the Rangers at Madison Square Garden, root for the World Champ Yankees at Yankee Stadium and the Mets at Shea Stadium. They place their bets at Aqueduct, Roosevelt, and Belmont Park racetracks in Queens, and they passionately follow the Jets and Giants at the nearby Meadowlands Stadium in East Rutherford, New Jersey.

Manhattan's dynamic nightlife has something to offer every fancy. Whether it's a blues club, a quiet cabaret, a dance club, a comedy club, a jazz bar, a sophisticated supper club, or a brewpub you're seeking, you'll have plenty of choice. There are lesbian and gay bars, cowboy bars, sports bars, and Irish pubs aplenty. And there are piano bars for every mood—the sophisticated Bemelmans Bar in the Carlyle Hotel (35 East 76th Street) and the atmospheric Silver Dollar Saloon at Bill's Nineties Cafe (57 East 54th Street). Then there's the lively Don't Tell Mama (343 West 46th Street) where the waitstaff is comprised of aspiring Broadway talents who each take a turn at the mike. And for a real theatrical all-out good time, there's Eighty Eight's (228 West 10th Street) where nearly everyone belts out showstoppers with gay abandon. For an evening of robust brass and reeds, there's the Mingus Big Band at Fez Under Time Cafe (at 380 Lafayette Street). Established by the widow of the late composer-bassist, the ensemble's blaring creativity and melding of melody against rhythm enlivens Thursday nights in the East Village.

And in this city that never sleeps, it is possible to shop, dine, and even work out around the clock. Jazz fans can revel at Small's (183 West 10th Street) in Greenwich Village all through the night and those with disco fever can dance the night away at Robots (25 Avenue B at East 3rd Street) in Alphabet City. East Village clubbers can refuel at Veselka (144 Second Avenue at East 9th Street), a colorful no-frills Polish eatery; pool sharks can cue up around the clock at Chelsea Billiards (54 West 21st Street) with its 45 pool tables, six snooker tables, and two billiard tables; more active sportsters can lace up for a game of hockey until 4 a.m. at the Sky Rink in the Chelsea Piers Sports and Entertainment Complex (Pier 61, 23rd Street at the Hudson River); and romantics can hop the Staten Island Ferry for a late night/early morning voyage and catch the moonlight shimmering over the Statue of Liberty as they head out and then feast on the incomparable city skyline at dawn on the return.

For many avid theater enthusiasts, New York is Broadway. Period. Many of us start out feeling that way. We breeze into the city to see as many shows as possible, choose a hotel in the theater district, eat in restaurants near whatever shows we are seeing, and seldom branch out into the world of Off-Broadway and almost never bother with Off-Off Broadway. After all, we reason, New York *is* Broadway and we want to see what all the shouting is about. But when we do venture off the Great White Way, we are rewarded with the intimacy of smaller theaters, a huge variety of quality productions, and fascinating—and sometimes daring—experimental theater.

15

And when all is said and done, if you take time to discover all the other pleasures and oddities this amazing spot on the planet has to offer, you will see that it is so much more than bright lights, traffic jams, massive billboards, tacky souvenir shops, street hustlers, hot dog vendors, and it is more than just a flashy entertainment pocket in a big concrete island. For in all the world, there is no place even remotely like it.

Lower Manhattan

Lower Manhattan, the oldest and most historic part of the city, is bounded by Chambers Street and the East and Hudson Rivers. Its major attractions include the **World Trade Center** (at 110 stories, the tallest structure in town), the **City Hall** district of majestic court buildings, the **New York Stock Exchange** where the fiscal fate of the world hangs in the balance, and **Fraunces Tavern** where George Washington wept while saying farewell to his officers at war's end in December 1783. The spirit of our first President can also be found at the **Federal Hall National Memorial** on Wall Street on the site where he took the oath of office on April 30, 1789, and at **St. Paul's Chapel** on Broadway at Fulton Street, where he worshiped.

The handsomely restored **South Street Seaport** is here as well. This vestige of New York's heyday as a great port in the 19th Century is located on the banks of the East River in an area adjacent to the picturesque **Brooklyn Bridge** and just minutes from **Wall Street**. It was here in the 1800s where you would find clipper ships from the China trade, as well as ships arriving from Europe. Its 18th and 19th Century warehouses are now restored harbor-view bars, restaurants, shops, and galleries. Fulton Street, a cobblestoned thoroughfare lined with restored 19th Century buildings, is its main street, while the **South Street Seaport Museum** is its cultural core. The museum's collections include more than one million urban archaeological artifacts as well as a fleet of ships docked at Piers 15 and 16.

Battery Park, an area created by landfill, takes its name from a line of British cannons that once overlooked the harbor in the late 1600s. It offers a sweeping view of New York Harbor and is the pushing off point for ferries to Liberty Island, Ellis Island, and Staten Island.

Lower East Side

The Lower East Side, one of New York's fascinating melting pot neighborhoods, is bordered by Houston Street, the Bowery, and the East River. This neighborhood was once home to many Jewish immigrants from Eastern Europe. The upwardly mobile among them moved uptown as quickly as possible, so that now the area is home to Chinese, Latin Americans, and African-Americans for the most part. But it is still possible to catch a taste of the Old Country with a knish at **Yonah Schimmel's Bakery** (137 E. Houston Street), a kosher dill at **Guss'** (35 Essex Street), where Peter Riegert courted Amy Irving in *Crossing Delancey*, or a hot pastrami at **Katz's Delicatessen** (205 E. Houston Street), where Meg Ryan got Billy Crystal's attention in *When Harry Met Sally*. However, the heart of the Lower East Side is Orchard Street, where hundreds of stores offer brand-name clothing and goods at discounts between 20 and 70 percent off the regular retail prices. A potpourri of street vendors add to the old-world marketplace atmosphere of the area.

Chinatown

New York's Chinatown is the largest Chinese-American community in America and ranks as the most exotic of the city's neighborhoods. You'll recognize it at once—pagodas rest atop its telephone kiosks and signs are in Chinese. Approximately 150,000 Chinese live here, along with a growing number of residents from Burma, Malaysia, Thailand, and Vietnam. The sidewalks of Mott Street, its main drag, teem with a profusion of vegetable stands and pungent fish markets. But to get Chinatown's true flavor, wander in and out of its narrow streets. There are huge segments of the area where the English language is hardly ever spoken.

A shopping spree along Canal Street and dim sum at the **Golden Unicorn** (18 East Broadway near Catherine Street) or **Triple Eight Palace** (88 East Broadway) makes for a colorful outing. No-ambience restaurants seem to characterize every city's Chinatown and they can be found here in abundance. And while the food can run the gamut from good to terrific, service tends to run the gamut from indifferent to really indifferent. For the most part, you can expect formica, paper napkins, soft drinks, and chaos.

Little Italy

Little Italy lies sandwiched between Chinatown and SoHo. In the 1800s the area drew Italian immigrants. Today, their food is the big draw. Mulberry Street north of Canal is lined with restaurants and shops selling wonderful Italian specialty foods. **Ballato's** (at 55 E. Houston Street between Mott and Mulberry Streets) is a local favorite for traditional Neapolitan homestyle cooking and offers wonderful fixed-price dinner bargains. And **Ferrara's** (at 195 Grand Street between Mott and Mulberry Streets) is *the* place for dessert. In operation for over 100 years, it is famous for its delicious cannolis, peasant pie, and Italian cheesecake.

The tenements and street life of the district along and around Mulberry Street from Spring Street to just above Canal Street were captured in scenes from "The Godfather" movies that were filmed there. And while this colorful ethnic neighborhood seems to be in danger of getting swallowed up by Chinatown and SoHo, it still manages to maintain its Italian bravado with its annual fall **San Gennaro Festival**, a week-long celebration when the air is scented with garlic and sausage, the street life takes a festive turn, and the sounds of Italian greetings fill the air.

SoHo

Within walking distance of Little Italy and Chinatown is the vogue neighborhood of SoHo (an acronym which comes from its location SOuth of HOuston Street). This area of 19th Century cast-iron architecture has since the 1960s flourished into a creative colony of writers, painters, and actors, and now brims with avant-garde boutiques, eclectic restaurants, and contemporary art galleries. Though it encompasses only a quarter of a square mile, it contains nearly 200 restaurants, 250 art galleries, more than 30 antique shops, over a dozen furniture emporiums, five museums, and over a hundred retail establishments.

The area has a kind of industrial chic with huge converted warehouses and 19th Century cobblestone showing through battered asphalt. One of the oldest of its 19th Century prefabricated cast-iron buildings is the **E. V. Haughwout Building** at 490 Broadway. Completed in 1857, it was a sophisticated retail store where Mary Todd Lincoln bought china for the White House.

18

Greene Street, the center of the **Cast-Iron Historic District,** is known for its continuous row of Renaissance and Neoclassical cast-iron buildings. Here, you can wander through an endless stream of galleries and vintage clothing and furniture stores. If you'd rather browse than buy, you might head for the museums of SoHo. The new **Guggenheim Museum SoHo** (at 575 Broadway at Prince), an annex of the Fifth Avenue museum, is housed in a landmark 19th Century red-brick structure with original cast-iron storefronts. It exhibits both contemporary works and pieces from the Guggenheim's permanent collection. And for a glimpse of experimental art, visit the **New Museum of Contemporary Art** at 583 Broadway. Also nearby is the **Museum for African Art** (593 Broadway), dedicated to traditional and contemporary art.

TriBeCa

TriBeCa (the triangle below Canal Street) is defined roughly by Canal Street to the north, Broadway to the east, and the Hudson River to the west. Its two main arteries are West Broadway and Hudson Street. Prior to the 1980s this area was pretty much a wasteland, but by then SoHo had come into its own and only the most successful of the new black-clad artistic gentry could afford its rents. Then, the spacious industrial buildings of TriBeCa began to catch the interest and spillover of artists in search of more space for less money. Now this once neglected area abounds in art galleries showing experimental works by young artists, trendsetting clothing shops, and restaurants with celebrated chefs. Robert DeNiro has his film production studio here and co-owns a number of the area's super hot restaurants. Along with Battery Park, it is one of New York City's most fast-changing areas. And while it may lack SoHo's more cohesive chic, it has attained its own cachet. Part of its scruffy charm lies in the fact that despite its upwardly fashionable climb, it retains the look and feel of a real working neighborhood.

Greenwich Village

Manhattan's bohemia, Greenwich Village has been home to such noncon-formist celebrities as Jack Kerouac, Allen Ginsberg, and Dylan Thomas (who drank himself to death in the **White Horse Tavern** at 567 Hudson Street). Eugene O'Neill, Mark Twain, Edgar Allen Poe, Tennessee Williams, Eleanor Roosevelt, Gypsy Rose Lee, Mikhail Baryshnikov, Dustin Hoffman, and Lenny Bruce are also part of the eclectic mix who have called it home. Bounded by the Hudson River, Broadway, Houston and 14th Streets, it has its own distinctive character and is one of the most picturesque neighborhoods in the city. Tree-lined streets, well-preserved Federal and Greek Revival townhouses, funky boutiques, antique shops, and trendy restaurants make it a popular destination to explore. And for jazz enthusiasts, no trip to the Village would be complete without making the rounds of its numerous jazz clubs.

A stroll through this quaint neighborhood displays just about every architectural style of the 18th and 19th centuries along with all sorts of delightful surprises and curiosities. At 75½ Bedford Street you'll see New York's narrowest house (just 9½ feet wide). Actor Cary Grant and poet Edna St. Vincent Millay both resided in this architectural oddity (though not together!). And Gay Street, lined with 1810-era row houses, has nurtured its share of creativity—it was at No. 14 that the play *My Sister Eileen* was conceived and at No. 12 where the early television icon Howdy Doody was born. No. 6 Leroy Street, built in 1880, was once the home of the city's flamboyant Mayor Jimmy Walker.

You'll find the part of Bleecker Street between Christopher and Bank Streets a pleasant stretch for browsing. Antique stores, book shops, trendy boutiques, and small cafes are in plentiful profusion along the route.

Over the years, **Washington Square Park** has served a variety of functions, from cemetery, to public gallows, to fashionable residential area. (It was also where Robert Redford tred *Barefoot in the Park*.) The building at No. 7 is where Edith Wharton once lived. And Eugene O'Neill wrote *The Iceman Cometh* during the period he lived at No. 38 South. Today, most of the buildings along Washington Square belong to New York University.

Greenwich Village also embraces one of the largest gay and lesbian communities in the country. Christopher Street (the heart of Manhattan's gay life) was the scene of the 1969 Stonewall riots that marked the birth of the gay liberation movement.

And while the Village has lost some of its charm to the retail trade of lower Broadway that has spread west and the throngs of teenagers who take over its streets on weekends, much of what made it attractive to earlier creative types is still here.

East Village

Between Broadway and the East River, Greenwich Village (or more accurately, the West Village) gives way to the East Village, an artsy, gritty neighborhood with a vibrant, scruffy personality all its own. **Tompkins Square Park** is its hub and **St. Mark's Place** its main drag. A beatnik haunt of the '50s and hippies' hangout of the '60s, it is still a haven for nonconformists and sports a proud grunge image. This is where an unknown rock star wannabe named Madonna started out.

Its relatively low rents attract innovative merchants and restaurateurs who might not be able to afford setting up shop in the more upscale neighborhoods. As a result, vintage kitsch abounds in its shops and street stalls, along with all that is trendy and cutting edge.

There's also a lively ethnic dining scene in this melting pot neighborhood. The stretch of East Sixth Street between First and Second Avenues, known as **Little India**, contains a plethora of Indian and Pakistani restaurants. For Eastern European fare such as pierogi, stuffed cabbage, blintzes, and kielbasa, head for Second Avenue (**Veselka** at 144 or **Ukrainian** at 140). And a taste of Italy can be found at numerous tiny pastry and cheese shops throughout the area.

Union Square/Gramercy Park/Murray Hill

These three vital neighborhoods span 14th to 39th Streets from Sixth Avenue to the East River and boast both the world's most famous skyscraper (the **Empire State Building**) and the city's first skyscraper (the wonderful Renaissance-style **Flatiron Building**.)

Back in the 1930s, the **Union Square** area was the gathering place for political rallies and much soapbox outrage. By the 1970s the neighborhood had deteriorated greatly and was taken over by drug dealers, kindred lowlifes, and other lost souls. But a massive renewal program in the 1980s transformed it. And today it is an animated area that embraces the city's large, lively **Greenmarket**, where farmers from all over the Northeast come with their fresh produce, cheeses, homemade bakery, flowers, fish, and New York State wines. The **Flatiron District** (rich in wonderful old buildings and high-profile shops) and the **Gramercy Park** neighborhood meet at Union Square, in an area that now includes some of the most dynamic restaurants in town.

And there's the charming **Gramercy Park**, New York's only private square. Surrounded by a cast-iron fence with a locked door, only residents who pay a yearly maintenance fee have keys. The park was established by landowner Samuel Ruggles in the 1830s when he chose to relinquish 42

21

potential building lots to create a leafy square reminiscent of those found in London. The area is modeled after London's Bloomsbury and Covent Garden neighborhoods. Beautiful 19th Century mansions characterize it. A stroll through its **Historic District** (East 18th to East 21st Streets along Lexington Avenue and Irving Place) is pure delight. Many of the Greek Revival townhouses that line the streets date from the 1840s and except for some 1920s apartment buildings on the Square's north side, little has changed since the days when Shakespearean actor Edwin Booth (brother of Lincoln's assassin and the foremost actor of his day) lived in the neighborhood. He transformed the elegant Gothic Revival brownstone that was his home (16 Gramercy Park South) into a social club for his fellow thespians. It is now the **Hampden-Booth Theater Library**, where tours are available by appointment only.

Teddy Roosevelt's birthplace, now a museum, can be found at 28 East 20th Street, near the park. The original Victorian brownstone where the young Rough Rider lived until he was 15 years old was torn down, but this is considered a near-perfect reconstruction of it. Also notable is the row of Greek Revival townhouses on the west end of the square. With their fanciful cast-iron verandas, they are reminiscent of New Orleans' French Quarter. And **Pete's Tavern** (at 129 East 18th Street) is notable not just as the oldest original bar in New York City but also as the place where O. Henry penned *The Gift of the Magi* (reportedly in the second booth to the right).

Residing in the **Murray Hill** area is the **Pierpont Morgan Library** (East 36th Street between Madison and Park Avenues). This beautiful palazzo-like building houses Old Master drawings, original music scores, and more than 1,000 illuminated medieval and Renaissance manuscripts. And the **Herald Square** area (around 34th Street and Broadway) is most famous as the home of **Macy's**, the world's largest department store.

Chelsea

Chelsea encompasses the area bounded by 34th Street to the north, 14th Street to the south, Sixth Avenue to the east, and the Hudson River to the west. Most of this land was acquired by Captain Thomas Clarke in 1750 and was named after London's Chelsea Hospital, an old soldiers' home. Until the 1830s, when it was developed into a residential district, it was one family's country estate.

In the 1880s, the West 23rd Street area briefly saw a profusion of theatrical enterprise, but in a few years the theater world had moved uptown.

Then, in the early 1900s its creative energy was regenerated when the country's motion picture industry moved in. Roomy lofts and theaters served as studios. But when the Astoria Studios in Queens built a more suitable facility and Hollywood's heydey began, Chelsea's movie business was history as well.

A longtime haven for artists and writers, today Chelsea includes an active gay community with Eighth Avenue rivaling Greenwich Village's Christopher Street as the main gay thoroughfare. And while still seedy in part, with tenements and row houses of mixed character, it is one of the up and coming neighborhoods of the moment. Large department stores (like fashionable **Barney's**), small boutiques, and bookstores make it another good shopping area. And within its eccentric boundaries resides the quirky **Hotel Chelsea** at 222 West 23rd Street (former home of O. Henry, Thomas Wolfe, Mark Twain, Tennessee Williams, Arthur Miller, and Sarah Bernhardt). It was here where drugged punk rocker Sid Vicious of the Sex Pistols stabbed and killed his girlfriend Nancy Spungeon. Also in Chelsea, you'll find the **Empire** (a 24-hour art deco diner at 210 Tenth Avenue) and the splendid enclave of Gothic architecture that is the **General Theological Seminary.** **Madison Square Garden, Penn Station,** and the imposing **Main Post Office** are here as well.

Recently, the **Chelsea Piers Sports and Entertainment Complex** has made a big splash in the area. Built on four renovated piers from the early 1900s, it has two indoor year-round ice-skating rinks, two outdoor roller rinks, an indoor jogging track, a 25-yard pool, an outdoor sundeck, 10,000 square feet of rock-climbing surface, a driving range, and a huge health club. The complex also includes restaurants, a microbrewery, shops, and a riverside park.

And the **Flower District** (Sixth Avenue between West 26th and West 30th Streets) adds an element of beauty to the area as its colorful bounty spills out onto the sidewalks early in the morning when florists arrive to select their blooms.

Theater District

The compact area from West 34th to West 59th Streets, from Avenue of the Americas to the Hudson River, contains the electric chaos of the **Theater District** and **Times Square.** Here street musicians, spirited dancers, magicians, mimes, rappers, and sidewalk salesmen mix with tourists and theatergoers in a sea of relentless motion and sound. Nearly 40 major Broadway theaters dot the area, along with a string of Off-Broadway houses (on the south side of 42nd Street) in an area known as **Theater Row.**

In the expanse below this Great White Way (around 34th Street and Seventh Avenue) there exists the permanent traffic gridlock and carnival atmosphere of the **Garment District**. Delivery trucks and racks of clothing crowd the streets and the buzz of commerce fills the air.

The flourishing **Times Square** area is in a state of change these days. Recently it has seen the opening of **Hansen's Times Square Brewery**, a brewpub serving German and British food; **O'Lunney's Times Square Pub**, an Irish bar and grill; and **Dine-O-Mat**, a diner steeped in World War II nostalgia. Theme restaurants continue to sprout up: **David Copperfield's** (specializing in magic), **Marvel Mania** (specializing in comics), and **Comedy Nation** (specializing in laughs). A Disney Hotel and entertainment complex of renovated theaters, upscale shops, and restaurants is under way to revitalize 42nd Street between Times Square and Eighth Avenue, replacing X-rated movie houses and pornography shops. About a dozen huge lighted signs throughout the complex are planned in the spirit of keeping with the general lively appearance of the Times Square billboard area. And of course to people around the world, mention of Times Square conjures up pleasant images of the biggest New Year's Eve party anywhere on earth.

Hotels, both grand and modest, and restaurants of endless variety abound, thriving on the theater enthusiasts who fill them in pursuit of convenient dining and sleeping quarters near the bright lights of Broadway. And upscale soup kitchens keep springing up all the time. Seinfeld fans wanting to go toe to toe with the "Soup Nazi" can find the real life inspiration for the classic episode at the Soup Kitchen International at 259A West 55th Street.

The stretch below Broadway throughout the area from Eighth to Twelfth Avenues known as **Hell's Kitchen** was once the toughest part of town. Today, while much of the tawdriness that has long characterized it still exists, it is undergoing considerable change and is a far cry from the days when its namesake gang ruled the streets.

Midtown

Midtown—roughly the area which extends from 39th to 59th Streets from Sixth Avenue (Avenue of the Americas) to the East River—is characterized by its stunning architecture. There's the art deco grandeur of the **Chrysler Building** with its world renowned stainless-steel sunburst spire creating the jewel of the city's skyline and the dazzling art deco interior of **Radio City Music Hall**. The famous **Rockefeller Center**, a striking example of modern architecture, is a complex of 19 individual skyscrapers. Its network includes the **NBC Studios**, the famous ice rink presided over by the renowned gilded sculpture of Prometheus, and more than 20,000 plants and flowers that change with the seasons. Its huge Christmas tree personifies the festiveness of the holiday season and from year to year is a landmark in its own right. The Beaux Arts styled **Grand Central Terminal** (42nd to 46th Streets between Lexington and Vanderbilt Avenues) is another example of the city's architectural brilliance. Its stunning 125-foot high vaulted ceiling twinkles with the constellations of the zodiac. Another fine example of Beaux Arts architecture is the **New York Public Library** (Fifth Avenue between West 40th and West 42nd Streets). In its shadow is **Bryant Park**, the city's elegant little park with a formal garden design.

Midtown also is home to the **United Nations**, as well as the peerless **Museum of Modern Art** (11 West 53rd Street), housing an extraordinary collection of 20th Century paintings, sculpture, and design. And at Fifth Avenue between East 50th and East 51st Streets, you'll find the lovely **St. Patrick's Cathedral**, a Gothic Revival structure dating back to 1878. It is the largest Catholic cathedral in the country.

And Midtown has a much more neighborhood feel—particularly along the numbered avenues—than its Theater District counterpart. Fabulous shops, wonderful hotels, and some of the best restaurants in town also lie within its boundaries making it the ideal choice for many visitors.

East Side/Upper East Side

This part of town is known as Manhattan's gold coast and is famous for its high style. It extends from 59th to 110th Streets and from the East River to Fifth Avenue. Along Fifth Avenue's **Museum Mile** (between 82nd and 104th Streets) many of the world's greatest works of art reside. A number of architecturally distinguished private residences, such as Andrew Carnegie's handsome Renaissance-Georgian mansion at 91st Street (now home to the **Cooper-Hewitt National Design Museum**) have been transformed into public institutions. Felix Warburg's French Gothic château (at 92nd Street) is now the **Jewish Museum** and the neo-Georgian Willard Straight townhouse (at 94th Street) is now the uptown branch of the **International Center of Photography**. And you'll find **The Frick Collection** at 70th Street, **The Metropolitan Museum of Art** at 82nd Street, and the **Guggenheim Museum** at 88th Street.

Fifth Avenue has also been home to many film and fashion celebrities, as well as the rich and famous from other walks of life. Jacqueline Kennedy Onassis lived at 1040 Fifth Avenue in an apartment facing Central Park. She regularly jogged around the Park's Reservoir which the city has now renamed in her honor.

Other notable houses on the East Side run the gamut from **Gypsy Rose Lee**'s former home at 153 East 63rd Street to **Gracie Mansion**, the Mayor's residence, on East End Avenue at 88th Street.

For the best in browsing, head for **Madison Avenue**, a delightful expanse of upscale bistros, charming boutiques, galleries, and exclusive shops of every kind. And to experience true urban charm, wander along the side streets between Fifth and Lexington Avenues where you'll find classic and Italianate townhouses and some of the city's finest restaurants. For ethnic character, stroll through **Yorkville**, the German-Hungarian neighborhood that lies between Lexington Avenue and the East River from 77th to 96th Streets.

And the dichotomy of Manhattan is probably nowhere more evident than it is at the juncture of the Upper East Side where one neighborhood's charm meets the neglect and degradation of another neighborhood at Spanish Harlem.

Central Park

The 843-acre patch of green (between Fifth Avenue and Central Park West and between 59th and 110th Streets) known as Central Park is one of varied splendors. It contains a lake with boat rentals, lush green sanctuaries, horse-drawn hansom cabs, skating rinks, an outdoor theater, a pocket-size zoo, a castle, a carousel, restaurants, and miles of jogging trails. It also comprises an area known as **Strawberry Fields**, a three-acre garden of peace honoring the late John Lennon. Maintained in his memory through an endowment by Yoko Ono, many of its shrubs and trees have been donated by various countries as a gesture toward world peace. An *Imagine* mosaic on the pathway and a handwritten note by Yoko Ono add a sense of poignance to the leafy scene.

A good way to experience the park is to take a two-hour bicycle tour offered by **Bite of the Apple Tours** (212/603-9750). The tour encompasses the park's main attractions and bicycle rental is included in the fee. For those wanting to leave the driving (or peddling) to someone else, there's a trolley tour (operated by Gray Line 212/397-3809). This one and a half hour tour includes a little walking and takes in scenic hot spots such as Strawberry Fields, Bethesda Terrace, and the Conservatory Garden.

Come to the park on a Saturday morning from June through September, when there's storytelling at the **Hans Christian Andersen Statue** (74th Street near Fifth Avenue). Tots sit on the statue's bronze lap and listen to fairy tales, myths, and stories from around the world. Afterwards you might venture to the Park's **Wildlife Conservation Center** (the zoo) and say hello to Gus, the 750-pound polar bear whose constant restless laps in his pool earned him a reputation as one more neurotic New Yorker. Though zoo officials contend he was just bored, an animal behaviorist was called in. Now Gus's environment has been stimulated with water toys and his food is hidden so he'll hunt for it.

And there are those who believe the park is home to at least two beautiful ghosts. One of its most enduring legends concerns the inseparable Van Der Voort sisters, who were so devoted to one another they resisted marriage in spite of their mother's best efforts. Their passion was skating in Central Park wearing their specially designed outfits—one red and one purple. After their mother's death, which left them in a state of genteel poverty, they were seldom seen in public except when they would go to the park to skate. In 1880, they died within months of one another. According to legend, their ghosts were first spotted during World War I, and over the years on fine clear nights guests at the Plaza Hotel have caught glimpses of the sisters gliding ethereally across the frozen pond in their signature dresses.

West Side/Upper West Side

The West Side and Upper West Side encompass the area bordered by 59th and 110th Streets and Central Park and the Hudson River. A quintessential New York neighborhood, it is home to **Lincoln Center**, as well as the **American Museum of Natural History** (where a 94-foot blue whale and more than 30 million other artifacts reside). A number of celebrities also call this part of town home. It is a neighborhood characterized by a relaxed, liberal, laid-back attitude.

Broadway is its main drag with Columbus and Amsterdam Avenues adding their own colorful mix of cafes, coffee bars, smart boutiques, junk stores, bars, and trendy restaurants. The stretch of Columbus Avenue between 65th and 86th Streets is a particularly eclectic shopping strip while Riverside Drive boasts grand architecture and a sweeping view of the Hudson River.

Turn-of-the-century brownstones and limestone row houses abound. The area also contains wonderful old apartment buildings along Central Park West, such as the grand dame of them all, the beautiful **Hotel des Artistes**. Its tenants over the years have included Isadora Duncan, Rudolph Valentino, and Norman Rockwell. And there's also the **Dakota**, an imposing German Renaissance-style mansion built in the late 19th Century, with its own impressive list of celebrity tenants such as Lauren Bacall, Madonna, Mia Farrow, and Yoko Ono. But, of course, most people remember it as the spot where ex-Beatle John Lennon was shot and killed in 1980 by a man who professed to be one of his biggest fans. It was also where *Rosemary's Baby* was filmed.

Morningside Heights/Harlem

Morningside Heights, the area between Cathedral Parkway and West 125th Street, is an area distinguished by educational giants. **Columbia University, Barnard College, Union Theological Seminary, and the Jewish Theological Seminary** dominate this exceptional academic community.

Harlem, the area that extends from the Harlem to the Hudson Rivers and from 125th Street to about 165th Street, is an African-American community rich in history and culture. Yet, few visitors enter the area because they associate it with racial tension and urban decay.

Originally a farming village in the 17th Century, it was an affluent white suburb in the 19th Century. After 1900 it became one of the largest urban black communities in the United States. W. C. Handy and Eubie Blake, two great musicians, lived in the **St. Nicholas Historic District** (also known as **Striver's Row**), an enclave of elegant townhouses on 138th and 139th Streets between Seventh and Eighth Avenues.

The famous **Apollo Theater** continues to be a draw for its concerts. And the **Schomburg Center for Research in Black Culture** is the nation's largest library devoted to black and African culture. Also notable is the **Studio Museum**, a small museum devoted to black artists.

For a sampling of the best of soul food, there's **Sylvia's** at 328 Lenox Avenue and **Copeland's** at 547 West 145th Street. And one of the very toughest tables to book in town is for dinner at **Rao's**, a fabulous Italian Restaurant at 455 E. 114th Street, known for its celebrity clientele, festive ambience, and wonderful food.

Since Harlem's interesting attractions are rather spread out, a good way to explore the area is to take a guided tour. Sunday gospel tours to the neighborhood's historic churches have become very popular.

THE BOROUGHS

While most visitors to New York City spend their time exclusively in Manhattan, the other four boroughs should not be altogether overlooked. Currently enjoying a tourism renaissance, Queens, Staten Island, Brooklyn, and the Bronx are showing off to more and more visitors each year. The Bronx Tourism Council has been so swamped with requests for tourist information it set up a Web site (http://www.ilovethebronx.com). Due to the increased demand for accommodations, Brooklyn recently broke ground on its first new downtown hotel in 50 years. And in a show of his faith in Queens, Magic Johnson has signed on to open the Magic Johnson Theater complex in the borough's Jamaica Center neighborhood in 1998.

Brooklyn

Nostalgia for the way New York used to be has fueled interest in Brooklyn. Often called "America's Home Town," its place as one of the most ethnically-diverse communities in the country is clearly reflected in its neighborhoods where you can sample the tastes of Mother Russia with blinis and borscht in Brighton Beach's busy **Little Odessa** or recall islandy specialties at dozens of Caribbean restaurants in **Flatbush**. And for top-notch Italian food, New Yorkers from all boroughs make their way to **Cucina** (256 Fifth Avenue) for the terrific specialties, great setting, and prices well below its Manhattan counterparts. Another excellent reason to venture to Brooklyn is to tuck into a steak at **Peter Luger** (178 Broadway). With the ambience of a German beer hall, there's nothing plush about the place, but it is continuously packed because it serves some of the most flavorful beef you'll ever find. For a romantic dinner, **The River Cafe** (1 Water Street at the Brooklyn Bridge) has one of the city's most scenic settings and creative American food that is a worthy match for the fabulous Lower Manhattan skyline vistas. And don't forget Brooklyn's other culinary enticement—**Coney Island** and **Nathan's** hot dogs.

One of the borough's truly great treasures is the **Brooklyn Academy of Music**, a world-renowned performing arts center, offering an iconoclastic selection of dance, music, and theater. And for a breath of heavenly-scented air on a nice warm day, venture to the **Brooklyn Botanic Garden** and take in the fragrant pleasures of the Japanese garden, the lilac grove, and the herb garden.

The New York Transit Museum (housed in a 1936 subway station) displays vintage subway cars, signaling equipment, and historic maps. Another popular tourist attraction is the **Brooklyn Museum** with collections of Egyptian and Middle Eastern art, European and American paintings, and decorative arts and textiles. And no trip to Brooklyn would be complete for animal lovers without a look at the **Prospect Park Wildlife Center**.

The Bronx

While the Bronx is pretty gritty in parts, it has much to offer visitors who venture there. Its nautical **City Island** is New York's answer to Cape Cod. More pastoral beauty can be found at both **Wave Hill** (a 28-acre public estate with elegant lawns and gardens, a superb view of the Hudson River, and a Greek Revival mansion where Mark Twain and Teddy Roosevelt were occupants) and at the **New York Botanical Garden** with mile after mile of sculpted lawns and gardens, a tropical rain forest, and an African desert. And while another popular destination is officially called the International Wildlife Conservation Park, it is mostly referred to as the **Bronx Zoo**. By whatever name, it draws more than two million visitors annually to see its more than 4,000 animals. And for literary types, there's the **Edgar Allan Poe Cottage** where the master of the macabre penned several of his most famous works. For old-world culinary pleasures, Arthur Avenue is a haven of terrific family-style Italian restaurants. **Dominick's** (at 2335 Arthur) and **Mario's** (across the street at 2342) are two such places.

Staten Island

On Staten Island, you might plan a picnic at historic **Richmond Town**. Actors in period costume preserve the look and feel of a 17th Century farming community. The oldest elementary schoolhouse still standing in the USA and an 1840s general store provide an authentic look back in time. And the **Snug Harbor Cultural Center** (formerly a home for retired sailors) beckons visitors with its beautiful Botanic Garden. It also has a children's museum, an art gallery, and a concert hall.

Queens

Queens contains the largest tract of undisturbed farmland in New York City. You'll find it at the **Queens County Farm Museum**, which offers hayrides, a petting zoo, and a glimpse of 18th Century farm life. In contrast, Queens also offers the sights of Hollywood at its **American Museum of the Moving Image** in **Astoria**. Here, a computer imaging room allows you to "try on" Marilyn Monroe's billowing white dress from *The Seven-Year Itch*. Its other attractions include Robin Williams' *Mrs. Doubtfire* mask. Also notable is the **Queens Museum of Art,** on the site of the 1939 and 1964 World's Fairs. It features exhibits of contemporary art and photography, as well as the world's largest scale architectural model, a 9,335-square-foot "Panorama of New York." And Astoria has another claim to fame as home to the largest Greek community outside Athens.

New York's second largest **Chinatown** can be found in the Queens neighborhood of **Flushing**. Its downtown streets teem with markets stocked with exotic fruits and fresh seafood, alongside tea shops, ginseng shops, dim sum banquet halls, bakeries, and dry-goods stores. For terrific food and bargain prices, **Joe's Shanghai Restaurant** (136-21 37th Avenue) is one of the best. **Jade Palace Seafood Restaurant**, another neighborhood favorite, is just across the street. And **KB Garden** (136-28 39th Avenue)—reminiscent of the large banquet hall restaurants found in Hong Kong—is another winner for dim sum.

THEATER

THEATER

When you return from a trip to New York City, chances are the first question you'll be asked by friends and colleagues is, "What did you see?" They're not talking about skyscrapers, monuments, or works of art. They're talking about theater, and more likely than not, they mean *Broadway.*

Day after day, all along this stretch known as the Great White Way, someone enters a Broadway theater for the first time. It could be a theater buff from Kansas City or Cleveland, a student group from Pittsburgh, or a pair of retired school teachers from Dubrovnik. They may see a blockbuster musical with extravagant sets and spectacular special effects, a heart-warming revival, a mesmerizing new drama, a ribald comedy, or maybe the brilliant stage comeback of a great star. The theater setting will be elegant, perhaps historic, and the experience itself unforgettable.

Many Broadway theaters carry famous names such as Ethel Barrymore, Eugene O'Neill, Lunt-Fontanne, Richard Rodgers, Booth, Helen Hayes, Gershwin, and Neil Simon. They all carry echoes from the past.

In 1926, Antoinette Perry (for whom the Tonys were named) starred in *The Ladder* in what is now the **Brooks Atkinson**. This theater was also the venue of Neil Simon's first Broadway play, *Come Blow Your Horn*. George Gershwin's Pulitzer Prize-winning *Of Thee I Sing* opened in 1931 and its success helped save the **Music Box** in that tough Depression year. Mary Martin became a star singing "My Heart Belongs to Daddy" at the **Imperial**. And the **Royale** showcased the gifts of Laurence Olivier in both *The Entertainer* and *Becket*. And when *A Chorus Line* moved to Broadway after its successful Off-Broadway run, the **Shubert** was home to its dancing feet for 6,137 performances. In 1962, Barbra Streisand made her Broadway debut here in *I Can Get It for You Wholesale* and later brought her magic to the **Winter Garden** in *Funny Girl*. The Byzantine-style **Martin Beck** premiered Arthur Miller's *The Crucible* and Tennessee Williams' *Sweet Bird of Youth*. It was here, too, that Elizabeth Taylor made her Broadway debut in Lillian Hellman's *The Little Foxes*. In 1970, Jimmy Stewart and Helen Hayes lit up the stage of the **Virginia Theater** in *Harvey*. And once upon a time, the **St. James** had a beautiful usherette we know as Lauren Bacall.

But beyond Broadway, there's innovative and experimental theater being performed in eclectic theater spaces scattered up and down Manhattan in what is labeled Off-Broadway and Off-Off-Broadway. Productions here are exhilarating and entertaining and often feature well-known performers. It was Off-Broadway where Bernadette Peters expressed true friendship in *Sally and Marsha*, Farrah Fawcett got revenge in *Extremities*, and Kathy Bates found love and lust in *Frankie and Johnny in the Clair de Lune*. Off-Broadway is also where *Driving Miss Daisy* and *Steel Magnolias* originated and where *The Fantastics*, the longest running play in theater history, is still going strong. And more recently two of Broadway's biggest hits, *Rent* and *Bring in da Noise, Bring in da Funk*, were spawned Off-Broadway. *Sunday in the Park with George*, *Crimes of the Heart*, and *The Heidi Chronicles* are other Broadway hits that were first performed Off-Broadway.

The terms Broadway, Off-Broadway, and Off-Off-Broadway tend to be as confounding as *Who's on First*. While Broadway is a street that runs the entire length of Manhattan, Broadway theaters are more accurately *around* Broadway and Times Square and not actually *on* Broadway. Aside from the geographical distinction, Off-Broadway and Off-Off Broadway theaters are much smaller than the grand Broadway houses. But what constitutes a Broadway theater is determined not just by location and size but, to some extent, politics. Membership is determined by the League of American Theaters and Producers, based in New York. Generally, Broadway houses are commercial theaters with at least 500 seats in the Times Square area from Broadway to Eighth Avenue between West 40th and West 53rd Streets.

To further confuse the issue, two not-for-profit Off-Broadway companies—the **Circle in the Square** and the **Roundabout Theatre Company**—moved to the Broadway district and became Broadway houses, although their ticket prices are at Off-Broadway levels. And even though the Lincoln Center's large **Vivian Beaumont Theater** is all the way up on West 65th Street, it is considered a Broadway house because of its size (and undoubtedly because the Tony voters could not ignore the quality of its offerings). The small **Mitzi Newhouse Theater**, also at Lincoln Center, is considered Off-Broadway. And while the 399-seat **Promenade Theater** (that gave us Edward Albee's brilliant *Three Tall Women* and Steve Martin's clever *Picasso at the Lapin Agile*) is physically on Broadway, it is an Off-Broadway theater.

In his 1969 book about the Broadway theater, "The Season," William Goldman predicted that virtually all straight plays would soon be produced Off-Broadway because the high costs "make doing anything but mass appeal plays a lunatic Broadway venture." And recently, even Neil Simon, the king of mass appeal, went to the Off-Broadway **Union Square Theater** with his comedy, "London Suite." His producer calculated that to open the show on Broadway, he would have to raise $1.6 million, but only $660,000 to do it Off-Broadway. Although big musicals may rake in record amounts on Broadway, the returns on plays are so meager and unpredictable that Off-Broadway is not only a neat sidestep to avoid disaster, but a good bet for making money.

While the bulk of Off-Broadway theaters can be found in Greenwich Village and the East Village, the area of West 42nd Street west of Ninth Avenue known as **Theater Row** boasts a concentrated collection of theaters and repertory companies of high quality offering an intriguing mixed bag of theater productions.

For complete listings of current theater offerings, consult *The New York Times'* Sunday "Arts and Leisure" and the Friday "Weekend" sections. Another excellent source is *Time Out New York*. Other good sources include *New York* magazine, *Village Voice*, and *Where* magazine (which you'll undoubtedly find in your hotel room). *The New Yorker* is another source, though its listings are not as comprehensive. The *New York Native*, *Christopher Street*, and *Homo-Extra* cover the gay scene. And my monthly newsletter *On and Off Broadway* will not only keep you current on what's playing on and off Broadway, but features six comprehensive restaurant recommendations in each issue. (Use the ordering information at the back of this book to receive two free issues.)

Among the many quality companies and theaters offering alternatives to Broadway's mainstream fare are the **Signature Theatre Company** (which presents the works of a single playwright each season), **Playwrights Horizons**, dedicated to the support and development of new American playwrights, composers, and lyricists and to the production of their work, and the **Manhattan Theater Club** which has garnered an impressive track record of sending young plays on to Broadway. The **Theater for the New City** presents contemporary and classical plays, along with compelling political dramas. And the **Bouwerie Lane Theatre**, the resident house of the **Jean Cocteau Repertory Company**, is devoted to producing the classics in rep.

The mission of the **American Place Theatre**, one of Off-Broadway's founding theater companies, is to offer audiences a challenging and provocative theatrical experience by developing and presenting new plays by living American playwrights and by producing theater which is meaningful to a diverse audience. Its numerous awards include a *Village Voice* Obie Special Grant and Citation for "uncompromising commitment to unconventional and daring plays." Productions over the years have included Sam Shepard's early work, as well as the casting of then-unknown actors such as Faye Dunaway and Dustin Hoffman.

The multistage East Village **Public Theater** (the late Joseph Papp's pride and joy) is one of the most consistently engaging theaters in the city. Writers such as Sam Shepard and David Rabe and actors such as Meryl Streep and the late Raul Julia were nurtured at the Public. Robert DeNiro and Kevin Kline have also graced its stages. Dedicated to showcasing new American playwrights and performers, it also offers new spins on Shakespeare and the classics. In the summer (from June to September), the Public's stages include Central Park's outdoor Delacorte Theater for **Free Summer Shakespeare in Central Park** productions.

The **Orpheum**, also in the East Village, introduced us to the *Little Shop of Horrors*. And today the inventive *Stomp* is still going strong with its creative noise.

The **Negro Ensemble Company** was founded in 1967 by actor Robert Hooks, playwright Douglas Turner Ward, and producer Gerald S. Krone to provide a continuously producing professional theatre in which black artists—performers, playwrights, directors, designers, and craftspeople—could oversee their own creative destiny. Since its founding, it has produced more than 300 new plays (both on and off Broadway) and won more than 40 major drama awards. Award-winning works first produced by the NEC include *Ceremonies in Dark Old Men*, *The River Niger*, and *A Soldier's Play*. The roster of artists who have distinguished its productions include Denzel Washington, Cleavon Little, Roscoe Lee Brown, Godfrey Cambridge, Phylicia Rashad, and Esther Rolle.

The **American Jewish Theatre**, devoted to the discovery, development and presentation of plays dealing with Jewish themes, stages contemporary plays and revivals of musicals. The **Jewish Repertory Theatre** also presents plays relating to the Jewish experience. And the **Irish Arts Center** is the premiere showcase for Irish dramas in America, staging both classics and the best new Irish plays straight from Dublin.

While Off-Broadway theaters may have as many as 499 seats, Off-Off Broadway venues comprise tiny spaces with fewer than 100 seats and its performers do not have to be card-carrying professionals. Another thing that sets them apart is that their less costly productions allow a greater degree of daring and risk-taking than even the Off-Broadway productions could afford. Another important distinction to both actors and audiences is that the intimacy of the smaller theaters allows the most subtle facial expressions of the actors to be seen from every seat in the house.

Off-Off Broadway is where you'll find the truly original, quirky, and sometimes weird, world of experimental and avant-garde theater. Tickets to these productions are seldom more than $15. Harvey Fierstein first presented his *Torch Song Trilogy* at **La Mama Experimental Theater Club,** one of the most respected of the Off-Off Broadway stages. Another is the **Ridiculous Theatrical Company** featuring theater of the absurd at its high camp best.

Theater venues Off-Off Broadway run a wide gamut. Tables and chairs in someone's loft comprise the theater space known as **Dixon Place.** This Off-Off gem provides a forum for emerging artists to show their works in progress.

The Wooster Group, whose members include Willem Dafoe and Spalding Gray, was founded in 1967 as an experimental theater collective and is one of the oldest and foremost avant-garde theater companies in America. In 1968, an old factory was transformed into **The Performing Garage,** a versatile performance space which has since served as the Group's home stage.

And **En Garde Arts,** one of the most original of all the companies, is completely site-specific. The streets and buildings of New York serve as its stage.

This is just a hint of what you'll find when you venture into the incredible world of New York theater. Over the years, theatergoers from around the world have been captivated by its magic. And it is a love affair that endures. For New York's lively world of theater continues to be its gift to the world.

THEATER VENUES AND COMPANIES

Broadway

Ambassador Theater
219 W. 49th St.
(between Broadway and 8th Ave.)
Telecharge: 212/239-6200 or
800-432-7250

Brooks Atkinson Theatre
256 W. 47th St.
(between Broadway and 8th Ave.)
Theater: 212/719-4099
TicketMaster: 212/307-4100 or
800-755-4000

Ethel Barrymore Theater
243 W. 47th St.
(between Broadway and 8th Ave.)
Telecharge: 212/239-6200 or
800-432-7250

Vivian Beaumont Theater
Lincoln Center
150 W. 65th St.
Telecharge: 212/239-6200 or
800-432-7250

Martin Beck Theatre
302 W. 45th St.
(between 8th and 9th Aves.)
Telecharge: 212/239-6200 or
800-432-7250

Belasco Theatre
111 W. 44th St.
(between Broadway and 6th Ave.)
Telecharge: 212/239-6200 or
800-432-7250

Booth Theatre
222 W. 45th St.
(between Broadway and 8th Ave.)
Telecharge: 212/239-6200 or
800-432-7250

Broadhurst Theatre
235 W. 44th St.
(between Broadway and 8th Ave.)
Telecharge: 212/239-6200 or
800-432-7250

Broadway Theatre
1681 Broadway
(at 53rd St.)
Telecharge: 212/239-6200 or
800-432-7250

Circle in the Square
1633 Broadway
(between 50th and 51st Sts.)
Telecharge: 212/239-6200 or
800-432-7250

Cort Theatre
138 W. 48th St.
(between Broadway and 6th Ave.)
Telecharge: 212/239-6200 or
800-432-7250

**Ford Center for the
Performing Arts**
213 W. 42nd St.
(between Broadway and 8th Ave.)
TicketMaster: 212/307-4100 or
800-755-4000

Gershwin Theater
222 W. 51st St.
(between Broadway and 8th Ave.)
TicketMaster: 212/307-4100 or
800-755-4000

John Golden Theatre
252 W. 45th St.
(between Broadway and 8th Ave.)
Telecharge: 212/239-6200 or
800-432-7250

Helen Hayes Theatre
240 W. 44th St.
(between Broadway and 8th Ave.)
TicketMaster: 212/307-4100 or
800-755-4000

Imperial Theatre
249 W. 45th St.
(between Broadway and 8th Ave.)
Telecharge: 212/239-6200 or
800-432-7250

Walter Kerr Theater
219 W. 48th St.
(between Broadway and 8th Ave.)
Telecharge: 212/239-6200 or
800-432-7250

Longacre Theatre
220 W. 48th St.
(between Broadway and 8th Ave.)
Telecharge: 212/239-6200 or
800-432-7250

Lunt-Fontanne Theatre
205 W. 46th St.
(between Broadway and 8th Ave.)
TicketMaster: 212/307-4100 or
800-755-4000

Lyceum Theater
149 W. 45th St.
(between Broadway and 6th Ave.)
Telecharge: 212/239-6200 or
800-432-7250

Majestic Theatre
247 W. 44th St.
(between Broadway and 8th Ave.)
Telecharge: 212/239-6200 or
800-432-7250

Marquis Theater
1535 Broadway
(at 45th St.)
TicketMaster: 212/307-4100 or
800-755-4000

Minskoff Theater
200 W. 45th St.
(between Broadway and 8th Ave.)
TicketMaster: 212/307-4100 or
800-755-4000

Music Box Theatre
239 W. 45th St.
(between Broadway and 8th Ave.)
Telecharge: 212/239-6200 or
800-432-7250

Nederlander Theater
208 W. 41st St.
(between 7th and 8th Aves.)
TicketMaster: 212/307-4100 or
800-755-4000

New Amsterdam Theatre
214 W. 42nd St.
(between 7th and 8th Aves.)
TicketMaster: 212/307-4100 or
800-755-4000

Eugene O'Neill Theatre
230 W. 49th St.
(between Broadway and 8th Ave.)
Telecharge: 212/239-6200 or
800-432-7250

Palace Theater
1564 Broadway
(at 47th St.)
TicketMaster: 212/307-4100 or
800-755-4000

Plymouth Theater
236 W. 45th St.
(between Broadway and 8th Ave.)
Telecharge: 212/239-6200 or
800-432-7250

Richard Rodgers Theater
226 W. 46th St.
(between Broadway and 8th Ave.)
TicketMaster: 212/307-4100 or
800-755-4000

Roundabout Theater Co.
1530 Broadway at 45th St.
Box Office: 212/869-8400

Royale Theater
242 W. 45th St.
(between Broadway and 8th Ave.)
Telecharge: 212/239-6200 or
800-432-7250

St. James Theatre
246 W. 44th St.
(between Broadway and 8th Ave.)
Telecharge: 212/239-6200 or
800-432-7250

Shubert Theatre
225 W. 44th St.
(between Broadway and 8th Ave.)
Telecharge: 212/239-6200 or
800-432-7250

Neil Simon Theatre
250 W. 52nd St.
(between Broadway and 8th Ave.)
TicketMaster: 212/307-4100 or
800-755-4000

Virginia Theatre
245 W. 52nd St.
(between Broadway and 8th Ave.)
Telecharge: 212/239-6200 or
800-432-7250

Winter Garden Theater
1634 Broadway
(between Broadway and 8th Ave.)
Telecharge: 212/239-6200 or
800-432-7250

Off-Broadway

Actor's Playhouse
100 Seventh Ave. So.
(between Bleecker and W. 4th)
Telecharge: 212/239-6200 or
800-432-7250
Greenwich Village

Altered Stages
212 W. 29th St.
(between 7th & 8th Aves.)
212/677-4079
Chelsea

American Jewish Theatre
307 W. 26th St.
(between 8th and 9th Aves.)
212/633-9797
Chelsea

American Place Theatre
111 W. 46th St.
(between 6th & 7th Aves.)
Telecharge: 212/239-6200 or
800-432-7250
Theater District

Judith Anderson Theatre
422 W. 42nd St.
(between 9th & 10th Aves.)
212/886-1889
Theater District

Astor Place Theater
434 Lafayette St.
(So. of Astor Pl.)
212/254-4370
East Village

Atlantic Theater
336 W. 20th St.
(between 8th and 9th Aves.)
Telecharge: 212/239-6200 or
800-432-7250
Chelsea

Bouwerie Lane Theatre
330 Bowery at Bond St.
Ticket Central: 212/279-42001
East Village

Carnegie Hall
154 W. 57th St.
(between 6th & 7th Aves.)
212/247-7800
Theater District

Century Center Theatre
111 E. 15th St.
(at Union Square East)
Telecharge: 212/239-6200 or
800-432-7250
Union Square

Chelsea Playhouse
125 W. 22nd St.
(between 6th & 7th Aves)
TicketMaster: 212/307-4100 or
800-755-4000
Chelsea

Cherry Lane Theatre
38 Commerce St.
(one block below Bleecker St.)
Telecharge: 212/239-6200 or
800/432-7250
Greenwich Village

Circle in the Sq. Downtown
159 Bleecker St.
(between Sullivan and Thompson)
212/254-6330
Greenwich Village

City Center
131 W. 55th St.
(between 6th & 7th Aves.)
212/581-1212
Theater District

Classic Stage Company
136 E. 13th St.
(between 3rd & 4th Aves.)
212/677-4210
East Village

Duffy Theater
1553 Broadway
(between 46th and 47th Sts.)
TicketMaster: 212/307-4100 or
800-755-4000
Theater District

Douglas Fairbanks Theater
432 W. 42nd St.
(between 9th and 10th Aves.)
Telecharge: 212/239-6200 or
800-432-7250
Theater District

47th Street Theater
304 W. 47th St.
(between 8th and 9th Aves.)
212/265-1086
Theater District

Greenwich House Theatre
27 Barrow St. (at 7th Ave. So.)
Telecharge: 212/239-6200 or
800-432-7250
Greenwich Village

Grove Street Playhouse
39 Grove St.
(between Bedford & Bleecker Sts.)
212/642-8202
Greenwich Village

John Houseman Theater
450 W. 42nd St.
(between 9th & 10th Aves)
Telecharge: 212/239-6200 or
800-432-7250
Theater District

Hunter College Playhouse
Sylvia & Danny Kaye Playhouse
E. 68th St. between Park and
Lexington Aves.
212/772-4448
East Side

Intar Theatre
420 W. 42nd St.
(between 9th & 10th Aves.)
Ticket Central: 212/279-4200
Theater District

Irish Arts Center
553 W. 51st St.
(between 10th and 11th Aves.)
Ticket Central: 212/279-4200
Theater District

Irish Repertory Theatre
132 W. 22nd St.
(between 6th and 7th Aves.)
212/727-2737
Chelsea

Jewish Repertory/Playhouse 91
316 E. 91st St.
(between 1st and 2nd Aves.)
212/831-2000
Upper East Side

Martin R. Kaufman Theater
534 W. 42nd St.
(between 10th and 11th Aves.)
Ticket Central: 212/279-4200
Theater District

La MaMa
74A E. 4th
(between Bowery and 2nd Ave.)
212/439-9128
East Village

Lamb's Theatre
130 W. 44th St.
(between 6th and 7th Aves.)
Telecharge: 212/239-6200 or
800-432-7250
Theater District

Liberty Theater
234 W. 42nd St.
(between Broadway and 8th Ave.)
Ticket Central: 212/279-4200
Theater District

Lucille Lortel Theater
121 Christopher St.
(between Hudson and Bleecker)
Telecharge: 212/239-6200 or
800-432-7250
Greenwich Village

MCC Theater
120 W. 28th St.
(between 6th & 7th Aves.)
212/727-7765
Chelsea

Manhattan Theatre Club
131 W. 55th St.
(between 6th and 7th Aves.)
212/581-1212
Theater District

Sanford Meisner Theatre
164 11th Ave. (at 23rd St.)
212/539-3841
Chelsea

Minetta Lane Theatre
18 Minetta Lane
(East of 6th Ave.)
212/420-8000
Greenwich Village

Mitzi E. Newhouse Theater
Lincoln Center
150 W. 65th St. at Broadway
Telecharge: 212/239-6200 or
800-432-7250
West Side

New Victory Theater
209 W. 42nd St.
(between 7th and 8th Aves.)
Telecharge: 212/239-6200 or
800-432-7250
Theater District

New York Performance Works
128 Chambers St.
(at W. Broadway)
212/726-1285
TriBeCa

New York Shakespeare Festival
Joseph Papp Public Theater
425 Lafayette St. (So. of Astor Pl.)
212/598-7150
East Village

New York Theatre Workshop
79 E. 4th St.
(between 2nd & 3rd Aves.)
212/460-5475
East Village

Ohio Theater
66 Wooster St.
(between Spring & Broome Sts.)
212/252-4031
SoHo

Orpheum Theater
126 Second Ave.
(between 7th and 8th Sts.)
212/477-2477
East Village

Joseph Papp Public Theater
425 Lafayette St.
(So. of Astor Pl.)
Telecharge: 212/239-6200 or
800-432-7250
East Village

Pearl Theatre Co.
80 St. Mark's Pl.
(between 1st & 2nd Aves.)
212/598-9802
East Village

Laura Pels at The Roundabout
1530 Broadway (at 45th St.)
212/869-8400
Theater District

Players Theatre
115 MacDougal St.
(at Minetta Lane)
Telecharge: 212/239-6200 or
800-432-7250
Greenwich Village

Playhouse Theatre
115 MacDougal St.
(between Bleecker and W. 3rd)
Telecharge: 212/239-6200 or
800-432-7250
Greenwich Village

Playwrights Horizons
416 W. 42nd St.
(between 9th and 10th Aves.)
Ticket Central: 212/279-4200
Theater District

Primary Stages
354 W. 45th St.
(between 8th and 9th Aves.)
212/333-4052
Theater District

Promenade Theatre
2162 Broadway
(at 76th St.)
212/580-1313
Upper West Side

Pulse Ensemble Theatre
432 W. 42nd St.
(between 9th & 10th Aves.)
212/333-7555
Theater District

Riant Theatre
161 Hudson St.
(between Hubert & Laight Sts.)
212/925-8353
TriBeCa

St. John's Church
81 Christopher St.
(betw. 7th Ave. So. and Bleecker)
Ticket Central: 212/279-4200
Greenwich Village

St. Luke's Church
308 W. 46th St.
(between 8th and 9th Aves.)
Telecharge: 212/239-6200 or
800-432-7250
Theater District

The Salon
432 E. 91st St.
(between 1st & York Aves.)
212/288-1125
Upper East Side

Second Stage Theatre
2162 Broadway at 76th St.
Telecharge: 212/239-6200 or
800-432-7250
Upper West Side

Selwyn Theatre
229 W. 42nd St.
(between Broadway and 8th Ave.)
Telecharge: 212/239-6200 or
800-432-7250
Theater District

Signature Theater Co.
425 Lafayette St.
(between 4th & 8th Sts.)
Telecharge: 212/239-6200 or
800-432-7250
East Village

SoHo Playhouse
15 Vandam St.
(between 6th Ave. and Varick St.)
212/691-1555
SoHo

SoHo Rep
46 Walker St.
(between Church St. & Broadway)
212/560-7387
SoHo

Sullivan St. Playhouse
181 Sullivan St.
(between Houston and Bleecker)
212/674-3838
Greenwich Village

Symphony Space
2537 Broadway
(between W. 94th & W. 95th)
212/864-5400
Upper West Side

Theater at St. Peter's Church
54th St. and Lexington Ave.
212/935-5820
Midtown

Theater for the New City
155 First Ave. at 9th St.
(between 9th and 10th Sts.)
212/254-1109
East Village

Theatre at St. Clement's
423 W. 46th St.
(between 9th and 10th Aves.)
Ticket Central: 212/279-4200
Theater District

Theatre East
211 E. 60th St.
(between 2nd and 3rd Aves.)
212/838-9090
East Side

Theater Four
424 W. 55th St.
Telecharge: 212/239-6200 or
800-432-7250
Theater District

Theater at Madison Sq. Garden
Two Pennsylvania Plaza
(7th Ave. betw. 31st & 32nd Sts.)
TicketMaster: 212/307-4100 or
800-755-4000
Chelsea

Theatre Off Park
224 Waverly Place
(between W. 11th and Perry Sts.)
212/627-2556
Greenwich Village

Theatre Row Theatre
424 W. 42nd St.
(between 9th and 10th Aves.)
Ticket Central: 212/279-4200
Theater District

Theatre 3
311 W. 43rd St.
(between 8th & 9th Aves.)
212/397-7841
Theater District

Thirteenth Street Repertory
50 W. 13th St.
(between 5th & 6th Aves.)
212/675-6677
Greenwich Village

Triad
158 W. 72nd St.
(betw. Amsterdam & Columbus)
212/799-4599
Upper West Side

Tribeca Performing Arts Center
199 Chambers St.
(between Greenwich & West Sts.)
Ticket Central: 212/279-4200
SoHo/TriBeCa

Ubu Repertory Theater
15 W. 28th St.
(between 5th and 6th Aves.)
212/679-7562
Gramercy Park/Murray Hill

Union Square Theatre
100 E. 17th St.
(at Park Ave. So.)
TicketMaster: 212/307-4100 or
800-755-4000
Union Square

Variety Arts
110 Third Ave. at 13th St.
Telecharge: 212/239-6200 or
800-432-7250
East Village

Victoria Theatre
235 W. 125th St.
(between Adam Clayton Powell
and Frederick Douglass Blvds.)
212/769-8183
Harlem

The Village Gate
240 W. 52nd St.
(between Broadway and 8th Ave.)
212/307-5252
Theater District

Vineyard Theatre
108 E. 15th St.
(at Union Square East)
212/353-3874
Union Square

Westbeth Theatre Center
151 Bank St. (at Washington St.)
212/741-0391
Greenwich Village

Westside Theatre
407 W. 43rd St.
(between 9th and 10th Aves.)
Telecharge: 212/239-6200 or
800-432-7250
Theater District

Wings Theatre
154 Christopher St.
(betw. Hudson & Greenwich Sts.)
212/627-2961
Greenwich Village

WPA Theater
519 W. 23rd St.
(between 10th and 11th Aves.)
212/206-0523
Chelsea

Getting Theater Tickets

At the box office or through ticket agents. Tickets for Broadway and Off-Broadway shows can be purchased at theater box offices or through ticket agencies such as **Telecharge** (212/239-6200 or 800-432-7250) or **Ticketmaster** (212/307-4100 or 800-755-4000). A surcharge ($2.00-$5.00 per ticket) will be added to the total of those purchased by ticket agents. **Ticketmaster has recently introduced a tickets-by-fax program.** To receive a free kit, fax your name and address to 212/307-4554 (or call 212/307-7171). The kit includes information on shows, seating charts, and special entertainment and dining offers. **Ticket Central** (212/279-4200) is the joint box office for Off- and Off-Off-Broadway shows.

By mail. If you wish, you may also order tickets in advance by mail by sending the theater a certified check or money order, several alternate dates, and a return self-addressed, stamped envelope. I don't really recommend this method. I prefer paying the small service fee charged by the telephone ticket agencies (listed above) that tell you what the available seat locations are for the dates of your choice.

Independent ticket agents such as **London Theatre & More** (800-683-0799), **Keith Prowse Tickets** (212/398-1430 or 800-669-8687), **Americana Tickets & Travel** (212/581-6660 or 800-833-3121), **Premiere Ticket Service, Inc.** (212/643-1274), **Theatre Direct** (800-334-8457) **(now offering ticket cancellation insurance at $5.00 per ticket)**, Golden/Leblang Theatre Ticket Service (212/944-8910 or 800-299-8587), and **Paramount Tickets and Tours** (800-232-7788) can be useful in obtaining hard-to-get tickets. **But keep in mind that this is a considerably more expensive way to secure seats. Brokers' fees vary.**

Half-Price Tickets. Day-of-performance tickets for a variety of Broadway and Off-Broadway shows may be purchased by **cash or traveler's checks** (but not by credit card) at the **TKTS booths** at the Times Square Theatre Center, located at 47th Street and Broadway, and at the Lower Manhattan Theatre Center on the mezzanine of 2 World Trade Center. The Times Square booth is open for matinee tickets on Wednesday and Saturday between 10:00 a.m. and 2:00 p.m. For evening performances, it is open from 3:00 to 8:00 p.m.; and for all Sunday performances from noon until 8:00 p.m. The World Trade Center branch is open weekdays from 11:00 a.m. to 5:30 p.m. and on Saturday from 11:00 a.m. to 3:30 p.m. For matinees and Sundays, you have to buy tickets the day before the performance. Telephone 212/768-1818 to confirm hours of operation.

Hit Show Club Discount Coupons. Vouchers for discount tickets (up to 50% off) are available at the Club's headquarters at 630 Ninth Avenue at 44th St., 8th floor. Phone 212/581-4211 for details. If you wish, you may send a stamped, self-addressed envelope and a list of the coupons you would like to receive. **Discount Coupons and flyers are also available at the Convention and Visitors Bureau at Two Columbus Circle (212/397-8200).**

Fund Tix. The Producers of Broadway's best have assigned house seats to The Actors' Fund for every Broadway show—even those sold out months in advance. Tickets are twice the box office price, half is a tax-deductible contribution. Call 48 hours in advance. Mon-Fri 10:00 a.m. - 4:00 p.m. AmEx, Visa, Master. 212/221-7301 x133.

Other ticket tips. Often you can get excellent single seats when pairs are either completely sold out or in the upper reaches of the balcony. My husband and I frequently buy choice seats to hit Broadway shows that are one in back of the other rather than taking seats together in less desirable locations. If you opt for the best seats, you will not have the pleasure of rubbing elbows during the performance, but you may have third and fourth row center seats instead of side-by-sides in the back of the house. I also like trying for house seats a few hours before a performance. These prime seats—reserved for various VIPs—are released for sale at face value an hour or two before the performance (and, on occasion, earlier in the day).

WEATHER

New York has four distinct seasons with spring and fall the obvious best times to visit. Winter weather is unpredictable—January and February can be stormy and severe. And in summer, July and August can be sweltering (with temperatures of 90°F and higher). But with good central heating and air conditioning the rule rather than the exception in restaurants, theaters, and museums, there's really no bad time to enjoy the abundance of indoor activities New York has to offer.

For recorded weather information, you may call 900/weather from anywhere in the United States (at a cost of 95 cents per minute). The following lists the average daily highs and lows throughout the year.

January	38/25°F	July	85/68°F
February	40/27°F	August	84/67°F
March	50/35°F	September	76/60°F
April	61/44°F	October	65/50°F
May	72/54°F	November	54/41°F
June	80/63°F	December	43/31°F

WHEN TO GO

As you will see by the following summary of yearly events, there is something interesting going on throughout the year. This summary is by no means exhaustive—it's merely a sampling. You may call the numbers listed for further information and details on the events mentioned or call the New York Convention and Visitors Bureau at 800-nyc-visit or 212/397-8222 for information on all the latest coming events and festivals.

January

Early in January, there's a one-day **Winter Festival on Central Park's Great Lawn** (near 81st Street) featuring cross-country skiing demonstrations, a winter fashion show, and a snow sculpture contest (212/360-3456). Also early in the month is the **Three Kings' Day Parade** when live camels, donkeys, children, and other celebrants weave their way through East Harlem (212/831-7272). Another popular event is the **New York National Boat Show** (212/216-

2000). Then the esteemed **Winter Antiques Show** comes to town late in the month (212/452-3067). A colorful highlight in late January-early February is the **Chinese New Year Celebration,** a lively street festival capped off by a festive parade that winds its way along Mott Street (212/373-1800).

February

For romantics, there's the **Valentine's Day Marriage Marathon** when couples marry atop one of New York's most famous landmark buildings, the Empire State Building (212/736-3100). The skyscraper has another big event later in the month with the **Annual Empire State Building Run-Up,** an invitational foot race in which 125 runners race up its 1,576 stairs (212/736-3100). Mid-month brings the crème of the canines to town for the **Westminster Kennel Club Dog Show** (212/465-6741). And music fans line the streets to Madison Square Garden to catch sight of the comings and goings of the glittery **Grammy Awards.**

March

March is a month of parades and flowers. Felines get to strut their stuff early in the month at the **International Cat Show** at Madison Square Garden (212/465-6741). And on St. Patrick's Day—when everyone is Irish and even the line running down Fifth Avenue is painted green—the **St. Patrick's Day Parade** makes its merry way through town. A little later in the month, there's the **Greek Parade** (718/204-6500). And then another kind of parade hits town when the **Ringling Brothers and Barnum & Bailey Circus** arrives for a two-month stay at Madison Square Garden (212/465-6741). And finally, you can put on your Easter bonnet for the **Easter Promenade,** the festive stroll along Fifth Avenue from 44th to 57th Streets (212/397-8222). The **Manhattan Antiques and Collectibles Triple Pier Expo** brings over 600 different exhibitors displaying formal furniture, arts & crafts, period pottery, textiles, statuary, art glass, jewelry, toys, folk art, and more to the West Side Piers (212/255-0020). And auto enthusiasts hit town for the world-famous **International Auto Show** at the Jacob K. Javits Convention Center (718/746-5300). The heady scent of flowers fills the New York Coliseum when the **New York Flower Show** arrives mid-month (212/757-0915). And there are more blooms to be found at **Macy's Spring Flower Show** (212/494-2922) and at the **Greater New York Orchid Show** at the World Financial Center (212/945-0505).

April

Sports fans everywhere rejoice in April. In New York, it means **opening day** at **Yankee Stadium** (718/293-6000) and **Shea Stadium** (718/507-8499) when the boys of summer officially take to the field for another season.

May

The beautiful month of May brings Navy and Coast Guard ships, aircraft carriers, and 10,000 uniformed personnel for **Fleet Week**. Then the sound of dancing feet fills the air with the **Annual Tap Dance Extravaganza,** which brings some of the world's best tap dancers to town to perform while great living legends of tap and jazz music are honored at various venues around town (201/935-5504). And the **American Ballet Theatre Season** at the Met begins (212/362-6000). This is also a good month for bikers with **Bike New York: The Great Five-Boro Bike Tour,** the two-wheel answer to the New York Marathon. This annual 42-mile bicycle tour starts in Battery Park in Manhattan and ends with a lively festival at Fort Wadsworth on Staten Island. The Brooklyn Botanic Garden hosts the **Annual Cherry Blossom Festival** (718/622-4433). And the Seventh Regiment Armory welcomes the **International Fine Arts Fair,** one of the art world's most important events, showing European and American works from over 70 galleries (212/472-0590). Then browse or buy at the **Washington Square Outdoor Art Exhibit** (212/982-6255). And foodies can spend the day sampling specialties from around the world at the **Ninth Avenue International Food Festival** stretching along Ninth Avenue from 37th to 57th Streets.

June

June is a month of street festivals, outdoor concerts, and parades that celebrate almost anything. For food fans (and who isn't), there's **Restaurant Week** when a variety of New York's best restaurants offer multi-course meals for $19.97. Participating restaurants change from year to year and some extend the special prix fixe menus until Labor Day, or even through the year. Full-page ads appear in *The New York Times* with details, and reservations fill up quickly. Food also figures prominently in the **Second Avenue Festival,** a street fair with music, games, arts and crafts, and all varieties of edibles (212/576-9000). Lincoln Center also gets in the act with its **Annual American Crafts Festival.** And there's the **Festival of St. Anthony,** another of the city's great street fairs, complete with games of chance, entertainment, and booth after booth of irresistible Italian goodies (212/777-2755). But it's not just the captivating aroma of sizzling sausages and spicy pizzas that fill the air in June. There's also music, music, music. **The New York Jazz Festival** occurs mid-month. The largest jazz event in New York, it features over 200 acts in ten different venues (212/219-3006). The **Washington Square Music Festival**, a season of free concerts featuring classical and jazz music, also begins mid-month (212/431-1088). And **SummerStage**, Central Park's summer-long series of outdoor concerts (rock, pop, folk, and jazz) gets launched (212/360-2777). Central Park's Delacorte Theater is the setting for **Free Shakespeare in the Park** productions starring top-notch performers during the **New York Shakespeare Festival** from June to August (212/539-8500). The **Metropolitan Opera** also offers free evening performances in the city parks from June to July (212/362-6000). And late in June, **Lesbian and Gay Pride Week** is kicked off with a zany parade that travels down Fifth Avenue to Greenwich Village (212/807-7433).

July

Fourth of July festivities include a colorful festival in Lower Manhattan, a parade of tall ships that sail up the Hudson River, and Macy's fabulous fireworks display over the East River (212/809-4900). The Museum of Modern Art's sculpture garden is the beautiful backdrop for its free weekend **Summergarden Concerts** by Julliard students through August. More beautiful music is made during the two-week **Mostly Mozart** concert series at Avery Fisher Hall toward the end of the month (212/875-5030). It commences with a free outdoor concert before moving indoors. And the wonderful **Lincoln Center Festival** (July and August) has a bit of everything, including ballet, contemporary dance, theater, opera, and Vietnamese puppets (212/lincoln).

August

The **Lincoln Center Out-of-Doors Festival**, a free performing arts festival, features live entertainment on the plaza from noon to sunset (212/875-5400). And the U.S. Open Tennis Championship, one of the major events on the tennis circuit, is held at the end of the month at Flushing Meadows Park in Queens (718/760-6200).

September

Broadway on Broadway, *the* free event of the year for theater enthusiasts, is a show celebrating Broadway with the songs and casts from virtually every Broadway production. A stage is erected in the middle of Times Square for this fabulous one-afternoon event early in the month (212/768-1560). Many other colorful affairs make this a great time to visit New York as well. **Little Italy's Feast of San Gennaro,** a week-long celebration of food and merrymaking Italian-style, is one of the city's most anticipated festivals (212/226-9546). And there's **Wigstock**—the most outrageous of galas—with thousands of gay and lesbian participants in a hugely colorful celebration of high fashion drag (212/620-7310). Parades abound: the **African-American/Caribbean Parade** (212/374-5176), the **German-American Steuben Parade** (212/207-7242), and, of course, the **Labor Day Parade** (212/374-5176). Then late in the month the two-week **New York Film Festival** begins at Lincoln Center (212/875-5610).

October

Ice Skating at Rockefeller Center (212/860-4455) glides in this month, along with yet more parades—the **Hispanic Day Parade** (212/864-0715), the **General Casimir Pulaski Day Parade** (212/254-1180), the **Columbus Day Parade** (212/249-9923), and the zany **Greenwich Village Halloween Parade** (212/758-5519). And for a really charming procession, visit the Cathedral of St. John the Divine for the **Feast of St. Francis of Assisi** when animals—great and small—are brought in to be blessed (212/662-2133).

November

The **New York City Marathon** takes the streets, traveling through all five boroughs before finishing at Tavern on the Green in Central Park (212/860-4455). And the **Big Apple Circus** pitches its tent this month in Damrosch Park at Lincoln Center and settles in until January (212/268-2500). Then late in the month comes one of New York's most enduring traditions, **Macy's Thanksgiving Day Parade,** marking the start of the Christmas season (212/494-5432). The best spot to view the parade is right in front of Macy's on 34th Street. Here, you'll have the best vantage point for seeing live performances by the casts of the Broadway musicals represented. Many New Yorkers, however, feel that the best part of the parade occurs the night before when the giant balloons are inflated. Spectators on Central Park West at 79th Street can watch as characters like Barney, Betty Boop, Snoopy, and the Pink Panther are pumped up with helium and air and brought to life once again.

December

This is when you can see New York at its most beautiful, all decked out in its festive holiday finery. Early in the month you can see it come to glowing life by catching the **Lighting of the Giant Christmas Tree at Rockefeller Center** (212/632-3975), the **Winter Garden Lighting Ceremony at the World Financial Center** (212/945-0505), the **Lincoln Center Holiday Tree Lighting** (212/lincoln), the **Harlem International Holiday Lighting Celebration in Central Park** (212/996-7563), and the **Lighting of the Giant Chanukah Menorah at Grand Army Plaza** (718/778-6000). And there's a public candlelight march to City Hall, **"Out of the Darkness,"** an observance of World AIDS Day (212/580-7668). The **Radio City Music Hall Christmas Spectacular** (212/247-4777) and the New York City Ballet's **Nutcracker** at Lincoln Center (212/750-5570) are just a few of the many holiday traditions that make the season so delightful. And, of course, come New Year's Eve there's the street bash to beat all, the **Annual New Year's Eve Celebration and Ball Drop in Times Square**, where a massive crowd gathers to cheer in the new year when the famous glowing ball drops at the stroke of midnight (212/768-1560). There's also a gala celebration, **First Night,** held at venues throughout the city. A purchased button is admission to events at various locations (212/922-9393). Other celebrations include a festive **Midnight Run** through Central Park starting at Tavern on the Green (212/860-4455) and **New Year's Eve Fireworks** at the South Street Seaport (212/732-5168).

USEFUL PHONE NUMBERS

EMERGENCY

Ambulance, Fire and Police 911
Doctors on Call (24 hours) 212/737-2333
Dental Service 212/679-3966
Pharmacy, Kaufman (open 24 hours) 212/755-2266

AIRLINES

Air Canada 800/776-3000
Air France 800/237-2747
Alitalia 800/223-5730
American 800/433-7300
America West Airlines 800/235-9292
British Airways 800/247-9297
Continental Airlines 800/525-0280
Delta Air Lines 800/221-1212
KLM Royal Dutch 800/374-7747
Lufthansa German Airlines 800/645-3880
Northwest 800/225-2525
Sabena Belgian Airlines 800/955-2000
Scandinavian Airlines 800/221-2350
Swissair 800/221-4750
TWA 800/221-2000
United Airlines 800/241-6522
USAirways 800/428-4322

CAR RENTAL

Avis 800/331-1212
Budget 800/527-0700
Hertz 800/654-3131
National 800/328-4567

LIMOUSINES

Absolute! Class Limousine . . . . 212/227-6588 or 800/546-6654
Bens Limousine Service . . . . 718/433-1212 or 800/227-5060
Gotham Limousine 888/227-7997
Imperial Limousines 212/229-9292
Lincoln Limousine 212/666-5050
Manhattan Int'l Limousine Network 800/221-7500
Millennium Limousine USA 212/807-9350
Showcase Executive 212/989-2201

PUBLIC TRANSPORTATION

Bus/Subway 718/330-1234
Amtrak 800/872-7245
Long Island Railroad 718/217-5477
Metro-North Railroad 212/532-4900
Port Authority Bus Terminal 212/564-8484
Taxis (lost property) 212/840-4734
Taxis (complaints) 212/221-8294

SIGHTSEEING COMPANIES

All American Stage Tours 800/735-8530
Americana Travel & Tours 718/375-9500
Bacon Yacht Charters 212/873-7558
Big Onion Walking Tours 212/439-1090
Brooklyn Museum/Botanic Garden Tour 718/638-5000
Central Park Bicycle Tour 212/603-9750
Central Park Trolley Tours 212/360-2727
Circle Line Sightseeing Yachts 212/563-3200
Circle Line Statue of Liberty Ferry 212/269-5755
Citywalks: Walking Tours of New York 212/989-2456
Discover NY with Kitt Garrett (customized tours) 212/750-5944
Express Sightseeing Cruises 908/872-2628
Field Studies Center of NY (technical tours) 212/575-8065
Gracie Mansion Conservancy Tour 212/570-4751
Gray Line New York Tours 212/397-2620

Harlem Spirituals 212/757-0425
Harlem Your Way! Tours Unlimited 212/690-1687
Just Brooklyn Tours 718/968-0352
Kramer's Reality Tour (Seinfeld's NY) 212/268-5525
Manhattan Shopping Sprees 212/594-5650
Marvelous Manhattan Tours Plus 917/865-5124
Metropolitan Opera House Backstage Tour 212/769-7020
New York Apple Tours (double-decker buses) 212/944-9700
New York Waterway Boat Cruises 212/902-8700
Radio City Music Hall Productions 212/246-4600
Seaport Liberty Cruises 212/630-8888
Shoppers Delight Tours (discount shopping by bus) 212/307-7050
Short Line Tours 212/397-2620
Sidewalks of New York (ghosts, celebrities, etc.) 212/662-5300
Sutherland Hit Show Tours 212/532-7732
V.I.P. Tours of New York (theater, architecture) 212/247-0366

TRAVEL SERVICES

Cary Airport Express Coach Bus 800/284-0909
Delta Water Shuttle 800/543-3779
Gray Line Airport Shuttle 212/315-3006
NY Convention & Visitors Bureau ... 212/397-8222 or 800/693-7291
Thomas Cook (currency exchange) 212/757-6915

MISCELLANEOUS

Consumer Complaints 212/487-4444
Dow Jones Report 212/976-4141
Time 212/976-1616
Weather 212/976-1212
Western Union 800/325-6000

ACCOMMODATIONS

 ★★★★★   **one of the world's best**
★★★★   **outstanding**
★★★   **deluxe**
★★   **very comfortable and pleasant**
★   **comfortable/good value**

While New York City has some of the most spectacular hotels in the world, with prices to match, a stay here may leave you with the feeling that never before have you paid so much for so little. Real estate is expensive in the Big Apple and those seeking lodging will find they are not only faced with a hefty daily rate but hotel taxes of 13.25 percent plus a $2.00 per night city occupancy charge. You can beat the high cost, however, by simply never paying full price. Nearly all hotels listed offer special weekend rates; some also offer weekend packages that include extras such as brunch, cocktails, fruit baskets and wine, free parking, or Broadway tickets. And some hotels are now offering supersaver rates, much as the airlines do, for advance booking (usually a month in advance). This gimmick can save you as much as 30-35 percent off the published rates. There are also times throughout the year when hotels offer special promotional rates and packages full of nice extras. Hotels also have reduced rates for members of certain groups, such as AAA or AARP. Government and military rates are also available, as are discounts (up to 50 percent) on adjoining rooms when families travel together. In general, it is best to bypass the centralized 800-number and call the property directly to get the best deal.

HOTEL DISCOUNTERS

Hotel discounters—also called hotel consolidators and hotel brokers—can be a traveler's best friend and make it possible for you to never pay full price for a hotel room. Discounts can be big—from 40 to 50 percent and sometimes as much as 65 percent. In a single call, you can find out what hotels (in a variety of price ranges) are available during the period you need accommodation. It's quite simple. And if you phone several different discounters to find out what their best deals are, it's a pretty sure thing that you'll find a bargain.

Discounters either arrange preferred rates with hotels (in the same way that travel agencies do for their best corporate clients) or pay in advance for large blocks of rooms at various hotels at special negotiated low rates. Hotels are happy for this business since it helps fill rooms, but have an agreement with discounters that they keep their advertising subtle. You may have skipped right over many such ads in your local travel section because of such subtlety. Often the ads are just small blocks that simply say "Discount Accommodations" and give an 800-number.

Be aware that some discounters list hotels at which they do not have negotiated special rates along with those at which they do. So when calling, it is important to indicate that you are only interested in finding out what they have available at a discounted rate.

There are various ways the discounters operate. Some require prepayment for a reservation, usually by credit card charge, and then issue vouchers. They may require several days' advance notice of a cancellation. Others, such as Quikbook, do not require prepayment and you can cancel without penalty up to the afternoon of your scheduled arrival. Among the discounters/consolidators:

Accommodations Express. 800/444-7666; fax 609/525-0111. Budget to luxury accommodations. Works with more than 80 percent of the city's hotels and offers from 10 to 40 percent discounts. Often has good last-minute deals. *Prepay/voucher. AE, DC, MC, V.*

Central Reservation Service. 800/548-3311 or 407/339-4116; fax 407/339-4736. Has 24-hour courtesy phones at LaGuardia. *Pay at hotel.*

Express Hotel Reservations. 800/356-1123 or 303/440-8481; fax 303/440-0166. Monday-Friday 9:00 a.m. - 6:30 p.m. Mainly moderate to deluxe hotels. Savings range from $30 to $80 per night. *Pay at hotel; credit card needed to guarantee. AE, MC, V.*

Hotel Reservations Network. 800/964-6835 or 214/361-7311; fax 214/361-7299. Awards 500 frequent-flyer miles on Northwest or Continental when three or more nights are booked. *Prepay/voucher. AE, Disc, MC, V.*

Quikbook. 800/789-9887 or 212/779-room; fax 212/779-6120. My favorite of the discounters. They offer a wide selection of hotels and do not require prepayment. *Pay at hotel.*

RMC Travel. 800/245-5738 or 212/754-6560; fax 212/754-6571. Reservations should be made at least 10 days in advance. *Prepay/voucher. AE, Disc, MC, V.*

Room Exchange. 800/846-7000 or 212/760-1000. Works with about 75 New York properties from budget to deluxe and offers 40 to 50 percent off published rates. *Prepay/voucher. All major cards.*

Take Time to Travel. 800/522-9991 or 212/840-8686; fax 212/221-8686. Works with economy to deluxe hotels. Offers up to 50 percent off published rates. *Prepay/voucher. AE, Disc, MC, V.*

DISCOUNT HOTEL MEMBERSHIPS

Half-off membership programs keep growing in popularity and in number. In general, they charge from $20 to $100 for a year's membership and a booklet listing thousands of hotels that offer half-price discounts to members. If it sounds too good to be true, often it is. Rooms are generally only discounted for those nights that hotels are expecting less than 80 or 85 percent occupancy. But if you are flexible and persistent, you can usually come up with a discounted room.

The Entertainment discount book is the best of the lot. Not only can you save as much as 50% on hotel rates, but the book also has coupons for restaurants, airlines, museums, movies, car rentals, and more. Issued annually for a number of cities, the book is priced at around $30.00 plus $3.00 for shipping and handling. Call 800/445-4137 to order or find out where you can obtain one for your city. Other companies selling discount memberships include the following:

America at 50 Percent Off ($19.95)	800/248-2783
Carte Royale ($39.95)	800/847-7002
Encore ($49.95)	800/638-0930
Great American Traveler ($49.95; $29.95 each year to renew)	800/331-8867
International Travel Card (aka ITC 50) ($49)	800/342-0558
Privilege Card International ($74.95 + $5.95/shipping)	800/236-9732
Quest International ($99)	800/638-9819

HOTELS

What follows is just a sampling of New York's many appealing hotels in a variety of price ranges. Prices listed are the published rack rates and are meant to serve as a comparative guideline only since rates fluctuate greatly throughout the year. And if you follow the above recommendations, you will never, ever, pay the published rate.

ALGONQUIN HOTEL ★★
59 West 44th Street (between Fifth and Sixth Aves.)
212/840-6800 or 800/228-3000
*Singles $230; doubles $250; suites $375-$550. **Special weekend rates.***

This turn-of-the-century theater district landmark hotel evokes another era. In the '20s it was the gathering place of the famed Round Table of clever literary types, including Dorothy Parker, George S. Kaufman, Robert Benchley, and Alexander Woollcott. Today, its wood-panelled Edwardian lobby has a certain nostalgic feel with its somewhat somber, genteel English club atmosphere. But while the hotel's historic appeal is undeniable, the small rooms and old-fashioned bathrooms are generally disappointing. More desirable are the signature suites, dedicated to the people and events that contributed to the hotel's reputation. They feature memorabilia related to these famous names, including the New Yorker, Vanity Fair, Playbill, James Thurber, and Dorothy Parker. Hotel conveniences include 24-hour front desk service, laundry/valet services, and 24-hour room service. But for the best of the Algonquin, come for the wonderful Oak Room cabaret.

BEACON HOTEL ★★
2130 Broadway (75th St.)
212/787-1100 or 800/572-4969
*$99-190. Pets allowed. **Special weekend rates and packages.***

You'll feel like a real New Yorker when you stay in this nice Upper West Side neighborhood. Lincoln Center is just a short walk away and the off-Broadway Beacon Theater is just downstairs. There's no food service here, but Zabar's and the Fairway Market are nearby, as well as many good neighborhood restaurants. Every room and suite features two double beds, an equipped kitchenette, and 78-channel cable TV. Dishes, cutlery, a coffee maker, and a hair dryer are also supplied. The closets are nice and roomy, the furnishings attractive, and the bathrooms have dressing-room style mirrors. A very good value for the money.

BEEKMAN TOWER HOTEL ★★★
3 Mitchell Place (First Ave. and 49th St.)
212/355-7300 or 800/me-suite
Studios $159-$279; one-bedroom suites $279-$359; two-bedroom suites $439-$499.
Special weekend rates, lower rates June-August.

This Manhattan East Suite Hotel is located in a charming East Side neighborhood near Sutton Place and the United Nations. Built in 1928, its distinctive tower is considered an art deco landmark. Accommodations are comfortable and attractive. Studios have sitting areas and kitchenettes. Suites feature traditional styling and some have terraces and river views. Both one- and two-bedroom suites are nicely appointed and each features a complete kitchen, including a full stove, refrigerator, coffee maker, and all the dishes, glasses, pots, and utensils needed to fix a full-course meal. Other amenities include hair dryers, irons and ironing boards, microwave ovens, and a 24-hour health club. And its Top of the Tower cocktail lounge, with a fabulous view and romantic piano music, is the perfect place to end an evening on the town.

BEST WESTERN WOODWARD HOTEL ★★
210 West 55th Street (Broadway)
212/247-2000 or 800/336-4110.
Singles and doubles $155-$165; suites $200-275.

This branch of the well-known chain offers a nice location for theatergoers and modest prices. Renovated in 1994, it has 131 guest rooms and suites. All rooms feature phones with modem capabilities and computerized concierge services, well-lighted work desks, and pay per-view movies. While there's no on-site fitness center, complimentary passes are available to Prescriptives Gym, a block and a half from the hotel. Room service is provided by the famous Carnegie Deli 21 hours a day. Executive Level rooms and suites include access to the Gold Crown Club which features complimentary continental breakfast, a video and CD library, and business support services. Executive Level rooms also offer more upscale amenities such as terry bathrobes and bathsheets, hair dryers and makeup mirrors, irons and ironing boards, coffee makers, refrigerators, and VCRs. Some rooms also have complete stereo systems with CD players.

BEVERLY HOTEL ★★
125 East 50th Street (Lexington Ave.)
212/753-2700 or 800/223-0945
Singles $139; doubles $149; studios $149-$159; one-bedroom suites $159-$209.
Continental breakfast included. **Special weekend rates.**

Originally designed by famed architect Emery Roth in 1927 as an apartment house, the Beverly's spacious rooms and suites reflect that past. It is one of the best buys in town and has long been a favorite of visiting United

Nations delegates. High ceilings, archways, and moldings give character to the homey rooms and suites. Traditionally decorated in a manner that is more pleasant than plush, it is the kind of place you can settle into comfortably. Studios and suites have the added convenience of fully-equipped kitchenettes. And while the bathrooms are old-fashioned, they are adequate. Some of the upper floor suites are particularly attractive and have private terraces with sweeping views of Midtown. Hotel amenities include multilingual concierge services, airport transfer service, a beauty salon, a 24-hour pharmacy, room service, laundry and valet service, and safe deposit boxes.

THE BOX TREE ★★★
250 East 49th Street (between Second and Third Aves.)
212/758-8320
Regular rooms $190 weekdays, $290 weekends; penthouse suites $230 weekdays, $330 weekends (weekend rates include a $100 credit in The Box Tree Restaurant).

Comprised of two adjacent four-story townhouses, this charmingly eccentric inn exudes pizazz and originality in its nine rooms and four penthouse suites. Each room is individually and elaborately decorated, some in the French manner, others in country English, Egyptian, Chinese, or Japanese style. Each has a working fireplace and its own personality. The ultimate for a romantic getaway.

BROADWAY BED & BREAKFAST INN ★
264 West 46th Street
212/997-9200 or 800/826-6300; fax 212/768-2807.
Singles $75-$85; doubles $85-$125; suites $150. Includes continental breakfast and 20% discount in restaurant.

Situated in the heart of the theater district and a stone's throw from Restaurant Row, this nifty newcomer is a nice find for those on a theater spree seeking nice, convenient lodging at an accommodating rate. Perched atop a friendly pub and a souvenir shop, it has the atmosphere of a European pensione. There are 40 rooms of varying size; most are on the small side but are pleasantly decorated in soft colors. All have air-conditioning and color cable TV. The larger rooms have baths with tubs and showers, others only showers. The suites, while not at all fancy, are pleasantly appointed with decent-sized bedrooms and sitting room/kitchenettes with microwaves and refrigerators.

THE CARLYLE ★★★★★
35 East 76th Street (Madison Ave.)
212/744-1600 or 800/227-5737
Singles $300-$450; doubles $330-$480; suites $500-$2,000. Pets accepted.

Old-world elegance abounds at this celebrated hotel that has hosted world leaders and the very rich and famous over the years. With a staff-to-guest ratio of two-to-one, service is extraordinary. The spacious rooms have the look of an English country house, and are comfortably charming rather than elegant. Even the single rooms are referred to as one-room apartments here. All accommodations include a private entrance foyer, ample closet space, a serving pantry or kitchen with refrigerator, VCR, premium cable TV, stereo, CD player, dedicated fax line, and multi-line speaker phones. The marble baths have whirlpool tubs and terrycloth robes. Several suites have private terraces; many have dining rooms and grand pianos. Perhaps the Carlyle's most endearing characteristic is that it is one of the rare grand hotels that projects a genuine friendliness and has a certain homey quality. Services even include dog walkers. (Yes, pets are welcome, too.)

CROWNE PLAZA ★★★
1605 Broadway (between 48th and 49th Sts.)
212/977-4000 or 800/243-nyny
Singles and doubles $219-$299. Small pets allowed. **Special weekend rates.**

A heart-of-the-theater district location at reasonable rates makes this upscale Holiday Inn an attractive choice for theatergoers. Guest rooms and suites are pleasantly appointed with modern furnishings and some boast impressive skyline or river views. All offer good amenities such as minibars, voice-mail and data port, irons and ironing boards, cable TV with a complimentary movie channel, coffee makers, makeup mirrors, hair dryers, in-room safes, and delivery of *USA Today* Monday through Friday. A 50-foot skylit pool—the largest indoor hotel pool in Manhattan—is a popular feature of the fitness center. The Crowne Plaza Club, located on the 43rd through the 46th floors, is the deluxe wing of the hotel. Rooms here are more luxuriously furnished and guests benefit from its separate check-in and check-out services. Other special amenities include two two-line phones, marble baths with terrycloth robes, and use of the Crowne Plaza Club lounge with complimentary continental breakfast, afternoon tea, hors d'oeuvres, and evening dessert, as well as beverages and snacks throughout the day.

DELMONICO HOTEL ★★★
502 Park Avenue (59th Street)
212/355-2500 or 800/821-3842
Suites $295-$550. Pets allowed. **Special weekend rates; lower rates in summer.**

A 1993 renovation to the tune of $7 million has made this apartment-suite hotel more appealing than ever. Once the elegant apartment residence of Lorenz Hart, Ed Sullivan, and Liza Minnelli, today it is the destination of both business and leisure travelers. Furnished to resemble a home-away-from-home, the one- and two-bedroom suites feature walk-in closets, spacious living rooms, dining rooms, and fully-equipped kitchens with all the conveniences you might want. Each suite is individually decorated, some with a nostalgic air and others with modern flair. A number also have wonderful terraces.

DORAL COURT ★★★
130 East 39th Street (between Park and Lexington Aves.)
212/685-1100 or 800-22-doral
Singles $175-$195; doubles $219-$235; suites $250-$500. **Special sale saver and weekend rates and packages.**

This very appealing European-style hotel is located in the charming Murray Hill area on a pretty tree-lined street. Guest rooms are over-sized and include features such as inviting foyers, walk-in closets, king-size beds, personal-sized refrigerators, and separate dressing alcoves. The charming country house decor is light and airy. Other amenities include VCRs, bathrobes, exercycles (on request), and use of the Doral Fitness Center nearby on Park Avenue. All suites offer full living rooms, walk-in kitchenettes, dining areas, and outdoor balconies. In its price range, it offers a lot more bells and whistles than most, and generously discounted weekend rates make it all the more irresistible.

DORAL PARK AVENUE ★★★
70 Park Avenue (38th St.)
212/687-7050 or 800/22-doral
Singles $185-$205; doubles $205-$225; suites $385-$650. **Special weekend rates.**

Rooms here are on the small side but are nicely decorated in a neo-classical style and have many comforts and much charm. They are equipped with refrigerators and some have serving pantries. The marble baths have hair dryers, makeup mirrors, and nice big towels.

DORAL TUSCANY ★★★
120 East 39th Street (between Park and Lexington Aves.)
212/686-1600 or 800-22-doral
*Singles $239; doubles $259; suites $400-$850. **Special sale saver and weekend rates.***

This charming European-style boutique hotel is surrounded by turn-of-the-century brownstones on a delightful tree-lined street in Murray Hill where a real neighborhood feel prevails. It is the kind of place that makes you want to return—again and again. Like its sister hotel next door, the Doral Court, it is loaded with amenities unusual in its price category. Rooms are spacious and full of personal style. Entrance halls, French doors, separate dressing/makeup rooms, Italian marble baths, walk-in closets, and personal mini-refrigerators are just a few of the nice extra touches that abound. If so inclined, you can work out at the nearby Doral Fitness Center or ask for an in-room exercycle.

DOUBLETREE GUEST SUITES ★★
1568 Broadway (at 47th St. and Seventh Ave.)
212/719-1600 or 800/325-9033
*Suites $199-$350; conference suites $250-$350. **Special weekend rates.***

Families appreciate the extra space and kid-friendly atmosphere at this Times Square hotel. Accommodations feature a separate bedroom and living space with sofa bed, dining table, wet bar, refrigerator, microwave, coffee maker, three phones with voice-mail, and two TVs. There's a floor of childproof suites and a Kids Club with a playroom, arts and crafts center, and computer and video games. In the same kid-friendly spirit, a special kids' room service menu, cribs, and strollers are also available. For those with business on their minds, there are conference suites large enough for small meetings.

DRAKE SWISSÔTEL ★★★
440 Park Avenue (56th St.)
212/421-0900 or 800/372-5369
*Singles $199-$355; doubles $199-$385; suites $350-$1,200. **Special weekend rates and packages.***

Swiss efficiency and a fabulous location—one block from the upscale boutiques of 57th Street, five blocks from Central Park, and within walking distance of Broadway theaters—are hallmarks of the Drake. Originally an apartment house, the spacious rooms have walk-in closets and some have the added bonus of a balcony or a fireplace. Each features an oversized desk and seating area, three telephones (including two multi-line speaker phones with call-waiting, voice-mail, and data port), an iron and ironing board, a mini-refrigerator, electronic safe, and a marble bathroom with a hair dryer and other upscale amenities. A recent renovation updated all the rooms and baths and added a fitness center. Geared to business travelers, a new business and conference center was also added which offers guests conference rooms with four free hours of use. And in an effort to appeal to families as well, a "Kidsôtel program" welcomes children with a backpack of goodies, TV movies, and bedtime stories by phone, along with milk and cookies.

ELYSÉE ★★★
60 East 54th Street (between Madison and Park Aves.)
212/753-1066 or 800/535-9733
Standard rooms $245; deluxe $265; junior suites $295; standard suites $325-$375; piano suite $775. Continental breakfast included.

Home of the legendary Monkey Bar, this small European-style hotel offers old-world elegance, pretty rooms with country French furnishings, and warm service. Generous amenities include a complimentary buffet continental breakfast with fresh fruit, cereals, assorted muffins, breads, Danish, bagels, croissants, yogurt, juices, coffee, and tea. Complimentary coffee, tea, hot chocolate, and cookies are available all day, and wine and hors d'oeuvres are served each weekday evening from 5 to 8 p.m. In-room goodies include bottled water, ice tea, and chocolate. Other in-room amenities include VCRs with complimentary video rental, voice-mail, and telephones with computer/fax capabilities. The Cardio Fitness Center—a health club two and a half blocks from the hotel—is offered to guests on a complimentary basis and provides all the exercise clothing required.

ESSEX HOUSE HOTEL NIKKO NEW YORK ★★★★
160 Central Park So. (between Sixth and Seventh Aves.)
212/247-0300 or 800/645-5687
*Singles and doubles $320-$365; suites $525-$2,500. Pets allowed. **Special weekend rates and packages.***

This New York landmark, overlooking Central Park, epitomizes classic art deco style. All rooms and suites feature three two-line speaker phones with data port, voice-mail, fax, in-room movies, safes, minibars, and VCRs. The all marble bathrooms come equipped with robes, scales, hair dryers, and upscale toiletries. They also have double sinks and separate bathtubs and shower stalls. A 1991 renovation enlarged the guest rooms that are now handsomely decorated in imitation Louis XVI or Chippendale. Guest services include weekday limousine service to Wall Street, free newspapers, and 24-hour room service. A European-style fitness center offers personal trainers, aerobics classes, massages, herbal wraps, and mud packs. The Nikko Kids Program furnishes coloring books, Frisbees, colorful bedding, and milk and cookies at bedtime. In-house restaurants include the charming garden-like Cafe Botanica and the luxurious Les Celebrities.

FITZPATRICK MANHATTAN HOTEL ★★
687 Lexington Avenue (between 56th and 57th Sts.)
212/355-0100 or 800/367-7701
Executive rooms $235-$250; one-bedroom suites $280-$295; Presidential suites $350. **Special weekend and holiday rates.**

This is New York's first Irish family-owned and operated hotel, and it prides itself on its wonderful Irish hospitality. All accommodations feature traditional cherry mahogany furnishings and beautiful fabrics ranging from deep prints to delicate pastels. Guest rooms offer a European-style trouser press, telephones with voice-mail, hair dryers, and makeup mirrors, and all suites include plush terrycloth robes, a second TV set, and a wet bar with a mini-refrigerator. Homey charm prevails. Sinead O'Connor, various Kennedys, and Mary Robinson, Ireland's President, have stayed here.

FLATOTEL INTERNATIONAL ★★★
135 West 52nd Street (between Sixth and Seventh Aves.)
212/887-9400 or 800/flatotel
Studios $265-$295; one-bedroom suites $299-$395; two-bedroom suites $465. Pets allowed. Continental breakfast included. **Special winter rates.**

For space and convenience, you can't do better than this sleek French suite hotel. The apartment-sized accommodations are truly spacious. Studios measure 750 square feet; one-bedrooms from 1,000 to 1,450 square feet; and two-bedrooms from 1,450 to 1,950 square feet. Every suite is turned out with European furnishings, has a large living room with a dining area, a fully-stocked gourmet kitchen, and a Jacuzzi bath. Other in-suite amenities include coffee makers, microwaves, full-sized stoves, double-door refrigerators, irons and ironing boards, and hair dryers. All the latest electronic goodies are offered as well—stereos with CD and tape players, remote-control TVs in each living room and bedroom, video cassette players, multiple telephone lines with data ports, and private voice-mail messaging. Other hotel amenities and services include a new fitness center, laundry/valet service, grocery shopping/delivery, in-room food service, and secretarial services. Private chef and catering services are also available. This is the kind of accommodation you can really settle into.

FOUR SEASONS ★★★★★
57 East 57th Street (between Madison and Park Aves.)
212/758-5700 or 800/332-3442
Singles $420-$615; doubles $490-$665; suites $825-$7,500. Small pets allowed.
Special weekend rates.

This glamorous I.M. Pei-designed skyscraper hotel opened in 1993 and features some of the most spectacular (and expensive) accommodations in town. From the columned Grand Foyer to the guest rooms, all is sleek and dramatic. The 367 exceptionally spacious guest rooms, including 58 suites, are some of the largest in New York (numbering as few as six per floor). Averaging 600 square feet, each has ten-foot ceilings, an entrance foyer, a sitting area, and a sycamore-panelled dressing room. Many feature full Central Park or city views; 23 have terraces. Room decor is stunning—each individually designed with every amenity you might want. There are oval partners desks with leather chairs, two-line speakerphones, well-stocked private bars, and in-room safes. Beautiful marble baths have tubs that fill in 60 seconds and separate glass-enclosed showers, TVs, terrycloth robes, and slippers. Hotel facilities include an impressive fitness center with state-of-the art exercise and cardiovascular equipment and spa services that include massages, facials, manicures, and pedicures. The business center covers all bases with everything from translators to paper shredders. There's around-the-clock room service, as well as one-hour pressing and valet service 24-hours a day.

THE FRANKLIN ★★
164 East 87th Street (between Lexington & Third Aves.)
212/369-1000 or 800/369-8787.
Singles $159-$169; doubles $179-$189. Includes free parking and continental breakfast.

This tiny charmer is one of The Gotham Hospitality Group's stylish redos. Located on the Upper East Side, it is situated in a neighborhood

71

abounding in museums, art galleries, boutiques, and reasonably-priced restaurants. The 53 guest rooms are terribly chic and terribly small. Packed with style, each features illuminated beds with billowing white canopies, custom-designed cherrywood and steel furnishings, TVs with built-in VCRs, and fresh flowers. (A word of caution: pack lightly when you stay here—your "closet" may be no more than six hangers on a foot-long rod.) Bathrooms have restored cast-iron tubs with European-style hand-held showers, stainless steel sinks set in black granite, oversized Irish cotton towels, and Neutrogena toiletries. A complimentary breakfast offers specially made granola, Gotham muffins, fresh-squeezed juices, and coffee. Afternoon tea is also provided.

GORHAM NEW YORK ★★
136 West 55th Street (between Sixth and Seventh Aves.)
212/245-1800 or 800/735-0710
Singles and doubles $180-$320; suites $210-$370; penthouse $395.

Ideally situated near Broadway theaters, Rockefeller Center, Carnegie Hall, the Museum of Modern Art, and Fifth Avenue shops, this European-style boutique hotel features sleek, newly renovated rooms reminiscent of an ocean liner. They are of good size and have fully-equipped kitchenettes with microwaves, refrigerator/freezers, wet bars, and coffee makers. The marble bathrooms are equipped with hair dryers, vanity mirrors, telephones, and digital water-controlled baths offering personalized water temperature and flow with the touch of a button. Suites have whirlpool tubs. Other amenities include a fully-equipped gym, 24-hour room service, secretarial services, and free newspapers.

GRAND HYATT NEW YORK ★★★
Park Avenue at Grand Central (Lexington and 42nd St.)
212/883-1234 or 800/233-1234
Singles $240-$300; doubles $265-$325; suites $450-$2,000. **Special weekend rates.**

A glitzy lobby greets you with a cascading waterfall, lots of greenery, and a 100-foot bronze statue at this towering structure built right over Grand Central Station. The hotel—a favorite of out-of-town sports teams—has a busy buzz throughout its public areas. In contrast, guest rooms are pleasantly subdued, decorated in soft pastels. Amenities include 24-hour room service, free newspapers, in-room pay movies, voice-mail and modem hook-up, hair dryers, and irons and ironing boards. Deluxe king rooms have separate seating areas. All bathrooms are luxurious and full of upscale amenities. Hotel conveniences include a theater ticket desk, a 24-hour front desk, and a variety of shops, commercial services, and boutiques.

HELMSLEY MIDDLETOWNE ★★
148 East 48th Street (between Lexington and Third Aves.)
212/755-3000 or 800/843-2157
Singles $150-$185; doubles $160-$200; suites $200-$450. Coffee, tea, and pastries included. **Special weekend rates.**

This pleasant property was converted from an apartment building and has retained a residential feel. Its 192 studio and one- and two- bedroom suites all have refrigerators and bathroom phones. The larger suites have complete walk-in kitchens and some have terraces.

HELMSLEY PARK LANE ★★★
36 Central Park South (59th St.)
212/371-4000 or 800/221-4982
Singles and doubles $255-$375; suites $500-$1,100. **Special weekend rates.**

This newly renovated hotel has a wonderful location. Near Carnegie Hall, Lincoln Center, Broadway theaters, and just steps from the shops of Fifth Avenue, it also boasts sensational Park views. The fact that Harry and Leona once chose this as their home base comes as no surprise. Glittering chandeliers, oriental rugs, and wall-to-wall marble greet you. Guest rooms are very spacious and luxuriously appointed. Bathrooms are equally luxurious and full of upscale goodies. Suites are palatial with huge windows displaying the splendors of Central Park.

HELMSLEY WINDSOR HOTEL ★★
100 West 58th Street (Sixth Ave.)
212/265-2100 or 800/221-4982.
Singles $150-$160; doubles $160-$170; suites $250-$425. Includes continental breakfast. **Special weekend and summer rates.**

This mid-priced hotel near Central Park not only has a very attractive location, but first-rate service and nice rooms. Carnegie Hall musicians often stay here. There's no restaurant or room service, but the area is full of interesting places to eat and is tremendously convenient. All told, this intimate, European-style hotel is a bargain for the neighborhood.

HOLIDAY INN DOWNTOWN ★★
138 Lafayette St. (between Howard and Canal)
212/966-8898 or 800-holiday.
Singles and doubles $89-$185; suites $175-$205.

This attractive branch of the popular chain is situated right at the crossroads of SoHo, Chinatown, and Little Italy—a fascinating area to explore abounding with shops, restaurants, and galleries. Rooms are pleasantly decorated with rosewood furnishings and Asian accents. They have combination-lock safes, voice-mail, coffee machines, and hair dryers. Suites have private fax machines.

INN AT IRVING PLACE ★★★
56 Irving Place (between 17th and 18th Sts.)
212/533-4600 or 800/685-1447
Single or double $275-$350. Continental breakfast included. No children under twelve.

A charming 19th Century townhouse turned inn with 12 guest rooms and lots of style. Big brass beds, Victorian armoires, and standing lamps add period charm. Modern amenities include VCRs and in-room fax machines. The inviting O. Henry Room has a fireplace and overlooks the courtyard garden. Verbena, Diane Forley's fab restaurant, is just downstairs.

INN NEW YORK CITY ★★★
266 West 71st Street (West End and Broadway)
212/580-1900; fax 212/580-4437
*Suites $195-$295. Self-service breakfast included. **Special weekend rates.***

This "inn" is really four apartment suites in a charming brownstone tucked away on a quiet Upper West Side street. There's no sign to announce it, but it is the kind of place you'll be very happy to search out. Each of the four suites is individually decorated. The spacious Parlor Suite, on the ground floor, has a piano, working fireplace, a stained glass ceiling, its own terrace, and a dining table set with china, glasses, and silverware. The Loft is furnished with antiques and reproductions and has a fireplace. The Vermont Suite is a duplex with its own entrance. The Spa Suite takes up a whole floor and comes with a spa room with a sauna and huge whirlpool. While the Spa Suite is probably the most popular, none disappoint. They are all lovely. Like an elegant home-away-from home, they are equipped with VCRs, telephone answering machines, CD players, washers and dryers, intercom security, and fully-equipped kitchens with stocked refrigerators.

INTER-CONTINENTAL NEW YORK ★★★
111 East 48th Street (Park and Lexington Aves.)
212/755-5900 or 800/327-0200.
Singles and doubles $250-$330; suites $475-$1,500. **Special weekend packages.**

An exhaustive enhancement program of all guest rooms was undertaken in 1994-1995 adding new life to the timeless charm of this likeable hotel. The lobby's signature brass bird cage with several varieties of beautiful birds remains a colorful focal point. Rooms, though not large, are nicely appointed with rich wood furnishings. Amenities include minibars, in-room movies, in-room videos, dual-telephone lines, 24-hour room service, babysitting and child services, a house physician, and pharmacy. A fitness center offers all the latest machines along with mini-TVs for diversion while you work out. A steam room, sauna, and massage therapy are also available.

THE KIMBERLY ★★★
145 East 50th Street (between Lexington and Third Aves.)
212/755-0400 or 800/683-0400
Deluxe guest rooms $195-$305 single, double supplement $25; one-bedroom suites $245-$415; two-bedroom suites $375-$655. **Special summer rates.**

Mostly a suite-hotel, The Kimberly also has 34 nicely decorated guest rooms with mini-refrigerators. The handsomely decorated suites feature separate dining and living areas, fully-equipped kitchens, and private terraces overlooking the city's panoramic skyline. Baths are sumptuous and contain deep soaking tubs and lots of marble. You can enjoy the New York Health and Racquet Club compliments of The Kimberly and also navigate the Hudson River aboard its 75' yacht with complimentary seasonal boarding on sunset and brunch cruises.

LOEWS NEW YORK ★★
569 Lexington Avenue (51st St.)
212/752-7000 or 800-23loews
Singles $185-$205; doubles $205-$225; suites $250-$850. **Small pets allowed.** **Special weekend rates.**

This functional hotel has a busy buzz all through the day and evening in its art deco-styled lobby. While the rooms are small and the decor is nothing to write home about, Loews enjoys a terrific Midtown location and is available through most of the hotel discount agencies at attractive rates. You can book a junior suite through the discounters for a little more than a regular room, and it's the only way to go here because you'll end up with a lot more space and comfort. There are various configurations of the junior suites—some are just large rooms with a separate sitting area at one end; others have handsome room dividers making the sitting room completely separate; some even have outdoor terraces. They are all quite spacious and the bathrooms have separate dressing/makeup areas. All of the rooms have mini-refrigerators, in-room safes, hair dryers, voice-mail, and bathroom phones. (Rooms above the 12th floor have coffee makers.) There's a concierge level with more upscale amenities and a club-like lounge where continental breakfast is offered in the morning and cookies, coffee, and tea in the afternoon. In the evening, hors d'oeuvres, sodas, and an assortment of wines are served.

THE LOWELL ★★★★
28 East 63rd Street (between Madison and Park Aves.)
212/838-1400 or 800/221-4444
*Singles $295; deluxe singles/doubles $385; junior suites $485; Garden Suite $785; Gym Suite $785; two-bedrooms suites $895-$955; Penthouse $1,655. Small pets allowed. **Special weekend rates.***

You'll know you're leading the good life if you stay at this posh flower-filled retreat with amenities fit for royalty. Its chic Upper East Side location near Central Park is just steps from the smart boutiques of Madison Avenue in an area abounding in restaurants, museums, and art galleries. The hotel has a charming European atmosphere. Antique furnishings and Chinese porcelains abound, and many of the rooms have wood-burning fireplaces. Amenities include a 24-hour front desk, babysitting and child services, in-room coffee makers, hair dryers, and minibars. Several years ago, the management installed a personal workout room for Madonna. Named the Gym Suite, it has a fireplace and terrace. But the most romantic and extravagant accommodation is the fabulous Garden Suite with two terraces, a rose garden, a trellised dining area, and a floricultural library. Awash in lace and chintz and scented with the flowers that surround you, it is as close to perfection as it gets.

LYDEN GARDENS ★★
215 East 64th Street (between Second and Third Aves.)
212/355-1230 or 800/me-suite
Junior suites $210-$250; one-bedroom suites $270-$280; two-bedroom suites $425-$485. Special weekend rates.

This Manhattan East Suite Hotels property is located on a pretty tree-shaded street near shops, art galleries, and good restaurants. It offers spacious suite accommodations with health club privileges, coin laundry facilities, in-room safes, premium cable channels, coffee makers, and microwaves.

LYDEN HOUSE ★★
320 East 53rd Street (between First and Second Aves.)
212/888-6070 or 800/me-suite
Studio suites $240-$250; one-bedroom suites $270-$280; two-bedroom suites $480. Special weekend rates; lower rates July-August.

Another member of the Manhattan East Suite Hotels group. This one has 80 spacious suites over 11 floors in the Sutton Place area, one of Manhattan's most desirable neighborhoods. Reminiscent of a small European hotel, its atmosphere is pleasant and homey. Each studio and one-bedroom suite has a full kitchen with a dining table, microwave oven, automatic coffee maker, and complimentary coffee service, as well as a large walk-in closet and individual climate control. Other amenities include health club access and premium cable channels. There are connecting suites, non-smoking suites, and penthouse suites.

MANSFIELD HOTEL ★★
12 West 44th Street (between Fifth and Sixth Aves.)
212/944-6050 or 800/255-5167
Standard rooms $195; suites $275; penthouses $650. Includes continental buffet breakfast and after-theater dessert buffet.

Rates at this smart boutique hotel include a long list of amenities, such as a generous continental buffet breakfast, cappuccino all day long in a pretty lobby salon, free parking, Monday evening music recitals, and nightly harp music accompanying a free after-theater dessert buffet. A $4 million restoration by the Gotham Hotel Group (also responsible for the stylish redos of the Wales, Franklin, and Shoreham hotels) has resulted in a stunning renovation. The fabulously chic lobby—full of beautiful architectural details—has a very Milan-feel. The breakfast buffet and after-theater dessert table are set up in a lovely library with a magnificent copper dome skylight and good collection of books. It's quite an elegant setting for tucking into the homemade granola, fresh fruit, soft-boiled eggs, croissants, and other baked goodies. Rooms are stylishly outfitted with sleigh beds with backlit iron and wire mesh headboards, white and beige cotton Belgian linens, and ebonized floors. All this and a location just steps from Fifth Avenue and minutes from the theater district. Is it too good to be true? Well, maybe. Since its opening, the Mansfield has received accolades galore from travel writers. But I doubt many of them have actually stayed there. While chic as can be, you might find the rooms lack some basic comforts when you actually settle in. Many of them are terribly small with minuscule TVs and only hand-held showers (no bathtubs). Drawer space is spare or non-existent, and many "closets" are just rods with hangers behind a mirror. Even some of the suites, while ever-so-chic, don't have traditional closets and drawer space, but have a black velvet-curtained contraption concealing hangers and racks in the living room and open pole-racks in the bedroom. All this said, the Mansfield is a terrific place to stay, particularly if you make your wish-list known in advance.

THE MARK ★★★
25 East 77th Street (Madison Ave.)
212/744-4300 or 800/the mark
Singles $355-$360; doubles $380-$385; suites $525-$2,400. **Special weekend and holiday rates.**

Part of The Leading Hotels of the World group, this intimate and sophisticated European-style hotel is a study in graceful nouvelle elegance. From its dramatic art deco facade to its landmark copper tower, it evokes character and style. The 180 generously proportioned rooms and suites abound in luxurious details with beautifully framed museum-quality prints and custom Biedermeier furniture. The luxurious baths have heated towel bars, imported bath crystals and potpourri, and deep soaking tubs. Some of the larger suites have libraries, wet bars, and landscaped terraces with views of Central Park.

MAYFAIR HOTEL ★★★★
610 Park Avenue (65th St.)
212/288-0800 or 800/223-0542
Singles $295, doubles $315; suites $440-$1,700. Includes breakfast. Very small dogs allowed. **Special weekend packages.**

78

Gracious and luxurious, the Mayfair surrounds you with a happy melding of efficiency, friendliness, and elegance. Built in 1925 by Secretary of Commerce Jesse Jones, this genteel hotel has an old-world ambience and a fabulous location near Central Park, the chic boutiques of Madison and Fifth Avenues, major museums, art galleries, and terrific restaurants. The hotel has 105 suites and 96 rooms (28 of which have wood-burning fireplaces) decorated in the tradition of understated European elegance. Its marble bathrooms have bathrobes, hair dryers, and telephone extensions. All suites and many of the rooms are equipped with a butler's pantry. Other niceties include a complimentary daily newspaper and shoeshine, four-line telephones with complimentary local calls, and a complimentary fitness center with a putting green.

MAYFLOWER HOTEL ★★
15 Central Park West (61st St.)
212/265-0060 or 800/223-4164
*Singles $165-$175; doubles $190-$210; suites $235-$285. Small pets allowed; grooming available. **Special weekly, weekend, and holiday rates; lower rates in July and August and mid-December through March 31.***

A longtime favorite of (nearby) Lincoln Center performers, this old timer's rooms reflect its past as a residential hotel. Spacious rooms, walk-in closets, serving pantries, and kitchenettes are some of the nice holdovers from its former life. Rooms are pleasantly furnished with traditional American reproductions in cherry. Some suites have terraces overlooking Central Park and the New York City skyline.

THE MICHELANGELO ★★★★
152 West 51st Street (between Sixth and Seventh Aves.)
212/765-1900 or 800/237-0990
*Superior rooms $295; deluxe rooms $325; Executive suites $375; deluxe one-bedroom suites $450-$550; two-bedroom suites $950; grand one-bedroom suite $750. Rates include continental Italian breakfast. **Special weekend rates.***

The rooms at this very Italian, very chic hotel are uniquely decorated in styles ranging from country French to art deco. Italian artwork adorns both public and private spaces and Italian music is heard throughout the hotel. Not only is the decor smart and beautiful, but the spacious guest rooms are among the most generously sized in town. And the gorgeous marble bathrooms feature oversized tubs, bidets, terrycloth robes, and even televisions. Other amenities include twice-daily housekeeping service, hair dryers, modem lines, Italian mineral waters, a 24-hour fitness center, overnight shoeshines, complimentary Wall Street limousine service daily, newspaper delivery, and a delicious Italian breakfast featuring expresso, cappuccino, and pastries. Its superb location is convenient to the exclusive shops of Fifth Avenue, Central Park, Carnegie Hall, Lincoln Center, Rockefeller Center, the Museum of Modern Art, and the theater district.

THE MILBURN SUITE HOTEL ★

242 West 76th Street (between Broadway and West End)
212/362-1006 or 800/833-9622
Studios $125-$140; one-bedroom suites $165-$200.

Located on a quiet side street on the Upper West Side, the Milburn is a favorite with families who appreciate its good value and roomy, cheerful accommodations. Studios or suites are available with a queen, king, or two twin beds. Each room includes a kitchenette equipped with a range, sink, refrigerator, microwave, and coffee maker. And the one-bedroom suites have a queen-sized sofa bed in the living room. The rooms all have modern furnishings and are decorated in bright colors. Colorful posters add another cheerful touch.

MILLENIUM HILTON ★★★★

55 Church Street (between Dey & Fulton Sts.)
212/693-2001 or 800/835-2220
Singles $250-$290, doubles $275-$355; suites $450-$900. **Special weekend rates and package plans.**

This high-tech high-riser is Lower Manhattan's only 4-star, 4-diamond hotel. During the week, it caters primarily to business travelers with amenities such as a 24-hour business center, in-room fax machines, dual-line phones with data port, and good work space. Leisure travelers move in on weekends when rates are reduced considerably. Rooms have teak and walnut furnishings and are well designed but on the small side. In-room amenities are more generous—premium cable channels, VCRs on request, umbrellas, irons and ironing boards, minibars, marble baths with telephones, lighted makeup mirrors, premium toiletries, and bathrobes and slippers. Upper floors offer spectacular views of Lower Manhattan and the Hudson and East Rivers. Other attractive features of the hotel include a fitness center with sauna and massage facilities and an indoor pool with a nice view of St. Paul's Chapel and poolside service. There's also a complimentary shuttle service to Midtown.

MILLENNIUM BROADWAY ★★★
145 West 44th Street (between Sixth Ave. and Broadway)
212/768-4400 or 800/622-5569
*Singles $245-$315; doubles $270-$320; suites $525-$3,500. Pets allowed. **Special weekend rates.***

This postmodern skyscraper hotel (formerly the Macklowe) not only boasts a location in the heart of the theater district action but also incorporates the restored landmark, beaux-arts 1902 Hudson Theater. The lobby—an expanse of cool black marble and African mahogany—is a study in art deco elegance. The rooms are on the small side, but nicely turned out in a sleek contemporary black and gray palette with custom furniture, cotton sheets and down pillows, and double pane windows (with some fabulous views). In-room amenities include hair dryers, minibars, modem lines, and 24-hour room service. Hotel amenities include a fitness center, business center, and an interactive TV system that allows you to book theater tickets and make restaurant reservations. There's also a welcome mat to pets.

MORGANS ★★★
237 Madison Avenue (between 37th and 38th Sts.)
212/686-0300 or 800/334-3408
*Singles $195-$240; doubles $220-$265; suites $395-$425. Pets shorter than 18 inches allowed. Complimentary continental breakfast. **Special weekend rates.***

There's no sign outside to announce this ultra-modern hotel (in the same low-profile manner assumed by its Paramount and Royalton relations). Inside it's all about style. A 1995 renovation by the hotel's original designer, Andrée Putman, brought ivory, camel, and taupe into what was once all black, white, and gray, adding just a dash of warmth to the crisp high-tech ambience. Rooms have custom-made furniture, including maple wall units and low-to-the-floor beds. Robert Mapplethorpe photographs add a striking element to the decor. The bathrooms are small, stark, and sterile-looking, or sleek and amusing—depending on your point of view. Amenities include health club privileges, bathroom phones, refrigerators, minibars, and VCRs. Morgan's eccentric style and high level of personal service attracts a pretty cool clientele. Mick Jagger, Billy Joel, Oprah, and Cher are among those who have bedded down here.

81

NEW YORK HELMSLEY ★★★
212 East 42nd Street (between Second and Third Aves.)
212/490-8900 or 800/221-4982
Singles $210-$260; doubles $235-$285; one-bedroom suites $425-650; two-bedroom suites $675-$800. Special weekend packages.

If big and busy turns you off, you might find the New York Helmsley off-putting when you arrive. But once you get past the check-in and into your room, you'll be delighted. This is one of the better values in its price category. Rooms are generously-proportioned, beautifully appointed, and constant upgrading keeps them fresh and inviting. Bathrooms are luxuriously outfitted with bathsheets, scales, full-length mirrors, hair dryers, makeup mirrors, and two new toothbrushes a day.

NEW YORK HILTON AND TOWERS ★★★
1335 Avenue of the Americas (between 53rd and 54th Sts.)
212/586-7000 or 800/445-8667
Singles $185-$295; doubles $252-$400; suites $500-$625. Pets allowed. Special family rates and weekend packages.

Big and brassy, this massive hotel always seems bursting with business meetings and conventioneers. Rooms are small, with singles particularly claustrophobia-inducing. While lacking pizazz and space, they are well-maintained and offer amenities such as individual climate control, first-run movies, minibars, coffee makers, hair dryers, irons and ironing boards, writing desks, and computer data ports. The Executive Tower, three floors of newly-decorated guest rooms and suites, has added conveniences for business travelers such as two separate telephone lines and a speaker phone on the desk. Its private concierge-staffed lounge and bar serves complimentary continental breakfast, afternoon tea, and hors d'oeuvres.

NEW YORK MARRIOTT EAST SIDE ★★★
525 Lexington Avenue (49th Street)
212/755-4000 or 800/228-9290
Singles and doubles $219-$249; suites $300-$670. Advance purchase discounted rates.

A recent renovation has improved this mid-priced business and tourist hotel (once the Halloran House). The lobby has a clubby old-world charm and the traditionally decorated guest rooms feature modern amenities such as minibars, coffee makers, irons and ironing boards, hair dryers, and in-room pay movies. The Concierge Level offers upgraded amenities. Hotel facilities include an exercise room and a business center. Its nice East Side location adds to its appeal and convenience. It is one block off Park Avenue, minutes from Rockefeller Center, St. Patrick's Cathedral, Fifth Avenue shopping, and the United Nations.

NEW YORK MARRIOTT MARQUIS ★★★
1535 Broadway (between 45th and 46th Sts.)
212/398-1900 or 800/843-4898 or 800/228-9290
Singles and doubles $250-$290; suites $425-$3,500. Small pets allowed. **Summer packages and advance purchase discounted rates.**

This is the kind of hotel that people tend to either really like or really not like. While far too big and busy to be a favorite of mine, I can appreciate its many attractive attributes. For theater enthusiasts with convenience in mind, the location is as good as it gets. Situated at Times Square, in the heart of the theater district, it is surrounded by 30 theaters (and actually houses the spectacular Marquis Theater). Rooms in this 50-story giant are pleasant and moderately roomy, and guest services are surprisingly efficient for a hotel of its size. (I once complained that my comforter was frayed and within five minutes it was replaced with a fresh new one.) Amenities include minibars, individual climate control, in-room safes, irons and ironing boards, coffee makers, and work desks. On the down side, the lobby is inconveniently situated on the 8th floor and the hotel's mega-size results in a sterile impersonal feel and long elevator waits. And, let's face it, a hotel with nearly 2,000 rooms loses bigtime on the charm-meter.

NEW YORK MARRIOTT WORLD TRADE CENTER ★★★
3 World Trade Center (West St. between Liberty and Vesey)
212/938-9100 or 800/831-4004
Singles and doubles $269-$369; suites $389-$1,750. **Special weekend and super saver rates and advance purchase discounted rates.**

This branch of the comfortable chain was the New York Vista prior to the World Trade Center bombing in 1993. Its forced closure brought about an impressive renovation that enlarged the rooms and resulted in a dramatic three-story atrium lobby with a sweeping waterfall and spiral staircase. Guest rooms are pleasantly decorated, have two-line phones, minibars, floor-to-ceiling windows, and nice marble baths. Situated between (and connected to) the twin towers of the World Trade Center, it is filled with shops and restaurants and is within walking distance of Wall Street and the financial district, as well as the Statue of Liberty and Ellis Island ferries, and the South Street Seaport. (But it is well off the Broadway theater path.) Facilities include a two-story health club (overlooking the Statue of Liberty) with an indoor pool, indoor jogging track, racquetball court, saunas, masseuse, exercise equipment, and aerobic classes.

NEW YORK PALACE ★★★★
455 Madison Avenue (between 50th and 51st Sts.)
212/888-7000 or 800-ny-palace
*Singles and doubles $295-$475, suites $550-$1,900. Small pets allowed. **Special weekend rates.***

This member of The Leading Hotels of the World group unites the opulent 1882 Villard House (designed in the style of a Roman palace) with a contemporary 55-story tower built in 1980. And it now has the culinary distinction of housing the celebrated Le Cirque restaurant. Guest rooms are all comfortably spacious—some are handsomely decorated in a very subdued manner while others are lavishly ornate. They contain such amenities as marble bathrooms with Caswell Massey and Crabtree & Evelyn toiletries, refrigerators, hair dryers, and three two-line telephones with personal voice-mail. All suites contain a full kitchen and 32-inch TVs.

NOVOTEL NEW YORK ★★
226 West 52nd Street (Broadway)
212/315-0100 or 800/221-4542
Singles and doubles $189-$229. Pets allowed.

There's enough comfort at this European chain to make up for its aesthetic shortcomings. Built above a gloomy commercial building with a grim little entranceway to the elevator, the hotel's colorful lobby on the 7th floor has a certain giddy appeal. The French modern room decor is nothing to write home about, but rooms have either a king bed or two double beds, spacious baths, soundproof windows, safes, hair dryers, minibars, and premium cable TV channels. There's also an exercise room, a business center, and some really good views. The location for theatergoers is terrific.

OMNI BERKSHIRE PLACE ★★★
21 East 52nd Street (at Madison Ave.)
212/753-5800 or 800/843-6664
Singles and doubles $355-$395; suites $695-$1,200. **Special weekend rates.**

This handsomely renovated Midtowner caters to an executive clientele during the week, but takes a romantic turn on weekends with chocolates and wine at bedside in rooms that are pretty and spacious. Stylishly decorated, they have a cozy appeal with their beamed ceilings, wingback chairs, and ottomans. Some have balconies. Amenities are all you might expect at this pricey level: nice marble baths with oversized tubs, terrycloth robes, free shoeshines, three two-line phones, in-room fax machines, minibars, and electronic bedside controls for TV, radio, air conditioning, lights, and door privacy sign. There's also an exercise room and a business center.

PARAMOUNT ★★
235 West 46th Street (between Broadway and Eighth Ave.)
212/764-5500 or 800/225-7474
Singles $135-$235; doubles $200-$255; suites $395-$475. Pets allowed. **Special monthly rates and weekend packages.**

Philippe Starck's design mastery has created a playful nouveau deco eyeful at this futuristic hipper-than-hip hostelry. In the heart of the theater district, it is frequented by a very artsy crowd. With its whimsical flair, it looks oh-so-good, but when you stay here you may feel your room is a case of style winning over standard conveniences. The stark white and pearly gray color scheme of the rooms is appealing and bright with dramatic bed headboards that are actually huge paintings with picture lights serving as reading lamps. Yet for all their élan, the bedrooms are minuscule and lack decent storage space. But for affordable chic at a great location for theatergoing, the Paramount does score bigtime.

LE PARKER MERIDIEN NEW YORK ★★★
118 West 57th Street (between Sixth and Seventh Aves.)
212/245-5000 or 800-543-4300
Singles $275-$295; doubles $300-$320; suites $375-$775. Pets under 15 pounds allowed. **Special weekend packages.**

An elegant three-story atrium greets you at this attractive French hotel. A stained glass roof, Doric columns, French tapestries, tall trees, beautiful marble floors, and two-story arched mirrors make it one of the most dramatic entrances in town. The contemporary-styled guest rooms in shades of sand and black were handsomely renovated in 1993 and have an art deco feel. All 100 suites offer views of Central Park and full kitchens. Odd-numbered guest rooms above the 26th floor also have wonderful views of Central Park. Club La Raquette, the hotel's bi-level fitness club is top-notch, featuring state-of-the-art equipment, aerobic and yoga classes, and racquetball, handball and squash courts. In addition, guests can work out under the supervision of a personal trainer. On the roof, there's a jogging track and a glass-enclosed heated swimming pool boasting unobstructed views of all of Central Park.

PENINSULA NEW YORK ★★★★
700 Fifth Avenue (55th St.)
212/247-2200 or 800/262-9467
Singles and doubles $365-$445; suites $700-$1,500. Pets allowed. **Special weekend rates.**

Elegant through and through, this turn-of-the-century landmark features beautiful (though not large) art nouveau-styled guest rooms decorated in soft grays and apricot. Bathrooms are luxurious and some have 6-foot soaking tubs. Fully stocked minibars, in-room safes, executive work desks, and fluffy bathrobes are other nice amenities you can expect. And there's a tri-level glassed-in fitness spa that allows you to work out with a view of St. Patrick's spires. A rooftop bar is another popular spot and the in-house restaurant is the elegant Adrienne.

THE PIERRE ★★★★
2 East 61st Street (Fifth Ave.)
212/838-8000 or 800/332-3442
Singles $325-$825, doubles $415-$825; suites $640-$2,100. Pets allowed. **Special weekend rates.**

This Central Park grande dame epitomizes elegance. Yet, for all its glamour, it has a genuine warmth about it that makes it one of the most comfortable of all the grand hotels in town. Over the years, it has been home to a number of tenants who kept apartments at the hotel. Elizabeth Taylor once owned a flat here. And celebrities such as Mary Tyler Moore and Barbara Walters have held wedding receptions in the hotel. Rooms are large, airy, and beautiful; suites are sumptuous. The bathrooms are not large, but are packed with all sorts of goodies. Conveniences include 24-hour room service, one-hour pressing service, overnight complimentary shoeshine, twice-daily maid service, and a helpful theater desk. Packing and unpacking services are also available on request. And there's a complimentary fitness center, handsomely decorated in Italian marble and hand-painted murals, with the latest in cardiovascular conditioning equipment and free weights. There's also a private massage therapy room. Lifecycles, stairmasters, and treadmills equipped with individual stereos and TV VCRs are other nice features of the facility.

THE PLAZA ★★★★
Fifth Avenue at Central Park South (59th St.)
212/759-3000 or 800/759-3000
Singles and doubles $275-$625; junior suites $495; suites $650-$1,200; specialty suites $1,500-$15,000. Pets under 15 pounds allowed. **Special promotions and weekend rates.**

Just the name of this legendary hotel evokes images of luxury and glamour. And the reality pretty much delivers the goods. Situated on the southwest corner of Central Park West and Fifth Avenue, it is one of the city's most celebrated movie sets and conveys a romantic atmosphere both inside and out. The lobby and public rooms of this official landmark have the grandeur and glow of a French Renaissance château. While some of the guest rooms are fairly ordinary and seem over-priced, many do have a spacious feel with high ceilings, beautiful moldings, and rich colors. Period details abound, including marble fireplaces, antiques, and crystal chandeliers. Canopy beds and oriental rugs enhance the elegance of some of the rooms. Throughout, amenities include spacious closets with satin-covered hangers, large dressers, armoire-concealed remote control TVs, and two phone lines with an extension phone in the bathroom. And as movies over the decades will attest, brunch at the Palm Court and a nip at the Oak Bar are quintessential New York experiences.

PLAZA ATHENEE ★★★★
37 East 64th Street (Madison and Park Aves.)
212/734-9100 or 800/447-8800
Singles and doubles $320-$475; suites $690-$2,900 Pets allowed. **Special weekend rates.**

French period furniture, fabric-covered walls, and draperies of hand-printed silk are just a few of the elegant touches that make the guest rooms in this grand, but intimate, hotel so special. Other pampering features include

87

Belgian sheets, robes by Porthault, and luxurious bathrooms. While some of the rooms are smallish, they are all charming and comfortable. Amenities include dual-line phones with data port, voice-mail, cable TV, luxurious toiletries, 24-hour room service, and a 24-hour fitness room. Suites are sumptuous; some have private patios or glassed-in balconies. Celebrities love the place. If you can afford it, you will, too.

PLAZA FIFTY ★★
155 East 50th Street (Third Ave.)
212/751-5710 or 800/me-suite
Guest rooms $189-$229; studio suites $219-$259; junior suites $229-$269; one-bedroom suites $259-$309; two-bedroom suites $479-$499; three-bedroom suites $549-$600. **Special weekend rates; lower rates in summer and winter.**

One of the Manhattan East Suite properties, Plaza Fifty enjoys a great East Side location and offers comfortable, roomy accommodations. Each suite features a full kitchen with coffee maker and complimentary coffee service. Business guests can take advantage of special amenities to fit their needs: telex, fax, audiovisual equipment, secretarial services, and in-room catering.

RADISSON EMPIRE ★★
44 West 63rd Street
(between Broadway and Columbus Ave.)
212/265-7400 or 800/333-3333
Singles and doubles $190-$235; suites $275-$600.

This pleasant hotel is nicely situated across from Lincoln Center and near Broadway theaters, and is just a block from Central Park. Its rooms and suites are small, but warmly decorated in the style of an English country inn with two-poster beds and floral comforters and draperies. Baths are also small but well turned out with heated towel bars, hair dryers, and telephones. Other amenities include in-room minibars, 24-hour room service, and complimentary full health club facilities in an adjacent complex. A very good value all around.

THE REGENCY ★★★★
540 Park Avenue (61st St.)
212/759-4100 or 800/233-2356
Singles and doubles $315-$395; suites $450-$800. Pets allowed. **Special weekend rates and shopping packages.**

Gracious through and through, this Loews flagship hotel has a serene elegance. While the entire hotel was renovated in 1993, it has retained its old-world character. Guest rooms are furnished with 18th Century reproductions, complemented by imported silks and antique prints. Soft shades of gray, green, and coral predominate. Some accommodations offer a private terrace overlooking neighboring rooftop gardens and some have an alcove kitchen. Other in-room amenities include a work desk, refrigerator, and personal safe. Large, beautiful marble baths feature a second telephone, TV, personal scale, robes, and fine toiletries. Suites and deluxe rooms have personal fax machines. Whirlpool and sauna, as well as the latest in exercise equipment, will be found in the fitness center. There's 24-hour room service, a business center, a barber, and beauty shop. The clientele here is an eclectic mix of rock stars, world leaders, and corporate suits. No one seems able to resist the personal service and Regency style.

RENAISSANCE NEW YORK ★★★
714 Seventh Avenue (between 47th and 48th Sts., Times Square)
212/765-7676 or 800/682-9222
Singles and doubles $255-$325; suites $425-$475. Continental breakfast included.
Special weekend rates.

At the crossroads of Broadway and Seventh Avenue, this branch of the Ramada chain offers upscale comforts in a heart-of-the-action setting. Rooms are of average size, but nicely appointed with good furnishings and quilts on the beds. Amenities include two-line speaker phones with call-waiting, hair dryers, VCRs, complimentary coffee, premium cable channels, minibars, and cotton robes. There's also a fitness center.

RIHGA ROYAL HOTEL ★★★
151 West 54th Street (between Sixth and Seventh Aves.)
212/307-5000 or 800/937-5454
One-bedroom suites $350-$450; two-bedroom suites $700-$900; Crown suites $1,200; Grand Royal suites $2,500-$3,000. Special family, weekend, and holiday rates.

This luxurious all-suite Japanese-owned property opened in 1990 with all the bells and whistles its international business and leisure clientele might desire. Situated in the heart of Midtown, it is near Broadway theaters, Fifth Avenue shopping, Carnegie Hall, museums, and many terrific restaurants. Each suite offers a spacious living room with bay windows, separate bedroom, a dressing area with vanity, and a marble bathroom with glass-enclosed shower and separate tub. Pretty mirrored French doors separate the living room and bedroom. Other amenities include a minibar with icemaker, computer and fax outlets, three two-line phones, two TVs, a video cassette player, electronic safe, hair dryer, bathrobe, personal scale, and luxurious toiletries. There's also a fitness center, business center, complimentary shoeshine, free Wall Street shuttle, and complimentary newspaper delivery daily. The Grand Royal suites have added conveniences such as kitchens, dining rooms, and oversized baths with whirlpool and sauna. And for the business executive who can afford it all, there are suites on the highest, most panoramic floors, that include the ultimate in executive convenience. Guests here are met at the airport and chauffeured in the hotel's town car. A private telephone line is provided which, when not answered, is automatically forwarded to the guest's complimentary cellular phone, or when necessary, back to voice-mail. Personalized business cards are provided with private phone and fax numbers.

RITZ-CARLTON NEW YORK ★★★★
112 Central Park South (59th St.)
212/757-1900 or 800/241-3333
Singles and doubles $329-$510; suites $750-$4,000. **Seasonal weekend packages throughout the year.**

Completely refurbished in 1993, this elegant hotel overlooks Central Park and is just minutes from Lincoln Center, Carnegie Hall, the Metropolitan Museum of Art, Fifth Avenue shopping, and Broadway theaters. Intimate and gracious, it has a country manor look and feel. Best yet, in spite of its fancy face, a sense of genuine friendliness prevails. Guest rooms have traditional European furnishings, Italian marble bathrooms, two dual-line telephones, modem hook-up capability, hair dryers, lighted makeup mirrors, bathroom scales, full-length mirrors, umbrellas, and VCRs upon request. You'll also find pampering touches like thick terrycloth bathrobes, a fully-stocked honor bar, and room service around the clock. Many of the rooms and suites offer sweeping views of Central Park or the New York City skyline, and several of the suites also have small terraces. But whether or not you spring for the park view, all rooms have the same quality decor and amenities. For those with really deep pockets, there's the Ritz-Carlton Suite with separate elevator key access, a marble foyer, a living room with fireplace, dining room, master bath with whirlpool, and four balconies overlooking Central Park. Business travelers will appreciate the convenience of complimentary limousine service to Wall Street each weekday.

ROGER SMITH ★★
501 Lexington Avenue (47th St.)
212/755-1400 or 800/445-0277
Singles $195; doubles $210; suites $275-$350. Small pets allowed. Continental breakfast buffet is included. **Special summer rates.**

Owned by an artist, colorful artwork decorates the rooms and public spaces of this delightful hotel. Guest rooms have antiques and quality early American furnishings, mini-refrigerators, and coffee makers; several have canopy beds, sofas, and extra space. Some of the suites have fireplaces and terraces—each has a butler's pantry. The hotel has a lot of personality and is a great place to stay—its individual style and good value make it a personal favorite. The only drawback I found was that during a week-long stay in one of the hotel's comfortable and appealing suites, the window air-conditioners were not up to the task of cooling the space during a hot September spell.

THE ROYALTON ★★★
44 West 44th Street (between Fifth and Sixth Aves.)
212/869-4400 or 800/635-9013
Singles $275-$330; doubles $295-$360; suites $425. Pets allowed. **Special weekend packages.**

A favorite of Hollywood celebrities, the dazzling Royalton has a whimsical, futuristic look. French designer Philippe Starck created a glamorous oasis of odd angles and vivid visuals at this shrine to the super-cool. Rooms have the sleek look of staterooms on a luxury liner. Beds have wraparound mahogany headboards and down comforters, and night tables are shaped like portholes. Many rooms have working fireplaces and some of the baths have five-foot round soaking tubs. The rooms are not large, but have style to burn. The in-house restaurant is the celebrated, celebrity-laden "44."

SALISBURY HOTEL ★★
123 West 57th Street (between Sixth and Seventh Aves.)
212/246-1300 or 800/223-0680
Singles $149-$189; doubles $169-$209; one-bedroom suites $239-$299; two-bedroom suites $299. Includes European-style continental breakfast. **Special weekend and summer rates.**

Past its no-frills lobby, the Salisbury is a pleasant find for those seeking roomy accommodations without breaking the budget. The decor is pleasantly traditional, nothing fancy, but loaded with homey comforts. Most of the apartment-sized rooms and all suites have serving pantries with refrigerators and sinks, and all rooms have large walk-in closets. Rooms on the top four floors also have coffee makers and microwave ovens. All suites now have two TVs. An Executive Floor offers rooms with fax machines and data port connections. The location is terrific—just across the street from Carnegie Hall and only two blocks from the shops of Fifth Avenue. Broadway theaters and Lincoln Center are easily within walking distance as well. Room service is now available from nearby Wolf's Sixth Avenue deli.

SAN CARLOS ★
150 East 50th Street (between Lexington and Third Aves.)
212/755-1800 or 800/722-2012
Singles $160-$180; doubles $170-$190; suites $200-$275. **Special weekend rates.**

This small hotel, while not luxurious, offers clean, comfortable accommodations and a residential feeling in the heart of Midtown. Guest rooms and suites have a cheerful, modern decor with kitchenettes, walk-in closets, remote cable TV, and data port phones on every desk. Good value all around.

SHELBURNE MURRAY HILL ★★★
303 Lexington Avenue (37th St.)
212/689-5200 or 800/me-suite
Studio suites $139-$259; one-bedroom suites $175-$290; two-bedroom suites $350-$470. **Special weekend rates.**

Located in the attractive Murray Hill section, this all-suiter has traditional European style and nicely-appointed studio, one- and two-bedroom suites with kitchens. A recent renovation has made it all the more appealing. Several suites offer balconies with views of the Empire State Building, and five penthouse suites open onto a spectacular rooftop garden. Other features include a health club with saunas, complimentary coffee and tea, microwave ovens, premium cable channels, room service, and business services.

SHERATON MANHATTAN ★★★
790 Seventh Avenue (51st St.)
212/581-3300 or 800/325-3535
Singles and doubles $204-$285; suites $350-$645. Pets allowed. **Special weekend rates.**

Much smaller than its sister hotel across the street, this Sheraton still has a big and busy feel. While nicely located for theatergoers, don't expect much pizazz in the guest rooms. Renovated since its days as the Sheraton City Squire, rooms have been greatly improved and include coffee makers, minibars, and premium cable channels, but they are still smallish and decor tends to be monochromatic. On the plus side, the hotel has a very nice fitness center featuring a wide variety of equipment such as exercise cycles, treadmills, stair climbers, free weights, and weight machines. There's also a sauna, sun terrace, and a heated indoor swimming pool. The Club Level, designed to accommodate business travelers, offers telephone data ports, complimentary continental breakfast, and a separate lounge with complimentary hors d'oeuvres.

SHERATON NEW YORK HOTEL & TOWERS ★★★
811 Seventh Avenue (between 52nd and 53rd Sts.)
212/581-1000 or 800/325-3535
Singles and doubles $285-$315; suites $400-$1,500. Pets allowed. **Special weekend rates.**

Geared to conventions and big business affairs, this nicely maintained Sheraton has a terrific location but a rather impersonal ambience. Surrounded by Broadway theaters, Fifth Avenue shopping, and within walking distance of most major attractions, it buzzes with activity throughout the year. Rooms are comfortable but on the bland side. Amenities include in-room movies, in-room safes, voice-mail, video checkout, writing desks, minibars, and coffee makers. There's a Club Level with separate check-in facilities and a separate lounge with complimentary hors d'oeuvres and a business service desk. A free continental breakfast is included for its guests. For more upscale amenities, the two floors designated as the Towers offer guests a private bar, breakfast buffet, down comforters, Frette sheets, fresh flowers, and terrycloth robes. Complimentary afternoon tea, cocktails, and hors d'oeuvres are served in its private lounge.

THE SHOREHAM ★★
33 West 55th Street (between Fifth and Sixth Aves.)
212/247-6700 or 800/553-3347
Standard rooms $225; suites $275; penthouse suites $375-$850. Includes breakfast. **Special weekend and holiday rates.**

This once dowdy property has been transformed into a smart European-style boutique hotel with nice amenities like free breakfast, afternoon tea, bedside books, backlit beds with perforated steel headboards, in-room VCRs, CD players, and Sunday chamber music. Compact rooms, tiny baths, but lots of style.

SOHO GRAND ★★★
310 West Broadway (Canal & Grand)
212/965-3000 or 800/965-3000
Singles and doubles $209-$369; penthouse suites $429-$1,149. Pets allowed.

This new 367-room hotel is the first to open in SoHo in more than a century. Its chic interior reflects its setting in the historic cast-iron architecture district with a striking iron staircase with translucent bottle-glass steps in the dramatic lobby. Guest rooms have smart custom-designed furnishings and are full of nice little details. Amenities include minibars, on-demand movies, two-line phones with voice-mail and data port, in-room safes, complimentary weekday newspapers, a fitness room, and free local phone calls. On the downside, while guest rooms have lots of style and generous amenities, many are quite small and storage space is pretty stingy.

ST. MORITZ ON THE PARK ★★
50 Central Park So. (59th St.)
212/755-5800 or 800/221-4774
*Singles $190-$250; doubles $215-$275; suites $210-$700. Pets allowed. **Special weekend rates.***

If location-location-location is your thing, you may be quite happy at this modestly priced (for the block) hotel with its fabulous Central Park South location. The closet-sized rooms are a big drawback though. A major renovation in the early '90s made the rooms more attractive and comfortable. But many who stay here feel that the best thing about the hotel is its location and the second-best thing is its ice cream parlor, Rumpelmayer's (where you can get great hot chocolate and killer banana splits). The Park View Club rooms and suites are by far the best bets. These newly decorated rooms and suites all have panoramic views of Central Park, updated furnishings, and extra amenities, including complimentary coffee, daily newspaper service, and a designated check-in area and express check-out. Some of these rooms and suites also offer nice private terraces for an exclusive view of Central Park.

ST. REGIS HOTEL ★★★★★
2 East 55th Street (between Fifth and Madison Aves.)
212/753-4500 or 800/759-7550
Singles and doubles $455-$565; suites $695-$5,000. **Special weekend packages.**

As reflected in the room rates (some of the highest in town), this beaux arts landmark is very, very grand. Fashionably situated at Fifth Avenue, it is near Central Park, Rockefeller Center, museums, art galleries, and some of the world's finest shops. Built in 1904 by John Astor, it was the most opulent hotel of its day. A massive top-to-bottom renovation in 1991 by ITT Sheraton restored its old-world grandeur while installing all the latest in high-tech amenities. Rich oak and mahogany panelling, sparkling chandeliers, and gleaming marble abound. The spacious guest rooms are lavish, each with its own sitting area. High ceilings, beautiful moldings, silk wall coverings, chandeliers, and Louis XV furniture surround you in luxury. The large marble bathrooms are similarly luxurious and packed with rich amenities. You'll find brass fixtures, two sinks, separate tub and shower stalls, hair dryers, makeup mirrors, personal scales, very fluffy robes, and Tiffany soaps, perfumes, and shampoos. Other amenities include afternoon sweets, complimentary mineral water, delivery of the newspaper of your choice, free local and credit-card calls, and use of a well-equipped fitness center. While guest rooms and amenities are lavish, it is the extraordinary service that really distinguishes the hotel and makes the stiff rates palatable for those who can afford staying here. Named for the patron saint of hospitality, the St. Regis's pampering services seem endless. Each floor has its own butler, who serves coffee or tea upon arrival and delivers fresh fruit and flowers each day. The 24-hour butler service also includes complimentary services such as packing, unpacking, and pressing clothes upon arrival. The hotel also houses one of the most celebrated restaurants in the country, the Mobil Guide 5-star, Lespinasse.

THE STANHOPE ★★★★
999 Fifth Avenue (81st St.)
212/288-5800 or 800/828-1123
Singles and doubles $350-$425; junior suites $450; suites $475-$2,500. **Special weekend rates and package plans.**

This gracious 1926 landmark hotel—across from the Metropolitan Museum of Art and Central Park—is in the heart of Museum Mile in a beautiful residential neighborhood. Baccarat crystal chandeliers, hand-loomed carpeting, Limoges porcelain, and extravagant floral displays are part of its very pretty picture. Guest rooms and suites are beautifully furnished in a Louis XV style with Asian accents. All accommodations offer two-line speaker phones, CD stereo systems, VCRs, in-room safes, minibars, terry bathrobes, and hair dryers.

SURREY HOTEL ★★★
20 East 76th Street (Madison Ave.)
212/288-3700 or 800-me-suite
*Studio suites $225-$265; one-bedroom suites $325-$405; two-bedroom suites $545-$630. Pets allowed. **Special weekend rates.***

This lovely all-suite lodging is located in an elegant tree-lined Upper East Side neighborhood of stately brownstones, international boutiques, museums, and galleries. Its other distinction is having one of the city's best restaurants (Daniel) on-site. Accommodations are in bright, oversized studios and one- or two-bedroom suites, some with kitchenettes, some with fully-appointed kitchens, and all with complimentary coffee service. Each suite has a distinct personality with graceful molded ceilings, beveled mirrors, and antique accents.

TUDOR ★★
304 East 42nd St. (between First and Second Aves.)
212/986-8800 or 800/879-8836
*Singles and doubles $245-$295; suites $325-$595. **Special weekend packages; lower rates May-September.***

A three-year refurbishment completed in 1991 upgraded this London-owned hotel near the United Nations. Rooms have been enlarged and furnished with classic English reproductions and have nice marble bathrooms. Amenities now include cable TV with in-room movies, minibars, hair dryers, and 24-hour room service. Many of the suites and executive rooms feature a jacuzzi bath and private terrace. Room decor and configuration varies quite a bit though. While many guest rooms have a British charm, I found others to be dark and dreary.

TRUMP INTERNATIONAL HOTEL & TOWER ★★★★★
1 Central Park West
212/299-1000 or 800/457-4000
*Parlor rooms $475-$525; one-bedroom salons $625-$675; executive one-bedroom salons $750-$800; two-bedroom galleries $1,350-$1,500; executive two-bedroom galleries $1,450-$1,650. **Special weekend rates.***

The Donald ponies up with the ultimate in amenities at this glitzy newcomer perched at the edge of Central Park, near Lincoln Center and Carnegie Hall. The 168-suite hotel has a Philip Johnson-designed bronze-and-glass facade, a restaurant run by celebrity chef Jean-Georges Vongerichten, and suites outfitted with Frette linens and Limoges china. The 168 luxury accommodations include 40 two-bedroom "galleries," 90 one-bedroom "salons," and 38 parlor studios, all featuring floor-to-ceiling windows, fully-equipped European-style kitchens, luxurious marble bathrooms, in-room entertainment centers including VCR and stereo with CD player, and telescopes for bringing the fabulous park views into focus. Giving hospitality a new spin, a Trump "attachée" is assigned to each guest upon reservation to provide comprehensive service before, during, and after each visit, with services running the gamut from stocking the refrigerator with a guest's favorites before arrival to arranging thank-you gifts for business associates after departure. Free local phone calls, complimentary local incoming/outgoing faxing from in-room fax machines, overnight pressing and shoeshines, personalized business cards and stationery, and complimentary cellular phones are some of the services that will undoubtedly attract business execs. For leisure time, the health spa features a 55-foot lap pool and state-of-the-art fitness equipment. Spa services such as massage (from Swedish and shiatsu to sport/deep tissue and reflexology) and herbal wraps are available. Spa services and exercise equipment can also be utilized in the privacy of the guest rooms. Needless to say, this level of high living doesn't come cheap.

U.N. PLAZA - PARK HYATT HOTEL ★★★★
1 United Nations Plaza (44th St. at First Ave.)
212/758-1234 or 800/233-1234
Singles and doubles $280-$300; junior suites $400-$500; one-bedroom suites $650-$1,200; two-bedroom suites $850-$1,500. **Special weekend rates and packages.**

This lovely hotel offers 427 gracious guest rooms starting on the 28th floor of a towering chrome-and-glass building directly across from The United Nations. All rooms have personal safes, minibars, clocks, hair dryers, dual-line phones with computer and fax hook-up capability, and fabulous views of the East River or the Manhattan skyline. Rooms are decorated with modern flair in soothing colors and attractive fabrics. While not large, they are comfortably roomy and the expansive view adds a sense of spaciousness. Complimentary services include delivery of *The New York Times*, weekday transportation to the financial district and Park Avenue, transportation to the theater district at 7:15 nightly (except Sunday), overnight shoeshines, and twice-daily maid service. The penthouse health club, overlooking the East River, offers state-of-the-art exercise equipment, massage and sauna facilities, and a glass-enclosed pool. There's also an indoor tennis court. I've always liked this hotel. Its far east location in a real neighborhood setting gives you the feel of city life and makes you forget you're a tourist. Attractive weekend packages make the tab a lot lighter.

WALDORF ASTORIA AND WALDORF TOWERS ★★★★
301 Park Avenue (between 49th and 50th Sts.)
212/355-3000 or 800/waldorf
Singles and doubles $179-$390; junior suites $400; suites $450-$950. Towers: singles and doubles $249-$435; suites $475-$6,500. Small pets allowed. **Special weekend rates.**

After a $200 million renovation by Hilton, this grand New York landmark hotel has been restored to its former glory and is more majestic than ever. *The quintessential New York hotel*, it has hosted every U.S. President since the early 1900s. Commanding a full city block in the heart of Midtown, it is within walking distance of Rockefeller Center, St. Patrick's Cathedral, the theater district, art galleries, and great shopping. Its dazzling art deco lobby personifies New York style and élan and has a constant buzz of activity; its multitude of upscale shops and restaurants includes the famous Peacock Alley and Sir Harry's Bar. The elegant guest rooms vary in size and no two are alike. Amenities include minibar/refrigerators, irons and ironing boards, hair dryers, on-demand movies, coffee makers, marble bathrooms, armoires, and two-line phones. The more expensive Waldorf Towers, occupying floors 28 to 42, is even more grand and has its own separate entrance and separate check-in. Furnished with authentic and reproduction English and French antiques, the rooms and suites in this hotel-within-the-hotel are graceful and charming. Some have full kitchens, maid's quarters, and dining rooms. Cole Porter kept a suite in the Tower for 25 years and wrote many of his famous lyrics on the Steinway grand piano that was a gift from the Waldorf. Today, the piano graces the lobby where a pianist plays nightly.

WALES HOTEL ★★
1295 Madison Avenue (between 92nd and 93rd Sts.)
212/876-6000
Singles and doubles $185; suites $245. Includes breakfast.

If you want to avoid the busy pace of Midtown, consider this turn-of-the-century Victorian. Located on the Upper East Side in the Carnegie Hill section, it is surrounded by historic mansions, Museum Mile, fashionable boutiques, and lively restaurants. But for theatergoing, it is somewhat out of the way. Lovingly restored by the Gotham Hospitality Group, its old-world charm has been polished to a high gloss. Intricate architectural details dress up the simple, comfortably old-fashioned furnishings of the guest rooms. Original fireplaces with carved mantles, oak woodwork, and marble have been beautifully restored. Amenities include afternoon tea and cookies, musical recitals, and Sunday chamber music concerts, along with room service and that amenity of the '90s—in-room VCRs.

WARWICK ★★
65 West 54th Street (Sixth Ave.)
212/247-2700 or 800/223-4099
Singles $220-$270; doubles $245-$295; suites $400-$500. **Special weekend rates.**

Built by William Randolph Hearst in 1927, this comfortable old hotel has seen its share of rising stars. In the '50s and '60s it hosted the likes of Elvis Presley and the Beatles. The top floor suite (now bookable for weddings) was once the home of Cary Grant. A one-time apartment building, many of its rooms are over-sized and have nice big walk-in closets, and some have terraces. Its Midtown location is quite handy for theatergoing and many terrific restaurants (including the fine on-premises Ciao Europa) are nearby. Amenities include two-line phones, premium cable channels, a business center, and exercise room. The rooms vary tremendously in size and decor. While many are huge by Midtown standards, there are also those that are small and drab. But the staff here is very eager to please and if you don't like your first assignment, you'll be shown others that are available.

WASHINGTON SQUARE HOTEL ★
103 Waverly Place (Sixth Ave. and MacDougal St.)
212/777-9515 or 800/222-0418
Singles $85; doubles $110-$117; quads $138. *Continental breakfast included.*

Nothing fancy, but if you want to stay in Greenwich Village, this modest hotel is the place. Popular with budget-conscious students and young Europeans, it boasts a terrific location overlooking Washington Square. Rooms are extremely small and interior ones can be dark and dreary, but they are clean and comfortable and overall good value. Amenities are spare—you may not have a remote for the TV and the towels are a little skimpy. But there's a good restaurant on-site (C-3) and a new exercise room with complimentary weight training and cardiovascular equipment for the exclusive use of hotel guests.

THE WESTBURY ★★★
15 East 69th Street (Madison Ave.)
212/535-2000 or 800/321-1569
Singles $315-$375; doubles $345-$405; suites $525-$1,750. Small pets allowed.
Special weekend rates.

Built in the late '20s by American polo player, Max J. Kramer, who named the hotel after his favorite polo field in Long Island, The Westbury creates the ambience of an old English country manor. Yards of floral chintz in warm tones of tan, red, and forest green grace the charming rooms and make you want to settle in for a long stay. Dark mahogany furniture, vibrant oriental and needlepoint carpets, and traditional English prints and drawings personalize each of the rooms and suites. The marble bathrooms are not large but have all the amenities you might want: hair dryers, scales, magnifying makeup mirrors, terrycloth robes and slippers, and imported designer toiletries from Britain. Other amenities include well-stocked minibars, in-room refrigerators, two-line phones, safes, and writing desks. There's also a complimentary fitness center fully equipped with stairmasters, treadmills, free weights, a sauna, and steam room. Suites are equipped with VCRs and fax phones.

WYNDHAM ★★
42 West 58th Street (between Fifth and Sixth Aves.)
212/753-3500 or 800/257-1111
Singles $120-$135; doubles $135-$150; suites $180-$360.

Over the years this pleasant old-timer has catered to a clientele of theater types who like to settle in for long runs. Those who have called it home include the Oliviers, the Cronins, Peter Ustinov, Harold Pinter, Eva Marie Saint, and Carol Burnett. Floral wallpaper, lace curtains, soft beds, low water pressure, and ancient furniture are part of its homey, eccentric charm. But this wonderful old place isn't for everyone. You won't find all the high-tech conveniences you may be accustomed to. A stay here is more like a visit with a sweet, maiden aunt. Situated in one of the most desirable areas in town, it is across the street from the Plaza, just off Fifth Avenue, and around the corner from Central Park. Those appreciative of its quirky, faded charm will be rewarded with one of the city's true bargains.

BED & BREAKFASTS

An economic alternative to staying in a hotel is to opt for the Bed & Breakfast experience. A growing number of travelers feel this European tradition is the best way to go. Rates can be as much as 60 percent less than what you would pay for comparable space in a hotel. And while New York State sales tax of 8¼ percent applies for stays of less than a week, guest don't pay the city's hotel tax of 5 percent.

This option ranges from renting a room in a private apartment with a resident host to staying in an unhosted apartment. To explore this alternative, contact one of the following services and ask for their brochure and sample list of the properties they represent. Be aware that not all services accept credit cards and some accept credit card payment for the deposit only. Also keep in mind that with the sometimes frequent modification of rosters, quality can be unpredictable. But if you make your requirements clear when booking, and if you don't require traditional hotel services, this might be just your cup of tea. In addition to lower accommodation costs, this type of travel gives you a better sense of what it means to be a New Yorker.

ABODE LTD.
P.O. Box 20022, New York, NY 10021
212/472-2000 or 800/835-8880 (except NY, NJ, PA, CT)
Deposit of 25 percent of total cost of stay is required. Deposit may be paid by check; balance of payment is to be paid upon arrival in cash or travelers checks or by an American Express credit card

Does not publish sample lists of accommodations; call for complete descriptions of current availabilities.

Accommodations range in size from studios to 3-bedroom apartments. Daily rates are $100-$300 with a large selection at $120-$135. Special rates can be arranged for extended stays.

AT HOME IN NEW YORK
P.O. Box 407, New York, NY 10185
212/956-3125 or 800/692-4262; fax 212/247-3294
Deposit of 25 percent of total charges (or one night, whichever is greater)
AE, MC, V

This Bed & Breakfast reservation service has a large international clientele, and represents over 300 B&Bs and private pied-a-terres. Accommodations are in modern luxury high-rise apartment buildings, private brownstones and townhouses, and artist lofts, as well as in some modest walk-up flats. All accommodations are periodically inspected to insure that they comply with the service's standards of cleanliness, comfort, privacy, and safety. Accommodations are located throughout the city and range from cozy rooms in hosted brownstones to spacious three-bedroom, two-bath unhosted apartments. (Absentee hosts usually leave breakfast fixings, maps, and menus of local restaurants.)

Sample Hosted (with private bath) Accommodations:

Host #LC-148. West 66th St., just off Central Park, near Lincoln Center. Single $80; double $90. An elegant B&B in a luxury high-rise 24-hour doorman/concierge building near Lincoln Center. Sunny guest room with connecting bath, double sofa bed, color cable TV, desk, and ample closet space. Terrace overlooks Central Park. (Smoking on terrace only.) The hostess is a young-hearted senior whose cheerful art is displayed throughout the apartment.

Host #MTW-25. West 57th St., corner of Sixth Ave. Single $80; double $90. Very private, bright guest room with connecting bath on 12th floor of modern 24-hour doorman/concierge high-rise building. Guest room extends from long hallway and has queen bed, desk, and private phone. The European hostess is a clinical psychologist.

Host #MTE-105. East 48th St., near Third Ave. Single $75; double $87; triple $110. Well-maintained older building with 24-hour concierge. Center courtyard. Guest Room 1 has queen bed and private bath ensuite; Guest Room 2 has a double and single bed with full bath outside door. The hostess is an actress/producer.

Sample Unhosted Accommodations:

Host #MTW-38. West 57th St. and Ave. of Americas. $135 for 1 or 2 persons ($15 for each additional). Weekly $875 for 1 or 2, $950 for more. Elegant, newly-furnished, spacious alcove studio in modern luxury doorman building near Carnegie Hall. Queen bed, queen sofa bed and matching love seat which converts to single bed. Fully equipped kitchenette with dishwasher, tile bath, brand new light parquet floors, color cable TV with movie channels, phone/answering machine, central A/C.

Host #LC-84. Lincoln Plaza at 64th St., between Central Park and Broadway. Daily $150. Spacious, luxurious 750 sq. ft. one-bedroom condo on 42nd floor of high-rise. Classic contemporary furnishings. Bedroom has queen bed and walk-in closet. Color TV, phone with answering machine, fax, A/C. Fully equipped kitchenette with dishwasher. Dining area off living room. Overlooks Lincoln Center and the Hudson River offering spectacular sunsets and dramatic city views.

Host #LC-239. Lincoln Center. Daily $135. Spacious 1-bedroom apartment in modern, luxury doorman building. Wall-to-wall white carpeting throughout. Bedroom has king bed and color cable TV. Living room has cushiony white upholstered sofas and loveseat, unusual stone coffee table, mirrored wall, many plants. Stereo with CD player and color cable TV with movie channels. Separate dining area, well-equipped kitchenette with microwave, dishwasher, and electric coffee maker. Laundry facilities in building, double-paned thermal windows, view of Fifth Ave. and Central Park.

BED & BREAKFAST NETWORK OF NEW YORK
134 West 32nd Street, Suite 602, New York 10001
212/645-8134 or 800/900-8134
Deposit of 25 percent is required. No credit cards.

Does not publish sample lists of accommodations; call for complete descriptions of current availabilities.

This reservations service has been in business since 1986. Accommodations vary from modest to quite luxurious. Prices range from $60 to $80 per night, single occupancy, for B&B accommodations. Entire apartments without hosts (and sometimes without breakfast) range from $90 to $325 per night, $600 to $2200 per week.

MANHATTAN HOME STAYS
P.O. Box 20684, Cherokee Station, New York, NY 10021
212/737-3868; fax 212/452-1604
Reservation must be confirmed with credit card; deposit taken only immediately before arrival.
MC, V

B&B accommodations and unhosted apartments.

URBAN VENTURES
38 West 32nd Street, Suite 1412, New York, NY 10001
212/594-5650; fax 212/947-9320
Deposit is not required if credit card guarantee is given; entire stay is charged to your card ten days before arrival.
All major cards.

Established in 1979, this was one of the first Bed & Breakfast reservation services in America. While it started with B&B accommodations, it is also a leading renter of unhosted apartments. Hosted B&B prices range from $70 to $115. Unhosted apartment rental prices are determined by location, view, furnishings, doorman (or no), and terraces. Studios range from $105 to $130, 1-bedrooms $125 to $190, and 2-bedrooms from $165 to $270. Apartment rental periods range anywhere from three nights to three years. Each apartment is inspected by a staff person and accurate descriptions are given to clients in advance. For stays longer than a month, apartments will be shown in advance. Apartments are thoroughly cleaned for your arrival, and if you wish to have cleaning services during your stay, that service can be arranged for an additional fee.

Sample Unhosted Accommodations:

Apt ID #69. Midtown/West, Central Park South. $260. A very fashionable 2-bedroom apartment with two marble bathrooms, 3 TVs, piano, massage chair, beautiful furnishings, queen bed, twins beds, and queen sleep sofa.

Apt ID #85. Midtown/West, 49th St. $240. A deluxe 2-bedroom, 1-bath apartment in the heart of the theater district in doorman building. Queen bed in each bedroom plus queen sleep sofa in small living room. Long hallway separates the bedrooms. Piano, TVs, VCR. Owner is an expert on theater.

RESTAURANTS

★GOOD ★★VERY GOOD ★★★EXCELLENT ★★★★OUTSTANDING

Restaurant closing hours tend to change with the flow of business throughout the year. And whether a restaurant serves brunch on Saturdays and Sundays is subject to the same fluctuation. It is always a good idea to make a reservation in advance to avoid disappointment.

Menu prices are listed to give you an idea of what you might expect to spend. Although every effort has been made to assure that the prices listed were accurate at the time of going to press, it is inevitable that there will be some changes. Menu selections and prix fixe offerings are also subject to change. Descriptions of a restaurant's culinary offerings are meant to give you an idea of its style of cooking and presentation, as well as a peek at the pleasures that lie in wait.

A note to readers:

Each restaurant listing is a recommendation rather than a review. Therefore, you will find the writeups generally affirmative. I've tried to include restaurants with a variety of cuisines, price ranges, and ambience. Each has something to offer that makes for a nice dining experience, whether it's the wonderful French cuisine served by candlelight in a romantic carriage house, the charm of a tiny bistro with the golden glow of days gone by, the joyful simplicity of an Italian trattoria, the dazzling decor and imaginative creations of a talented chef in a restaurant hailed as one of the world's best, or the lazy pleasure of brunch in a sun-dappled garden oasis that seems far removed from the concrete world you've left behind. I like every restaurant in this book; I've talked to locals, hotel concierges, tourists, hotel managers, restaurant managers, chefs, and people in elevators to find out what they like. Still, some wonderful restaurants may have been overlooked. If you discover a terrific restaurant I've missed, please write and tell me about it for inclusion in future editions. If you have a bad experience, I would like to hear about that as well.

CHELSEA

Chelsea

Jakob K. Javits
Convention Center

THEATER DISTRICT/GARMENT CENTER

W. 34th St.

W. 33rd St.

Broadway

Lincoln Tunnel

W. 32nd St.

General
Post Office

Madison
Square
Garden
Center

Pennsylvania
Station

Pennsylvania
Central Railroad Yards

W. 31st St.

W. 30th St.

W. 29th St.

FUR
DISTRICT

W. 28th St.

12th Ave.

Chelsea Park

FLOWER
DISTRICT

W. 27th St.

W. 26th St.

11th Ave.

10th Ave.

9th Ave.

Penn Station
South

8th Ave.

7th Ave.

Avenue of the Americas (10th Ave.)

W. 25th St.

W. 24th St.

W. 23rd St.

West
Park

W. 22nd St.

W. 21st St.

W. 20th St.

UNION SQUARE/GRAMERCY PARK/MURRAY HILL

W. 19th St.

West St.

HUDSON
RIVER

W. 18th St.

W. 17th St.

W. 16th St.

10th Ave.

9th Ave.

8th Ave.

7th Ave.

W. 15th St.

Avenue of the Americas (6th Ave.)

W. 14th St.

GREENWICH VILLAGE

ALLEY'S END ★★   American
311 West 17th Street (between Eighth and Ninth Aves.)
212/627-8899
Dinner - Daily 6:00 - 11:00 p.m.
Master, Visa, Discover

A small neon knife and fork at the end of an alley off West 17th Street lets you know you've reached your destination when you undertake the adventure of finding this hidden gem. If you hesitate for a moment or two before venturing any further, you'll be all the more delighted once you do. For inside you'll find a charmingly funky set of dining areas and gardens that will make you forget from whence you've come. While all seating is indoors, the dining room is built around an outdoor garden and waterfall that gives the space an engaging split personality. Ivory-tinted brick walls, full-length windows, and a skylit ceiling enhance the appealing garden-like setting and allow you—for a time—to feel far away from the city streets you've left behind.

The good American bistro food will add to the feeling that you've finished first at a scavenger hunt. You might start with homemade soup of the day served with onion focaccia toast ($5.00), grilled sausage with pearl onions, lentils, and dried cranberries ($7.50) or risotto with lobster stock with a grilled jumbo shrimp ($8.00). Particularly recommended for the main course are the grilled boneless breast of chicken with garlic mashed potatoes and julienned vegetables ($10.00), center-cut grilled pork loin with apple cider Bourbon sauce served with wild rice, cranberries, pecans, and red Swiss chard ($11.00), grilled shell steak in a red wine mushroom sauce with horseradish new potatoes and green vegetables ($16.75), and oven-roasted salmon in a mustard sauce with four-grain pilaf and squash ($13.25). Desserts (around $6.00) might be almond cake with a wild cherry sauce, ginger cake with cinnamon ice cream served with apple-raisin compote, or a seductively light bread pudding.

CHELSEA BISTRO & BAR ★★   French
358 West 23rd Street (between Eighth and Ninth Aves.)
212/727-2026
Dinner - Monday through Thursday 5:30 - 11:00 p.m.;
Friday and Saturday 5:30 p.m. - Midnight; Sunday 5:00 - 11:00 p.m.
All major cards

New on the scene in March 1995, Chelsea Bistro & Bar quickly achieved rave reviews, and for good reason: the food is wonderful and the waitstaff energetic, friendly, and knowledgeable about the menu. It is the kind of

109

neighborhood bistro that is immediately embraced by those lucky enough to have it in their neighborhood. A sophisticated and casually elegant rendering of an authentic Parisian bistro, the dining room features polished brass railings, miles of velvet curtains, gilded mirrors, frosted cut glass shades, a brick fireplace, and dried floral bouquets on each table. Walls are lined with Impressionist and Post-Impressionist prints and the ceiling sports a lacy-patterned paper border. Candlelight and French music combine nicely and enhance the cozy feel of the place. There's also a wonderful glass-enclosed candlelit terrace room with French lace curtains, cream and green wicker chairs, and an entire wall of French mirrored louvered doors.

This pretty place has also been captured on film as the site of a recent filming of the TV shows, *Law & Order* and *Homicide* in an episode that involved a police officer of the *Homicide* cast coming from Baltimore and taking the assistant D.A. from the *Law & Order* cast to dinner at "the most elegant restaurant" in town.

The menu offers contemporary French bistro fare prepared with up-to-the-minute flair by French chef Philippe Roussel. His signature starter dishes are ravioli of pheasant ($8.00), warm flan of wild mushrooms with a Port wine sauce ($6.50), and a tart of herb goat cheese and caramelized onions ($7.50). Favorites among mains are escallop of salmon served with horseradish sauce and spinach flan ($17.50), roasted, marinated free-range chicken with mashed potatoes ($16.00), seafood "choucroute" with shellfish sausage, lobster sauce, savoy cabbage, and root vegetables ($19.00), escallop of veal stuffed with wild mushrooms in a Port sauce ($20.00), braised lamb shank with fettuccine and autumn vegetables ($18.00), and hangar steak with a red wine sauce, confit of shallots, and lyonnaise potatoes ($19.50). The changing variety of desserts ($5.50 to $7.50) might include frozen banana soufflé with walnuts, warm flourless chocolate cake, or bread pudding.

DA UMBERTO ★★   Italian
107 West 17th Street (between Sixth and Seventh Aves.)
212/989-0303
Lunch - Monday through Friday Noon - 3:00 p.m.
Dinner - Monday through Thursday 5:30 - 11:00 p.m.;
Friday and Saturday 5:30 - 11:30 p.m.
American Express only

This is a real neighborhood kind of place, the kind you'd find tucked away on a small street in Tuscany. Once you get past its dreary frontage and enter this lively trattoria, passing the abundant antipasto table, hearing the accents of the flirtatious Italian waiters, and catching the heady aromas drifting from the display kitchen in back, you will be truly transported. Its two dining rooms are spare and attractive, with sponged ochre walls, gentle lighting, and a wall of wine racks. One of the most animated dining scenes in Chelsea, its noise level makes it impractical for a romantic rendezvous but great fun otherwise.

The best way to start a meal here is with a selection from the enticing antipasto table ($9.00). Other choices include prosciutto and melon ($9.00), minestrone ($5.75), and carpaccio ($9.00). Of the mains, a house favorite is the veal chop in a Cognac sauce ($28.00). Veal scaloppine ($18.00), Florentine steak for two ($54.00), and chicken paillard ($16.00) are other popular choices. The pastas are fabulous. The lively gnocchi all'arrabbiata ($14.00) and robust lasagna ($16.00) are particularly good. The mushroom risotto ($18.00) is another winner. Keep in mind that the menu is supplemented with a lengthy recitation of daily specials with an emphasis on fresh fish and game. The dessert bounty is fairly staggering as well and the house tiramisú is considered the best in NYC.

FRANK'S RESTAURANT ★★   Steakhouse
85 Tenth Avenue (15th Street)
212/243-1349
Lunch - Monday through Friday 11:30 a.m. - 4:00 p.m.
Dinner - Monday through Saturday 5:00 - 11:00 p.m.;
Sunday 4:00 - 10:00 p.m.
All major cards

Frank's is a family-run no-nonsense man's kind of place where beef is king and portions are huge. This hungry man's heaven was founded in 1912 in the heart of the meat-packing district. After a 1994 fire, it relocated around the corner from its original 14th Street site and lost a little of its nostalgic steakhouse ambience in the transition. But while its new setting is bigger and brighter with high ceilings and an inviting bar along one wall, no attempt was made to gussy it up like its uptown competition. It is still a big, boisterous two-fisted booze and beef sort of place (with a cigar room in back) where you come to tuck into plate-filling portions of superb quality meat, calories be damned.

A good way to start a meal here is with the shrimp cocktail served with a nice, spicy cocktail sauce ($3 per jumbo shrimp). Other good options include wild mushrooms sautéed in olive oil and garlic ($7.50), onion soup gratiné with

111

parmesan and Swiss cheeses ($5.50), and tomato and onion salad ($5.00). Main course standouts are the excellent steaks: succulent shell steak ($27.50), tender filet mignon ($26.50), and full-of-flavor skirt steak ($21.00). Best of all is the 40-ounce T-bone for two ($53.00). Other good choices include a veal chop cut thick and grilled ($26.50), three loin of lamb chops ($26.50), and grilled chicken with mustard and tarragon ($19.00). The fettuccine Bolognese ($18.00) is also pretty good. And the hand-cut steak fries are fabulous ($5.50). Other good sides include block potatoes for two (mashed potatoes baked with cheese and prosciutto) ($6.50) and spinach with garlic and oil ($6.00). For dessert, the choice is easy—New York cheesecake ($5.50).

GASCOGNE ★★   French
158 Eighth Avenue
(between 17th and 18th Sts.)
212/675-6564
Lunch - Monday through Friday and Sunday Noon - 3:00 p.m.
Dinner - Monday through Thursday 6:00 - 10:30 p.m.;
Friday and Saturday 6:00 - 11:00 p.m.;
Sunday 5:00 - 10:00 p.m.
All major cards

When you enter Gascogne, it's like stepping off Eighth Avenue into the French countryside. Loaded with character, its duplex dining room with walls of rough sandstone and partially exposed brick is reminiscent of a Gascony farmhouse. It overlooks a beautiful shaded garden illuminated by banks of colored lights creating a romantic alfresco oasis of tranquillity in warmer months and, come the winter holidays, a miniature wonderland with a festive Christmas tree and snowmen.

This is not a place for calorie counting. The cuisine is the robust fare of Gascony, a pastoral region in the southwest of France, home of Armagnac, foie gras, and cassoulet. For starters, the house specialty is the warm fresh foie gras with seasonal fruits ($18.00). Other good starters: escargots in garlic butter served in phyllo dough with a chive beurre blanc; St. James mussels gratinées with garlic butter and parsley; and a warm goat cheese salad with potatoes and fresh herbs (each $8.00). As for the main, the house specialty is the cassoulet Toulousain ($21.00). Other notable choices (each well priced at $21.00): free-range roasted baby chicken with a walnut sauce; filet mignon flambé with an Armagnac, black, pink, and green peppercorn sauce; roasted rack of lamb with garlic and fresh rosemary; free-range rabbit fricassée with white wine, wild mushrooms, baby onions, and fresh herbs; and fondue Gascogne (a traditional fondue with duck magret and three sauces). Seafood is good here as well. Try the fresh roasted trout with almonds or the baked salmon in papillotte with white wine and a julienne of vegetables (each $19.00). The kitchen's finesse extends to the dessert course, with choices that include frozen Armagnac soufflé and thin puff pastry-crusted apple tart with green apple sorbet. There's also vanilla ice cream with crème de marrons and hot chocolate fudge and prune ice cream with Armagnac in an almond pastry shell. Desserts (each $7.00) are all homemade, including the ice cream.

   A pre-theatre menu is available from 6:00 to 8:00 p.m. (three courses for $25.00, including a glass of Armagnac). If you're seeing a dance performance at the Joyce—just across the street—dining here is definitely a perfect way to start the evening.

LE MADRI ★★★   Italian
168 West 18th Street (Seventh Ave.)
212/727-8022
Lunch - Daily 11:30 a.m. - 2:30 p.m.
Dinner - Monday through Saturday 5:30 - 11:30 p.m.;
Sunday 5:30 - 10:30 p.m.;
All major cards

   With its panache and high style, this glamorous Tuscan trattoria has captured the affections of the fashion and publishing crowd. Its large airy dining room is one of casual elegance, with a vaulted ceiling, pale yellow walls, a huge wood-burning pizza oven decorated with Farnesi tiles, and tables well spaced for privacy. A spacious, wood-planked patio (under a striped tent) with umbrellaed tables and potted trees provides a nice option in pleasant weather.

   Opened in 1989 by sage restaurateur Pino Luongo, and in keeping with his view that the best restaurants in Italy are the family-oriented trattorias which draw inspiration from home cooking, this restaurant was named Le Madri ("the mothers" in Italian). It quickly gained a local following, and today the wonderful regional Italian food coming out of the kitchen keeps it high on the list of the city's best Italian restaurants. The seasonal menu offers many super starters such as warm goat cheese encrusted with walnuts and served with baby greens and beets ($8.50), grilled portobello mushrooms drizzled with garlic-balsamic oil and served with Tuscan bruschetta ($8.50), beef carpaccio with baby artichokes, arugula and parmesan shavings ($9.00), and fried calamari with a spicy roast pepper-tomato sauce ($8.00). There's an excellent selection of pastas including half-moon ravioli of spinach and ricotta tossed with mixed mushrooms ($16.00), basil tagliolini with shrimp, scallops, asparagus, and olive oil ($17.00), and spaghetti with tomato, olive oil, garlic, and crushed red pepper ($14.00). Gnocchi is a specialty here with a preparation that changes daily ($15.00). There are many other commendable dishes when it comes to the main course. Favorites include grilled tuna with seared endive and zucchini with an olive-caper-tomato vinaigrette ($25.00), roast Amish free-range chicken breast with a crispy potato cake, mushrooms, and a medley of vegetables ($21.00), braised veal shank served with portobello mushrooms and saffron risotto ($24.00), loin of lamb roasted with thyme and mustard, served with asparagus and black olive-mashed potatoes with apple chips ($23.00), and veal chop seared with herbs and accompanied with wood-oven roasted vegetables and potatoes ($28.00). It's all so good. The dessert choices are pretty standard: crème brûlée, tiramisú, gelato, and tarts (each $8.00).

EAST SIDE

East Side

UPPER EAST SIDE

E. 73rd St.

E. 72nd St.

E. 71st St.

New York
Hospital/
Cornell
University
Medical
College

E. 70th St.

E. 69th St.

CENTRAL
PARK

Hunter College

E. 68th St.

EAST RIVER

E. 67th St.

*Rockefeller
University*

E. 66th St.

E. 65th St.

E. 64th St.

Franklin D. Roosevelt Dr.

Roosevelt Island

Zoo

E. 63rd St.

E. 62nd St.

5th Ave.

Madison Ave.

Park Ave.

Lexington Ave.

3rd Ave.

E. 61st St.

2nd Ave.

1st Ave.

York Ave.

E. 60th St.

Queensboro Bridge

E. 59th St.

MIDTOWN

ARCADIA ★★★   American
21 East 62nd Street (between Fifth and Madison Aves.)
212/223-2900
Lunch - Monday through Saturday Noon - 2:30 p.m.
Dinner - Monday through Saturday 6:00 - 10:00 p.m.
All major cards

Warmth and charm abound at this much-loved tidy townhouse restaurant.
A beautiful arcadian mural surrounds the pretty flower-filled dining room and
soft lighting gives it a decidedly romantic feel. Like its namesake—a legendary
region of Greece with lush pastures and fruitful valleys where the gods loved
to frolic—its setting evokes pastoral images and forms a lovely background for
the culinary creations of chef-owner Anne Rosensweig. Her innovative and
elegant American cooking has earned her star status among the city's great
chefs.

The three-course dinner prix fixe is $58.00. There are at least a half-
dozen choices in each category, with tantalizing starter options such as
buckwheat fried oysters with a mizuna and fried lemon salad; corn cakes with
crème frâiche and caviar (+$5.00); Arcadian Caesar salad with arugula and
brioche croutons; and mustard-crisped crab cake with sweet pea greens. Your
main choice might be: crispy roast chicken with red potatoes, morels, and favas;
toasted sesame tuna with asparagus and rock shrimp ravioli; or the signature
chimney-smoked lobster with tarragon and celery root cakes (+$7.00).
Desserts are American classics and oh-so-good. A house specialty is the
chocolate bread pudding with Brandy custard.

**A pre-theatre menu offers three courses for $30.00 at the 6:00 p.m.
seating, a wonderful value in this special restaurant.**

ARIZONA 206 ★★★   Southwest
206 East 60th Street (between Second and Third Aves.)
212/838-0440
Lunch - Monday through Saturday Noon - 3:00 p.m.
Dinner - Monday through Thursday 5:30 - 11:00 p.m.;
Friday and Saturday 5:30 - 11:30 p.m.; Sunday 5:30 - 10:30 p.m.
All major cards

This animated spot radiates a lively spiritedness. It is the only
Southwestern restaurant to receive three stars from *The New York Times* (and
it has done it twice). Yet, as you pass the long, busy bar to a small rustically-

styled area, you may begin to wonder where the restaurant is located. The space seems too small for a restaurant with such a large, enthusiastic following. But after dining here once, you'll understand why—the food is fabulous enough to make up for any shortcomings in the space. And while its wood-burning fireplace, soft desert colors, adobe-style walls, wooden booths, and wood plank floors may be reminiscent of Santa Fe, the smart-looking young crowd and noise level are pure New York.

Starters will stimulate your tastebuds, especially the fabulous crisp potato and salmon quesadilla with mango-epazote sauce, crème fraîche, and black caviar ($10.00) and the spicy shiso scallop with tempura crust and sesame-soy sauce ($8.00). Other winners include chile relleno of crab with fresh corn, carrot-ginger butter, black beans, and habanero sauce ($12.00), and petite tuna tacos with wasabi tobikko (flying-fish roe), potato, cucumber, and tropical salsa ($10.00). Of the equally vibrant mains, house specialties are the lobster tamale with wild mushrooms, cactus and poblano, with beurre-soy ($28.00) and terrific sage-roasted chicken with blue corn stuffing, green chile mashed potatoes, and honey-baked shallots ($20.00). Other good choices might be Peking duck tamale with ancho-plum sauce, cucumber, and scallion ($26.00) and wild striped bass with green chile tempura and a garlic sauce ($24.00). Even desserts have a Southwest flair—warm fruit empanaditas with honey vanilla ice cream and hazelnut praline sauce ($7.50), sorbet tacos with tropical fruits and candied citrus ($7.50), and a Cajeta (caramelized goat milk) banana split with toasted almonds, crisp plantains, and cinnamon ice cream ($7.50). Another sweet temptation is a pineapple tart layered with phyllo, spicy pecans, and lime yogurt ice cream ($7.50).

There's an adjacent cafe with a breezy Southwest decor, similar food, and lower prices. And in warm weather, sidewalk tables are another option.

AUREOLE ★★★★   American
34 East 61st Street
(between Madison and Park Aves.)
212/319-1660
Lunch - Monday through Friday Noon - 2:30 p.m.
Dinner - Monday through Saturday 5:30 - 11:00 p.m.
All major cards

Aureole is the kind of restaurant that catches your eye as you walk by and makes you long to be inside. Its soaring two-story front window allows a peak at its charming flower-filled interior. Situated on two floors of a graceful townhouse once owned by Orson Welles, its elegance has a rustic feel. Extravagant floral arrangements, dried flowers in twig baskets, and wildlife reliefs on sandstone walls set the whimsical tone of the main floor dining room. The airy upper level affords an atrium-like view of the lower dining space and offers a more private atmosphere. And for warm weather dining, there's an elegant little summer garden with geraniums and ivy spilling out of white planters and climbing a white trellis.

Charlie Palmer, the brilliant chef/owner, once aspired to a career in professional football. His career shift is a present to all who dine here. He opened Aureole in 1988 after perfecting his craft at La Côte Basque and The River Cafe, and it has been a hot ticket ever since. (Aureole was voted the No. 1 restaurant for food by New Yorkers in the 1997 *Zagat Survey* and placed No. 2 as overall favorite.)

Palmer calls his cooking progressive American—by whatever name, it is wonderful. His inventive, ever-changing menu is determined by market availability. **Dinner is prix fixe only, with three courses for $63.00.** Starter offerings might include hot lobster vichyssoise with spring leeks and potato crisps; balsamic poached artichoke salad with tomato coulis, crisp shallot, and mesclun greens; oak-smoked salmon with vegetable citrus salad, smoked salmon mousse, and sourdough toasts; or the signature starter, sea scallop sandwiches in crisp potato crusts. Recent offerings from the ever-changing list of mains: garlic-crusted chicken with slow-roasted artichoke, a purée of barlito beans, tomato oil, and fresh rosemary; veal medallions with wild mushroom cannelloni; grilled lamb loin with a crisp tomato quesadilla; and charcoaled filet mignon with roasted shallots, country potatoes, foie gras-stuffed morels, and crisp parsnip. Desserts are delicious and such spectacular architectural wonders, they defy description. These edible sculptures have many components, such as the white chocolate cheesecake that comes with a round of chocolate mousse wrapped in a ribbon of chocolate, on top of which rests three chocolate wafers intersected by a white crescent. Well, go see for yourself.

There's also an $85 tasting menu available to the entire table at dinner. But a less costly way to sample this terrific restaurant is at lunch when a $32 four-course prix fixe is offered.

CAFE GRECO ★   Continental
1390 Second Avenue
(between 71st and 72nd Sts.)
212/737-4300
Lunch - Daily Noon - 4:00 p.m.
Dinner - Daily 5:00 - 11:00 p.m.
All major cards (except for pre-theatre menu)

Wood and brass, high ceilings, abundant floral displays, and generous hospitality make for a relaxed atmosphere at this pleasant, family-run restaurant. The soothing pastel decor and prices—especially the fixed price offers—make it all the more attractive.

The menu seems to scan the Mediterranean with no clear commitment to any one port, but everything is good and the dishes are the kind that mix and match happily. Starter offerings include grilled octopus ($5.00), Greek salad ($5.00), mussels marinara ($5.00), spanakopita ($5.00), and Caesar salad ($4.00). Good main choices are chicken Marsala ($12.95), penne with black olives, capers, and fresh tomato ($10.95), jumbo shrimp scampi ($13.95), grilled or blackened swordfish ($13.95), grilled whole striped sea bass ($15.95), grilled sirloin ($13.95), and grilled lamb chops ($18.95). The changing assortment of desserts are $4.00 each.

A $9.95 fixed price lunch menu is available from noon to 4:00 p.m. on weekdays; on weekends there's a $10.95 fixed price brunch menu available from noon to 4:00 p.m. with a drink and two courses; a $16.95 three-course pre-theatre menu is available from 5:00 to 6:30 p.m. daily; and a $21.95 fixed price dinner menu with three courses is available from 5:00 to 11:00 p.m. daily. (As noted above, no credit cards are accepted for the pre-theatre special.)

CAFE PIERRE ★★   French
(Hotel Pierre)
Fifth Avenue at 61st Street
212/940-8185
Lunch - Daily Noon - 2:30 p.m.
Dinner - Daily 6:00 - 10:30 p.m.
All major cards

This celebrated cafe has a subdued elegance. Soft shades of yellow and gray with silver accents, etched Italian mirrors, imported silks and satins, ornate fabric-draped mirrors, and cloud murals on the ceiling all combine to create a soft, soothing ambience. Both the tables and waiters are dressed to the nines, and among the sophisticated looking diners there's usually a famous face or two. And if you're in the mood for some old-fashioned cheek to cheek dancing, you can do so here on Friday and Saturday evenings.

Chef Bertrand Vernejoul's modern interpretations of classical French cuisine highlight the seasonal menu that always includes a good selection of alternative cuisine low in calories, cholesterol, sodium, and fat. You might start with a warm terrine of roasted eggplant with red bell peppers and goat cheese ($11.00), open ravioli with tomatoes, spinach, and mozzarella ($12.00), or Maine crab salad with a lemon confit and chive vinaigrette ($15.00). For the main, steamed filet of red snapper with tomato fondue and grilled eggplant ($25.00) and roasted rack of lamb in an herb crust with sautéed artichokes ($29.00) are house specialties. Other good options include sea scallops with onion compote, potato gnocchi, and scallions ($26.00), bowtie pasta with grilled Gulf shrimp, artichokes, fresh tomatoes, and black olives ($25.00), grilled filet of beef with garlic whipped potatoes and a red wine sauce ($28.00), and roast free-range chicken with asparagus risotto and a lemon-thyme sauce ($24.00). Good desserts include a crisp Napoleon of poached plums with orange crème brûlée ($9.00), hazelnut meringue with mixed berry and pineapple frozen yogurt ($8.50), and lemon curd tart with strawberries ($8.00).

A pre-theatre menu is offered with three courses for $34.00, with four or five choices in each category. This is a nice way to step into the elegant atmosphere of yesterday without breaking the budget.

CIRCUS ★★   Brazilian
808 Lexington Avenue (between 62nd and 63rd Sts.)
212/223-2965
Lunch - Daily Noon - 5:00 p.m.
Dinner - Daily 5:00 - 11:30 p.m.
All major cards

A pretty setting and well-prepared Brazilian standards make this a consistent winner. Its delightful decor is highlighted with a circus painting by Axel Sande. A working fireplace, along with colorful banquettes and curtains, add a homey warmth to the chic playfulness of the room. Samba sounds dance in the background. And in spring and summer, the front opens and sidewalk tables allow a look at the activity along this busy stretch of Lexington Ave.

The traditional Brazilian fare served here has been given a light touch and it is all quite good. Start on a pleasant note with a baked empanada filled with chicken and hearts of palm ($7.00). Another nice opener is soft polenta with sage and shallots served with a choice of veal sausage ($9.00), chicken liver ($8.00), or diced sirloin ($10.00). Other good choices include homemade mozzarella with fresh tomato, hearts of palm, and basil ($7.00) and black bean soup ($5.00). Good mains include a grilled skewered combination of chicken, beef, and veal sausage served with vegetable rice ($18.00), pan-seared medallions of filet mignon with onion, served with rice and black beans ($19.00), country-style beef chunks served on a bed of mashed potatoes with black bean broth ($17.00), crispy chicken chunks with fresh herbs, garlic, rice, and beans ($14.00), shrimp, halibut, clams, scallops and mussels cooked in a light saffron broth ($19.00), and pan-seared salmon coated with mixed herbs and served on a bed of black bean sauce ($18.00). There are delightful pastas as well—shells tossed with broccoli tips, parmesan, and homemade veal sausage ($14.00) and penne with a light tomato sauce with chopped tomato, mozzarella, and basil ($14.00). Feijoada, Brazil's national dish, a black bean stew with lean cuts of pork, beef, and sausage, served with collard greens and rice ($18.00) is served only on Saturdays and Sundays.

CONTRAPUNTO ★★   Italian
200 East 60th Street (Third Ave.)
212/751-8616
Monday through Thursday Noon - 11:00 p.m.;
Friday and Saturday Noon - Midnight;
Sunday 2:00 - 10:00 p.m.
All major cards

This chipper second-story pasta palace has a winning combination with its appealing all-day menu, cheerful ambience, and great vantage point for people-watching. Situated just opposite Bloomingdale's, across the street from the off-Broadway Theatre East, and amidst a host of movie theaters, the all white dining room with floor-to-ceiling windows and an open kitchen has a pleasing vibrancy and busy buzz about it.

Contrapunto isn't just for convenience though—you can also get a terrific meal here. You might start with white bean soup with extra virgin olive oil and parmesan ($6.50), grilled rustica bread salad with green olives, tomato, and ricotta ($5.50), grilled quail with polenta ($10.00), or prosciutto with warm greens ($10.00). Pastas—innovative and delicious—are served in either starter or main course portions. Choices include tagliarini with squid, tomatoes, and jalapeño ($8.50/$14.00), ruffled pasta with sausage, white beans, and escarole ($9.50/$16.00), fettuccine with wild mushrooms, truffle oil, and parmesan ($9.75/$16.50), and buckwheat pappardelle with braised duck, pearl onions, and dandelion greens ($10.00/$17.00). Among mains, house specialties include wild striped bass with leeks, cockles, shellfish broth, and lemon-olive oil ($18.00) and grilled leg of lamb with roasted eggplant, greens, and herbed tomato sauce ($20.00). Also good: roast chicken breast with polenta ($14.50); grilled salmon with artichokes and a tomato-black olive vinaigrette ($16.00); and roasted duck breast with glazed turnips, pearl onions, coriander, and honey ($21.00). And for dessert, the winner is the chocolate hazelnut cake with raspberry sauce and vanilla ice cream ($7.50). Also popular are the house-made gelati and sorbet selections.

IL TOSCANACCIO ★★★   Italian
7 East 59th Street (between Madison and Fifth Aves.)
212/935-3535
Lunch - Monday through Friday Noon - 3:00 p.m.
Dinner - Daily 5:30 - 11:30 p.m.
All major cards

This is another triumph for restaurateur Pino Luongo, a spirited Florentine whose restaurants are known for their chic settings and terrific food. (Le Madri, Coco Pazzo, and Coco Pazzo Teatro are other Manhattan pleasures to his credit.) Il Toscanaccio (Naughty Tuscan) has an earthier, more rustic ambience than the others—it replaces Amarcord, Luongo's rather formal restaurant which previously occupied this space. The sunny dining room now has a nice informal feel to it, with vibrant linens, lively murals, and a long wooden table laden with colorful vegetables and huge baskets of bread at its center. Its joyful ambience is echoed in a huge, playful mural of Sophia Loren, Catherine di Medici, and Dante dining together.

You can't go wrong with any of the delicious starters. Choices include an assortment of Tuscan specialties ($8.50), baby octopus stewed in a spicy tomato sauce on toasted garlic bread ($9.00), pasta e fagioli (the traditional pasta and bean soup) ($8.00), a delicious Tuscan-style onion soup with whole peas and an intense peppery flavor ($8.00), and a wonderfully simple dish of eggs, tomato, and garlic ($8.00). There are several really good salads—my favorite is the seasonal chopped variety with tomatoes, cannellini beans, mushrooms, onions, carrots, parsley, and parmesan ($7.50). Also good is a salad of baby artichokes, thinly-sliced and tossed with lemon, olive oil, and shaved parmesan ($9.00). The simplest of the pasta offerings is a wonderful homemade tagliatelle with old-style tomato sauce ($16.50). More intricate options include spaghetti with chunks of lobster, fresh tomatoes, and herbs ($21.50), spaghetti with clams and arrugola, hot red pepper, garlic olive oil, and tomato ($17.00), linguine with scallops, mussels, clams, and calamari ($17.00), penne with sausage, pancetta, onions, tomatoes, and herbs ($16.00), and a daily preparation of risotto (p/a). Of the mains, a fabulous choice is the fritto misto (a delicious mix of fried seafood and vegetables in an edible basket of fried potatoes) ($27.00). If you like lamb stew, you'll love the version served here in a bowl of bread ($24.50). Other good choices include stewed veal with potatoes, assorted vegetables, white wine, and tomato, served in homemade zoccolo bread ($22.50), pounded breast of chicken, breaded and pan-sautéed and served with arrugola, tomato, and onion ($21.50), ribeye steak grilled and served with roasted potatoes, cranberry beans, and tomato ($28.00), and filet of fish of the day stewed with garlic, tomato, herbs, and hot chile pepper, served with soft polenta ($25.00). Desserts are $8.00. For chocolate lovers, the choice way to end a meal here is with the soft-centered chocolate cake. Others might opt for the poundcake with pine nuts, raisins, and berries.

JO JO ★★★   French
160 East 64th Street
(between Lexington and Third Aves.)
212/223-5656
Lunch - Monday through Friday Noon - 2:30 p.m.
Dinner - Monday through Friday 6:00 - 11:00 p.m.;
Saturday 5:30 - 11:00 p.m.
All major cards

Relentlessly chic, this casually elegant bistro has been wildly popular since the day it opened. Its beautiful townhouse setting makes it as pretty from the street as it is inside. Graceful windows, a cheerful awning, and handsome moldings greet you outside. Inside, the two-story restaurant has a decidedly Parisian feel. Its downstairs dining room imparts a breezy sophistication with warm yellow walls, crimson banquettes, pretty mirrors, and a floor of tiny tiles. The upstairs rooms are pretty, too, and have a more relaxed atmosphere, especially the parlor room in back with its Victorian sofas and tall fireplace (perfect for an after dinner drink).

Chef/owner Jean-Georges Vongerichten (whose childhood nickname was JoJo) was the forerunner of the '90s movement toward healthier cooking, starting the trend of replacing cream and butter with Asian spices, herb-infused oils, exotic vinaigrettes, and vegetable broths. And he is nothing short of masterful at creating stunning, delicious, and relatively guilt-free cuisine.

While the menu is somewhat limited—with eight or ten choices in each category—choosing a starter is still difficult with appealing choices such as goat cheese and potato terrine ($10.00), creamless sweet pea soup with roasted vegetables and croutons ($8.00), tuna spring roll ($10.00), crab salad with mango, cumin crisps, and a grainy mustard ($11.00), and shrimp dusted with orange powder, artichoke, and basil ($12.00). Mains display the same diversity with choices that include slowly-baked salmon with crisp potato, celeriac, herb salad, and horseradish condiment ($24.00), roasted chicken with chickpea fries ($18.00), roasted duck breast with caramelized pear, pommery mustard sauce, and red cabbage ($24.00), and roasted veal chop with asparagus broth and a compote of shallots and tarragon ($28.00). Desserts ($7.00-$8.00) are fabulous. Reward yourself with the awesome soft-centered chocolate cake.

A four-course dinner prix fixe is $55.00 and a four-course vegetable prix fixe is $35.00. There's also a three-course lunch prix fixe for $25.00. The menus are set and change often.

L'ABSINTHE ★★   French
227 East 67th Street
(between Second and Third Aves.)
212/794-4950
Daily 6:00 - 11:00 p.m.
All major cards

This wonderful place imparts the golden glow of days gone by. Its setting is a handsome mix of bistro posters, polished brass, etched glass, old-fashioned chandeliers, huge imported mirrors, ancient clocks, pretty floor tiles, and lace curtains. It has the feel of a 1920s Parisian brasserie and is packed with a chic 1990s clientele. Waiters dart about in traditional bistro-brasserie garb and the sound of animated conversation fills the room with a convivial buzz. This is the sort of place that reminds you of tiny back streets and Paris nights. In warm weather, the front opens and tables spill out onto the sidewalk adding to the impression that the Seine can't be far away.

Chef Partner Jean-Michel Bergougnoux, originally from Lyon, has cooked in such prestigious American kitchens as Lutèce, La Cygne, and Raphaël. Here, he presents a menu of both innovative contemporary dishes with seasonal ingredients and a light touch and a selection of old-fashioned hearty bistro dishes. Once seated, you'll be welcomed with delicious tiny peppery cheese puffs to nibble while you contemplate whether to start with sautéed calamari with gnocchi ($8.50), endive salad with roquefort and smoked duck breast ($9.00), or the terrific house specialty—Beaujolais-style warm poached sausage with potatoes and lentils ($8.50). And in keeping with brasserie tradition, mains include terrific renditions of hanger steak with sautéed potatoes and a red wine sauce ($22.50) and roasted free-range chicken with wild mushrooms and mashed potatoes ($20.50). Other good options include a wonderful Moroccan-style salmon served with couscous and preserved lemons ($23.50) and veal risotto with fava beans and fresh coriander ($22.50). And for dessert, you couldn't find a better apple tart ($9.00) in Paris. This buttery, flaky wonder is served warm with honey ice cream. The second best dessert is the warm chocolate cake with a crunchy exterior and melting center ($9.00). This course alone is bistro at its best.

LA GOULUE ★★   French
746 Madison Avenue (65th St.)
212/988-8169
Lunch - Daily Noon - 3:30 p.m.
Dinner - Daily 6:00 - 11:30 p.m.
All major cards

Loaded with charm and conviviality, La Goulue captures the spirit of an authentic turn-of-the-century Parisian bistro. Its name refers to the Moulin Rouge dancer immortalized by Toulouse-Lautrec, and its atmosphere might just beckon you back to that other time and place. Period mirrors, lace curtains, much brass, and dark wood panels contribute to its look, while a chic clientele contributes to its cachet. In fact, the chance of a nice payoff at people-watching here is great. And now with a dynamic young chef, Philippe Schmit, the food is finally as good as the setting.

An outstanding way to start is with the warm potato and goat cheese tarte Tatin with smoked duck breast ($9.50). Other good options include salmon tartare with a gazpacho-style coulis ($9.50) and New England crabmeat salad with avocado in an aromatic vinaigrette ($11.00). There's also a very good selection of French and New York cheeses served with country bread toasts ($12.00). Main courses well worth consideration are the pan-roasted tuna steak on a salad of fennel, tomatoes, lemon, and basil ($23.00), grilled Maine sea scallops with herb jus and summer green peas risotto ($23.00), and roasted veal chop in sage jus with homemade gnocchi ($25.00). And for true bistro bliss, there's steak in a green peppercorn sauce with homemade frites

($26.00) and free-range chicken breast roasted on a bed of mashed potatoes and sweet garlic ($20.00). Daily desserts are delicious bistro classics.

LE VEAU D'OR ★   French
129 East 60th Street (between Lexington and Park Aves.)
212/838-8133
Lunch - Monday through Saturday Noon - 4:00 p.m.
Dinner - Monday through Saturday 5:30 - 11:30 p.m.
All major cards

This old-fashioned French bistro opened in 1937, and its timeless appeal is evident from the many affectionate loyalists who keep coming back week after week and year after year. Its pleasantly timeworn, cozy appearance and classic bistro comfort food offer the kind of authentic atmosphere that makes the place seem forever 1950s Paris.

Its menu also seems etched in time with classic starters like celeri remoulade, baked onion soup, and paté du chef. **The price of the main includes both an appetizer and dessert.** And you'll find all the classic bistro dishes among the list of mains—things like frog legs ($25.00), seafood casserole ($26.00), roast duck with cherry sauce ($24.00), roast baby chicken with white wine and mushrooms ($24.00), coq au vin ($24.00), roast rack of lamb ($30.00), and steak au poivre ($29.00). Desserts are bistro favorites as well: chocolate mousse, parfait au rhum, meringue glacée, and crème caramel.

A three-course $19.95 prix fixe menu is available at both lunch and dinner. Starter choices might be vichyssoise, artichoke vinaigrette, or celeri remoulade. Main selections include sautéed chicken in a tarragon sauce with pasta, fish of the day, and steak frites. Dessert choices include chocolate mousse, crème caramel, and peach melba.

MANHATTAN CAFE ★★   American
1161 First Avenue (between 63rd and 64th Sts.)
212/888-6556
Monday through Friday and Sunday noon - 11:00 p.m.;
Saturday 5:00 - 11:00 p.m.
All major cards

This is the kind of restaurant that has a lot of curb appeal. It looks so inviting with its hunter green canopies, flower boxes, and fresh white window trim. There's also a refurbished bronze doorway from the old Biltmore Hotel. And if you peek inside you'll see the green velvet chenille and mahogany chairs, French art deco chandeliers suspended from pressed tin ceilings, fresh cut flowers, and crisp white table linen. Persian carpets, brocade draperies, and rich mahogany panelling create a warm and clubby ambience for dining. And a 110-year old mahogany and oak bar (taken from the ballroom of the Astor Hotel) with its original decorative moldings, gives the bar an old-world elegance.

The fare is American steakhouse and it covers a lot of territory and does it quite well. Starters on the extensive menu include lobster cocktail ($15.75), oyster cocktail ($10.25), smoked salmon ($12.75), stuffed mushrooms ($8.75), fried calamari ($9.75), and New England clam chowder ($5.75). There's much diversity in the list of mains, as well. Choices include Cajun chicken with corn stuffing ($24.75), broiled filet of New England flounder ($24.75), blackened Cajun swordfish ($28.75), poached filet of salmon ($28.75), filet mignon ($29.75), prime rib ($28.75), veal chop ($29.75), rack of lamb ($29.75), sliced sirloin in a Cognac and peppercorn sauce with steakhouse stuffing ($29.75), veal piccata ($25.75), and a pair of thick pork chops with a cranberry-sweet potato sauce and vegetable stuffing ($26.75). There's even a fair selection of pasta dishes—linguine with white clam sauce ($18.95), gnocchi Bolognese ($18.95), and spaghetti and meatballs ($18.95).

MARCH ★★★   New American
405 East 58th Street
(between First Ave. and Sutton Pl.)
212/754-6272
Dinner - Monday through Thursday 6:00 - 10:00 p.m.;
Friday and Saturday 6:00 - 10:30 p.m.;
Sunday 5:00 - 9:00 p.m.
All major cards

March's warm hospitality and beautiful townhouse setting allow you to feel as though you're dining in a gracious private home. Situated in a charming turn-of-the-century townhouse off Sutton Place, its atmosphere is intimate and romantic. Comprised of two dining rooms featuring 12-foot ceilings, teak floors, fabric-covered banquettes, candlelit lamps, and antique furnishings, it is luxurious and very pretty. Dried flowers, frosted hanging wreaths, and needlepoint tapestries add to its allure. There's also a glass-enclosed rear dining room that overlooks a garden and is used for both individual dining and small private parties. From its rear door, a staircase descends to a brick-paved garden patio with ivy-clad trellises, lush flowerbeds, and flowering trees. And for an intimate alfresco dinner, the charming newly-landscaped green and white canopied wildflower garden makes spring and early summer seem like the perfect time to dine here. Yet, there is something special about March at any time of year. On cold evenings, a fire blazing in the fireplace at the elegant entrance, along with the warmth of the welcoming host, contribute to the feeling that you're about to be embraced by the good life, at least for the evening.

Chef Wayne Nish and amiable host Joe Scalice, friends from their days at La Colombe d'Or, opened this very personal restaurant in 1990 and it has consistently earned high marks from local restaurant critics as well as its legion of well turned out diners. Its menu reflects the multi-ethnic culinary style of the very gifted Mr. Nish whose occasional Asian spin stems from his Japanese-Maltese background. **He offers a prix fixe menu for $59.00 which includes an amuse gueule, choice of eight starters, mains, and desserts, and finishes with coffee and pralines.** The menu changes approximately twice a season. Starters are unfailingly special—perhaps smoked trout and bacon with lettuce and tomato; seared rare tuna in a sesame seed crust with caramel soy; ricotta and goat cheese gnocchi with braised greens and wild mushrooms; or venison salad with quinoa pilaf and Chinese black beans. Mains are wonderful as well with choices such as five-spice salmon with wild mushrooms; poached breast of chicken with spicy cider sauce and potato pancakes; aged sirloin with garlic whipped potatoes and caramelized shallots, and roast rack of Colorado lamb with sweet mustard and Israeli couscous (+$5.00). Dessert choices might be the refreshing house specialty grapefruit and grapefruit sorbet with gin syrup and coriander seed, warm walnut tart with hazelnut ice cream, or vanilla custard with sugar-glazed bananas, bittersweet chocolate, and candied cashews.

There is also a four-course tasting menu, available all evening, which includes an amuse gueule, three courses, and a mini dessert sampler and finishes with coffee and pralines. This is priced at $70.00 and is available with three glasses of selected wines for $90.00.

After 8:00 p.m., a seven-course tasting menu is available which includes an amuse gueule, five courses, a sorbet course, and a grand dessert sampler and finishes with coffee and pralines. This is priced at $85.00 and is available with four glasses of selected wines for $115.00.

If you're feeling really flush, there's a nine-course Gourmand Menu prepared with 24 hours notice for $175.00 including five to seven glasses of wine.

PARK AVENUE CAFE ★★★   American
100 East 63rd Street (at Park Ave.)
212/644-1900
Lunch - Monday through Friday 11:30 a.m. - 3:00 p.m. (Dim Sum on
Saturdays with 11:15 and 1:15 reservations)
Brunch - Sunday 11:00 a.m. - 2:30 p.m.
Dinner - Monday through Saturday 5:30 - Midnight; Sunday 5:30 - 9:30 p.m.
All major cards

American folk art, antique toys, and arrangements of dried wheat set a
cheerful tone at this fanciful American cafe. And chef David Burke's inventive
American cuisine is as whimsical as the decor.

Everything is wonderful, starting with the bounteous basket of fabulous
bread that welcomes you. Stunning presentations and a flair for creative
combinations of flavors are Burke's trademark. His colorful repertoire includes
starters such as tomato-spinach and ricotta ravioli with arugula ($12.50),
Chinese-style ribs with grilled prawns and asparagus ($12.50), gazpacho with
avocado, spiced shrimp, and Jack cheese quesadilla ($9.50), and lobster wonton
soup ($10.00). Of the main courses, a sensational sample of Burke's
inventiveness is a dish called Duck! Duck! Duck! ($28.50). He created three
distinctive recipes for this dish—the first consists of marinated, very lean
domestic duck breast that he grills and slices diagonally as in flank steak; the
second component of the dish is a meatloaf made from ground duck, eggs,
crumbled cornbread, and sweet potato purée; and the third is a foie gras duck
dumpling on cranberry sauce atop celery and passion fruit sauce. Other good
choices among mains include onion-crusted roast organic chicken with potatoes
($25.50), baby rack of lamb with roast shallot ravioli and cauliflower purée
($29.50), seared salmon with ginger, cracked pepper, soba noodles, and Asian
mushrooms ($28.00), mustard-crusted tuna teriyaki ($29.50), and grilled ribeye
steak with Cabernet potatoes ($33.50). Desserts ($8.50) are both beautiful to
behold and delicious. Choices might be warm strawberry fritters with a
rhubarb charlotte, crisp apple tart with Tahitian vanilla ice cream, chocolate
mousse cake, or fresh mango and lemon tart with lemongrass sauce.

The setting here seems perfect for Sunday brunch when the menu entices
with the likes of silver dollar almond pancakes with passion fruit butter and
maple syrup ($14.50), raspberry, banana, and pecan waffles with maple syrup
and whipped yogurt ($14.50), a French toast loaf with preserves ($15.00), an
omelette with wild mushroom hash and a red pepper sauce ($16.50), and ribeye
steak and poached eggs with tomato and spinach strudel ($24.50). And how
about starting with housemade jelly doughnuts and fruit salad ($10.50)?

THE POLO ★★   American
(Westbury Hotel)
Madison Avenue at 69th St.
212/439-3907
Lunch - Monday through Saturday Noon - 2:30 p.m.
Brunch - Sunday Noon - 2:30 p.m.
Dinner - Daily 6:00 - 10:00 p.m.
All major cards

Paisley banquettes, soft leather armchairs, elegant dark panelling, shiny brass sconces, and walls adorned with sporting prints set the clubby tone in this handsome dining room in the venerable Westbury Hotel. The atmosphere is subdued and relaxed, with beautiful table settings, soft piano music, and an attentive staff to enhance the luxurious feel of the place.

The innovative new American cuisine of Executive Chef Kerry Heffernan is touched with European accents and an emphasis on bold flavor combinations. His menu changes with the seasons, always with daily specials reflecting the freshest ingredients available from the market and the dishes they inspire. One of his signature dishes is a starter of grilled Louisiana shrimp with artichokes, haricots verts, and an orange-tarragon sauce ($14.00). Other tempting starters include smoked Canadian salmon with Napa mustard slaw ($13.00) and cannelloni of buttercup squash with Parma ham and sage ($11.00). Good mains include filet of pork with spiced endive, celery root, and roast Hudson Valley apples ($21.00), loin of Colorado lamb with polenta, escarole, and parmesan ($28.00), Black Angus sirloin with a crisp potato cake, grilled portobello mushrooms, and a Bordelaise sauce ($30.00), and seared spice-crusted tuna with Swiss chard, fingerling potatoes, lemon coulis, and thyme ($26.00). Daily desserts might include warm chocolate cake with toasted almond and dark chocolate ice creams and warm rhubarb tart.

Sunday brunch is also an elegant affair here. The set price is $33.50 and includes a sampling of selections from a buffet of shrimp, seafood, smoked salmon, charcuterie, and vegetable salads. Then order a main course from a choice of poached farm eggs on toasted potato bread with smoked salmon and herb hollandaise, Black Angus sirloin with Bordelaise sauce and shoestring potatoes, seared salmon with a mustard vinaigrette, and buckwheat waffles with hickory smoked bacon and a warm fresh berry compote. End with a selection from the dessert table of assorted seasonal fruit tarts, pastries, cakes, and fresh fruits.

THE POST HOUSE ★★★   Steakhouse
28 East 63rd St. (between Park & Madison Aves.)
212/935-2888
Lunch - Monday through Friday Noon - 4:00 p.m.
Dinner - Daily 5:30 - 11:00 p.m.
All major cards

With its impressive collection of American artifacts, prized paintings, and deep taupe leather banquettes and armchairs, this venerable restaurant has a polished style all its own. It is easily one of the smartest looking steakhouses in town.

One of its best starters is a plate of cornmeal-fried oysters served over homemade coleslaw ($10.75). Other good openers include Maryland crab cocktail ($12.75), whole chilled baby lobster ($13.75), and coconut shrimp ($12.75). For the main, Post House classics include a terrific Cajun rib steak ($34.00), filet au poivre ($29.75), and prime rib ($29.75). This is also the sort of steakhouse where it is possible to venture off the red-meat trail and still eat very, very well. Other fine options include a wonderful grilled chicken breast with corn, shiitake mushrooms, and country ham ($23.00), triple lamb chops ($29.75), rack of baby lamb ($29.75), and broiled sole with lemon butter ($22.50). Daily specials might be honey-roasted free-range chicken with fig and prosciutto stuffing ($25.50), grilled double pork chop with orange and ginger glaze and mashed sweet potatoes ($25.50), or roast loin of lamb with apple and mint chutney ($29.75). The elegant and irresistible desserts ($7.50) come in hungry-man portions: there's fudgy chocolate cake filled with vanilla ice cream and served in a pool of Valhrona milk chocolate sauce; banana cream pie; and the Post House chocolate box (a Belgian semi-sweet chocolate box filled with white and dark chocolate mousse).

SEL ET POIVRE ★★   French
853 Lexington Avenue (between 64th and 65th Sts.)
212/517-5780
Lunch - Daily Noon - 4:00 p.m.
Dinner - Sunday through Thursday 4:00 - 10:30 p.m.;
Friday and Saturday 4:00 - 11:00 p.m.
All major cards

This upscale bistro is comfortably elegant and has all the attributes to make it a neighborhood prize. Its atmosphere is cozy and unpretentious, with white walls, dark beams, and vintage black and white photos of Parisian street life setting a pleasant backdrop. Intimate and charming, with four sidewalk tables out front, it is reminiscent of the neighborhood bistros of Paris.

Executive Chef Bernard Teisseidre presents a menu of country-style bistro favorites, tossing in a few international curves along the way, such as in one of his most popular starters, clams posillipo ($9.50), which are served in their shells in a light red sauce perfect for dipping. Other good starter choices include onion soup with a country bread and Swiss cheese crust ($5.95), arugula, endive, and watercress salad with roquefort cheese ($7.50), mussels marinières ($8.50), and warm garlic sausage wrapped in brioche ($8.95). House specialties among mains include roasted chicken with frites ($16.95), steak frites with salad ($16.50), steak au poivre with frites ($22.95), bouillabaisse ($19.95), grilled tuna with sweet red peppers in a raspberry vinegar sauce ($19.95), and poached salmon on a bed of vegetables in a Pernod sauce ($19.95). Crisply roasted duck in an orange sauce ($19.50), porcini mushroom-filled ravioli in a tomato sauce ($14.95), and fettuccine and chicken in a cream and black pepper sauce ($15.95) are other good choices.

A pre-theater menu is available from 4:30 to 6:00 p.m. with three courses for $15.95. There's also a good prix fixe lunch with three courses for $11.95.

Weekend brunch is nice here with a prix fixe of $12.95. It includes an assortment of breads, coffee or tea, and seasonal fruit, along with a main course. Choices include eggs Benedict, strawberry macadamia nut crêpes, French toast with caramelized apples, and penne provençale.

THE SIGN OF THE DOVE ★★★   Modern American
1110 Third Avenue (65th St.)
212/861-8080
Lunch - Tuesday through Friday Noon - 2:30 p.m.
Brunch - Saturday and Sunday 11:30 a.m. - 2:30 p.m.
Dinner - Monday through Friday - 6:00 - 11:00 p.m.;
Saturday 5:30 - 11:00 p.m.; Sunday 6:00 - 10:00 p.m.
All major cards

With all the beauty and glamour a special evening deserves, "the Dove" has an air of celebration about it. You look around wondering what each table is celebrating or what big deal is being sealed. While it has long been renowned as one of the most beautiful restaurants in New York, for a time its culinary achievement was in no way a match for its knockout looks. But now when you dine here, you'll be dazzled as much by the food as you are by the pretty place in which it is served.

Housed in three converted brownstones, the Dove's four dining areas are separated by graceful brick arches with wrought-iron filigree. Lavish flowers, hand-painted chests, classical statuary, flagstone floors, oriental carpets, skylights, and tall plants combine to create a spectacularly romantic garden oasis. And on pleasant days, when its retractable skylit ceilings open to the sky and an ever so slight breeze plays across your face, you'll know you're living the good life.

The delicious basket of bread that greets you comes from the restaurant's own bakery up the block, Ecce Panis. It's all quite wonderful. **The 2-course prix fixe dinner price is determined by the entrée.** From an ever-changing menu, you'll choose from starters that seem to scan the globe: pumpkin tortelloni with warm ricotta, sage butter, and parmesan bread crumbs; seared sea scallops with a pesto of black beans and Thai basil; baby artichoke and mushroom pisto with a warm goat cheese beignet; and cold grilled tuna with ginger aïoli. Mains might be braised rabbit with mustard spätzle with sweet and hot peppers, portobellos, and pearl onions ($35.00); stuffed breast of chicken with braised greens and whole garlic cloves ($30.00); filet mignon with herbed roesti potatoes ($45.00); crispy salmon with polenta gnocchi ($35.00); and monkfish medallions wrapped in prosciutto with spring onions and mashed potatoes ($30.00). Desserts are wonders—temptations like a warm tart of cranberries, pears, and apples; chocolate-hazelnut gâteau with spiced raspberry compote; vanilla custard cake with caramelized bananas, passion fruit jus, and bon-bons; and chocolate soufflé cake with vanilla ice cream.

A pre-theater menu is available Monday through Friday with 5:30 or 6:00 reservations and offers any two courses for $32.00 or three courses for $39.00.

YELLOWFINGERS DI NUOVO ★   American
200 East 60th Street (Third Ave.)
212/751-8615
Monday through Thursday 11:30 a.m. - 1:00 a.m.;
Friday and Saturday 11:30 a.m. - 2:00 a.m.;
Sunday 11:30 a.m. - Midnight
All major cards

This animated American bistro offers an appealing Italian-influenced all-day menu and late hours. It's open-kitchen turns out an eclectic, contemporary array of well-prepared specialties, and its glassed-in sidewalk cafe offers a front row view of this busy neighborhood in motion. A favorite lunch spot for Bloomies' shoppers, it's also great before or after a movie or a production at the off-Broadway Theatre East (just across the street).

Good starters include warm white bean hummus with roasted tomato salad and pane nuda ($6.00) and fennel-fried calamari with a tomato-green olive dipping sauce ($7.00). Fa'Vecchia, a delicious pizza-like bread, is served with a variety of toppings such as fennel sausage, roasted peppers and onions, ricotta, and mozzarella ($12.00), prosciutto, charred tomatoes, arugula and red onion salad, and parmesan cheese ($12.50), and Japanese eggplant, sweet peppers, mozzarella, and goat cheese ($11.50). Good sandwich combos include grilled turkey breast on pepper brioche with sun-dried cranberry chutney ($11.50) and grilled eggplant, mozzarella, peppers, tomatoes, and pesto on focaccia ($9.75). Generous salads are a house specialty with offerings like shrimp and roasted vegetables with a lemon-garlic vinaigrette ($14.50) and rosemary chicken with peppers, eggplant, celery and a lemon-garlic vinaigrette ($14.50). Other specialties include good grilled chicken with garlic mashed potatoes, green beans, and a wild mushroom sauce ($15.00), grilled marinated steak and fries with mustard butter and mixed greens ($16.00), and grilled yellowfin tuna with black bean and arugula salad and a roasted pepper-garlic sauce ($15.00). And in keeping with the pleasures that precede them, desserts are delightful. Choose from a selection that includes bittersweet chocolate tart with whipped cream and fresh strawberries ($5.50), warm apple streusel pound cake with vanilla ice cream and caramel sauce ($5.50), and lemon ricotta cheesecake with sun-dried cherry compote ($5.50).

EAST VILLAGE

East Village

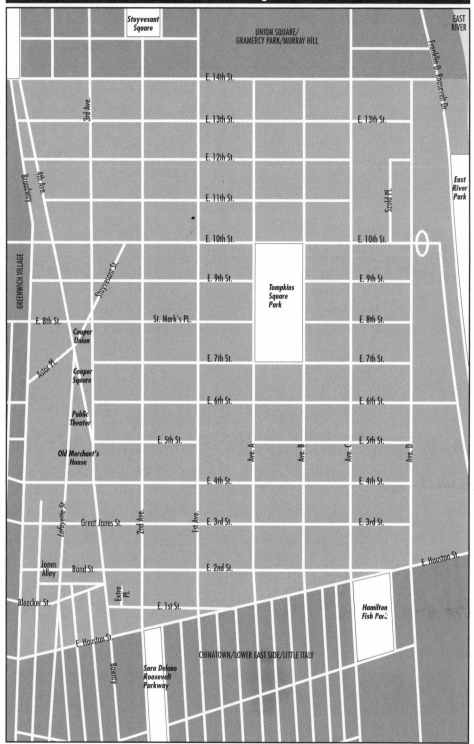

COL LEGNO TRATTORIA ★★   Italian
231 East 9th Street
(between Second and Third Aves.)
212/777-4650
Dinner - Tuesday through Sunday 6:00- 11:30 p.m.
American Express only

As you enter this simple Tuscan trattoria, the heady scent of aromatic wood, fragrant sauces, and fresh bread greets you. The spare no-frills setting is comfortable, unpretentious. Black lacquered tables and chairs, black and white photos on brick and tin walls, and tiled floors set the scene.

Authentic Tuscan specialties are featured, with meat, fish, and game cooked over aromatic wood for distinctive flavor. Delicious pastas, soups, vegetables, and desserts are made daily on the premises. And, happily, the prices are just as pleasing as what appears on your plate. For starters, there's a good bruschetta ($3.95), polenta with sautéed mushrooms ($5.95), and mozzarella and tomatoes ($6.95). Excellent pizzas prepared in a wood-burning oven come topped with sweet sausage, garlic, mozzarella, and tomato sauce ($7.95) or with wild mushrooms, fresh tomato, mint, and garlic ($9.95), along with several others combinations. The vegetable dishes are all quite fine, too. Feel virtuous eating steamed spinach dressed with olive oil and lemon ($4.95), white beans simmered in a flask with wine, sage, garlic, and olive oil ($5.95), or thinly-sliced roasted potatoes layered with thyme and parmesan cheese ($5.95). The freshly-made pastas are hardly run of the mill with choices like pappardelle in a sauce of ground wild boar, tomato, and rosemary ($12.95) and tagliatelle in a wild mushroom sauce flavored with mint. More traditional choices include spinach lasagna ($12.95) and spaghetti with a fiery sauce of tomato, onion, pancetta, and hot peppers ($11.95). Dessert choices are simple—gelati, a fresh fruit plate, or tiramisú (each $4.95).

CUCINA DI PESCE ★★   Italian
87 East 4th Street (between Second and Third Aves.)
212/260-6800
Dinner - Monday through Thursday 3:30 p.m. - Midnight;
Friday and Saturday 2:30 p.m. - 1:00 a.m.;
Sunday 2:30 p.m. - Midnight
No credit cards

Hearty portions and bargain basement prices keep this subterranean East Villager packed in spite of its no-reservations/no-credit cards policy and long waits. Great free mussels at the bar do help make the wait more agreeable. And in warm weather, a good people-watching sidewalk cafe increases seating. The restaurant itself is snug and pleasantly old-fashioned with statues, French mirrors, and antique frames. And its situation—on the same block as the La MaMa theater complex and near several other off-Broadway houses—makes it all the more congenial for theatergoers.

Good starters include mushrooms stuffed with vegetables and topped with melted mozzarella ($4.95), smoked salmon on a bed of endive with watercress and capers ($4.95), grilled portobello mushroom ($5.95), fried calamari with a spicy red sauce ($5.95), and a cold seafood antipasto plate with marinated scallops, shrimp, calamari, and mussels on a bed of red leaf lettuce ($6.95). The fresh homemade pasta is very good indeed with choices that include Sicilian lasagna ($7.95), large spinach ravioli ($6.95), fusilli with sun-dried tomatoes, gorgonzola, and capers in a cream sauce ($6.95), seafood fettuccine with shrimp, scallops, and crabmeat in a marinara or light cream sauce ($8.95), and shells with sautéed eggplant, fresh tomato, and roasted peppers, topped with ricotta cheese ($6.95). Winning mains (served with linguine marinara) include sea scallops broiled with lemon and butter and topped lightly with parmesan ($10.95), stuffed brook trout (a whole fish, boned and stuffed with shrimp, scallops, and crabmeat) ($9.95), grilled salmon, topped with sautéed mushrooms in a lemon dill sauce ($9.95), and shrimp scampi ($9.95). While seafood definitely reigns supreme here, there are other good options as well—chicken Marsala ($7.95), boneless breast of chicken topped with eggplant, prosciutto, and mozzarella in a white wine tomato sauce ($8.95), chicken Parmigiana ($8.95), veal Parmigiana ($9.95), and veal Marsala ($8.95).

Between 3:30 and 6:00 p.m., there's a $9.95 pre-theater menu that includes soup, salad, wholewheat bread, and a main course.

DANAL ★★   Contemporary American
90 East 10th Street
(between Third and Fourth Aves.)
212/982-6930
Lunch - Wednesday through Friday Noon - 3:00 p.m.
Brunch - Saturday and Sunday 11:00 a.m. - 3:00 p.m.
Dinner - Tuesday through Sunday 6:00 - 10:00 p.m.
All major cards

Unless you live in the neighborhood, Danal is pretty much a buried treasure. And once discovered, it's the kind of prize you want to keep to yourself. Sweet and tiny, it's like dining in your grandmother's attic. There are mismatched chairs and all sorts of interesting objects—bird cages, old pitchers, framed photos, hanging baskets of dried flowers—scattered amidst the old farmhouse tables. But there are also lace curtains, a pair of sofas, and a decorative fireplace to add a sense of order. It is just the sort of neighborhood restaurant we'd all like to have as a neighbor.

The service is casual and friendly, and while the menu changes daily, the food is consistently delicious. There are always wonderful salads, pastas, meat dishes, and homemade desserts. Starters might include roasted eggplant soup ($3.00), baked brie with beets on mixed greens ($6.50), and roast corn and goat cheese tart ($5.00). The salad niçoise with seared tuna steak ($15.00) is a big favorite when on the list of mains. Other pleasing recent mains have been filet of beef with artichoke cream sauce and mashed potatoes ($16.00), pork tenderloin with apples, cabbage, and a sweet potato ($16.00), grilled trout with pecan butter and wild rice ($16.00), penne with chicken sausage, peppers, and cheese ($13.00), and grilled salmon remoulade with couscous ($15.00). Desserts are the kind that deserve to be enjoyed slowly—and if you're sharing, you'll wish you weren't. The changing array might include pumpkin bread pudding, 3-berry cobbler, pear tarte Tatin, crème brûlée tart, and banana cheesecake ($4.50).

FIRST ★★   Eclectic
87 First Avenue (between Fifth and Sixth Sts.)
212/674-3823
Brunch - Sunday 11:00 a.m. - 3:00 p.m.
Dinner - Monday through Thursday 5:30 p.m. - 2:00 a.m.;
Friday and Saturday 6:00 p.m. - 3:00 a.m.; Sunday 4:00 p.m. - 1:00 a.m.
All major cards

You get a lot of bang for your bucks at this wonderfully eclectic East Villager. While its name pays tribute to the avenue on which it is located, its owners chose its East Village site not because of any particular fondness for the area, but for its affordable rent. That focus is a big gain for those who dine here. The food is wonderfully inventive—as well as just plain wonderful—and the prices are much lower than they would be for such prime fare in a more upscale neighborhood. The dining room has a trendy and casually sophisticated flair with a long brick wall, a soft color scheme, and comfortable big, round banquettes. All in all, a fabulous find.

Chef Sam DeMarco describes his spirited global cuisine as having inner-city flavor. His seasonal menu is a mix of French, Greek, Spanish, Moroccan, Indian, Colombian, Chinese, and Italian fare. Oh, and homey American, too. The winter menu offers intriguing starter choices such as a terrific hot shrimp cocktail with horseradish crust, seasonal greens, and lime vinaigrette ($9.00), pumpkin gnocchi with wild mushrooms, sage, and truffle-scented broth ($8.00), black bean soup with chorizo sausage, cilantro, sour cream, and crisp tortillas ($6.00), frisée roast beet salad with walnuts, bacon, and warm blue cheese fondue ($8.00), sautéed veal sausage with potato latke, apples, onions, and sour cream ($7.00), and a wonderful dish of steamed mussels in wasabi broth (Japanese horseradish) with sticky rice, scallions, and sesame oil ($7.50). The skillfully prepared mains also scan the globe with good choices like spaghetti and meatballs with plum tomato sauce, reggiano shavings, and ricotta cheese ($13.00), Southern-fried chicken with mashed potatoes and corn-on-the-cob ($13.00), grilled hanger steak with mushroom hash, spinach, crisp onions, and Cabernet sauce ($17.00), venison steak with braised red cabbage and whipped potatoes ($18.50), stuffed rotisserie chicken with roast acorn squash, green beans, and cranberry dressing ($14.00), pan-seared sea scallops with corn risotto, chicken livers, escarole, and roast garlic butter ($16.50), and grilled salmon with sautéed spinach and gratin potatoes ($16.00). There are nightly specials as well. If it's Sunday, it's roast suckling pig ($18.50) and Monday is Latin Nite with paella ($19.00). Desserts ($5.00) are scrumptious, especially the warm chocolate pudding cake with coffee ice cream. There's also a yummy banana cake with ice cream and créme anglaise and a nice apple tart with vanilla ice cream and caramel sauce.

IL BUCO ★★   Mediterranean
47 Bond Street (between Bowery and Lafayette St.)
212/533-1932
Tuesday through Thursday 6:00 p.m. - Midnight;
Friday and Saturday 6:00 p.m. - 1:00 a.m.;
Sunday 6:00 - 11:00 p.m.
Cash only

Captivating aromas greet you as you enter this quirky charmer. By day, it's an antique shop; in the evening, it becomes a wine and tapas bar, taking on the ambience of a European taverna with candlelight amid a backdrop of various bric-a-brac. Its walls are lined with antique radios and other odds and ends for sale. Aging tricycles, plastic purses, and pretty quilts coexist with furniture also on the trading block, giving the place a funky split personality that is part Grandma's attic and part discount house.

The menu, like the decor, is a delightful potpourri of tapas and appetizers, and it is all so good. Mix, match, and share. Choices include bruschetta ($5.00), prosciutto croquettes ($6.00), grilled baby calamari with fresh tomato ($7.00), frisée salad with pears, walnuts, and big chunks of blue cheese ($8.00), Serrano-style ham with fresh figs or melon in season ($10.00), saffron risotto cakes with sautéed wild mushrooms ($12.00), seared tuna and corona beans ($12.00), and grilled baby lamb chops ($16.00). The wine selection (from the cellar said to be the inspiration for Edgar Allen Poe's *The Cask of Amontillado*) includes Italian, French, and Spanish—with a few Alsatian and South African—wines mostly in the $20-$40 range. Desserts (around $6.00) vary daily.

INDOCHINE ★★   French Vietnamese
430 Lafayette Street
(between Astor Pl. and 4th St.)
212/505-5111
Dinner - Daily 5:30 p.m. - Midnight
All major cards

With a clientele of fashion models (with names like Cindy, Christy, and Bianca) and fashion model wannabees competing with the tantalizing decor, dining here has long been a visual as well as a culinary affair. And fun. Once among the hottest tickets in town, it went through a cooling off period. Though there are still some complaints about long waits during prime time, it is enjoying a season of renaissance and is red hot once again. Its setting combines manilla-colored walls with banana leaf murals, dark green banquettes, and white tablecloths for a tropical look. Tall greenery and exotic flower arrangements amid soft candlelight add to the sensuous feel of the place.

The comprehensive Vietnamese menu seldom changes. You can expect terrific starters and good authentic mains when you dine here. It's always tempting to make a meal of appetizers with choices like fried spring rolls with shrimp, bay scallops, and fresh crabmeat ($8.50), spicy salad of thinly-sliced filet of beef ($10.75), steamed Vietnamese ravioli filled with chicken, shiitake mushrooms, and bean sprouts ($8.50), lightly-fried squid stuffed with shrimp and served with grilled vegetables ($9.75), fish soup with scallops, shrimp, coconut milk, and rice vermicelli ($6.50), and sweet and sour shrimp soup with tamarind, pineapple, and tomato ($6.50). Among the mains, the house specialty is a crispy whole sea bass with lemongrass ($18.75). Other top choices include filet of sole with coconut milk steamed in a banana leaf ($17.75), grilled chicken breast stuffed with lime leaf, lemongrass, and coconut milk

($14.75), grilled whole prawns with crushed ginger, scallions, and angel hair pasta ($17.25), filet of beef with vegetables in a light sauce ($17.50), and boned roast duck with ginger and bean sprouts ($17.50). Sticky rice Indochinese-style with bits of pork ($3.50) or the house rice sautéed with green peas, shrimp, and egg ($3.75) is a must.

A pre-theater menu is offered from 5:30 to 7:00 p.m. with three courses for $19.50. Reserve in advance when you're attending a performance at the Public Theater—it's just across the street.

LANZA ★★   Italian
168 First Avenue (between 10th and 11th Sts.)
212/674-7014
Lunch - Daily Noon - 3:00 p.m.
Dinner - Sunday through Thursday 4:00 - 11:00 p.m.;
Friday and Saturday 4:00 p.m. - Midnight
All major cards

Stained glass, a stamped-tin ceiling, and colorful murals of carefree Italian scenes create an appealing old-fashioned ambience in this turn-of-the-century restaurant that was caringly restored several years ago. It is an enduring East Village favorite that seems to get better all the time. Ceiling fans, fresh flowers, and a generously endowed table of appetizers complete its gracious setting. A pleasant garden is another nice feature.

Good homestyle Italian food and some fabulous prix fixe specials make it a wonderful bargain. Even the prices on the regular menu are gentle by most standards. Starters include fried zucchini ($5.95), Caesar salad— Lanza's specialty ($5.95), and fresh mushrooms sautéed in olive oil with garlic and hot pepper ($4.95). Mains could be whole boneless trout sautéed in olive oil with garlic and rosemary ($11.50), veal scaloppine ($12.50), shell steak with sautéed mushrooms ($15.95), spaghetti with plum tomatoes, basil, and mozzarella ($9.95), or linguine with freshly shucked clams in olive oil and garlic ($9.95).

A prix fixe dinner menu with three courses for $15.50 is available Monday through Saturday from 4:00 to 6:30 p.m. and on Sunday from 3:30 to 6:30 p.m. There are a half-dozen choices in each category. You might start with clams oreganata, a mozzarella and tomato salad, or ripe melon and prosciutto. Main choices include fusilli with tomato and prosciutto, chicken parmesan, trout with garlic and rosemary, and veal Marsala. For dessert: black and white chocolate cake, cannoli, or ricotta cheesecake. **A prix fixe lunch is**

also a good buy with two courses (starter and main or main and dessert) for $8.50.

There's also a terrific late night pasta prix fixe available daily from 9:00 p.m. with three courses for $11.95. There's a choice of six starters and about 16 different pasta choices (tortellini Alfredo, homemade ravioli with a creamy ricotta filling, rigatoni in marinara sauce, straw and hay with cream, peas, and prosciutto, seafood linguine, ziti Bolognese, and calamari in a white wine sauce—to name a few). Then choose from about five desserts.

LOUISIANA COMMUNITY BAR AND GRILL ★★   Cajun
622 Broadway
(between Bleecker and Houston Sts.)
212/460-9633
Dinner only - Monday through Thursday 6:00 - 11:00 p.m.;
Friday and Saturday 6:00 p.m. - Midnight;
Sunday 5:00 - 10:00 p.m.
All major cards

A festive ambience is the order of the day—every day—at Louisiana Community Bar and Grill. Decorated to evoke an authentic Louisiana shotgun bar and with live music seven nights a week, the atmosphere is engagingly raucous, always fun. This is a place where cold Dixie beer and Cajun martinis mix with blues, jazz, zydeco, and Cajun bands, to form a merry backdrop for good Cajun and Créole food. Until 1992, this was K-Paul's New York with the present owners in partnership with famed New Orleans superchef Paul Prudhomme. Although Prudhomme is no longer involved, his spirit echoes throughout, particularly in the kitchen where the recipes he inspired still make up the heart and soul of the menu.

Your starter might be fresh Louisiana oysters ($8.00 half-dozen), Gulf Coast nachos with spicy crawfish, Jack cheese, guacamole, and salsa ($8.00), jalapeños stuffed with shrimp and cheese and wrapped in bacon ($8.00), fried green tomatoes with cream gravy ($7.00), crawfish enchilada in a red chile sauce ($7.00), or a cup of seafood okra gumbo ($6.00). The mains are generously proportioned and delicious with choices like blackened pork chops with onion gravy ($15.00), blackened yellowfin tuna with sauce piquant ($19.00), vegetarian jambalaya with basmati rice and sauce piquant ($13.00), grilled salmon with crawfish magnolia sauce ($16.00), shrimp and andouille creole with rice ($17.00), blackened prime rib with browned garlic butter and potatoes ($20.00), and slow-roasted chicken with jalapeño mashed potatoes and pecan gravy ($15.00). Desserts—divine. Favorites are the coconut cake with freshly grated coconut ($5.00), sweet potato pecan pie ($5.00), and warm bread pudding with whipped cream ($4.00).

MARION'S CONTINENTAL RESTAURANT   Continental
& LOUNGE ★★
354 Bowery (between Great Jones and East 4th Sts.)
212/475-7621
Brunch - First Sunday of each month
(seatings at 12:30 and 2:00 p.m.)
Dinner - Sunday through Thursday 6:00 - 11:30 p.m.;
Friday and Saturday 6:00 p.m. - 2:00 a.m.
Visa, Master

This funky East Village hideaway has a look of sophisticated mischief. Its retro supper club ambience and laid-back attitude, along with boozy refreshments like Manhattans, Vodka Gibsons, and Rob Roys will transport you back to the 1940s and put you in a wee small hours of the morning mood. Opened in the 50s by model Marion Nagy, it quickly became a hangout for movie stars and politicians—with its prime corner banquette once reserved for John and Jackie Kennedy. In 1973, Ms. Nagy closed her well-loved domain to enjoy more time with her family. In 1990, several years after her death, her son and a business partner reopened, taking care to leave its personality much as it was. And with a tip of a hat to its glamorous originator, fashion brunches are held on the first Sunday of each month featuring the work of local designers. At other times it is open only for dinner. They also do themes every so often (Chinese New Year, the Flower Show, Beach Party, etc.).

The fare is mostly French and Italian, but food isn't really the main draw here. It's the atmosphere and the bar scene that the crowd seems to savor. When it comes time to order, though, the Caesar salad ($4.95) is a definite winner. Other good options include marinated asparagus and white bean salad ($5.50), deep-fried calamari with a fresh herb dip ($5.50), and shrimp fritters with a chipotle mayonnaise ($6.50). Mains that please include grilled chicken breasts with a roasted red pepper sauce ($10.50), grilled Thai barbecued pork medallions ($10.25), grilled sea scallops with ginger and cilantro ($10.50), linguine with clams ($9.95) and a good steak au poivre ($13.95).

There are daily specials and a pre-theatre "yellow plate special" with soup, salad, entrée, and coffee for a modest $9.95. You can't beat that.

ROETTELE A.G. ★   Swiss/German
126 East 7th Street
(between First Ave. and Avenue A)
212/674-4140
Lunch - Monday through Saturday Noon - 3:00 p.m.
Dinner - Monday through Thursday 5:30 - 11:00 p.m.;
Friday and Saturday 5:30 - 11:30 p.m.
All major cards

This cozy alpine charmer is the kind of place you might find in the Swiss countryside. Comprised of three small dining areas, it has the kind of kitsch you don't expect to find in the East Village. Year-round Christmas lights, wooden beams, uneven floors, red and white tablecloths, votive candles, and German artifacts set the stage, and waitresses dressed in lederhosen and dirndls add to the old country feel of the place. On Thursday evenings, live entertainment provides more atmosphere and merriment. And while faux grapevines sweep along the ceiling inside, the backyard garden is completely covered with real grapes and is a delightful option for warm weather dining.

The Swiss-German fare has many French and Italian influences and is quite good. Starters include fried crab cakes with a tomato butter sauce ($6.00), roasted red peppers and fresh mozzarella ($5.25), baked brie with fresh assorted fruit and toasted almonds ($7.50), grilled shrimp and smoked mozzarella pizza ($7.00), and chopped salad with pepperoni, Swiss cheese, and a cucumber dressing ($3.50). House specialties include veal strips sautéed with shallots and mushrooms in a light white wine sauce, served with rösti ($16.00), and sauerbraten served with spätzle and red cabbage ($14.50). Other mains worth considering include pork tenderloin ($16.50), baked chicken breast with artichokes and parmesan ($14.50), paella with mixed seafood, chorizo, and chicken ($17.50), and grilled mahi with fresh tomatoes, garlic, kalamata olives, and a balsamic vinaigrette ($16.50). Desserts are delicious. There's a wonderful Swiss nut torte served with raspberry whipped cream ($4.00), a moist linzer torte ($4.50), and rich chocolate mousse ($5.00).

A prix fixe menu is offered all evening with soup or salad, a main course, and coffee for $12.95.

TELEPHONE BAR & GRILL ★   American/English
149 Second Avenue
(between 9th and 10th Sts.)
212/529-5000
Lunch - Monday through Saturday 11:30 a.m. - 5:00 p.m.;
Brunch - Sunday 10:30 a.m. - 4:00 p.m.
Dinner - Daily 5:00 p.m. - Midnight
All major cards

Shiny red British phone booths out front let you know you've arrived at this pub-styled eatery. Inside, you'll find a smart and cozy atmosphere, replete with exposed brick walls adorned with whimsical murals, pressed copper ceilings, stained glass windows, and an attractive marble and cherrywood bar. A handsome back room has a fireplace and a charming library-like ambience that is especially appealing on cold winter evenings.

Good starters include fresh salmon cakes with citrus sour cream ($7.00), goat cheese bruschetta ($6.00), fried calamari with a tomato-basil sauce ($7.00), Stilton cheese fritters with cranberry-orange relish ($6.00), smoked trout filet with horseradish dressing ($6.50), barbecued chicken wings with a blue cheese dipping sauce ($6.00), and grilled shrimp ($7.00). Good salad selections include grilled chicken breast with spinach, bacon, tomato, red onions, sesame seeds, and a feta cheese dressing ($9.50) and a smoked salmon salad ($6.50). As for the mains, the kitchen does just honors to the typically English dishes (served in copious portions)—shepherd's pie ($9.00) and New York Times fish and chips ($9.00). And there are some good all-American choices as well, like the rotisserie chicken dinner with challah apple stuffing and mashed potatoes ($12.25), chicken pot pie ($9.00), and grilled sirloin with a creamy mustard sauce, mashed potatoes, and onion rings ($16.00).

Brunch choices include either a Mimosa, Bloody Mary, or fresh orange juice and coffee or tea served with a mixed bread basket and raspberry butter. The menu offers much choice. Selections include blue corn tortillas topped with scrambled eggs, Monterey Jack cheese, chipotle sauce, and sour cream ($8.95), a country-style breakfast of two pancakes and eggs with bacon or bangers ($8.95), pancakes with fresh fruit and maple syrup ($7.75), a fried egg sandwich on an English muffin with bacon, tomato, fresh mozzarella, and watercress ($6.95), steak and eggs ($9.75), vegetarian eggs Benedict (spinach and tomato on an English muffin with poached eggs and a citrus hollandaise) ($7.25), traditional eggs Benedict ($9.25), and a nice variety of omelettes served with new potatoes or grits ($8.25).

TIME CAFE ★   American
380 Lafayette Street
(between Great Jones and East 4th Sts.)
212/533-7000
Lunch - Monday through Friday Noon - 4:00 p.m.
(light fare menu between 4:00 - 6:00 p.m.)
Brunch - Saturday and Sunday 10:30 a.m. - 4:00 p.m.
Dinner - Daily 6:00 - Midnight
All major cards

This popular pretty-people hangout features a huge desert mural along one wall, cacti plants on each table, and a laid-back attitude. Also on the premises is a Moroccan lounge called Fez, which offers jazz, cocktails, and a limited Time Cafe menu, dessert, and coffee. A large outdoor cafe is another attraction, and is packed all day long.

The cafe's lengthy menu of healthy and innovative American fare is enticing and varied with starters like arugula salad with beets and roquefort cheese served with a sherry walnut vinaigrette ($5.50), Mediterranean salad with cucumbers, feta cheese, baby artichokes, beets, and crostini topped with diced tomatoes and yogurt ($5.75), quesadillas with black beans, jalapeños, onions, and Jack cheese ($6.50), and grilled portobello mushrooms served with arugula, radicchio, and goat cheese ($6.50). There's also an assortment of spicy tapas with marinated grilled chicken, shrimp, and beef served with flour tortillas and tomatillo sauce ($7.75) and good pizzas ($9.75). Among the pasta offerings are fettuccine with portobello mushrooms, roasted peppers, arugula, sun-dried tomatoes, and herbed ricotta cheese ($11.00), penne with sun-dried tomatoes, basil and walnut pesto, topped with parmesan cheese ($11.25), and shells with shrimp, corn, sun-dried tomatoes, poblano and jalapeño peppers in a clam broth ($12.75). Good mains include a market salad with grilled daily vegetables, lentil salad, tabbouleh, and sesame-coated goat cheese ($12.50), grilled pork tenderloin with a papaya corn chutney, grilled pineapple, and jalapeño oil ($14.75), smoked free-range chicken tortilla with pinto and black beans, tomatillo, salsa, guacamole, and Jack cheese ($15.25), crispy whole free-range chicken, roasted with garlic, cumin and thyme, served with polenta ($15.50), roasted striped bass with sautéed portobello and shiitake mushrooms, basil oil, and sun-dried tomato sauce ($15.75), grilled yellowfin tuna with stir-fried vegetables and wild rice in a vegetable broth with ginger ($16.50), and a ten-ounce barbecued burger with tomato, onion, romaine, and chili pepper-dusted fries ($8.25). Desserts are good, too—offerings include homemade brownies with expresso ice cream and chocolate sauce ($4.00), warm homemade gingerbread with pumpkin ice cream ($4.50), warm sugarless apple-raisin pie ($4.50), raspberry tiramisú ($5.00), and peanut butter mousse cake layered with milk chocolate ($5.00).

WINDOWS ON INDIA ★   Indian
344 East 6th Street (corner of First Ave.)
212/477-5956
Lunch - Daily Noon - 4:00 p.m.
Dinner - Daily 4:00 p.m. - 1:00 a.m.
All major cards

This pleasant place—one of the most appealing in the East 6th Street lineup of aromatic Indian restaurants—offers exceptional value. The attractive garden-like dining room has an open, airy feel, and in nice weather two sides of windows open to the breeze.

The well prepared cuisine is that of Southern and Northern India, Bangladesh, and Indonesia. Good starters include vegetable fritters ($1.95), skewers of meat, onion, and herbs from the tandoor ($3.25), shrimp cooked Bengal style and served with poori ($3.25), an assortment of vegetarian appetizers ($4.95), and an assortment of appetizers from the tandoor ($4.95). Indonesian mains to consider include spicy grilled lamb on skewers ($7.50), and jumbo shrimp with coconut in cream sauce ($8.50). Mains from the tandoor include beef kebabs ($7.50), mixed grill ($8.95), and salmon ($15.95). Other good mains are chicken, lamb, or beef curry ($5.50), spicy chicken, lamb, or beef vindaloo ($5.95), lobster vindaloo ($9.95), and vegetarian curry ($5.50). All mains are served with rice, vegetable, dal, and relish. For dessert, choices include Indian pudding flavored with rose water ($1.75), homemade cheese balls fried and soaked in sweet rose water ($1.95), and homemade ice cream with pistachios and saffron ($1.95).

A variety of special set dinners also offer tremendous value, with three courses for $11.95 or $13.95.

GREENWICH VILLAGE

Greenwich Village

CHELSEA

UNION SQUARE/GRAMERCY PARK/MURRAY HILL

10th Ave.
9th Ave.
West St.
7th Ave.
5th Ave.
4th Ave.
Broadway

W. 14th St.
W. 14th St.
E. 14th St.

W. 13th St.
W. 13th St.
E. 13th St.

Jackson Square

Hudson St.

Little W.12th St.
W.12th St.
E.12th St.

Seravalli Playground

Bloomfield St.

Gansevoort St.
Greenwich Ave.
W. 11th St.
E. 11th St.
University Pl.

Horatio St.
Waverly Pl.
W. 10th St.
E. 10th St.

Jane St.
Greenwich St.
8th Ave.
W. 4th St.
W. 9th St.
E. 9th St.

W.12th St.
Abingdon Square

Bethune St.
W. 8th St.
E. 8th St.

Greene St.
Mercer St.

Bank St.
Bleecker St.
Gay St.
MacDougal Alley
Wash. Mews

Hudson St.
Waverly Pl.

W. 11th St.
Washington Sq. North
Waverly Pl.

Perry St.
W. Wash. Place
Washington Square

Wash. Sq. West
Wash. Place

Charles St.
W. 4th St.
Washington Sq. South
West 4th St.

Grove St.
Jones St.
Cornelia St.

W. 10th St.
New York University (NYU)

Washington St.
W. 3rd St.

Christopher St.
Commerce St.

West St.
Father Demo Square

Bedford St.

Barrow St.
7th Ave. S.
Bleecker St.

Morton St.
Carmine St.
MacDougal St.
Sullivan St.
Thompson St.
La Guardia Pl.
Mercer St.
Broadway

HUDSON RIVER
Walker Park
Downing St.
EAST VILLAGE

Leroy St.
W. Houston St.

Clarkson St.

W. Houston St.

SOHO/TRIBECA

ANGLERS & WRITERS ★   American
420 Hudson Street
(corner of St. Luke's Place)
212/675-0810
Daily 9:00 a.m. - Midnight
Afternoon Tea 3:00 - 5:00 p.m.
Personal checks accepted

This charmingly offbeat spot is one-of-a-kind. Owned by avid angler and aspiring writer Craig Béro (who also owns the delightful Village Atelier on the same block), Anglers & Writers pays homage to both passions. Its walls are covered with vintage fishing paraphernalia and shelves of books. Antique china, fresh flowers, and handmade doilies add a homespun feel to the mix and aromas of the past fill the room. The rustic and homey ambience has a genuine authenticity. Charlotte Béro left the farm town of Algoma, Wisconsin, to bake the pies, cakes, and breads for her son's restaurant; berries come from the farm owned by his high school sweetheart; his grandmother's silver coffeepot displays flowers; and some of the mismatched china and tableware was gathered by Wisconsin neighbors at farm sales. If you have fond memories of Mom's pies cooling in the window or of stealing a slice of warm cake before it was iced, you'll find Anglers & Writers a nostalgic pleasure.

The menu recalls home cooking with hearty harvest soup with chicken and vegetables ($3.50), old-fashioned lamb stew ($12.50), roast chicken with dressing ($10.50), chicken pot pie ($9.50), turkey casserole ($10.00), and Bourbon-glazed baked country ham with candied sweets ($11.50). There is also pasta of the day ($10.50), salad niçoise ($9.00), hot open-face roast turkey sandwiches with gravy and stuffing ($7.50), gnocchi Bolognese ($8.75), and French peasant omelettes with ham, cheese, tomato, and onion ($7.00). Saturday and Sunday brunch offers its own delights including buttermilk pancakes (blueberry or cherry) with brandied maple syrup ($7.50), French toast with Montmorency cherries, strawberries, and bananas ($7.75), eggs Benedict ($8.75), fisherman's omelette with salmon, cream cheese, and spinach ($8.75), and French crêpes (apricot/apple and farm cheese stuffing and glazed cherry sauce) ($7.75). The changing selection of nostalgic desserts might include apple rum raisin cake, banana cream pie, apple sour cream pie, carrot cake, cherry pie, key lime pie, lemon meringue pie, raspberry pie, and sweet potato pie (pies $4.25, cakes $4.75).

ANTON'S ★★   Eclectic
259 West 4th Street (Perry St.)
212/675-5059
Brunch - Sunday Noon - 4:00 p.m.
Dinner - Tuesday through Sunday 5:30 - 11:30 p.m.
All major cards

A friendly feel pervades this winsome chef-owned West Villager where the charming reception and service allow you to feel like a guest and not just a customer. Jazz tapes in the background and a very pleasant ambience add to the mellow mood of the place.

The delicious cooking of Anton Linder is an eclectic mélange with Austrian-Italian leanings. You might start with polenta tarts with gorgonzola and tomatoes ($5.75), lamb sausage on an arugula and lentil salad ($5.25) or the always satisfying soup of the day ($4.50). Good pasta choices include penne with a Vodka and bacon sauce ($12.50) and spaghetti with artichokes, spinach, and shiitake mushrooms ($12.00). Also good are mains such as rack of lamb with Italian vegetables ($21.00), Viennese schnitzel ($15.00), New York shell steak with mushrooms and a red wine sauce ($20.00), and duck with a sour cherry sauce ($16.00).

Sunday brunch offers good omelettes (spinach and cheddar, Virginia ham and potato, or tomato, onion, and mushroom) (each $7.00). Eggs Benedict ($7.00) and steak and eggs ($12.00) are other popular options. Pasta and salads are also on hand.

ARLECCHINO ★★   Italian
192 Bleecker Street
(between Sixth Ave. & MacDougal St.)
212/475-2355
Lunch - Daily Noon - 4:00 p.m.
Dinner - Daily 4:00 - Midnight
American Express only

A light-hearted whimsical decor creates a festive mood in this delightful Village trattoria. Harlequin costumes, masks, and puppets adorn the walls of its two dining areas creating a colorful and playful background for dining on some seriously good Italian fare.

Its menu is quite comprehensive and wild mushrooms are featured in many of the dishes. To start, choices include carpaccio with grana cheese ($8.00), wild sautéed mushrooms ($8.00), baked clams ($7.50), and spiedino Arlecchino (a house specialty with slices of bread and mozzarella in a special sauce) ($7.00). Among the many nice pasta offerings are pappardelle with fresh tomato, onions, and ham ($11.00), fettuccine with wild mushrooms, sun-dried tomatoes, and zucchini ($12.50), rigatoni with spinach and wild mushrooms ($11.50), homemade ravioli stuffed with mushrooms and crab in a pink sauce ($12.00), and linguine with smoked salmon and cream ($12.50). Other mains include breast of chicken with mozzarella ($14.00), grilled veal with wild mushrooms ($16.50), grilled baby lamb chops with rosemary and white wine ($16.50), medallions of beef breaded and grilled with herbs ($16.50), shrimp sautéed in white wine and lemon ($17.00), and pan-fried squid ($13.50).

ASTI ★   Italian
13 East 12th Street
(between University Pl. and Fifth Ave.)
212/741-9105
Dinner - Tuesday through Thursday 5:30 p.m. - 12:30 a.m.;
Friday and Saturday 5:30 p.m. - 1:00 a.m.
All major cards

At Asti, every night is a celebration of song, of opera, and just about everybody sings—waiters, bartenders, the owners. And from time to time, a talented customer or two or a visiting professional may rise for a spontaneous performance that thrills the room. But every night, arias from great operas, as well as popular songs and classics, are sung with zeal by the Asti group. You may remember a scene from *Big* where Tom Hanks and his young friend are serenaded by singing waiters—it was here at Asti's. And the roster of visiting celebrities who have tucked into its ragu over the years, and sometimes even joined in song, is both lengthy and diverse—Babe Ruth, Julie Andrews, Leonard Bernstein, Carol Burnett, Richard Burton, Van Cliburn, Noel Coward, Joe DiMaggio, Greta Garbo, Judy Garland, Richard Gere, King Hussein, Caroline Kennedy, Rocky Marciano, Groucho Marx, Paul Newman, Luciano Pavarotti, Gloria Swanson, and Arturo Toscannini, to single out just a few. Hundreds of signed photos line the walls and attest to the rich history of this enjoyable place that has been dispensing opera, pasta, and merriment since the 1920s. Rich in atmosphere, warm-hearted, and wholly gleeful—but what about the food, you ask. Well, it's secondary here, but it's not bad. Go for the fun of it.

Appetizers include baked clams oreganata ($11.75), stuffed artichoke ($11.75), and fresh roasted red peppers and anchovies ($11.75). Pastas are standards like cannelloni alla verdi ($18.50), fettuccine Alfredo or carbonara ($18.50), and spaghetti marinara ($16.75). Time-honored classics among mains include calamari with pasta ($21.75), seafood linguine ($22.75), chicken cacciatora ($20.75), veal parmigiana ($23.75), and sirloin steak with green peppercorns and a Cognac sauce ($27.75). Homemade desserts to consider are the rum cake ($7.25), tiramisú ($8.25), and chocolate mousse ($7.25).

A fixed price dinner menu is offered at $39.00. It includes a glass of wine, a choice of appetizer, a salad, a choice of entrée, a choice of dessert, and coffee or tea. There's also a fixed price supper menu at $26.50 available on Friday and Saturday after 10:30 p.m. and on Sunday, Tuesday, Wednesday, and Thursday after 10:00 p.m. It includes a glass of wine, a choice of any pasta from the menu, and a choice of dessert, plus coffee or tea.

BORGO ANTICO ★   Italian
22 East 13th Street
(between Fifth Ave. and University Pl.)
212/807-1313
Lunch - Daily 11:30 a.m. - 4:30 p.m.
Dinner - Daily 5:00 p.m. - Midnight
All major cards

This amiable spot entices from the get-go, with charms that include hand-painted Sicilian tiles, alabaster Spanish sconces, reproductions of Medieval Italian tapestries, and antique Italian wood furnishings. Its name in Italian means "old little village" and its Tuscan farmhouse ambience echoes that theme. The atmosphere is cozy, but large, well-spaced tables keep it from feeling cramped.

Its zesty Emiglio-Tuscan fare changes with the seasons and the kitchen focuses on the natural flavors of each dish, keeping the sauces very simple. Moderately priced game in season and homemade pasta are house specialties. Virtually everything on the menu is made on the premises, from the freshly baked focaccia and breadsticks to the individual tiramisú. It is all so pleasing. You might start with venison carpaccio with mushrooms, artichokes, and reggiano ($9.00), goat cheese tart with roasted red pepper sauce and prosciutto ($8.50), polenta with the chef's daily choice of accompaniment ($6.50), New Zealand mussels in a white wine sauce ($7.00), panzanella (tomato, bread, onions, endive, and basil) ($5.50), or country minestrone ($5.50). The homemade pastas are wonderful, with choices like wholewheat pappardelle with roasted tomato, aged ricotta, and roasted garlic ($12.00), gnocchi with broccoli rabe, tomato, and sausage ($12.00), fresh saffron tagliolini with shrimp, arugula, and tomato ($13.00), linguine with New Zealand clams ($13.00), and fettuccine with meat sauce ($12.00). Current offerings among mains include braised rabbit with olives and leeks ($16.00), medallions of beef sautéed with herbs and balsamic vinegar ($19.00), filet of salmon roasted in paper with fresh vegetables ($15.00), roasted loin of pork with beans and spinach ($17.00), and lamb chops with potato purée and string beans ($19.00). Desserts (each $6.00) include wonderful temptations such as an upside-down sponge cake with peaches and Italian crêpes filled with white chocolate mousse and sautéed in strawberries and balsamic vinegar. Borgo Antico's wine list features affordable vintages from over 15 regions in Italy, with an assortment of reds and whites in the $18-$29 range, as well as a few select wines between $30 and $60.

CAFE DE BRUXELLES ★★   Belgian
118 Greenwich Avenue (W. 13th St.)
212/206-1830
Lunch - Daily Noon - 3:00 p.m.
Dinner - Daily 5:00 - 11:30 p.m.
All major cards

Lace curtains, a great zinc bar, pink seats, and a funky '50s look give this pleasant Belgian brasserie a kitschy and cozy appeal. It is a relaxed setting for the lusty and well-prepared Belgian cuisine that makes it unique.

Its signature frites are fabulous, among the best in town. Parchment paper-lined silver cups of them are served around the room accompanied by homemade Belgian mustardy, garlicky mayo—a gift from the chef to please one and all. Starters are delicious, with choices such as wild mushrooms in puff pastry ($7.50), sautéed potatoes with beans, bacon, and endives in sherry vinegar ($6.75), and homemade country pâté ($4.00). Main dish specialties include a rich and delicious dark Belgian beer stew of beef ($15.50) and a Belgian bouillabaisse ($16.50). Other good mains include grilled salmon with summer roast vegetables ($17.50), sirloin steak with a green peppercorn sauce ($18.50), and loin of lamb with rosemary ($19.50). Look for daily specials, as well, and throw back a Belgian beer.

CAFE LOUP ★★   French
105 West 13th Street
(between Sixth and Seventh Aves.)
212/255-4746
Lunch - Monday through Friday Noon - 3:00 p.m.
Brunch - Sunday Noon - 3:30 p.m.
Dinner - Sunday and Monday 5:30 - 11:30 p.m.;
Tuesday through Saturday 5:30 p.m. - Midnight

This wonderful neighborhood art-filled bistro is the kind you'd like to have in the brownstone next door. The service is warm, the food is consistently good and moderately priced, and there's a nice selection of wine by the glass. Inviting in every way, it's easy to see why it's a longtime neighborhood favorite.

The quintessentially French bistro menu offers long-standing favorites such as country-style pâté served with two mustards, cornichons, and olives ($6.00), escargots baked with butter, garlic, shallots, and parsley and napped with a hollandaise sauce ($6.50), and green leaf salad with sourdough croutons and a creamed anchovy-garlic dressing ($5.00) for starters. The well prepared mains include reliable standards with some surprising twists. There's seared raw yellowfin tuna set over organic sunflower sprouts, served with Asian slaw, soy-ginger dipping sauce, and a garnish of tiny garlic sprouts ($14.50), a half farm-raised chicken with paprika and garlic, served with shallot-flecked mashed potatoes and a tarragon jus ($14.50), grilled Colorado rib lamb chops served with mashed potatoes, various house vegetables, and a sauce of Cabernet and reduced pan juices ($19.50), and grilled marinated skirt steak served with French fries and a caramelized shallot glaze ($16.00).

There's a fixed-price three-course dinner available every evening for $25.00.

CAFFE ROSSO ★   Italian
284 West 12th Street (W. 4th St.)
212/633-9277
Brunch - Saturday and Sunday Noon - 4:00 p.m.
Dinner - Daily 5:00 p.m. - Midnight
All major cards

This rustic little charmer is perched on a quiet West Village street. Inside, its windows offer a romantic glimpse of Village life with views of the cobble-stoned, tree-lined streets that highlight its quaint appeal. The atmosphere is country Italian, with fresh flowers, worn wooden floors, a tiny oak bar, red velvet drapes, and old-fashioned chandeliers. It's also a friendly place, a neighborhood favorite.

The food is Northern Italian and quite good. Menu selections include starters of mixed grilled vegetables ($8.50), carpaccio with arugula and sliced parmesan cheese ($10.00), homemade mozzarella, tomato, and basil ($7.50), sautéed wild mushrooms, baby string beans, and warm mozzarella ($10.00), mussels in tomato sauce with toasted bread ($8.00), and spinach salad with shrimp, avocado, tomatoes, bacon, mushrooms, and croutons with a mustard vinaigrette ($8.50). The pasta offerings are extensive. Select from spaghetti with olive oil, garlic, and hot pepper ($8.00), black linguine in a light spicy tomato sauce ($13.00), rigatoni with tomato, prosciutto, and onions ($12.50), penne with spinach, wild mushrooms, and sun-dried tomatoes in a light pink sauce ($12.00), penne with fresh salmon, smoked mozzarella, and arugula in a pink sauce ($14.00), and seafood risotto (two person minimum $30.00). Other good choices include boneless breast of chicken stuffed with prosciutto, spinach, and mozzarella in a brown sauce ($17.00), veal scaloppine ($17.00), filet mignon in a Cognac pepper sauce ($21.00), grilled salmon with a mustard sauce ($19.00), whole grilled red snapper ($19.00), and grilled jumbo shrimp ($20.00). If you're in the market for dessert, there's gelato (chocolate, vanilla, and hazelnut) ($6.00), triple chocolate mousse cake ($6.00), and baked pear zabaglione ($6.00) among other straightforward offerings.

CENT 'ANNI ★★   Italian
50 Carmine St.
(between Bleecker and Bedford Sts.)
212/989-9494
Lunch - Monday through Friday Noon - 3:00 p.m.
Dinner - Daily 5:30 - 11:30 p.m.
All major cards

This simple Florentine trattoria has a storefront setting and a faithful following who claim it just gets better with every passing year. Its name celebrates the classic toast "May you live 100 years." The sentiment and the nice service underscore what a pleasant place this is.

The starter list, with its many delicious offerings, presents the first dilemma. Choices include a wonderful seafood salad of lobster, shrimp, bay scallops, and squid ($9.00), along with more robust fare such as the zucchini stuffed with meat, cheese, and broiled with butter ($6.00) and the baked soup of beans, cabbage, leek, toast, and cheese ($9.00). Other selections include portobello mushrooms broiled with olive oil, garlic, and fresh basil ($9.00) and a mozzarella, tomato, and basil salad ($9.00). The pastas are outstanding. Favorites include homemade green and white fettuccine in a sauce of cream, butter, and smoked salmon, with sun-dried tomatoes, mint, and onions ($16.00), angel hair pasta in a light tomato sauce with lobster and clams ($16.00), linguine in a tomato sauce with Vodka and red pepper ($13.00), and penne in a sauce of olive oil, grappa, shiitaki mushrooms, and basil ($13.00). Half portions are $8.50. Other choices to tempt include double cut loin of pork roasted with white wine, garlic, and rosemary, served in a brown sauce ($18.00), chicken breast sautéed in white wine with garlic, butter, basil, wild mushrooms, and fresh tomatoes ($16.00), baby rack of lamb, split and grilled ($22.00), a mixed grill plate of rabbit, lamb, sausage, and quail ($24.00), a large grilled porterhouse steak for two ($45.00), tender squid sautéed in oil, garlic, tomatoes, and spices ($14.00), and shrimp and bay scallops sautéed with butter, garlic, thyme, Cognac, and a hint of tomato.

DA SILVANO ★★   Italian
260 Sixth Avenue (between Bleecker and Houston Sts.)
212/982-2343
Lunch - Monday through Saturday Noon - 5:00 p.m.
Dinner - Daily 5:00 p.m. - 11:30 p.m.
All major cards

A country-style trattoria, Da Silvano is at its best in spring and summer when its very appealing sidewalk cafe comes to life. Set well back from traffic, it provides a delightful setting and good people watching. Inside, there's an elegantly rustic ambience, with exposed brick walls, an antique wine cupboard, colorful ceramics, white tablecloths, and a partially open kitchen.

This longtime Greenwich Village Tuscan favorite attracts a smart crowd and a throng of regulars who have learned how to navigate the somewhat uneven menu. And it is worth navigating, particularly for the terrific pastas. Starters are robust and also quite good, especially the bread salad with roasted peppers, tomatoes, cucumber, and onions ($6.50) and the grilled sausage with broccoli rabe in olive oil and garlic ($9.50). Favorites among pastas are spaghetti puttanesca with tomato, garlic, black olives, capers, and anchovies ($12.50), rigatoni with double-smoked bacon, sage, garlic, white wine, cream, and tomato ($13.50), penne with olive oil, tomato, minced garlic, and hot red pepper ($12.50), and spinach and ricotta ravioli sautéed in butter and sage ($12.50). Main offerings include grilled veal chop marinated with olive oil and sage ($24.50), grilled shell steak, sliced thin and topped with green peppercorns and rosemary ($19.50), and large prawns sautéed in olive oil and topped with a julienne of fennel, celery, scallions, and tomatoes ($24.50).

E & O ★   French Vietnamese
100 West Houston Street
(between LaGuardia Pl. and Thompson St.)
212/254-7000
Daily Noon - Midnight
All major cards

E & O (Eastern and Oriental), with its high ceilings, purring fans, rattan banquettes, Asian graphics, and bird cage lanterns, has an exotic prettiness about it. Shades of blue, green, and apricot color the room and tall columns add to the airy feel of the space. There's also a sultry red lounge, the Suzie Wong Room, open from 10:00 p.m. until 2:00 a.m. for late night rendezvous.

The French Vietnamese menu (like the kitchen) has not yet found its stride but does offer a good selection of starters. Ordering several to compose a meal is often the best way to dine here. Signature dishes include a green papaya salad ($6.50), spicy filet mignon salad with cucumber, bean sprouts, lemongrass, and fresh basil ($10.00), and shrimp ravioli with fresh herbs and fried shallots ($7.00). Other choices include grilled squid with chili sauce ($5.50), grilled Asian eggplant ($5.00), and vegetable spring rolls ($6.00). For the main: roasted whole baby chicken with coriander and lemongrass marinade with lime chili sauce ($15.50), crispy duck with ginger sauce ($17.00), filet mignon with haricots verts, mushrooms, and basil ($18.00), and sautéed sea scallops with eggplant and beans in a light coconut curry sauce ($16.50). Dessert might be coconut rice pudding ($6.00) or a refreshing sorbet ($6.00).

ENNIO & MICHAEL ★★   Italian
539 LaGuardia Place
(between Bleecker and West 3rd Sts.)
212/677-8577
Monday through Saturday Noon - 11:00 p.m.;
Sunday 1:00 - 10:00 p.m.
All major cards

This merry Italian restaurant has a comforting homespun ambience and is a longtime Village favorite, though not always at the same address. Its warm atmosphere, cordial staff, and reliably good cooking have all contributed to making it a pleasant place to dine at each location. Originally a simple storefront, it acquired a few upscale comforts at its second location. And now at its third and present address, it is notably more stylish with cloth-draped ceilings, carpeting, white tablecloths, and photographs by local radio personality Cousin Brucie. But its endearing family feel still prevails. And in warm weather, its outdoor cafe—set back from the street—is reminiscent of those found along so many boulevards in Europe and is ever so pleasant.

Good starters here include delicious french-fried shoestring zucchini ($5.75), large mushrooms roasted with wine and garlic ($8.25), baked clams ($6.50), slices of prosciutto with fresh mozzarella and melon ($8.25), and avocado stuffed with crabmeat ($7.75). Nice pasta choices are the gnocchi with mozzarella in tomato sauce ($12.75), spaghetti puttanesca ($12.25), a rousing rigatoni with fresh tomato sauce, prosciutto, onions, and olive oil ($12.75), and mushroom risotto with a Vodka sauce ($14.75). Other good options for the main include breaded chicken topped with radicchio and melted mozzarella ($14.75), chicken cacciatore ($14.75), veal sautéed with wine and baked with eggplant and mozzarella ($16.75), veal sautéed with wine and prosciutto over spinach ($16.75), eggplant parmigiana ($11.75), sausage and peppers ($13.75), and jumbo shrimp sautéed in lemon butter ($17.75). Daily specials are always good bets as well.

GOTHAM BAR AND GRILL ★★★   American
12 East 12th Street
(between Fifth Ave. and University Pl.)
212/620-4020
Lunch - Monday through Friday Noon - 2:15 p.m.
Dinner - Sunday through Thursday 5:30 - 10:00 p.m.;
Friday and Saturday 5:30 - 11:00 p.m.
All major cards

This extravagantly chic restaurant, situated in a former warehouse, has a striking postmodern decor and very tall food. Its bi-level design features mustard-colored pillars and platforms that divide the open high-ceilinged loft space and make it seem less cavernous and allows each table a surprising sense of intimacy. Billowing parachute-style fabric-draped lights float over the well-spaced tables, exotic floral arrangements punctuate the room, and a statue of liberty oversees it all. For a stylish, hip New York brasserie experience, this is the real thing. Its renowned chef, Alfred Portale, comes from a background in jewelry design and his creations—now culinary—still dazzle. His exceptionally innovative fare carries his signature style of soaring dimensions, resulting in lofty salads, spiralling pastas, high-rise mains, and towering desserts.

The menu changes seasonally and its starter list is always full of interesting and delicious choices such as herbed ricotta ravioli with mushrooms, parmesan, and white truffle oil ($13.00), smoked duck breast with basmati rice and yogurt salad with apricot-cherry chutney ($12.00), seafood salad with scallops, squid, Japanese octopus, lobster, and avocado, dressed in lemon and extra virgin olive oil ($14.00), grilled and roasted vegetable salad with aïoli, goat cheese, and basil oil ($13.00), and vegetable risotto with roast quail, asparagus, peas, and chervil butter ($16.00). Excellent mains include wild striped bass in warm vinaigrette with fingerling potatoes, corn, fava beans, and tomatoes ($28.00), roasted Maine lobster tail with beets, baby bok choy, couscous, ginger, and scallions ($33.00), grilled saddle of rabbit with steamed spinach, white beans, and young fennel ($28.50), squab and grilled foie gras with sweet corn, creamy polenta, and cranberry beans ($29.00), roast organic free-range chicken with select vegetables and shoestring potatoes ($26.50), rack of lamb with Swiss chard, roast shallots, and garlic mashed potatoes ($31.00), and grilled New York steak with crushed white peppercorns, a marrow mustard custard, and deep-fried shallots ($29.50). And you'll probably find the changing selection of towering desserts ($7.50-$8.50)—from a sensational chocolate bread pudding served with vanilla ice cream and chocolate sauce to a warm apple tart served with vanilla ice cream and a cranberry compote—impossible to resist.

GRAND TICINO ★★   Italian
228 Thompson Street
(between West 3rd and Bleecker Sts.)
212/777-5922
Monday through Saturday Noon - 11:00 p.m.
All major cards

This wonderful old place recalls an earlier Greenwich Village. With its old-fashioned ambience and all the spirit and intimacy of a family-owned restaurant, it projects a comfortable charm and real warmth. Opened in 1919, it has a long history of serving good homey Italian food to neighborhood regulars as well as to many famous writers and artists. In times gone by, Edna St. Vincent Millay and Eugene O'Neill have supped here; more recently, Robert DeNiro. And scenes from *Moonstruck* were filmed here, capturing everyone's ideal of a small, romantic Village restaurant.

While the menu won't knock you out with innovation, it will surely contain many of your old favorites. You might start with an assortment of hot appetizers ($8.00), baked clams ($7.25), prosciutto and melon ($7.00), fried calamari ($6.75), or egg drop and spinach soup ($8.00). Pastas are all quite good—the selection includes linguine with white or red clam sauce ($12.50), spaghetti carbonara ($11.95), a nice spicy penne Arrabbiata ($10.95), homemade ravioli ($11.95), and seafood risotto ($15.50). Mains include lemon filet of sole ($15.25), calamari marinara ($13.50), shrimp in a spicy red sauce ($16.50), veal piccata ($15.25), breast of chicken with prosciutto and fontina cheese ($13.50), and medallions of beef in Barola ($21.25).

A pre-theatre menu with three courses is a nostalgic $19.19.

GRANGE HALL ★★   American
50 Commerce Street (corner of Barrow St.)
212/924-5246
Breakfast - Saturday 11:00 a.m. - 3:00 p.m.;
Sunday 10:30 a.m. - 3:00 p.m.
Lunch - Monday through Friday Noon - 3:00 p.m.
Dinner - Monday 5:30 - 11:00 p.m.;
Tuesday through Saturday 5:30 - 11:30 p.m.;
Sunday 5:00 - 11:00 p.m.
American Express

Tucked away on one of the most delightful streets in the West Village, Grange Hall is also just steps from the Cherry Lane Theatre. Housed in a restored '30s era speakeasy, its original art deco interior includes soaring columns and a wing-shaped period mahogany bar. There's also soft lighting, comfortable booths, and a large social realist-inspired mural of farmers. And while the crowd may be NYC cool, the place still has the feel of the heartland.

The specialty here is food from the American farm with an emphasis on seasonal vegetables and organic meats. The menu offers a nice selection of small dishes that can be taken as either a starter or a side to your main—things like acorn squash baked with maple syrup ($4.00), potato pancakes with fresh scallion sour cream ($4.75), freshly made sausage of the day with seasonal relish or chutney ($5.50), red cabbage braised with apples ($3.75), and scalloped potatoes ($4.75). There's always a nice selection of homemade soups, both vegetarian and meat-based (cup $3.50, bowl $4.50) and good salads like red pear with watercress and endive, Maytag Farms blue cheese, and a mustard-white wine vinaigrette ($7.50). Notable choices among mains include oven-roasted organic half chicken with fresh corn and currant relish ($12.25), cranberry-glazed center cut pork chops with poached apples ($12.75), baked freshwater trout with wild rice ($14.75), and shell steak with fried Idaho potatoes and homemade sweet pickles ($16.25).   Desserts ($5.00) revive memories of childhood treats with a super iced devil's food layer cake, homemade seasonal fruit pies, wild rice pudding, and vanilla angel food cake with fresh fruit.

This is also a fine stop for weekend breakfasts when offerings include hazelnut cream French toast with a pear-cranberry compote ($6.25), scallion scrambled eggs and smoked salmon trout on sourdough toast ($7.75), oatmeal wholewheat pancakes with apples and pecans ($6.50), and grilled Virginia ham steak and three eggs with fried cornmeal mush ($6.75).

GROVE ★★   French/American
314 Bleecker Street (Grove St.)
212/675-9463
Brunch - Saturday and Sunday 11:00 a.m. - 3:00 p.m.
Dinner - Monday through Thursday 6:00 - 11:00 p.m.;
Friday and Saturday 6:00 p.m. - Midnight; Sunday 5:30 - 11:00 p.m.
All major cards

In the pretty dining room at Grove, all is harmonious and serene. It has a crisp, cool look with wood floors, cream walls with halogen sconces, big vases of beautiful flowers, a slate blue ceiling, and rotating artwork from local artists. While the interior of this charming French/American bistro is indeed inviting, its wonderful flowery outdoor garden is even more so. It seats 70 during warm weather; in winter half is enclosed and heated.

Inside or out, moderate prices and wonderful food make this a delightful place to dine. Good starters include thick butternut squash soup ($6.00), goat cheese tart with grilled tomato ($6.00), perfectly crisp-fried calamari with chipotle mayonnaise ($6.00), and steamed mussels with white wine and shallots ($7.00). Among mains, good choices include penne with baby eggplant, wild mushrooms, and tomato ($11.00), grilled chicken with mashed potatoes and wild mushrooms ($13.00), grilled pork chop with two-potato gratin, spinach, and chutney ($12.00), hanger steak with shallots, white wine, and French fries ($16.00), and pan-roasted monkfish ($17.00).   For dessert, surrender to the apple tartelette served with caramel sauce and topped with a dollop of vanilla ice cream ($6.00).

GUS' PLACE ★★   Greek
149 Waverly Place
(between Christopher St. and Sixth Ave.)
212/645-8511
Lunch - Daily Noon - 4:00 p.m.
Dinner - Daily 5:00 - 11:30 p.m.
All major cards

The light, cool decor is appealing and the service is warm and friendly at this delightful taverna.   An abundance of fresh flowers and a spiralling grapevine mural set a lighthearted tone and an affable staff and warmhearted owner make you feel like an old friend returning to the fold.

You'll find some of the best Greek-inspired Mediterranean cooking in Manhattan here. This is the sort of place with such tempting "small plates" or starters that it's hard to resist making a meal by combining several. Notable among the irresistible choices are the phyllo turnovers with three fillings (wild mushrooms, shrimp and crabmeat, and country sausage) ($8.50), spinach, leek, and feta pie ($6.00), a basket of tiny fried fish ($6.50), steamed mussels with garlic, white wine, tomato, and ouzo ($7.50), and crisp-roasted quail on a bed of lentils and hot garlic greens ($9.00). But, ultimately, the large plates are just too good to skip. Choices include orzo and Gulf shrimp with walnuts, garlic, herbs, and feta cheese ($16.50), linguine with littleneck clams, lemon, garlic, and parsley ($15.50), roast vegetable tart with goat cheese and a charred tomato sauce ($13.50), grilled tuna with white beans, cilantro, orange, and fried leeks ($19.50), 10-ounce rib steak rubbed with green and black peppercorns with sautéed sweet onions and garlic mashed potatoes ($19.50), lamb moussaka in an eggplant shell served with tzatziki ($15.00), and Greek-style cassoulet with garlic sausage, braised lamb, preserved duck, smoked bacon, gigantes beans, and herbed bread crumbs ($17.50).   For dessert: baklava ($5.00), dark chocolate hazelnut cake ($6.50), warm almond and semolina cake with fresh berries ($6.00), poached pear with three-nut baklava and a ginger curl ($7.50), and warm bread pudding with pear, apple, and quince with fig ice cream and warm caramel sauce ($7.00).

A theatergoers discount of 20 percent is offered to guests seated between 5:00 and 6:00 or after 10:00 p.m. Cash only.

HOME ★★   American
20 Cornelia Street (between Bleecker and West 4th Sts.)
212/243-9579
Breakfast - Monday through Friday 9:00 - 11:30 a.m.
Lunch - Monday through Friday 11:30 a.m. - 3:00 p.m.
Brunch - Saturday and Sunday - 11:00 a.m. - 4:00 p.m.
Dinner - Monday through Saturday 6:00 - 11:00 p.m.;
Sunday 5:30 - 10:00 p.m.
American Express only

An open kitchen, farmhouse decor, and blues music in the background set the stage for real home-cooking, but better. This delightful place is just a narrow sliver of a room simply decorated, informal, and totally inviting. It's the kind of place you'd like to call your home-away-from-home and would pop into often for a comforting breakfast or comfortable dinner if it were in your neighborhood. A sweet sun-dappled back garden is one more pleasant aspect of Home on nice days and a perfect spot for a lazy weekend brunch.

From its tiny kitchen come tantalizing starter creations like delicious blue cheese fondue with rosemary, caramelized shallots, and walnut bread toasts ($7.00), grilled shrimp on a warm frisée salad with potatoes, red onion, and tarragon ($8.00), and goat cheese, roasted beet, and grilled leek salad ($7.00). Favorites among the so-good mains include cumin-crusted pork chops with barbecue sauce, rosemary mashed potatoes, and grilled scallions ($15.00), roasted leg of lamb with split peas, red onion, marjoram, and lemon ($15.00), grilled New York State trout with a sweet potato sauce, a wild mushroom pancake, and artichokes ($15.00), peppered Newport steak with escarole and a garlic potato cake ($16.00), and roasted chicken with sautéed greens and spicy onion rings with homemade catsup ($14.00).

LA METAIRIE ★★   French
189 West 10th Street (West 4th Street)
212/989-0343
Lunch - Monday through Friday Noon - 3:00 p.m.
Brunch - Saturday and Sunday Noon - 3:00 p.m.
Dinner - Sunday through Thursday 5:00 p.m. - Midnight;
Friday and Saturday 5:00 p.m. - 1:00 a.m.
American Express

With a look that personifies everyone's image of a perfect French country inn, La Metairie is the sort of place you can't walk past in the evening without longing to be inside with someone you love. From outside, you note its white picket fence, charming duck sign, and white-trimmed windows that reveal the intimacy of the candlelit interior. And when you dine here, you'll find it even more alluring with a charming rustic decor that has logs stored along the ceiling ledge, huge dried flower arrangements here and there, and candle sconces on fresh whitewashed walls with dark wood trim.

The cooking is as homey and French as the atmosphere and just as nice. Start with smoked salmon cannoli with cucumber salad ($9.00), terrine of duck with pear and dried cherry compote ($6.00), or endive and arugula salad with spiced pecans and gorgonzola cheese ($7.00). Mains are just as satisfying with choices that include grilled chicken breast with ricotta cheese and herb polenta ($15.00), roast cod with olive mashed potatoes, roasted garlic, and tomato butter ($17.00), lobster risotto with wild mushrooms and truffle butter ($22.00), and filet of beef sautéed with Port wine and garlic ($23.00). Desserts are excellent as well—check the day's offerings.

LA RIPAILLE ★★   French
605 Hudson Street
(between W. 12th and Bethune Sts.)
212/255-4406
Dinner - Monday through Saturday 5:30 - 11:30 p.m.
All major cards

For a romantic evening, La Ripaille has it all: candlelight, pretty fresh flowers, and a totally charming, totally French mood. Stucco and natural brick walls, a stately old grandfather clock, and reproductions of medieval tapestries lend the look and ambience of a rural French inn.

The upscale bistro fare is very good indeed. The pick of the appetizers are wild mushrooms flambéed in Cognac in a light puff pastry ($7.00), warm garlic sausage in olive oil on a bed of potatoes ($7.50), and broccoli mousse with a light lemon butter sauce ($5.75). The pasta offerings are quite nice as well—linguine with smoked salmon, shallots, and chives ($14.50), penne with sun-dried tomatoes, black olives, and garlic ($12.00), and fresh spinach-stuffed ravioli in a light cream sage sauce ($13.50). Other notable mains include grilled swordfish in a fresh basil sauce ($18.75), chicken breast stuffed with spinach and fresh garden vegetables ($15.50), veal scaloppine ($17.50), and shell steak in a green peppercorn sauce with French fries ($18.75).

A $19.95 three-course menu is available from 5:30 to 6:30 p.m.

MARY'S ★★   New American
42 Bedford Street
(between Carmine and Leroy Sts.)
212/741-3387
Dinner - Daily 6:00 p.m. - Midnight
American Express only

Mary's faded elegance has a nostalgic appeal, and is a favorite of romantic gays. Situated in an 1820 townhouse, its creaky wood floors, federal-style draperies, Venetian chandeliers, and handsome fireplaces cast a dreamy spell. Yet the place has a homey feel and its ambience is one of casual charm. A small private dining room, calling itself the Angie Dickinson Room, adds a sense of fancy displaying the film star's youthful beauty in a variety of photos that line the walls.

While its look is one of antiquity, its menu is strictly New American. You might start with butternut squash-apple soup ($4.50), steamed mussels with prosciutto, garlic, white wine, and tomatoes ($7.50), or sautéed wild mushrooms with sage polenta, vermouth, and chives ($6.95). The mains are just as appealing. Good choices include pan-roasted chicken breast with an apple-leek stuffing ($13.95), grilled pork loin with mashed sweet potatoes ($14.25), sautéed crab cakes with lobster sauce and basil orzo ($15.50), tenderloin of beef wrapped in bacon with mashed potatoes and a horseradish sauce ($18.50), and wild mushroom ravioli ($12.95). The daily desserts ($5.50) are the homey variety—chocolate raspberry tarte, apple pie, and crème brûlée.

ONE IF BY LAND, TWO IF BY SEA ★★★   Continental
17 Barrow Street
(between Seventh Ave. So. and W. 4th St.)
212/228-0822
Dinner - Sunday through Thursday 5:30 p.m. - Midnight;
Friday and Saturday 5:30 p.m. - 1:00 a.m.
All major cards

This quintessentially romantic restaurant has a setting made for special occasions. Housed in the landmark carriage house and stable formerly owned by Aaron Burr, it is exquisite. Tall candles and fresh roses grace every table, and a pianist at a grand piano fills the balconied space with love songs. Adding to the seriously romantic ambience and glorious scene are four working fireplaces and a pretty viewing garden with greenery studded with tiny white lights.

The menu embodies a well-chosen variety of favorites from land and sea, prepared with sophistication and artfully presented. Among starters, a house specialty combines warm lobster medallions and shrimp in a chervil broth with leek fondue and a rich Champagne-beet reduction ($15.00). Other good openers include crab cakes with opal basil aïoli and cilantro oil ($11.00), and an excellent Caesar salad ($8.00). The signature main is individual Beef Wellington ($35.00), rich and delicious. Another excellent choice is roasted boneless breast of chicken with sour cream mashed potatoes and a mushroom ragout ($26.00). Other good options include grilled rack of lamb with yukon gold potatoes and a mint jus ($33.00) and grilled American-cut veal chop with herbed potato pie ($33.00). Favorite mains representing the sea include anise-seared tuna with spicy mango salsa and a red wine glaze, served with basmati rice ($32.00), crispy-skin filet of Maine salmon with wild mushroom potatoes ($30.00), and pan-seared fresh diver scallops with a sweet and sour couscous cake, sautéed shrimp, and wasabi crème fraîche ($28.00). Sweet enticements ($7.50) include bittersweet chocolate mousse torte with roasted and caramelized banana, fresh raspberry gratin with lemony pound cake and vanilla ice cream, frozen white chocolate cheesecake with fresh raspberry and passion fruit sauce, and strawberry shortcake ($7.50).

PARIS COMMUNE ★   French
411 Bleecker Street
(between Bank and West 11th Sts.)
212/929-0509
Lunch - Monday through Friday 11:00 a.m. - 3:00 p.m.
Brunch - Saturday and Sunday 10:00 a.m. - 3:30 p.m.
Dinner - Daily 6:00 - 11:00 p.m.
All major cards

A country French atmosphere abounds at this decidedly cozy and informal bistro. Its intimate atmosphere is enhanced by glowing candles and on cool evenings a blazing fireplace. Prices that are quite reasonable make it all the more pleasant. And if the food doesn't dazzle, neither does it displease. It is simple bistro fare, competently prepared and served by an affable staff in a setting that has a comfortable warmth. Dining here has a familiar feel, even on a first visit, and when you leave, you know you'll want to return.

For a hearty starter, order the good onion soup au gratin ($4.50). Other nice openers include smoked salmon with capers and onion ($6.00), escargots ($7.00), and warm goat cheese salad ($6.00). Among the four or so pastas available are tri-colored fettuccine with hot sausage in a fresh tomato sauce

($10.00) and penne with chicken and shiitake mushrooms ($12.00). Other good mains include a refreshing niçoise salad plate with grilled tuna ($14.00), chicken Basque-style (pan-seared and simmered with prosciutto, hot and sweet peppers, and tomatoes) ($12.00), grilled spiced pork chops with apple chutney ($14.00), roasted monkfish with basil aïoli ($16.00), and grilled leg of lamb with onion marmalade ($16.00). End with a fruit tart ($5.00).

PETER'S BACKYARD ★   Steakhouse
64 West 10th Street
(Between Fifth and Sixth Aves.)
212/477-0076
Brunch - Saturday and Sunday 11:00 a.m. - 4:00 p.m.
Dinner - Daily 5:30 p.m. - Midnight
All major cards

You can catch the ambience of Old New York at this classic 1940s steakhouse/tavern. It occupies a charming brownstone (dating back to 1882) on a delightful stretch of 10th Street. In days gone by, Humphrey Bogart, Lauren Bacall, Marilyn Monroe, Arthur Miller, and Andy Warhol were part of its regular celebrity clientele. Now, after more than a decade-long absence, it has made a gorgeous comeback. Pale yellow stuccoed walls, high ceilings, wrought iron chandeliers, a balcony circling the dining room, and paintings by local artists create a pretty backdrop.

In classic steakhouse fashion, the menu is brief. The arugula, pear, and stilton cheese salad ($6.50) is a terrific starter. Also good is the Caesar with chopped anchovy and shaved parmesan ($6.50) and steamed mussels with garlic, tomato, onions, and herbs ($9.50). There are some good pasta choices such as fettuccine pomodoro ($10.95), rigatoni tossed with eggplant ($10.95), and penne puttanesca ($10.95). The house specialty among mains is the porterhouse steak ($24.95). Other meaty choices include a veal chop with mushroom sauce ($19.95), filet mignon ($20.95), and medallions of pork with apple Calvados sauce ($16.95). For a lighter repast, there's grilled chicken breast ($15.95) and daily fish specials served with steamed vegetables. The signature dessert is a panatone cake soaked in Grand Marnier.

A $21.95 three-course prix fixe menu is available from 5:30 to 8:00 p.m. with three or four choices in each category.

PO ★★★   Italian
31 Cornelia Street
(between Bleecker and W. 4th Sts.)
212/645-2189
Lunch - Wednesday through Sunday 11:30 a.m. - 2:30 p.m.
Dinner - Tuesday through Thursday 5:30 - 11:00 p.m.;
Friday and Saturday 5:30 - 11:30 p.m.;
Sunday 5:00 - 10:00 p.m.
American Express only

Po's simple setting makes the drama of the cooking a happy surprise. This wonderful little place is situated on a tiny street in the heart of the West Village, and has a very appealing quality whether you're on the outside looking in or lucky enough to occupy one of its 12 tables. Its interior is comfortably stylish with white wainscotting, polished wood floors, big square mirrors, and softly revolving ceiling fans.

The modern Italian fare served here is innovative and delicious. Co-owner/chef Mario Batali puts a lively spin on traditional Bolognese and Tuscan specialties and the results are dazzling. Surprisingly gentle prices for such sophisticated cooking is another nice surprise. When you arrive, you'll be greeted with fabulous white bean bruschetta, an indication of the pleasures to come. You might go on to steamed clams in a spicy mint brodetto ($8.00), roasted beets with lentils, watercress, and taleggio ($6.00), or grappa-cured salmon with crushed lemon crostini ($7.00). The white bean ravioli with balsamic vinegar brown butter ($10.00) is one of Batali's signature dishes, but the pastas are all wonderful. Other options include gnocchi with fresh tomato, green olives, and Coach Farm ricotta ($10.00), spaghetti in a spicy porcini sauce ($12.50), and linguine with clams, pancetta, and hot chilies ($12.50). Of the other mains, you can't go wrong with the grilled chicken paillard with fresh tomatoes, smoked mozzarella, and black olive vinaigrette ($13.00), veal piccata ($14.00), grilled salmon with scallion crushed potatoes and blood orange citronette ($13.00), or roasted monkfish in a tangy sweet pea broth with braised leeks and lemon saffron vinaigrette ($15.00). The warm apple tart with hazelnut gelato is a favorite dessert.

For pasta lovers, there's a five-course pasta tasting menu for $25.00. There's also a $29.00 six-course tasting menu.

TARTINE ★★   French
253 West 11th Street (W. 4th St.)
212/229-2611
Lunch - Monday through Friday 11:30 a.m. - 4:00 p.m.
Brunch - Saturday and Sunday 10:30 a.m. - 4:00 p.m.
Dinner - Tuesday through Sunday 5:30 - 10:30 p.m.
No credit cards

A sweet charm emanates from this homey café/bakery. Brick and wood-covered walls, a wood floor, and photos of lighthouses and boats give the tiny space a comfortable warmth. Situated on a wonderfully quaint block, its six sidewalk tables provide another delightful option on pleasant days.

The food is terrific and the prices gentle. Good starters include French onion soup ($3.75), herbed goat cheese salad with tomatoes and walnuts ($7.25), and escargots with parsley and garlic butter ($6.50). Main selections include chicken pot pie with dumplings and mushrooms, served with a green salad ($8.75), beef mignonettes with French fries ($11.25), and grilled salmon with citrus vinaigrette and julienned vegetables ($10.25). Desserts are old-fashioned comforting favorites like strawberry shortcake ($3.75), caramelized apples over puff pastry served warm with vanilla ice cream ($4.50), and a selection of fabulous custard-filled tarts (lemon, pear, plum, apricot, mixed fruit, strawberry, blueberry, blackberry, and raspberry) ($3.50-$4.25).

Saturday and Sunday brunch is wonderful here and quite popular. Main dishes are all $8.75 (OJ, coffee or tea included). Choices include eggs Florentine with fresh spinach, homemade hollandaise, and roasted potatoes; perfect eggs Benedict; French toast on home-baked brioche with roasted potatoes; apple pancakes; and a choice of omelettes served with roasted potatoes.

VILLA MOSCONI ★   Italian
69 MacDougal Street
(between Bleecker and W. Houston Sts.)
212/673-0390
Lunch - Monday through Saturday Noon - 3:00 p.m.
Dinner - Monday through Saturday 5:00 - 11:00 p.m.
All major cards

Villa Mosconi, with its warm, old-fashioned atmosphere, is the other side of trendy. With a minimum of style, it maxes when it comes to comfort and good Italian homestyle cooking. This is a family operation of a kind you find so often in Italy where brothers and cousins and in-laws all pitch in, a feeling of genuine hospitality abounds, and everyone who comes to dine is treated like a friend.

Generous portions and moderate prices have kept this a neighborhood staple. Menu choices are almost overwhelming. The extensive starter options include good stuffed mushrooms ($7.50), baked clams ($7.75), fried calamari for two ($12.00), and meat-filled dumplings in broth ($5.25). You certainly can't go wrong with any of the homemade pastas. Again, the choice is great. Opt for the homemade ravioli, manicotti, or cannelloni ($11.25) and you'll be happy. Other good choices are gnocchi with a pesto sauce ($12.50), tortellini with a meat filling ($12.25), and fettuccine Bolognese ($11.25). And this is the kind of Italian restaurant that still serves spaghetti and meatballs ($11.75). Among other mains, selections include chicken with prosciutto and cheese in a wine sauce ($13.25), veal with fresh mushrooms in a Marsala sauce ($13.75), veal parmesan ($13.25), filet mignon in a Marsala sauce ($17.25), stuffed zucchini ($10.75), and mozzarella omelette ($10.75). Good seafood specialties are the trout sautéed in lemon and wine ($15.00), shrimp marinara ($15.50), and broiled bay scallops ($15.70). In season, the grilled soft shell crabs are a treat at $16.75. And each day of the week carries its own specials. If it's Wednesday, you'll be offered veal and peppers ($11.95) and mussels in white wine ($10.25).

A $19.95 three-course dinner available until 6:00 p.m. is yet another good option for early diners.

VILLAGE ATELIER ★★   French/American
436 Hudson Street
(corner of Morton St.)
212/989-1363
Lunch - Monday through Friday 11:30 a.m. - 3:00 p.m.
Dinner - Daily 5:30 - 11:30 p.m.
American Express, Personal checks

Village Atelier gives off a cozy, old-fashioned feel in its country cottage setting. Situated in an 1820s village brownstone with cherry wainscoting, fieldstone walls, hand-hewn beams and a pressed tin ceiling, the romantic wildflower-filled interior emanates charm. American country antiques from owner Craig Béro's family farm in Wisconsin enhance its quaint appeal. And with only 13 tables, it has a genuine aura of intimacy and is nice for a quiet lunch or dinner.

The food is all so good—a delightful blending of rustic French with a strong American affection. Of the starters, house specialties are the crispy confit of duck, croquettes of goat cheese, mesclun, and fruit compote ($8.00) feuilleté of asparagus and wild mushrooms with shallots and lemon thyme ($8.50), and Maine crab cakes with cracked grain mustard ($9.00). There's a nice risotto with garlicky pan-roasted shrimp ($16.00) and a housemade pasta composed daily ($13.00). Good mains include a terrific herbed roast chicken with sage-prune stuffing, gravy, and parmesan mashed potatoes ($15.00), sautéed duck breast, crispy confit, risotto-mushroom cake, acorn squash, with a Port wine and raspberry sauce ($17.00), and filet mignon with roasted vegetables ($19.00). The pan-sautéed brook trout with hazelnuts in a lemon-caper sauce ($17.00) is a specialty of the house and grilled Atlantic salmon with wild rice, almonds, and horseradish butter with sun-dried tomatoes and black olives ($18.00) is another winner. Don't leave without trying one of the delicious mom-made desserts.

YE WAVERLY INN ★   American
16 Bank Street (Waverly Pl.)
212/929-4377
Lunch - Monday through Friday 11:30 a.m. - 3:30 p.m.
Brunch - Saturday and Sunday 11:00 a.m. - 3:30 p.m.
Dinner - Monday through Thursday 5:00 - 10:30 p.m.;
Friday and Saturday 5:00 - 11:30 p.m.; Sunday 5:00 - 10:00 p.m.
All major cards

Ye Waverly Inn, originally a carriage house built in 1844, is situated on a charming residential street in the West Village. With four small dining rooms, low ceilings, old-fashioned wooden booths, and provincial wallpaper, it has the feel of a colonial inn. For warm weather dining, its pretty flower garden is quite pleasant. But the three working fireplaces inside make fall and winter the time it is most romantic and cozy. This quaint, warm place looks like a page from yesteryear, is as welcoming as a neighborhood tavern, and everyone on the staff seems eager to please. If the food were as good as its setting is charming, this would be a multi-star restaurant.

The food is traditional American with a New England bias. The homemade breads, muffins, and cobblers are delectable. For starters, choices include chicken vegetable soup ($4.75), baked corn pudding ($4.75), ragout of

175

wild mushrooms with grilled polenta ($7.00), warm asparagus salad with baby bliss potatoes, toasted pine nuts, and lemon zest mayonnaise ($7.25), and baked brie wrapped in pastry with sour cherry preserves ($7.00). You'll have to forego the calorie count when choosing a main with favorite specialties like roast turkey with cornbread stuffing, giblet gravy, and fresh cranberry compote ($11.75), French peasant meatloaf baked in a flaky crust, with house gravy ($11.25), Southern-fried chicken ($11.75), and the house specialty, chicken pot pie ($12.75). Other fare includes seafood ravioli in a lemon basil butter sauce served with sturgeon caviar ($15.75), penne with cilantro pesto and grilled portobello mushrooms ($13.75), zucchini-wrapped red snapper with roasted tomato cumin orange sauce ($16.50), filet mignon with a green peppercorn Cognac sauce ($18.75), and grilled chicken breast marinated with lemon and ginger, served with curried butter ($14.25). All main courses are served with a choice of salad or vegetables. For an additional $5.50 you'll get soup, salad, coffee, and dessert.

You can't beat the weekday pre-theater special here. **From 5:00 to 7:00 p.m., Monday through Thursday, $13.50 gets you soup, a main course, vegetables, and dessert and coffee.**

Saturday and Sunday afternoon is a great time to dine here when a Champagne brunch is offered. The set price is $11.50 and includes a complimentary cocktail or a glass of Champagne or house wine, buttermilk biscuits, muffins, strawberry butter, a main course, and coffee or tea. You can't go wrong with choices like eggs Benedict, Eggs Waverly (scrambled eggs with onions, sour cream, and bacon in a puff pastry shell), leek and brie omelette, wild mushroom frittata, challah bread French toast served with bananas and cinnamon, and chicken pot pie.

MIDTOWN

Midtown

CENTRAL PARK

EAST SIDE

THEATER DISTRICT

Avenue of the Americas (6th Ave.)

W. 59th St. — E. 59th St.
W. 58th St. — E. 58th St.
W. 57th St. — E. 57th St.
W. 56th St. — E. 56th St.
W. 55th St. — E. 55th St.
W. 54th St. — E. 54th St.

Museum of Modern Art

W. 53rd St. — E. 53rd St.
W. 52nd St. — E. 52nd St.
W. 51st St. — E. 51st St.
W. 50th St. — E. 50th St.

Rockefeller Center

Rockefeller Plaza

W. 49th St. — E. 49th St.
W. 48th St. — E. 48th St.
W. 47th St. — E. 47th St.
W. 46th St. — E. 46th St.
W. 45th St. — E. 45th St.
W. 44th St. — E. 44th St.
W. 43rd St. — E. 43rd St.
W. 42nd St. — E. 42nd St.
W. 41st St. — E. 41st St.
W. 40th St. — E. 40th St.
W. 39th St. — E. 39th St.

5th Ave.
Madison Ave.
Park Ave.
Lexington Ave.
3rd Ave.
2nd Ave.
1st Ave.

Sutton Pl.

Beekman Pl.

Franklin D. Roosevelt Dr.

Park Ave.

Grand Central Terminal

Vanderbilt Ave.

The United Nations

EAST RIVER

Bryant Park

New York Public Library

Tunnel Exit St.

Tunnel Entrance St.

Tudor City Pl.

Queens Midtown Tunnel (Toll)

UNION SQUARE/GRAMERCY PARK/MURRAY HILL

ANCHE VIVOLO ★★   Italian
222 East 58th Street (between Second and Third Aves.)
212/308-0112
Lunch - Monday through Friday Noon - 3:00 p.m.
Dinner - Monday through Saturday 5:00 - 11:30 p.m.
All major cards

Anche Vivolo's understated dining room, done in soft pastels, is quietly pretty and thoroughly comfortable. Cozy cane chairs and mirrors reflecting beautiful flower arrangements add warmth to the sedate room. A cordial welcome, good classic Italian cuisine, and outstanding prix fixe early offers and late night specials make it a pleasant haven for a regular clientele and a nice piece of serendipity for anyone who pops in just because it looks so pleasant from the outside looking in.

You might start with a big plate of delicious fried zucchini for the table ($5.50) then move on to starters such as beef carpaccio with rucola and parmesan ($7.50), rolled eggplant with cheese and tomato ($5.95), and a seafood salad of calamari, conch, octopus, mussels, and celery with extra virgin olive oil and lemon ($6.95). Good pasta choices include linguine with garlic, anchovies, basil, oregano, and tomato ($11.95), capellini primavera ($11.95), and fettuccine with diced tomato, rucola, and shrimp ($12.95). Main selections include boneless brook trout sautéed with tomato, black olives, capers, garlic, basil, and oregano ($13.95), broiled veal chop accompanied with a white bean salad ($18.95), salmon in a mustard sauce ($15.95), breast of chicken sautéed with mushrooms, garlic, lemon, parsley, and shrimp ($14.95), and veal scaloppine with fresh asparagus, artichokes, and seasonal mushrooms in a lemon, butter, and white wine sauce ($15.95).

The pre-theater menu is offered from 5:00 to 6:30 p.m. It includes three generous courses for $18.95 with a great deal of choice in each category. Starter selections include a mozzarella, tomato, and basil salad; fried calamari; and mussels in a light tomato sauce. There are at least fourteen mains to choose from, including veal scaloppine with artichokes, fresh tomato, and a wine sauce; linguine with clams; rigatoni Bolognese; filet of sole in a white wine sauce; grilled minute steak with sautéed onions, peppers, and roasted potatoes; and a combination of the veal and chicken specialties of the day. Dessert selections include various daily specials as well as menu standards such as chocolate mousse, ricotta cheesecake, and cannolis.

Another terrific deal is the late night dinner menu offered after 9:00 p.m. It includes three courses for $14.95 and again the choice is great. There are about ten starter options with good choices such as a Caesar-type salad with polenta croutons; a salad of endive, chopped tomato, and bacon; and a mozzarella and tomato salad. Over two dozen mains are offered, with selections that include mussels in a light tomato sauce; farfalle with broccoli and sweet sausage; rigatoni with tomato, onion, and pancetta; fettuccine with veal dumplings in a spicy tomato sauce; green and white pasta strips with shrimp, zucchini, garlic, tomato, and parmesan; scaloppine of veal rolled with mozzarella and prosciutto with a mushroom-Marsala sauce; and ricotta and spinach ravioli prepared with butter and sage. Finish with dessert and coffee and you've had one sweet deal.

AQUAVIT ★★★   Scandinavian
13 West 54th Street
(between Fifth and Sixth Aves.)
212/307-7311
Lunch - Monday through Friday Noon - 2:30 p.m.
Brunch - Sunday Noon - 3:00 p.m.
Dinner - Monday through Saturday 5:30 - 10:30 p.m.
All major cards

A soaring eight-story glass-enclosed atrium houses the main dining room in this cool, sophisticated art-filled Scandinavian restaurant where every element of the design is a visual treat. Situated in a landmark mansion that was once the residence of the John D. Rockefeller family, its dramatic setting includes a cascading two-story waterfall, colorful hanging sculptures, and towering birch trees. Though undeniably romantic by candlelight, it is almost more striking during the day when light pours in and accentuates the calm of the waterfall.

While there was a period when the setting outshined the food, that is no longer the case. Now when you dine here, you'll find a nice balance in the beautiful space and the beautiful food. **The main dining room's menu is a $58.00 prix fixe with three courses.** Starter choices might be mixed greens with a root vegetable julienne, toasted walnuts, and roasted tomatoes; lobster bisque with grilled shrimp; smoked venison salad; and smoked salmon with buckwheat potato blini and goat cheese cream. Main selections include phyllo-wrapped salmon with orange fennel broth, braised greens, and a sweet potato cake; mushroom-crusted Icelandic cod with grilled new potatoes; sun-dried cherry-crusted rack of lamb with lemon-rosemary sauce and a tomato and eggplant Napoleon; loin of Arctic venison with oven-dried lingonberry sauce and apple-potato gratin; and seared beef tenderloin with beer-braised potatoes and onions. For dessert: assorted cheeses with Port wine crème brûlée; warm chocolate cake with white chocolate sorbet; Swedish cheesecake; or a deliciously different ice cream sandwich-like creation made with mascarpone ice cream between thin layers of gingerbread on a plate drizzled with licorice sauce.

A pre-theater menu is offered from 5:30 to 6:15 p.m. with three courses for $39.00.

The upstairs cafe offers a more casual atmosphere in a stylish bar setting, along with a very appealing menu. At dinner, first course choices include mixed field greens with a red wine vinaigrette and garlic herb croutons ($8.00), fish soup ($8.00), traditional gravlax with a mustard sauce and dill ($9.50), and smoked salmon with horseradish cream ($10.50). For the main, good choices include assorted hors d'oeuvres ($17.50), pan-seared Atlantic salmon with herb sauce with tomatoes on a potato pancake ($18.50), roasted chicken with seasonal vegetables and apples ($17.00), diced tenderloin of beef with potatoes and onions ($20.00), and Swedish meatballs with lingonberries, a cucumber salad, and mashed potatoes ($16.00). **A pre-theater menu with three courses here is $25.00.**

ARCIMBOLDO ★★   Italian
220 East 46th Street
(between Second and Third Aves.)
212/972-4646
Lunch - Monday through Friday 11:45 a.m. - 3:00 p.m.
Dinner - Sunday through Thursday 5:30 - 11:00 p.m.;
Friday and Saturday 5:30 p.m. - Midnight
All major cards

The first thing you notice about Arcimboldo is how pretty it is. The interior, designed by David Barrett, pays homage to the 16th Century Italian artist, Giuseppe Arcimboldo, who created portraits using fruits, flowers and vegetables. Stucco-finished walls, dreamy shades of peach, and rosso marble floors are reminiscent of Italian country palazzos. And with delightful trompe l'oeil murals, beautiful chandeliers, terraced dining areas, and whimsical asparagus columns, the decor strikes a happy balance between elegance, humor, and comfort. Live piano music nightly adds to its romantically festive atmosphere. Dining here is just delightful.

The food is wonderful. Of the starters, I particularly like the Sicilian eggplant tart with fresh mozzarella, hints of parmesan, and fresh basil ($6.50). The Tuscan-style minestrone garnished with pesto ($5.95) is another nice way to start a meal here. Other popular starters—broiled portobello with extra virgin olive oil and a touch of balsamic vinegar ($8.95), carpaccio of marinated Norwegian salmon ($11.50), and a sampling of vegetarian antipasti from the buffet ($6.95). Good pasta selections include rigatoni with fresh tomato sauce, basil, diced eggplant, and fresh mozzarella ($10.95), spaghetti with baby clams ($13.50), homemade meat ravioli with fresh tomato and basil ($10.95), homemade ravioli stuffed with eggplant, fresh basil, and mozzarella in a delicate tomato sauce ($10.95), penne in a spicy tomato sauce with fresh parsley, garlic, and extra virgin olive oil ($11.95), and linguine with shrimp, clams, and calamari ($14.95). Other main options include fresh grilled salmon ($16.95), batter-fried jumbo shrimp, calamari, baccale, and fresh vegetables ($14.95), medallions of veal, grilled and garnished with fresh tomato and mozzarella ($17.50), baby rack of lamb seasoned with fresh rosemary ($22.50), and rolled breast of veal stuffed with spinach and pignoli nuts in a white wine sauce ($16.50). Good thin crust pizza is another temptation—it comes in a variety of interesting topping combos such as shrimp, onions, and arugula ($12.50), gorgonzola and radicchio ($13.95), olives, artichokes, ham, and mushrooms ($14.50), and fontina, mozzarella, gorgonzola, and parmesan ($12.50). When the platter of sweet concoctions is brought around for your consideration, think tiramisú.

Sundays at Arcimboldo means "Opera With Taste." Professional singers from the Metropolitan Opera offer a selection of arias at 7:00 and at 9:30 p.m. The chef prepares a prix fixe four-course dinner of regional specialties for $40.00. Each month, a different composer or style of opera is highlighted. Dinner is served during piano solos, and guests are welcome to stay for both performances. Reservations are recommended.

ARTUSI ★★   Italian
36 West 52nd Street
(between Fifth and Sixth Aves.)
212/582-6900
Lunch - Monday through Friday Noon - 3:00 p.m.
Dinner - Monday through Saturday 5:30 - 10:30 p.m.
All major cards

Artusi—named after 19th Century cookbook author Artusi Pellegrino, who wrote Italy's most famous cookbook, *Science in the Kitchen and the Art of*

Eating Well—replaces the pleasant Cesarina. With well-spaced tables, mirrored walls, and attractive banquette seating along the perimeter, it appears much the same. Its setting is comfortable, its elegance subdued. The big difference is in the kitchen. Its owners (Lake Como's luxurious Villa d'Este) decided it was time for their Manhattan restaurant to undergo a metamorphosis and hired chef Mauro Mafrici, who has worked at Felidia and at San Domenico in Imola, Italy, and who fosters an affection for the old master's cooking.

There is much on his menu to attract new admirers to the original Artusi's style of cooking. Thinly-sliced roasted pork loin with eggplant, new potato salad, and sun-dried tomatoes ($8.50) and tuna in a veal sauce with arugula salad ($9.00) are a few of the chef's adaptations from the original recipe book. Also good is a mélange of vegetables with grilled scallops, yellow pepper purée, and fresh onions ($9.00). Pastas are unusual and also very good. Selections include tortelloni filled with peas in a light tomato sauce with crispy pancetta ($18.00) and white lasagna with artichoke sauce ($18.00). There's also a terrific risotto with fresh wild mushrooms and quail ($19.00). Mains are just as interesting and quite generously proportioned. Choices include roasted red snapper with a bouquet of spring vegetables and aromatic herbs in a Spumanti wine sauce ($24.00), roasted rack of lamb with peas and leeks ($23.00), leg of rabbit roasted with honey and herbs and served on soft polenta ($22.00), veal medallions with chanterelle sauce, mashed potatoes, and spinach ($23.00), and grilled spicy baby chicken with zucchini sauce, roasted leeks, and potatoes ($22.00). Desserts are excellent, especially the frollino pastry filled with peaches, zabaglione, and mascarpone cheese with scoops of blueberry sorbet ($7.00) and chocolate hazelnut meringue with chocolate zabaglione served with a small sour cherry tart (also $7.00).

BOUTERIN ★★   French
420 East 59th Street (between First Ave. and Sutton Pl.)
212/758-0323
Lunch - Monday through Friday Noon - 2:30 p.m.
Dinner - Monday through Saturday 5:00 - 10:30 p.m.
All major cards

Bouterin's ambience is one of sheer charm. Hand-painted curtains, apricot and green walls, rustic bric-a-brac, and mismatched crockery impart the feel of a restaurant in the Provençal countryside. Rushes of extravagant flowers, low-burning candles, and soft amber lighting add to its immense appeal. Chef-owner Antoine Bouterin, who spent 13 years polishing his craft at Le Périgord, created this gorgeously rustic restaurant as an affectionate

183

tribute to his grandmother Marguerite, whose Le Café de l'Epicerie in St. Rémy was launched in 1915. When you dine here, you have to feel how pleased she would be.

Not every dish is a winner. But so much of Bouterin's food is delicious and the room in which it is served is so lovely and transporting, dining here has a very special feel. A personal favorite, I would happily tip-toe through this menu any day of the week. Slow-cooking and the exuberant use of fresh herbs are trademarks of the talented chef. Starter standouts are grand-mère's vegetable soup ($9.00), eggplant caviar with parsley blinis ($7.00), and seafood risotto ($9.00). Other good choices include provençale vegetable tart with basil sauce ($9.00) and crab cake ($12.00). Among mains, good choices include a simple, old-fashioned country roast chicken and sautéed potatoes ($18.00), sea bass filet with bouillabaisse sauce ($25.00), grilled salmon filet with rosemary béarnaise and spinach mousseline ($19.00), and grilled peppered steak with a Cognac sauce and potatoes au gratin ($27.00). Of the signature slow-cooked dishes, the old-fashioned beef daube stewed with red wine and garlic with carrots and onions ($22.00) is delicious, but the lamb stew ($21.00)—cooked for seven hours and meant to be eaten with a spoon—can be disappointingly flat and stringy. When it comes to dessert, opt for the floating island when available—the whipped, poached egg whites drizzled with caramel sauce create a velvety, sweet finale that will take some of the sting out of stepping back out on dreary old 59th Street.

On Sundays a prix fixe menu is available with three courses for $28.00.

THE BOX TREE ★★   French
250 East 49th Street (between Second and Third Aves.)
212/758-8320
Lunch - Monday through Friday Noon - 2:30 p.m.
Brunch - Sunday Noon - 2:00 p.m.
Dinner - Daily 5:30 - 10:30 p.m.
Amex, Visa, Master

A warm, romantic feeling pervades this glorious antique and flower-filled townhouse. Beautiful artwork, Tiffany windows, and three working fireplaces echo the ambience of a gracious English mansion and combine to create one of the most romantic destinations in town.

The spectacular ambience comes at a considerable cost with its five-course prix fixe dinner menu a stout $86.00. But while the food is suitably elegant and mostly wonderful, it is not quite as impressive as its splendid setting.   Starter enticements might be house-cured salmon with a fresh horseradish sauce, prosciutto with fresh pears, blini with salmon caviar and chilled Vodka, and marinated quail with warm potato salad and olives. A soup course follows with selections such as a chilled cucumber and yogurt soup and Maine lobster bisque.   For the main, perhaps medallions of veal with wild mushrooms, filet of beef with cracked corriander and Armagnac, breast of duck with green peppercorns, or roast pheasant with juniper berries. Then an endive and cress salad is served with stilton and Port before the elegant sweet finale.

CAFE CENTRO ★★   French
200 Park Avenue
(45th St. and Vanderbilt Ave.)
212/818-1222
Lunch - Monday through Friday 11:30 a.m. - 5:00 p.m.
Dinner - Monday through Saturday 5:00 - 10:00 p.m.
All major cards

Reminiscent of the grand cafes of Europe, this luxurious brasserie's rich interior is accented with gold leaf, handsome murals, Lalilique-inspired chandeliers, and stately columns topped with sculpted pewter friezes of frolicking animals. A glassed-in kitchen and huge rotisserie fireplace complete its saucy, flamboyant look.   But since coming on the scene in 1994, Cafe Centro has proven to be more than just a sassy new face in town.   Here, executive chef Stephane Becht, from the Alsace region of France, offers a menu of delicious French bistro fare with American influence and a Moroccan slant.

Within this polished evocation of Parisian art deco, there also resides an all-American Beer Bar, featuring its own menu of more casual fare (including a great burger) and more than 20 different kinds of beer.   And in warm weather, it has one of the most appealing sidewalk cafes in town—glass-fronted and pleasantly decked out with cheery red umbrellas and flower boxes bursting with colorful blooms.

Dinner at Cafe Centro might start with sea scallops provençale, pan-seared with walnut butter and herbs ($8.50), curly endive with smoked bacon and cheese-garlic croutons ($8.00), pan-seared calamari stuffed with basil and salmon ($8.00), clams on the half shell ($1.50 each), or black bean soup ($7.25).   From its ever-changing list of mains, selections include lamb steak with baby potatoes, carrots, and mushrooms ($18.50), steak frites ($18.00), boeuf bourguignon with fettuccine ($17.50), herb-roasted chicken with creamy mashed potatoes ($16.95), roasted stuffed turkey with chestnut sauce ($18.00), grilled mahi mahi with sun-dried tomato and black olive tapenade and oyster sauce ($18.50), rigatoni with marinated chicken and Merguez sausage ($17.50), duck cassoulet ($17.00), and a delectable chicken bisteeya with almonds, raisins, honey, and orange flower essence in a phyllo pie ($16.00). For dessert: twice-baked apple with raisins and walnuts wrapped in phyllo dough and topped with whipped cream ($6.50), almond macaroons filled with Kahlua and expresso parfait ($6.50), roasted pecan tartelette with a vanilla sauce ($6.50), and warm flourless chocolate cake with a saffron and Grand Marnier sauce ($6.50).

Daily three-course prix fixe dinners are also offered. The $22.50 prix fixe might be black bean soup, fresh herb-roasted chicken, and marquise au chocolat. And the $27.50 prix fixe could be salad, rotisserie of the day, and vanilla crème brûlée-chocolate tart.

CAFE DU PONT ★★   French
1038 First Avenue
(between 56th and 57th Sts.)
212/223-1133
Lunch - Daily Noon - 3:00 p.m.
Dinner - Daily 5:00 - 10:00 p.m.
All major cards

This tiny neighborhood charmer has a simple and pretty setting with a burgundy backdrop and nice paintings. A spirited, welcoming staff rounds out its homey congeniality.

The cuisine is eclectic French with things like smoked salmon and pumpernickel with marinated red onions, capers, and sour cream dill sauce ($9.00), mussels marinières with white wine, garlic, and shallot sauce ($7.00), and a good Caesar salad with anchovy caper vinaigrette ($6.50) highlighting the starter list. For the main, choose from good renditions of sautéed brook trout amandine with a tarragon mustard sauce ($18.00), Atlantic fish stew, in a classic bouillabaisse style, with red snapper, shrimp, mussels, and clams ($22.00), herb-roasted chicken with a wild mushroom sauce ($15.50), veal scaloppine piccata sautéed with a lemon butter sauce ($19.50), steak au poivre with pommes frites ($23.00), and rack of lamb with braised northern white beans and carrots with a Port shallot sauce ($24.00). There are nice pasta options as well—fresh fettuccine with smoked salmon and dill with a pink sauce ($17.50), linguine Bolognese ($16.00), and ravioli stuffed with spinach and

186

cheese with a basil pesto sauce ($15.50). A nice entrée salad of grilled vegetables with balsamic vinaigrette ($15.00) is also available.

Between 5:00 and 6:30 p.m., a three-course prix fixe menu with a wide variety of choices is offered for $19.95. Credit cards, however, are not accepted with the prix fixe dinners.

CAFE NICHOLSON ★★   American
323 East 58th Street (between First and Second Aves.)
212/355-6769
Dinner only - Wednesday through Saturday 5:30 - 9:00 p.m.
All major cards

This antique-filled charmer will lull you into a mellow frame of mind with its romantic turn-of-the-century setting and caring service. Perched unimpressively under the ramp to the 59th Street Bridge, its interior is a delicious surprise. Decorated with elaborate 19th Century hand-painted tiles, beautiful paintings, and pottery from around the world, it has a fanciful and seductive appeal.

The main drawback to dining here is finding out when it is open. Its delightfully eccentric owner opens only when the spirit moves him and when his travel bug isn't biting. But when you do find that open window, you will be pleasantly rewarded for your patience. The menu is simple and the food simply delicious. **A set price of $43.50 covers three courses with red and white wine included.** To start, choices include cheese soufflé (a house specialty), pickled herring with dill, and shrimp with dill. For the main, you choose from a list that includes free-range roast chicken with herbs, filet of salmon, roast leg of lamb, crab cakes with a pepper sauce, and filet mignon. For dessert, the chocolate soufflé is legendary.

CHIAM ★★   Chinese
160 East 48th Street (between Lexington and Third Aves.)
212/371-2323
Lunch - Daily 11:30 a.m. - 3:00 p.m.
Dinner - Daily 3:00 p.m. - Midnight
All major cards

This cool and sophisticated oriental oasis has an impressive wine list and upscale decor that sets it apart from the typical Chinese restaurant. Its gracious service, terrific food, and handsome black and white motif win raves from locals who flock here for gourmet dim sum. They also appreciate the English-speaking waiters who are helpful with the extensive choices on the well-balanced menu.

Starter selections might be hot and sour soup ($3.95), seafood bisque ($5.75), Cantonese egg roll ($3.75), four crispy shrimp balls ($6.75), broiled stuffed mushrooms ($6.00), and barbecued spare ribs ($10.25). But the favorites are the dumplings, with choices that include four cilantro seafood dumplings ($6.75), four steamed chrysanthemum chicken dumplings ($5.75), four steamed pork dumplings ($5.75), and eight spicy sautéed dumplings ($6.50). There are lots of delicious choices among the mains as well. Choose from a list that includes Szechuan prawns ($19.50), salmon with ginger and scallions ($19.50), steamed lemon chicken ($14.75), shredded pork with a spicy garlic sauce ($14.95), crispy beef l'orange ($16.95), roast duck with plum sauce ($17.50), Peking duck ($36.00), and sesame crispy chicken ($15.50). There are a number of good pasta and rice specialties as well—pan-fried angel hair with seafood ($16.95), beef fettuccine ($11.95), angel hair with clams and black bean sauce ($10.95), and fried rice with chicken and shrimp ($12.95). Perhaps the nicest feature of Chiam's menu is its diversity, including a nice selection of alternative/spa cuisine for the health conscious. These dishes are all plain steamed, with no oil, corn starch, soy sauce, sugar, or salt. Selections from this healthy list include steamed catch of the day with ginger and scallions ($19.50), steamed lobster with lemon and ginger ($22.50), beef tenderloin with seasonal vegetables ($14.95), and prawns and scallops with seasonal vegetables ($19.50).

CHIN CHIN ★★★   Chinese
216 East 49th Street
(between Second and Third Aves.)
212/888-4555
Lunch - Daily 11:30 a.m. - 4:00 p.m.
Dinner - Daily 4:00 p.m. - Midnight
All major cards

This top of the line Chinese restaurant ranks with the very best in town. It's also a good place for people who ordinarily don't like Chinese restaurants. Chin Chin is by no means ordinary. For one thing, the interior doesn't look at all the way Chinese restaurants usually look. While some are dreadfully ornate and others dreary, Chin Chin fits neither mold. Its postmodern design is stark and handsome. The dining rooms have creamy off-white walls, recessed lighting, and polished dark wood wainscoting. Sepia portraits of generations of the Chin family line the walls, and in the back dining room brilliant pottery lends a cheerful touch. There's also a nice rear garden room enclosed with skylights.

The eclectic menu features delicious specialties from many different provinces of China. A good kick-off for this culinary adventure are the wonderful steamed Shanghai dumplings ($7.00) or the steamed vegetable dumplings ($7.00). You also can't go wrong with the barbecued spare ribs ($10.75), crispy fried squid ($7.50), spring rolls ($4.50), scallion pancakes ($4.50), hot and sour soup ($3.50), chunky fish chowder ($4.00), Maine lobster roll ($18.50), or the shredded chicken salad with eggplant ($9.50). Good vegetable dishes include eggplant with garlic sauce ($8.00) and a Chinese ratatouille casserole ($12.50). Pasta is good here, too. Try the angel hair with fresh greens ($10.50) or the angel hair with assorted seafood ($15.00). Other good main dishes include lemon chicken ($14.50), boneless duckling l'orange ($17.50), lobster with ginger and scallions ($21.50), clams with black bean sauce ($15.50), sautéed leg of lamb with leeks ($16.50), moo shu pork with crêpes ($14.50), veal medallions with a spicy peppercorn sauce ($17.50), crisped orange beef ($17.50), and Chin Chin steak with asparagus ($18.50). Desserts include a variety of pies and cakes (each $5.00) as well as a selection of homemade sorbets and ice cream (each $4.00).

A special Peking duck dinner is available at $28.00 per person (for two or more people). It includes a choice of soup; then crispy duck skin with pancakes, hoisin sauce, and scallions; followed by sautéed shredded duck meat, fried rice, and poached spinach; and for dessert, sorbet or ice cream.

CIAO EUROPA ★★   Italian
63 West 54th Street
(between Fifth and Sixth Aves.)
212/247-1200
Lunch - Daily Noon - 3:00 p.m.
Dinner - Daily 4:00 - 11:30 p.m.
All major cards

Ciao Europa's setting pays homage to a more formal era. Its dining room, on two levels, has high ceilings, iron chandeliers, and huge Elizabethan-style murals, giving it the look of a drawing room in a European castle. Yet it has a comfortable feel and not a bit of stuffiness.

The food is quite good. To start, try the house specialty of sautéed shrimp wrapped in prosciutto with a Grand Marnier glaze ($11.50). Other good starters include fried calamari in a spicy marinara sauce ($11.75), smoked sea scallops with cold caponata ($11.75), and a chopped salad with zucchini, tomato, and olives ($6.75). The pastas are all wonderful, but the house specialty is half-moon shaped pasta filled with chopped broccoli and shrimp ($14.75). Other good choices include spaghetti with fresh Alaskan crab and tomato ($16.75) and pappardelle with mushrooms, asparagus, sun-dried tomatoes, pine nuts, and a touch a pesto ($15.25). There is also a risotto of the day. Other delicious options include the boneless breast of chicken filled with apple and mozzarella ($17.75), veal scaloppine topped with mozzarella, sun-dried tomatoes, and asparagus ($18.75), grilled sliced shell steak with sautéed leeks and Montepulciano wine served with gorgonzola polenta ($21.75), and red snapper baked in parchment with vegetables ($21.75). The changing assortment of desserts ($7.00) does justice to what has come before.

A pre-theatre menu is offered from 5:00 to 7:00 p.m. with three courses for $24.95. You might start with mushrooms sautéed in extra virgin olive oil with garlic and fresh herbs, penne in a light and spicy tomato and Vodka sauce, or chopped lettuces with zucchini, olives, and tomato. For the main: jumbo shrimp with capers and Champagne; angel hair pasta with tomato, ricotta cheese, and pesto; chicken in a tangy garlic-lemon sauce; or veal scaloppine. Finish with a choice of daily desserts and coffee or tea.

An after-theatre menu is served from 10:00 to 11:30 p.m. with three courses for $19.97. To start, either soup of the day or mixed organic baby greens. Main choices include linguine in a red or white clam sauce; chicken chunks in garlic, white wine, and herbs; chicken Caesar; and veal scaloppine. Then select one of the daily desserts and coffee or tea.

CIBO ★★   Contemporary American
767 Second Avenue (42nd St.)
212/681-1616
Lunch - Monday through Friday 11:30 a.m. - 3:00 p.m.
Brunch - Sunday 11:30 a.m. - 3:30 p.m.
Dinner - Sunday through Thursday 5:30 - 10:00 p.m.;
Friday and Saturday 5:30 - 11:00 p.m.
All major cards

Cibo's setting projects a comfortable warmth with its simple lines, pale wood, and warm earthy tones of chocolate, night blue, and sand. Its walls of eggshell and gilded copper are inlaid with shallow shelves holding potted plants and hand-painted Italian dishes. The big, well-spaced tables, comfortable burled walnut chairs, and casual, upscale atmosphere make it a popular choice with the local lunch crowd. In the evening, the atmosphere is more serene, and various dining nooks (including four cozy booths separated by wire mesh curtains) make the 125-seat dining room a bit cozier. The food is wonderful and dining here is made all the more pleasant by the absolute niceness of the staff.

The contemporary American menu shows a definite Tuscan affection in harmony with the restaurant's name, which means "food" in Italian. Setting a course for the pleasures to follow, the bread basket that greets you is wonderful. I particularly enjoyed the moist focaccia with big chunks of zucchini. The menu changes with the seasons. In winter, you'll find nice, warming starters like creamless butternut squash soup with blue cheese and toasted walnuts ($6.00), roasted lobster and corn chowder ($9.00), and potato and cheese ravioli with porcini mushroom broth ($8.00). In the summer, refreshing starters include cucumber gazpacho with cold poached shrimp and feta cheese ($8.00) and tuna tartare with black olives, crisp potatoes, and organic arugula ($9.00). Specialties of the house among mains: salmon with a ginger crust ($17.00) and braised lamb shank with couscous and roasted shallots ($17.00). Other good options include grilled New York strip steak with sautéed spinach, sweet potato gratin, and black olive essence ($21.00), seared veal chop, potato-mushroom pancake, and porcini jus ($22.00), double-cut smoked pork chop with whipped potatoes and roasted apple butter ($18.00), and braised rabbit with butternut squash gnocchi and sage-toasted chanterelles ($19.00). Good homemade pasta choices include fettuccine with lobster, peas, fresh tomato, and crispy prosciutto ($18.00), spaghetti with tomato sauce and crispy basil ($13.00), and pappardelle with braised chicken ragu and a lemon-garlic essence ($16.00). The delicious dessert bounty includes cheddar-crusted deep apple pie with caramel ice cream with apple chips ($8.00), pumpkin tart with ginger ice cream and ginger snaps ($7.00), and sugar-roasted fig with an almond Napoleon and Port essence ($7.00).

The Sunday prix fixe $19.97 brunch offers a choice of any beverage, an appetizer, and main dish. Starters are straight from the regular menu. And there's quite a nice selection of mains—morning delights like French toast with ricotta, walnuts, and maple syrup; scrambled eggs with bacon and a potato pancake; a three-egg omelette with asparagus, tomato, basil, and fontina; and poached eggs with toasted ciabatta, crispy prosciutto, and tomato sabayon.

There's also a popular Sunday supper with three courses for $24.95.

CINQUANTA ★   Italian
50 East 50th Street
(between Park and Madison Aves.)
212/759-5050
Lunch - Daily Noon - 3:00 p.m.
Dinner - Sunday through Thursday 3:00 - 11:30 p.m.;
Friday and Saturday 3:00 - Midnight
All major cards

Cinquanta features good Tuscan cuisine in a comfortable setting in a four-story brownstone. The pleasant dining rooms and nice service make for an enjoyable, if not exciting, dining experience.

Good starter choices would be the baby shrimp with white beans, red onions, rosemary, and virgin olive oil ($9.00), a warm salad of smoked salmon, rice, and chopped arugula ($8.00), and Florentine vegetable soup on toasted country bread ($8.00). There's an extensive choice of pastas, including ricotta gnocchi with mixed wild greens and spinach with a tomato and basil sauce ($15.00), linguine with manila clams ($16.00), risotto with scallops and fresh baby artichokes ($17.00), and a house specialty of "pinci di zia pina," a handmade pasta of arugula, scallions, garlic, and herbs with roasted garlic, zucchini, and broccoli rabe ($16.00). Pastas are available in half portions for $10.00. Other good choices include whole grilled red snapper ($23.00), monkfish sautéed in a white wine sauce ($19.00), breast of chicken sautéed with garlic, rosemary, and exotic mushrooms ($16.00), veal scaloppine with gorgonzola ($18.00), filet mignon with a purée of olives, red wine, and a touch of cream ($24.00), and T-bone steak Florentine-style ($26.00).

Good value prix fixe menus are offered daily. Prices vary with the menu.

DARBAR ★★   Indian
44 West 56th Street
(between Fifth Ave. and Ave. of the Americas)
212/265-1850
Lunch - Daily Noon - 2:45 p.m.
Dinner - Monday through Thursday 5:30 - 11:00 p.m.;
Friday and Saturday 5:30 - 11:30 p.m.; Sunday 5:30 - 10:00 p.m.
All major cards

The setting is lovely and authentic at this terrific Indian restaurant considered one of the best in town. Housed in a pretty duplex townhouse, its decor is elegant and stylish without being stuffy or intimidating. Exquisite tapestries and beautiful hammered brass hangings adorn the walls and a spiral staircase connects its two levels. The first level is the more romantic of the two, with some of its tables tucked intimately behind carved wooden screens, while the second level boasts tall elegant windows. But wherever you sit, this is a lovely place to sample really fine Indian cuisine.

You might start with a delicious fritter-type appetizer—thinly-sliced onions lightly fried in a flour batter ($8.75), vegetable samosas ($8.75), or shrimp lightly marinated in sour cream and herbs then batter-fried ($12.95). Favorites among the tandoori specialties: chicken darbari (boneless chicken marinated in yogurt, fresh garlic, and ground spices, then broiled in the tandoor) ($19.95) and small tender leg of lamb first marinated in fresh garlic, ginger, and special spices, then roasted in the tandoor and served with basmati rice ($23.95). Other specialties include lamb or beef cooked with fresh spinach, green coriander and fragrant herbs ($18.95), crab malabar (succulent pieces of crabmeat simmered in onions, tomatoes, and fennel seed, sprinkled with coconut) ($23.95), and a sensational lobster dish called malai khasa where the lobster is gently cooked in a coconut cream ($23.95). Tops among the vegetarian specialties are the bayngan bhurta (whole eggplants partially cooked on skewers in the tandoor, then chopped and mixed with tomatoes, onions, and spices and simmered gently) ($13.95) and a selection of garden fresh vegetables and cheese cooked in a spice-laced cream, then sprinkled with nuts ($13.95). The most popular desserts are the cardamom-flavored rice pudding with nuts ($6.50) and fig ice cream ($6.50).

DAWAT ★★   Indian
210 East 58th Street (between Second and Third Aves.)
212/355-7555
Lunch - Daily 11:30 a.m. - 2:45 p.m.
Dinner - Sunday through Thursday 5:30 - 10:45 p.m.;
Friday and Saturday 5:30 - 11:15 p.m.
All major cards

Decorated in shades of salmon and blue-green, with clusters of wooden folkloric figurines spotlighted on the walls, Dawat has a pleasant upscale ambience. Lighting is gentle, tables well-spaced for privacy, and a glass-encased tandoor dominates the backdrop. While generally regarded as the best Indian restaurant in the city, it has recently had its ups and downs (including a demotion to 1-star status from *The New York Times*). But lately, it seems to be hitting the mark more and more like days of old.

The guiding light behind the menu is Indian actress and cookbook author Madhur Jaffrey. Dishes run the gamut from Bombay street fare to robust home-style cooking to the most sophisticated favorites of the royal families. Starter standouts are the shrimp enlivened by garlic, mustard seeds, and curry leaves ($9.95) and curry leaf-flavored potato cakes served with a special red pepper chutney with almonds and mint ($5.95). The breads are fabulous, especially the onion and black pepper kulcha (a crisp, pizza-like bread from the tandoor oven, filled with caramelized onions and dusted with coarse black pepper) ($5.95) and the poori (deep-fried wholewheat puffed bread) ($3.95). Of the mains, winners include salmon smothered in a fresh coriander chutney and steamed in a banana leaf, served with basmati rice ($22.95), Cornish hen with green chilies ($16.95), and chicken tikka masala ($15.95). The terrific tandoor oven specialties include king-size shrimp marinated in mild spices ($21.95), chicken (whole $16.95, half $10.95), and boneless cubes of lamb marinated in yogurt, garlic, and ginger ($16.95). The vegetarian specialties are wonderful—fresh homemade cheese, grated and cooked with green peppers, tomatoes, and onions ($12.95), long green peppers stuffed with fennel-flavored potatoes ($12.95), and spicy potatoes flavored with whole and ground cumin seeds ($12.95). Dinner specials include a vegetarian thali with Ms. Jaffrey's selection of vegetables, split peas, rice, breads, chutneys, and relishes ($23.95), a low calorie combination of chicken or fish with assorted vegetables, salad, chutneys, relishes, and bread ($23.95), Dawat's Special (a soup, tandoori chicken, seekh kabab, fish tikka, lamb gosht, a vegetable, nan bread, and vegetable biryani) ($23.95). Desserts are nothing to get excited about unless caramelized grated carrots with pistachios and whipped cream ($4.95) tempts you. Otherwise, opt for the refreshing mango or coconut ice cream ($4.95).

Prix-fixe lunch specials for $12.95 and $13.95 are abundant, delicious bargains.

EAMONN DORAN ★   Irish/American
998 Second Avenue (between 52nd and 53d Sts.)
212/752-8088
Lunch - Daily 11:00 a.m. - 4:00 p.m.
Dinner - Daily 4:00 p.m. - 4:00 a.m.
All major cards

This must be one of the friendliest spots in town and the most obliging. Food is served until 4:00 a.m. every day of the year, including Christmas and Thanksgiving. It's an Irish pub gone upscale. The regulars are a varied lot from the United Nations, international rugby, and theater, to tourists from

194

around the world. The bar, with an extensive list of international beers, is pleasantly boisterous and convivial and you'll hear more than a few brogues. The dining room in back is a more sedate retreat but offers the same pub-like warmth and some nice continental dishes.

Good starters include oysters Rockefeller ($10.95), crab-stuffed mushrooms ($5.95), and Irish smoked salmon ($10.95). Two of the specialties among the mains have been featured on *Live with Regis & Kathie Lee*—Gaeltach chicken (half a roast chicken with ham and stuffing) ($14.95) and braised lamb stew ($13.95). Other good choices include grilled Norwegian salmon with a dijon sauce ($16.95), roasted rack of lamb with rosemary ($21.95), and chateaubriand for two ($40.95). All mains are served with fresh vegetables and a choice of potato or rice. Several pasta dishes make nice choices, too—penne with shrimp and bacon ($12.95) and fettuccine with chicken and peas in a pink Vodka cream sauce ($11.95). The fact that this is an Irish pub hasn't been lost altogether in the continental slant of the kitchen. There's also steak and kidney pie ($12.95), shepherd's pie ($10.95), bangers and mash ($9.95), and fish and chips ($11.95).

A three-course prix fixe menu is offered all evening for $26.50. And, yes, it does include Irish Coffee.

8½ ★★   Italian/Colombian
208 East 52nd Street (off Third Ave.)
212/759-7373
Lunch - Monday through Friday Noon - 3:00 p.m.
Dinner - Daily 5:00 - 10:00 p.m.
All major cards

With its name inspired by the Academy Award-winning Fellini film, 8½ is endearingly eclectic and full of whimsical charm. Graceful brick arches, mirrors, and amusing paintings highlight the decor. Listed in *The Best Places to Kiss in and Around New York City*, its Southern Italian menu even seems couple-oriented with its claim that every appetizer, pasta or main course serves two. In fact, some of the pasta dishes would actually accommodate a third wheel.

The good homestyle Italian offerings emphasize freshness and abundance. Nice starters include stuffed eggplant ($12.50), mozzarella and tomato salad ($12.50), stuffed mushrooms ($11.00), and grilled vegetables ($14.50). When ordering pasta, you choose from among cappellini, linguine, and penne, then also choose from a selection of sauces that includes white or red clam ($18.00), primavera ($14.50), amatriciana ($15.50), garlic and oil ($15.00), meat sauce ($17.50), seafood ($24.50), and marinara ($12.50). Mains also entice with choices such as a juicy, whole roasted chicken with roasted potatoes, onions, tomatoes, and herbs ($24.50), a recipe of the chef's mother. Other good options include veal Milanese ($20.50), chicken cacciatore ($24.95), and pork chops with peppers ($20.50). There's also a menu of Colombian specialties such as yucca fritters filled with cheese ($5.95), three beef empanadas ($5.95), shrimp and scallops marinated in lime ($9.95), rice and chicken casserole ($13.50), jumbo Pacific shrimp sautéed with a touch of tomatoes, bread crumbs, garlic, and herbs, served on a garland of rice ($22.50), and flank steak marinated and oven-roasted, served with potatoes covered with onions, scallions, and melted cheese ($16.95). For dessert, try the pineapple flan ($5.95) or the three-fruit mousse cake ($5.95).

FASHION CAFE ★   Eclectic
51 Rockefeller Plaza
(on 51st St. between Fifth and Sixth Aves.)
212/765-3131
Daily 11:00 a.m. - 1:00 a.m.
All major cards

Supermodels Claudia Schiffer, Elle MacPherson, Naomi Campbell, and Christy Turlington are part of the ownership of this theme-park of fashion. Designed to give the effect of walking through the lens of a camera, the cafe's central area features the latest in audio-visual systems. Three rooms off this studio-like area are each designed to look like one of the fashion capitals of the world—New York, Paris, or Milan. Fashion designers from around the world are represented in the memorabilia on display which includes the Armani suit worn by Sean Connery in the film *The Untouchables*, a Versace red plastic suit worn by Elton John, two Givenchy dresses worn by Audrey Hepburn in *Breakfast at Tiffany's*, and a Thierry Mugler red robot outfit worn by Iman. There's more, of course, much more. But don't look to find the high fashion crowd here; you're much more likely to find a sea of tourists and a high noise level. But, along with the eye-catching video graphics and fashion shows, it is possible to eat fairly well here, as long as you keep your expectations at a reasonable level.

The same menu is served all day and is designed to suit just about any mood or ethnic fancy. Under appetizers, you'll find things like Thai spring rolls served with a spicy and sweet dipping sauce ($5.95), smoked chicken quesadillas ($7.95), New England clam chowder served San Francisco-style in sourdough bread ($4.95), and Elle's shrimp on the barbe' with julienne vegetables and a tomato-corn salsa ($8.95). Of the salads, the cobb ($10.95) is the clear winner. Sandwiches come with fries, garden walnut slaw, and a pickle. The selection includes a good roast chicken club ($9.95) and a veggie burger, as well as the beefy variety (each $7.95). The pizzas are good and come in a variety of guises, including Southwestern and Hawaiian ($9.95 to $11.95). Mains are served with potatoes and vegetables and include Claudia's New York strip steak ($15.95) and Naomi's fish and chips ($9.95). When it comes to dessert, think fruit and you'll end up with the cafe's best offerings—the poached pears with vanilla ice cream and raspberry sauce ($4.95) and apple pancakes served warm with caramel sauce and cinnamon ice cream ($5.95).

FELIDIA RISTORANTE ★★★   Italian
243 East 58th Street
(between Second and Third Aves.)
212/758-1479
Lunch - Monday through Friday Noon - 3:00 p.m.
Dinner - Monday through Saturday 5:00 - 11:30 p.m.
All major cards

In the sea of terrific Italian restaurants on the East Side, Felidia still manages to shine. Namesake owners, Felice and Lidia Bastianich, celebrate the cuisine of their homeland—a region in Northeastern Italy called Istria—in a handsome townhouse setting. Its attractively rustic dining rooms are set on two levels. The balcony level with skylights and lush greenery is the nicest of the two. But whitewashed walls, terra-cotta floors, and pretty flower arrangements create a cozy look throughout the candlelit rooms. And Felidia's wine cellar has a fame of its own, regarded as one of the finest in the country.

A good way to start a meal here is with the calamari with green beans and polenta ($12.00), breast of veal stuffed with seasonal vegetables ($10.00), warm mozzarella and artichokes with tomato purée ($12.00), grilled polenta with warm octopus salad and red onions ($10.00), or the delicious hearty seasonal vegetable soup served with parmesan toast ($9.00). The homemade pastas are both delicious and inventive—among them, quill-shaped pasta with broccoli and homemade sausage ($18.00), ravioli stuffed with porcini, shiitake, and oyster mushrooms in a light mushroom sauce ($20.00), taglioni in a zesty tomato, basil, and hot pepper sauce ($16.00), and diamond-shaped pasta in a light seafood sauce of shrimp, scallops, and clams ($22.00). Of the dry pastas, the spaghetti with lamb ragu and artichokes ($18.00) is a terrific choice. If you favor risotto, there's a good one with assorted mushrooms ($18.00). When it comes to the main, the kitchen shows off with the likes of lobster and skate in a spicy sauce garnished with polenta ($29.00), seared salmon with a chive-mustard sauce and asparagus ($27.00), a butterflied and breaded veal chop pan-fried with mozzarella and tomato ($28.00), herb-infused seared breast of chicken with garden greens, cherry tomatoes, and basil dressing ($25.00), roasted rosemary-infused rack of lamb ($29.00), and a superb osso bucco with vegetable barley risotto ($26.00). For a refreshing finale, try the cooked pear stuffed with pistachio in a mixed berry sauce ($8.00). Even better is the warm pear tart with chestnut ice cream ($8.00).

FIFTY-SEVEN FIFTY-SEVEN ★★★   American
Four Seasons Hotel
57 East 57th Street (between Madison and Park Aves.)
212/758-5757
Lunch - Monday through Friday 11:30 a.m. - 2:00 p.m.
Brunch - Saturday and Sunday 11:00 a.m. - 2:00 p.m.
Dinner - Daily 6:00 - 10:30 p.m.
All major cards

Fifty-Seven Fifty-Seven—simply named for its address—has the endearing quality of being both luxurious and completely unstuffy. The postmodern decor by I. M. Pei, which has received the James Beard Foundation award for best restaurant design in the United States, features soaring 22-foot high ceilings, three tall scagliola marble-like wall panels, bronze chandeliers, Dakota Jackson chairs, and cherrywood tables. Yet, for all its sophistication, the decor has a quiet and rather minimalist look that allows the creations that appear on your plate to be the real star attractions here.

Executive chef Susan Weaver brings to the menu innovative contemporary American cuisine with regional and Mediterranean influences. She also puts her own lively stamp on alternative cuisine with reduced calories, cholesterol, sodium, and fat. Recent pleasures on the seasonal menu have included starters such as Maryland crab cake, farmer's greens, and roast pepper aïoli ($17.00), pomegranate-glazed duck salad with Israeli couscous and pear barbecue sauce ($16.00), and lobster Caesar salad ($19.00). Flavorful light openers like creamless tomato soup with chives and oven-roasted yellow tomatoes ($10.00) and marinated swordfish and asparagus with a sour cherry and citrus vinaigrette ($17.00) are delicious examples of Ms. Weaver's flair at alternative cuisine. And for a light main, the grilled swordfish with warm potato salad, horseradish mustard and citrus juices, and baby beet greens ($27.00) is a winner. Other good mains include grilled shrimp Manhattan-style with clam chowder and rosemary bagel chips ($26.00), open chicken ravioli with white beans, roast bell peppers, asparagus, and aged gouda ($24.00), herb-roasted rack of lamb with braised lamb and red wine potato pie, chanterelles, and green beans ($31.00), and char-grilled New York steak with sautéed spinach and rosemary cream potato pot pie ($30.00). A vegetarian sampling tray offers five varied vegetable dishes for $25.00. Highlights among desserts for chocolate lovers ($10.00) include a wonderful sticky chocolate cake with cashew caramel sauce and banana ice cream, double-chocolate cake with white chocolate fudge ice cream, and chocolate crème brûlée with pine nut pistachio biscotti. Other nice choices include spiced pumpkin layer cake with lemon-poppy seed ice cream and crumble pie with pear, quince, and apple with candied vanilla and blueberry sauce.

The weekend brunch menu is also inviting with offerings like lemon ricotta hot cakes with applewood-smoked bacon ($19.00), French toast with brandied bananas and applewood-smoked bacon ($19.00), two eggs any style with roasted potatoes, tomatoes, asparagus, and breakfast meats ($17.00), egg white frittata with tomato, herbs, and spinach ($17.00), and smoked salmon with a bagel, tomato, red onion, and dilled quail eggs ($20.00).

A pre-theater menu is offered from 6:00 to 7:00 p.m. with three courses for $42.00. There are four choices in each category of items from the regular menu. There is also a different three-course prix fixe offered every day (available all evening) for $45.00.

THE FOUR SEASONS ★★★★   American
99 East 52nd Street
(between Park and Lexington Aves.)
212/754-9494
Lunch - Monday through Friday Noon - 2:15 p.m.
Dinner - Monday through Friday 5:00 - 9:30 p.m.;
Saturday 5:00 - 11:15 p.m.
All major cards

The Four Seasons surrounds you with luxury. In 1990 it was designated an architectural landmark, making it the first Manhattan restaurant to receive such status. The interior's quintessential modernism style of less-is-more (created by Philip Johnson, the father of American architecture) sets a quiet backdrop for a lavish art collection which includes the world's largest Picasso tapestry and a massive James Rosenquist painting. Twenty-foot window walls curtained by shimmering, dancing chain metal creates another dramatic visual effect.

Two distinctively different dining rooms and dining experiences actually comprise the restaurant. The Grill Room has long been a handsome arena for the power lunch bunch. Influential personalities like Henry Kissinger, financial movers and shakers, and the publishing world's top suits and hot properties are regulars here. (Yet, it is told, Jackie O's entrance once brought all conversation to a halt.) While the Grill Room has a wood-panelled masculine glamour, the Pool Room is pure romance. Some of the best tables in town are those next to its fourteen-foot square white marble reflecting pool. Four towering illuminated trees, one at each corner, add to the magic of the room.

The menus in both rooms change with the seasons. The summer menu's list of starters includes an excellent tuna carpaccio with ginger and coriander ($17.00) and delicious crab salad with baby artichokes and black truffles ($18.50). Other notable choices include prosciutto with figs ($16.50), a platter of littlenecks or cherrystones ($13.00), a selection of oysters ($15.00), chanterelle ravioli with sage ($17.50), sautéed foie gras with peaches ($25.00), and chilled sweet pea, corn, and lobster soup ($11.50). Among the beautifully prepared mains are medallions of veal with chanterelles and vegetable fettuccine ($36.50), crab cakes with mustard sauce ($37.50), Maine lobster (broiled, poached or steamed) ($48.00), Dover sole ($45.00), grilled lamb chops with string beans ($37.00), aged prime skillet steak with smothered onions ($40.00), and steamed vegetables with wild rice and herb oil ($30.00). Ruth Reichl, *The New York Times'* food critic, says the most perfect duck in the city is served here ($79.00 for two). Also for two—and delicious—is roast rack of lamb with chanterelles and string beans ($85.00) and chateaubriand ($90.00). Outstanding accompaniments are the roesti potatoes ($7.00) and corn and jalapeño cakes ($7.50). Temptations on the dessert cart include blackberry shortcake with Vodka orange sauce, white chocolate and macadamia tart, and (a longtime favorite) chocolate velvet cake (each $8.50). Or you might plan ahead and order one of the wonderful soufflés—raspberry, apricot, or praline ($9.50)—at the beginning of your meal.

While dining here is an exceptional experience, it is also a very pricey one. But, happily, it is possible to do so at a relative bargain. **Both the Pool Room and the Grill Room offer a three-course prix fixe until 6:15 p.m. for $43.50.**

FRESCO RESTAURANT ★★   Italian
34 East 52nd Street
(between Park and Madison Aves.)
212/935-3434
Lunch - Monday through Friday 11:30 a.m. - 3:00 p.m.
Dinner - Monday through Saturday 5:30 - 11:00 p.m.
All major cards

Pale shades of green and yellow, colorful paintings, and pretty floral displays enliven this warm and friendly family-owned Tuscan restaurant. Once discovered, it's the kind of place people return to because of the wonderful food, abundant portions, and the genuinely warm welcome. A restaurant without attitude or pretensions, Fresco brims with its own brand of style and grace.

The sensational thin crust pizzas are winning openers ($13.00). Another good appetizer for the table is the cornmeal-dusted calamari and battered artichokes fried and served with a duo of sauces ($14.00). Other good starters include semolina gnocchi wedges baked with parmesan and topped with a hearty sausage ragu ($10.00), a grilled portobello mushroom stuffed with garden tomatoes, fontina cheese, and basil pesto ($9.00), and a salad of frisée, endive, and shaved fennel in a light citrus vinaigrette with toasted almonds and orange segments ($9.00). The pastas are outstanding. An all-time favorite is the penne baked with pancetta, parmesan, and cream ($17.00). Other good choices include rigatoni with broccoli and grilled chicken ($18.00), spaghetti with veal and chicken Bolognese ($18.00), bucatini with crab sauce ($19.00), and penne with a sauce of garden tomatoes, garlic, basil, and roasted eggplant, finished with fresh mozzarella ($17.00). There's also a homemade ravioli of the day ($17.00). Of the mains, good choices include a double-cut pork chop marinated with rosemary and a hint of molasses, then grilled and served with a roasted onion stuffed with mashed potatoes, pancetta, and fontina cheese ($26.00), roast loin of veal served with a lemon-scented spaghetti pie, roasted snap peas, summer squash, and baby carrots ($26.00), grilled double breast of chicken served with a terrific grilled bread salad and roasted summer vegetables ($24.00), beef brisket braised with carrots, onions, wine, and a hint of tomato, served with creamy polenta and red cabbage ($22.00), grilled center cut of tuna with tomato puttanesca salsa on a nest of fried onions ($26.00), and grilled filet of halibut served on a bed of crispy potatoes with a light pesto sauce with asparagus and pan-seared oyster mushrooms ($27.00). Look for the daily desserts.

GIOVANNI RISTORANTE ★★   Italian
47 West 55th Street (between Fifth and Sixth Aves.)
212/262-2828
Lunch - Daily Noon - 4:00 p.m.
Dinner - Daily 4:00 - 11:00 p.m.
All major cards

With a highly-stylized and sophisticated interior, Giovanni has several distinct personalities. Each forms a nice backdrop for the authentic, rustic cooking inspired by the cuisine of the northeastern most regions of Italy. For an alfresco mood, there's the Pavilion Room, featuring trompe l'oeil paintings that create the illusion of a canopy overhead and hint at the Italian countryside in the distance. Then there's the Card Room, where playful murals of cards from Italy's oldest games adorn the walls, and the European-styled Club Room, where cigar enthusiasts can relax with a glass of Port and a smoke.

The food is quite good and the menu offers generous choice. To start, good options include smoked salmon with a potato pancake and horseradish-crème fraîche ($9.75), grilled scallops on a bed of mesclun greens ($11.75), grilled polenta with portobello mushrooms and a touch of balsamic vinegar ($9.00), and homemade mozzarella rolled with prosciutto and slow-roasted tomatoes ($9.75). The delicious homemade pasta specialties include ravioli filled with ricotta and spinach with butter and fresh sage ($12.75), gnocchi with a wild mushroom sauce ($13.75), fettuccine Bolognese ($13.50), and risotto with mascarpone cheese and spinach ($18.00). (Appetizer portions of pasta dishes are available for $9.75.) Notable among mains are the breast of chicken sautéed with vegetables and served with soft polenta ($16.00), grilled veal chop with mashed potatoes ($26.00), grilled sirloin served with herbed potato chips and rucola salad ($24.00), and horseradish-encrusted sea bass with mashed potatoes and a chive sauce ($19.75).

IL VAGABONDO ★   Italian
351 East 62nd Street (between First and Second Aves.)
212/832-9221
Lunch - Monday through Friday Noon - 3:00 p.m.
Dinner - Monday through Saturday 5:30 p.m. - Midnight;
Sunday 5:30 - 11:00 p.m.
All major cards

This comfortable trattoria features the city's only indoor boccie court. It has a clamorous, merry atmosphere and no one seems to mind that the decor is, well, no decor at all. The game of boccie—somewhat like lawn bowling—has been a favorite Italian sport since the days of the Roman Empire. You can try your hand at it here or just watch the practiced neighborhood regulars.

The menu has the same straightforward no-frills approach as the decor. Critics may scoff at the food, but the robust saucy pastas and veal dishes can be quite good. Meat entrées come with either a side of pasta or a vegetable or salad. Good pasta choices include a rich homemade gnocchi ($10.25), lasagna ($10.25), linguine with clam sauce ($12.00), and spaghetti and meat balls ($10.25). Other good choices are the chicken parmigiana ($13.50), veal piccata ($14.50), roast pork ($14.00), and veal roast ($14.50).

JIMMY SUNG'S ★★   Chinese
219 East 44th Street (between Second and Third Aves.)
212/682-5678
Lunch - Daily Noon - 3:30 p.m.
Dinner - Daily 5:00 - 10:30 p.m.
All major cards

Elegant Chinese fare is served in suitably lavish surroundings at this still largely undiscovered restaurant. A huge green and gold awning flanked by two gold Buddha statues greet you outside. Inside, the lavish decor has a festive feel and host Jimmy Sung's welcome is warm. You immediately sense you are about to have a pleasant dining experience, and I don't think you'll be disappointed. The roomy tables are beautifully set and well-spaced for privacy. Brocade chairs, sculpted arches, cherrywood panelling, and rich carpeting lend a plush ambience. Ornate brass peacock-fountain chandeliers cast a soft glow and piano music adds another mellow note.

The lengthy menu offers the traditional cooking from several regions of China. There's the hot and spicy flavors of Hunan cooking and the Canton stir-fry specialties that are the essence of Chinese cooking. The menu also encompasses inventive Shanghai dishes, as well as Manchurian cuisine which combines Chinese, Japanese, Korean, and Russian flavors.

Popular choices among starters include pan-fried dumplings ($6.75), sweet and pungent baby ribs ($6.95), crispy shrimp patties ($6.95), pan-fried scallion pancakes ($5.25), shredded duck salad ($8.25), and cold noodles with sesame sauce ($6.50). House specialties among mains include prawns with fresh asparagus ($13.95), fresh scallops with sesame sauce served with vegetables on a sizzling platter ($16.25), filet of sole, lightly breaded and cooked with a special sweet and sour sauce (market price), Peking duck served in Peking pancakes with scallion brushes and Hoisin sauce ($32.00), and assorted seafood in a bird nest ($17.50). Other good mains include cashew chicken ($12.50), moo shu chicken with pancakes ($12.50), sliced duck with Peking sauce ($13.25), beef with oyster sauce ($12.95), shredded pork with garlic sauce ($12.50), lamb with scallions ($13.95), prawns with a hot spicy ginger sauce ($15.95), and salt-baked fresh cuttlefish with chili ($13.95). Vegetarian choices include a delicious vegetable pie with house pancakes ($17.95) and four kinds of braised vegetables in a savory sauce ($13.50).

A six-course prix fixe is available nightly for $30.00.

LA CARAVELLE ★★★   French
33 West 55th Street (between Fifth and Sixth Aves.)
212/586-4252
Lunch - Monday through Friday Noon - 2:30 p.m.
Dinner - Monday through Saturday 5:30 - 10:00 p.m.
All major cards

Old-fashioned in the nicest sense, La Caravelle's setting is quietly elegant and its service smooth and formal. It has been around since 1960 when it captured the attention and affection of the Kennedys (who managed to steal its chef for the White House), giving it instant glamour and many years of fame as a place to see and be seen. Later, it went through a period of decline when it was considered a bit too stuffy and its cuisine too rich and heavy for today's more health-aware diners. But current owners Andre and Rita Jammet have rejuvenated it with a softer look and lighter menu. The lovely Jean Pagès postwar murals of Parisian park scenes and street life have been beautifully restored. And peach shantung banquettes, shaded lamps, and festive flower arrangements give the room a fresh look.

While main courses are lighter than before, the courtly tableside carving and elegant service are holdovers from earlier days. The food now is a wonderful blend of classic and modern French with a few Asian accents. **The dinner menu is a three-course prix fixe for $62.00.** Choices among starters include: tartare of yellowfin tuna with avocado pear and lime vinaigrette; wild mushroom fricassée in puff pastry; oysters and clams of the day; and mussel cream soup with saffron. For the main: filet of bass steamed in lemon verbena with a vegetable compote; calico scallops and shrimp in thin pasta layers; truffled pike quenelles in a lobster sauce; filet of beef in a red wine sauce;

venison in a grand veneur sauce; and rack of lamb for two (+$12.00). There's always a nice assortment of desserts to choose from, but the house specialties are the divine soufflés (+$5.50). **A five-course tasting menu is also available for $75.00; a larger tasting menu is $90.00, and at lunch there's a three-course prix fixe for $36.00.**

You can capture the spirit and sample the cuisine of this wonderful classic at a real bargain with the pre-theater menu which applies for orders taken by 6:30 p.m. It includes three courses with many choices in each category for $40.00. For example, you might start with mixed greens with a shallot dressing, oysters and clams of the day, crispy rolls of minced duck with curry, or an assortment of salads and terrines. Selections from the list of mains include grilled smoked salmon, roasted chicken with a light cream Champagne sauce, crispy duck with cranberries, veal kidney with a dijon mustard sauce, and beef hanger steak with a shallot sauce. Your dessert choice might be crème brûlée with berries, a chocolate surprise, or one of the soufflés (+$6.00).

LA CÔTE BASQUE ★★★★   French
60 West 55th Street (between Fifth and Sixth Aves.)
212/688-6525
Lunch - Daily Noon - 2:30 p.m.
Dinner - Daily 6:00 - 10:00 p.m.
All major cards

Since opening in 1979, La Côte Basque has been regarded as one of New York's most enchanting restaurants. Then suddenly in 1995, chef/owner Jean-Jacques Rachou discovered his landlord was not renewing his lease. Fortunately, he was able to relocate his legendary restaurant—with all of the elements that made its ambience special—just one block west to the space that had housed La Scala. The dark wooden cross beams, the bar, the old-fashioned table lamps, and even the revolving door are the same. And, most important, the signature murals of the Basque coast and countryside and charming faux flung-open windows (giving diners the impression of overlooking a bustling harbor) have been magically transported to the new quarters. Now, La Côte Basque seems better than ever and continues to provide the kind of dining experience that memories are made of. Long after you've dined here, the feel of the charming dining room, the extravagant food, and the generous hospitality play on your mind. And when the occasion calls for something special, chances are you'll think of it once again.

While the warm ambience and flawless service have not changed, the classic French cuisine has been updated to reflect changing tastes. **The dinner menu is a three-course prix fixe for $59.00 ($33.00 at lunch).** First course choices include: house oak-smoked salmon with celery and cucumber salad; jumbo asparagus with truffle oil and parmesan; and grilled vegetables with goat cheese and tomato in a ginger sauce. Among mains, the house specialty is the cassoulet. Other superb choices include: black bass filet in a crust of potato with red wine sauce and braised leeks; grilled chicken breast with artichokes, onions, mushrooms, potatoes, and tomatoes; roasted duckling with honey, Grand Marnier, and a black cherry sauce; filet mignon with potato, morel sauce, and shallots; roast rack of lamb with braised potatoes and Boston lettuce; and venison steak with vegetables. And to end on a dazzling note, opt for the chocolate cube filled with a sensational expresso mascarpone on double-chocolate sorbet, or a classic like crème brûlée or chocolate soufflé. But the sweet part of the evening doesn't end with dessert. Delicious cookies and candied fruits next appear and then a box of handmade chocolates. Be mindful when dining here that it may very well spoil you for other places.

LA GRENOUILLE ★★★★   French
3 East 52nd Street (between Fifth and Madison Aves.)
212/752-1495
Lunch - Tuesday through Saturday Noon - 2:30 p.m.
Dinner - Tuesday through Saturday 5:45 - 11:30 p.m.
All major cards

Flower-filled and so romantic, La Grenouille has the grand, elegant look of an earlier era. Red velvet banquettes, gold-leaf wall sconces, and charming little silk-shaded lamps on elegantly-set tables combine with breathtaking floral displays to present one of the prettiest pictures in town.

Daniel Orr and Mark Matyas, co-executive chefs, form a perfect union in producing what many consider to be Manhattan's best French food. That they are both American comes as a surprise to many.

The seductive atmosphere and superb classic French cuisine of La Grenouille has long attracted the well-heeled and celebrity crowd of regulars you will see at the power room at the front. But dining on the exquisite fare created by Orr and Matyas is a splurge for most of us. Expect a big bill. **Dinner is prix fixe $77.00.** At that price, dining here is no time to start counting calories, so indulge in the exquisite lobster ravioli or rich lobster bisque to start. Other sumptuous selections include: a fricassée of vegetables;

an assortment of hors d'oeuvres which could include grilled portobellos, lentils with walnuts, curried wild rice, poached salmon, shrimp, and beets with fennel; and a classic French split pea soup served with cheese twists. For the main: chicken in an old-fashioned Champagne sauce; filet of beef in a heady Armagnac sauce; grilled sole in a mustard sauce; or the signature dish of frogs' legs in a sauce of butter, tomatoes, and garlic (+$7.50). Desserts are rich tricks as well; the Grand Marnier soufflé is legendary.

The three-course $43.00 prix fixe lunch offers a less extravagant opportunity to sample the fare and ambience of this timeless restaurant.

LA MANGEOIRE ★★   French
1008 Second Avenue (between 53rd and 54th Sts.)
212/759-7086
Lunch - Monday through Friday Noon - 2:30 p.m.
Dinner - Daily 5:30 - 10:30 p.m.
(closed on Sundays during July and August)
All major cards

Rich in atmosphere, La Mangeoire captures all the warmth of the sunny side of France. With straw hanging from the ceiling, dried flower arrangements scattered amidst abundant fresh floral displays, colorful pottery decorating the small rooms, and beautiful soft paintings against Mediterranean blue and stucco walls, it has a rustic country French ambience that is thoroughly inviting.

The Southern French food is wonderfully satisfying. House specialties among starters include a Mediterranean-style fish soup with garlic croutons ($8.50), caramelized onion tart ($7.50), and a terrific beef daube and spinach ravioli with tomato, basil, and parmesan ($9.00). Of the main courses, house specialties are the bouillabaisse-style roasted monkfish ($20.00) and the provençale-style rabbit with garlic mashed potatoes ($22.50). Other winners include herb-grilled shrimp with mint tabbouleh ($25.00), veal stew with tomatoes and onion and niçoise gnocchi ($19.50), roasted rack of lamb with kidney beans and sage juice ($26.00), Black Angus sirloin steak and potato cake ($26.00), and breast of chicken with a purée of wild mushroom filling ($18.00).

A three-course pre-theater menu is offered until 6:45 p.m. for $19.97 and a three-course prix fixe menu for $25.00 is offered all evening. And there's a "Flavors of the Côte d'Azur" five-course tasting meal of regional dishes selected by the chef for $44.00—a nice way to sample the considerable talents of Patrick Bruot.

LA RESERVE ★★★   French
4 West 49th Street
(between Fifth and Sixth Aves.)
212/247-2993
Lunch - Monday through Friday Noon - 3:00 p.m.
Dinner - Monday through Saturday 5:30 - 11:00 p.m.
All major cards

Reminiscent of the well-mannered genteel atmosphere of another era, La Reserve's ambience is one of quiet elegance. Its dining rooms are picture-perfect with beautiful Venetian chandeliers, high ceilings, mirrors, soft peach fabric banquettes, and wall-to-wall murals of a wildlife reserve. It is indeed romantic and tranquil, with service that is polished and rather formal. Despite its hushed atmosphere and serious service, it has a cozy and comfortable feel, and is the kind of place you immediately think of for a celebratory evening.

The classical French cuisine is unfailingly special. **The three-course prix fixe is $54.00.** It features starter temptations like grilled quail salad with green peppercorn vinaigrette, cream of lobster soup with lobster dumplings, smoked duck breast salad with beets and goat cheese, scallops and salmon with dill, and duck terrine with mixed nuts. The superb mains include filet of grilled red snapper with couscous, filet of bass in coriander jus, lobster and scallops in a sauce of exotic fruits and spices, veal medallions with rosemary, saddle of rabbit with roasted garlic, grilled chicken with herbs, and aged sirloin in a red wine sauce. The groaning dessert cart carries an astonishing assortment of goodies. Alternatively, you might order one of the fabulous soufflés.

A pre-theatre menu is offered from 5:30 to 6:45 p.m. with three courses for $39.50.

LE COLONIAL ★★★   French Vietnamese
149 East 57th Street
(between Lexington and Third Aves.)
212/752-0808
Lunch - Monday through Friday Noon - 2:00 p.m.
Dinner - Sunday through Thursday 5:30 - 11:30 p.m.;
Friday and Saturday 5:30 - Midnight
All major cards

Designed to evoke the bygone days of French colonial Southeast Asia, Le Colonial's seductive setting includes lazy ceiling fans, fringed lamps, exotic potted palms, black rattan chairs, and walls graced with grainy period photographs. While outrageously chic, it manages to project an air of friendliness. A lovely lounge upstairs has pretty Oriental rugs, rattan sofas, low tables, and a sultry "play-it-again-Sam" atmosphere.

The menu is the creation of noted author/chef Nicole Routhier, who has published two award-winning books on Vietnamese cuisine. The dishes here are lighter and more subtly seasoned than in many Vietnamese restaurants, the food is served family style, and it's all so enjoyable—one of my favorite places to dine in Manhattan.

First course specialties of the house are the Vietnamese spring rolls made with shrimp, pork, and mushrooms ($6.50) and soft salad rolls with shrimp, lettuce, bean sprouts, rice and aromatic herbs in rice paper, served with a peanut dipping sauce ($6.50). Another popular way to start a meal here is with the hearty oxtail soup with rice noodles and beef tenderloin ($5.00). Also good are the crispy fried vegetable spring rolls ($6.50), grilled shrimp wrapped around sugar cane with angel hair noodles, lettuce, mint, and peanut sauce ($8.00), and the Colonial salad, a refreshing mix of greens, pineapple, cucumber, bean sprouts, and herbs with a tamarind vinaigrette ($6.50). House specialties among mains are grilled beef brochette with five spices over angel hair noodles ($15.00) and oven-roasted chicken with lemongrass and lime dipping sauce ($14.50). Another favorite is the ginger-marinated roast duck with tamarind dipping sauce ($16.00). Notable seafood choices include filet of catfish simmered in a clay pot with fresh chili and black pepper ($16.00) and sautéed jumbo shrimp with eggplant in a curried coconut sauce ($17.00). The caramelized lemon tart ($6.50) is a nice finish.

A $24.00 pre-theatre dinner menu is offered between 5:30 and 7:00 p.m. It includes three courses, plus coffee or tea.

LE PÉRIGORD ★★★   French
405 East 52nd Street (First Ave.)
212/755-6244
Lunch - Monday through Friday Noon - 3:00 p.m.
Dinner - Daily 5:00 - 10:30 p.m.
All major cards

For years, Le Périgord has been one of the most popular of Manhattan's big-name French restaurants. The first time I went there, I had been passing by and stopped in to make a reservation. Having scanned a number of reviews that read like valentines, my expectation was to be dazzled the moment I stepped inside. But as I stood at the front, looking around, I wondered what all the shouting was about. While the flower arrangements were pretty and the display of appetizers near the entrance was colorful and enticing, the ceilings were low and the room seemed rather bland. But when you dine here the perspective is altogether different, as the extravagance of the food and the warmth of the service bring life to the sedate room.

For over a dozen years, Antoine Bouterin had performed the culinary wizardry that won Le Périgord three or more stars on a regular basis. Now that he's opened his own restaurant (Bouterin) on East 59th Street, Pascal Coudouy (formerly of Gascogne) has taken over the kitchen. He has added a provincial touch to the traditional French fare this old-timer is known for. And dining here is still a special treat. **The dinner menu is a three-course prix fixe for $52.00 ($32.00 at lunch).** To start, you might sample an assortment from the cold buffet. Other good options include crab cake with salad and saffron mayonnaise; vegetable tart with goat cheese; and lobster bisque. For the main, you can't go wrong with choices like salmon in a potato crust with a red wine sauce; sautéed red snapper with leeks in a peppercorn sauce; rack of lamb with olives and rosemary, served with a gratin of potatoes with goat cheese (+$4.00); roasted rabbit with peas and potatoes; roast duck with seasonal fruits; and country-style beef stew. Tempting choices abound for dessert, but the soufflés (+$5.00)—chocolate, Grand Marnier, and Armagnac—are really special.

Theatergoers who reserve in advance for pre-theater dining and, of course, leave by 8:00 p.m. receive a 20 percent discount (on drinks and wine as well as the meal).

LES SANS CULOTTES ★   French
1085 Second Avenue (at 57th St.)
212/838-6660
Lunch - Daily Noon to 3:00 p.m.
Dinner - Daily 5:00 - Midnight
All major cards

All decked out in red, white, and blue, this sprightly bistro (at each of its three locations) has a French Revolution decor and a thoroughly cheerful air about it. Chances are good you'll find it easy on the spirit and good for a hearty, unpretentious bistro meal. You will definitely leave stuffed and amazed at how little you've spent in the process.

210

The complete dinner offer at $19.95 starts you off with a bountiful basket of whole vegetables, a rack of sausages to hack off to your heart's content, rolls, and a crock of pâté. Main choices are bistro standbys like grilled salmon, crisp duck with an orange sauce, chicken with a tarragon sauce, grilled shell steak, and baby rack of lamb with a garlic sauce. Chocolate mousse, ice cream with chestnuts, or crème brûlée might be your dessert choice. If you don't want the complete dinner, other main choices to consider include veal piccata ($11.95), coq au vin ($11.95), sea scallops provençale ($13.95), and minute steak with shallots ($15.95). While the food may not be memorable, it's hard not to like a place that treats you so generously and has such a merry personality.

LESPINASSE ★★★★   French
St. Regis Hotel
2 East 55th Street (at Fifth Avenue)
212/339-6719
Lunch - Monday through Saturday Noon - 2:00 p.m.
Dinner - Monday through Saturday 6:00 - 10:00 p.m.
All major cards

Named after an 18th Century French literary patron, Lespinasse is a study in monochromatic elegance. A beautiful Waterford chandelier, soaring ceilings, arched alcoves, gilded moldings, and lush paintings combine to create a look of serene grandeur. Widely-spaced tables are luxuriously set, elegant armchairs are oversized, and wonderful floral displays add a burst of color to the almost too sedate room.

While the quiet opulence may lack pizazz, the food has it in abundance. Here East meets West in a dynamic ethno-fusion cuisine. Acclaimed chef Gray Kunz, a Singapore-born Swiss who trained in Switzerland under Freddy Giradet, was once a chef at the Regent Hotel in Hong Kong. His affection for that cuisine is evident in his style of cooking. His provocative Asian-accented French creations are about as good as it gets. *Wine Spectator*, in March 1995, called Lespinasse one of the top three restaurants in America, and in 1996 *Gourmet* magazine named it the best restaurant in New York City.

The menu is both seasonal and driven by the freshest ingredients available on a given day. A superb starter is the herbed risotto and mushroom fricassée ($22.00). Other good options include marinated crabmeat with avocados, melon, and citrus ($18.00), shrimp, scallop, gravlax and lemon-cucumber salad ($23.00), and chilled yogurt tarragon soup ($16.00). Notable among the terrific mains are roast lobster with onions, leeks, and garlic ($38.00), plantain-crusted striped bass with kaffir and bell pepper essence ($34.00), spice-glazed grilled salmon with bean and sweet corn stew ($35.00), pan-roasted veal steak and kidney with spinach and paprika cream ($35.00), and rack of lamb on a curried eggplant tart with carrot emulsion ($36.00). Desserts ($9.50) are outstanding—a favorite is the chocolate-banana soufflé with banana-topped chocolate ice cream.

A five-course prix fixe is $98.00 and a special vegetarian tasting menu is $76.00.

LUTÈCE ★★★   French
249 East 50th Street (between Second and Third Aves.)
212/752-2225
Lunch - Tuesday through Friday Noon - 2:00 p.m.
Dinner - Monday through Thursday 6:00 - 10:00 p.m.;
Friday and Saturday 5:30 - 10:00 p.m.
All major cards

Though the beloved André Soltner, one of the greatest French chefs in the world, has taken his final bow from the celebrated stage he created, the show goes on at Lutèce with chef Eberhard Müller. And it still astonishes.

In late 1994, after thirty-four years, Mr. Soltner sold his perennial four-star restaurant to the Ark Restaurant chain. For Mr. Müller, following such a legend might have been daunting. But he is recognized as a culinary force in his own right, having earned an outstanding reputation during his time at New York's best seafood restaurant, Le Bernardin. Before taking over the kitchen at Lutèce, he worked alongside Mr. Soltner for six months. Since then, he has slowly been putting his own distinctive stamp on this venerable institution. But his respect for Soltner has guided the changes he's made, so that while his lighter menu reflects today's health consciousness and his own personal style, it is not a complete departure from the past. Aware that people come to Lutèce with great expectations, he is in the kitchen six days a week continuing Mr. Soltner's tradition of not opening the restaurant if the chef isn't there.

After a much-needed sprucing up, the new Lutèce looks much like the old Lutèce, but is prettier. Soft yellows, peach, and sienna combine to create a pleasant backdrop of color. Beautiful flowers add to the palette. The barroom in front, with its Paris mural and zinc bar, is still cramped, but the upstairs dining rooms have a lighter, soft new look, and the summery main dining room, converted from an outdoor garden space, retains an alfresco atmosphere with its charming latticework and huge spray of flowers.

The dinner menu is prix fixe $60.00 ($38.00 at lunch). You'll get off to a wonderful start with choices like warm lobster salad with mango and basil; chicken consommé with cheese and herb ravioli; and escargots and wild mushrooms in phyllo. Chef Müller's brilliance with seafood shines through in mains such as sautéed red snapper with asparagus vinaigrette; pan-roasted salmon round on endive and basil; and Dover sole with parsley and brown butter (+$10.00). But one of the most raved-about mains is the guinea hen and cabbage, with the white meat served in moist slices while the dark is mixed with carrots and wrapped in a ruffled leaf of savoy cabbage. Other delicious choices include veal medallions with a vegetable curry and sirloin strip steak in a red wine sauce (for two). Desserts are also delicious: rich Calvados ice cream; sautéed bananas in phyllo with banana cashew ice cream with passion fruit sauce; and strawberry-rhubarb pie with strawberry ice cream.

MANHATTAN OCEAN CLUB ★★★   Seafood
57 West 58th Street (between Fifth and Sixth Aves.)
212/371-7777
Lunch - Monday through Friday Noon - 4:00 p.m.
Dinner - Monday through Saturday 5:00 - 11:30 p.m.; Sunday 5:00 - 11:00 p.m.
All major cards

The ambience at this sophisticated fishhouse is one of chic simplicity and elegance. Sleek and spacious, its stylish interior features graceful Grecian columns and Picasso ceramics mounted behind glass. Tranquil lighting, comfortable seating, and roomy tables enhance its feel of luxury. The fact that it is generally regarded as one of the city's top seafood restaurants is reflected in the prices—the final tab can easily make your head swim.

When you allow yourself this indulgent nautical treat, you'll be rewarded with seafood that is always gleaming fresh and delicious. Among starters, both the clam chowder ($6.75) and fish soup ($6.75) are excellent choices. Sliced artichoke with smoked salmon and a chervil vinaigrette ($9.50) and vine-ripened tomatoes with feta cheese, vidalia onions, and olive oil ($10.50) are refreshing cold appetizers. Of the warm starters, top choices include baked oysters with morel cream ($12.50) and grilled scallops with tomato-onion compote and asparagus vinaigrette ($11.50). Outstanding main choices include swordfish au poivre ($29.75), crab cakes ($29.75), grilled swordfish with cream of lentils, curry, and crisply-fried onion rings ($27.75), steamed or broiled lobster ($16.75/lb), salmon marinated with tandoori spices, cucumbers, tomatoes, and cilantro sauce ($27.75), and soft shell crabs with wilted greens, potatoes, and a peanut curry sauce ($27.50). The shoestring potatoes ($6.75) are sensational. Vegetable sides like asparagus ($7.75) and sugar snap peas ($7.50) are nicely done, but surely inflate the bill. Desserts are usually American classics—there's generally a good cobbler, along with fruit tarts, warm chocolate cake, and an irresistible caramel-pecan sundae.

MICKEY MANTLE'S ★   American
42 Central Park South
(between Fifth and Sixth Aves.)
212/688-7777
Monday through Saturday Noon - Midnight;
Sunday Noon - 11:00 p.m.
All major cards

For an all-American outing with the family, consider this pleasant sports-themed restaurant. Its museum-quality memorabilia include the uniforms of Mantle, Babe Ruth, and Joe DiMaggio. It also houses an interesting sports art gallery with vintage photographs, lithographs, and paintings. Huge TV monitors are tuned to the games of the day or replays of magic moments from yesterday, many of which feature No. 7—the Bronx Bomber—hitting them long and hard from both sides of the plate. Since his death in the summer of 1995, those moments hold even more nostalgia for fans who remember the excitement that filled the stadium when he stepped up to the plate. Now when you stop here for lunch or a late-night burger and brew, you'll hear people around you talking about a game they saw him win in extra innings or maybe about seeing one of his famous tape-measure home runs.

The thing is no one really comes here for the food—they come because the name on the door says Mickey Mantle's or because it has a convenient all-day menu and late hours, or because it has a nice sidewalk cafe facing Central Park. But the food is better than you might expect. Good starters include fried calamari with a spicy tomato sauce ($6.95), blue corn nachos with guacamole and salsa ($7.95), and Southern-fried chicken fingers with a honey mustard sauce ($7.95). The most popular mains include a good chicken pot pie ($12.95), wild mushroom ravioli with fresh thyme, chopped tomatoes, spinach, and white wine ($13.95), and grilled filet mignon served with fresh asparagus and mashed potatoes with cream gravy ($19.95). The menu also features "Mickey's Favorites"—rib-sticking items like chicken-fried steak with mashed potatoes and cream gravy ($16.95), hickory-smoked baby back ribs with vegetable/chili slaw and fresh cornbread ($16.95), herb-roasted breast of chicken with sweet potato pancakes and fresh chunky applesauce ($15.95), and beef chili with melted Jack cheese and blue corn tortillas ($13.95). The menu covers many other bases, with low-cal specials, sandwiches, and burgers. A Little League Menu features children's portions of things like spaghetti and meatballs ($6.95) and macaroni and cheese ($6.95). Desserts are geared to little leaguers as well with offerings of hot fudge/brownie sundaes ($6.50) and chocolate chunk rice pudding with fresh strawberries ($4.95).

MONKEY BAR ★★★   American
Hotel Elysée
60 East 54th Street (between Madison and Park Aves.)
212/838-2600
Lunch - Monday through Friday Noon - 2:30 p.m.
Dinner - Monday through Thursday 6:00 - 10:45 p.m.;
Friday 6:00 - 11:30 p.m.; Saturday 5:30 - 11:30 p.m.;
Sunday 6:00 - 10:00 p.m.
All major cards

Situated on the main floor of the Hotel Elysée, the legendary 1930s Monkey Bar was a chic watering hole in its glory days for a celebrity crowd with recognizable first names like Tennessee and Tallulah. Closed for several years, it reopened in late 1994 after a fabulous redesign by David Rockwell that included the addition of a striking restaurant full of 1930s Manhattan glamour. And now the famous bar that once stood alone still holds its own. Currently one of the hottest spots in town, its decor has been described as a "celebration of urban wit." The frolicking monkey murals have been restored and have even increased in number. Oversized "stuffed olive" bar stools perch humorously along the rich mahogany bar and, in keeping with the past, a piano man croons in the background. **Jackets are required in both the restaurant and bar, except on Sundays.**

Fashioned in the spirit of the great supper clubs of days gone by, the dining room's knockout style encompasses arresting etched art deco glass screens evoking the Manhattan skyline and lush burgundy velvet and wood columns that divide the upper and lower dining levels. The room is alive with color—hyacinth blue, buttery yellow, and tropical greens. Jungle-patterned banquettes add an extra dash of pizazz to the rear of the restaurant and deco-styled forest green velvet chairs surround colorfully set tables that have seen the likes of Barbara Streisand, Mike Wallace, Hugh Grant, and Warren

Christopher. And while its ambience evokes the look and feel of a New York supper club of yesterday, its prices will certainly remind you that time has marched on.

The fusion-driven menu includes wonderful starters such as fried green tomatoes with barbecued spare ribs, crisped runner beans, and watercress ($11.00), smoked trout and Belgian endive salad with pea shoots, radish, shiso, and wasabi ($11.00), asparagus salad with roasted beets, grilled leeks, and roquefort cheese ($12.00), ricotta ravioli with grilled vegetables, spaghetti squash, and tomato broth ($10.00), and a Monkey Bar seafood salad of fresh shrimp, bay scallop seviche, and fried squid with cucumber, cilanto, and lime ($14.00). Mains display the same diversity with choices such as vegetable-stuffed trout with pesto risotto, zucchini chips, and red pepper broth ($24.00), baked lobster with roasted zucchini, fennel, and toasted couscous ($30.00), roast Amish chicken breast with spicy garlic glaze, shoestring potatoes, and broccoli rabe ($19.00), grilled Black Angus steak with a baked potato, fabulous buttermilk onion rings, and Swiss chard ($29.00), roast rack of lamb with macaroni and goat cheese, chopped vegetables, and rosemary jus ($32.00), and roast cod with mashed potatoes, roasted carrots, and celery root chips ($23.00). For dessert, the Baked Alaska ($9.00) is a winner. A chocolate soufflé cake forms its base and intense homemade caramel ice cream tops it, studded with roasted almonds covered with hundreds of tiny stars of meringue. Other delights include devil's food cake with chocolate icing, pistachio ice cream, and chocolate sorbet ($9.00), warm apple tart with a cinnamon crust and vanilla ice cream ($8.00), coconut crème brûlée with glazed pineapple and sugar cookies ($8.00), and, of course, banana cream pie with chocolate curls, bruléed bananas, vanilla, and chocolate sauce ($8.00).

MONTEBELLO ★★   Italian
120 East 56th Street
(between Park and Lexington Aves.)
212/753-1447
Lunch - Monday through Saturday Noon - 3:30 p.m.
Dinner - Monday through Saturday 3:30 - 10:30 p.m.
All major cards

A much-loved restaurant among well-heeled locals, Montebello's success stems from its uncompromising quality of ingredients and obvious neighborhood affection. There's much hand shaking and cheek kissing during the comings and goings here. And while the place has a rather European feel and a slight formality, the atmosphere is warm and the welcome very genuine even for newcomers. The setting is serene and comfortable. There's a handsome bar at the front and an attractive dining room beyond with shaded wall sconces, dramatic floral arrangements, and nicely appointed tables with starched napery and tiny sprays of delicate flowers.

The fare is Northern Italian and very good. Nice starters include eggplant stuffed with fresh ricotta ($8.75), fried mozzarella ($8.75), baked clams ($9.75), and fresh roasted peppers with anchovies ($8.75). The pastas are all really delicious—choices include spaghetti primavera ($16.75), white and green noodles in a cream sauce with peas and prosciutto ($17.75), linguine with white or red clam sauce ($17.75), gnocchi Bolognese ($16.75), and angel hair with crabmeat, tomatoes, and shallots—a house specialty ($20.75). Another specialty of the house is shrimp in a spicy red sauce with spaghetti ($23.75). Other good mains include filet of sole with white wine, capers, and olives ($19.75), chicken with prosciutto, cheese, and peas ($18.75), veal topped with prosciutto, mozzarella, and roasted peppers ($21.00), breaded veal chop with tomato and rugola ($24.00), Italian sausage with peppers and mushrooms ($18.75), and lamb chops sautéed with garlic, white wine, and rosemary ($27.00).

A pre-theatre four-course dinner for $26.75 is available from 5:00 to 6:30 p.m.

NANNI'S ★★   Italian
146 East 46th Street
(between Lexington and Third Aves.)
212/697-4161
Lunch - Monday through Saturday Noon - 3:00 p.m.
Dinner - Monday through Saturday 5:30 - 10:30 p.m.
All major cards

Nanni's provides both an atmospheric and edible walk down memory lane with its old-fashioned ambience and homey cooking. It's a solid choice for terrific pasta and veal dishes and its convivial, old-school atmosphere is always a pleasure.

Start with the hot fish antipasto ($10.00), mozzarella with tomato and basil ($8.50), roasted peppers with anchovy ($7.50), eggplant with ricotta and spinach ($8.00), or the pasta and bean soup ($8.00), and you won't go wrong. One of the house specialties is the angel hair pasta ($18.00). Other delicious pasta choices include fettuccine Bolognese ($18.00), seafood linguine ($22.00), rigatoni with a spicy tomato and basil sauce ($18.00), linguine with clam sauce ($18.00), and seafood risotto ($23.00). There's also a good selection of seafood, notably shrimp with garlic, tomatoes, and mushrooms ($26.50), swordfish with capers ($24.50), and fresh salmon with Barolo and mushrooms ($24.50). The house specialty among many good veal dishes is the chop stuffed with cheese and prosciutto ($27.00). Another all-time favorite is the veal parmigiana ($24.50). Also good is the breast of chicken with prosciutto and cheese ($23.50) and broiled sirloin ($27.00). Main courses are served with vegetable and salad. Dessert selections are $6.50.

NIRVANA PENTHOUSE ★★   Indian
30 Central Park South, Penthouse - 15th Floor
(between Fifth and Sixth Aves.)
212/486-5700
Lunch - Daily Noon - 3:00 p.m.
Dinner - Daily 3:00 p.m. - 1:00 a.m.
All major cards

When you step off the elevator at the penthouse level at 30 Central Park South, you enter an exotic and colorful other world. Sitar music accompanies what is truly a visual treat. You walk through a beautiful bar area to the festively appointed dining room which boasts one of the city's most breathtaking panoramic views of Central Park. Colorful Indian tents overhead, beautiful fabrics, and candlelight highlight the romantic atmosphere. Indian diplomats dine here, along with familiar faces such as Bill Cosby, Phil Donahue, Marlo Thomas, and Brooke Shields.

Menu selections are large, with many interesting regional dishes as well as a nice selection of special vegetarian dishes. While the food may play second fiddle to the glorious view, it is still quite good and dining here is very, very pleasant. You might start with vegetable samosas ($6.95), meat samosas ($7.95), a vegetarian appetizer platter with a vegetable turnover, onion fritter, corn dumpling, and a crisp lentil wafer served with tamarind chutney ($8.95), or Mulligatawny soup ($6.95). The lengthy list of good vegetarian mains (accompanied by basmati pilaf) includes cauliflower and potatoes cooked with ginger, green chilies, and spices ($16.95), cauliflower, eggplant, and green peas, cooked with aromatic spices ($17.95), and braised fresh vegetables blended with basmati rice, raisins, and almonds ($17.95). Chicken and meat specialties (also accompanied by basmati pilaf) include chicken vindaloo (a Goanese specialty with tender pieces of boneless chicken marinated in cayenne pepper and a fiery-hot curry sauce) ($19.95), tender pieces of chicken slowly cooked with onions, fresh herbs, and ground spices ($18.95), beef braised with spinach and spices ($19.95), and morsels of braised lamb in a mildly seasoned cream sauce ($21.95). Be sure to order one of the delicious Indian breads—potato paratha (flaky wholewheat bread stuffed with spiced potatoes and fresh herbs) ($6.95), garlic naan (fine wheat flour bread stuffed with chopped garlic) ($6.95), or tandoori-baked bread stuffed with homemade cheese and spices ($7.95), to name just a few of the delicious options. For dessert, try the coconut rice pudding garnished with raisins and almonds ($3.95).

A prix fixe "theater dinner" is offered from noon until 1:00 a.m. every day for $6.00 above the cost of the main course. It includes assorted appetizers, a main course selection, basmati rice, dessert, and Darjeeling tea or Nirvana coffee.

PALM ★★   Steakhouse
837 Second Avenue (between 44th and 45th Sts.)
212/687-2953
Lunch - Daily Noon - 3:30 p.m.
Dinner - Monday through Friday 3:30 - 11:30 p.m.;
Saturday 5:00 - 11:30 p.m.; Sunday 4:00 - 10:00 p.m.
All major cards

While this quintessential New York steakhouse has a stripped-down decor, everything else defines excess. Gigantic plate-filling juicy steaks and succulent lobsters and no-nonsense waiters are part of its time-honored tradition and "he-man" ambience. Opened in 1926, it has generations of devoted regulars. (There's even an annex across the street, Palm Too, to take care of the overflow.) Its yellow smoke-stained walls with amusing caricatures of newspaper legends and other famous faces speak of the power and glitz that make up the celebrity crowd of this unique city from year to year.

The menu is classic steakhouse fare with starters like shrimp cocktail ($12.00), clams Casino ($10.00), crabmeat cocktail ($14.50), lobster cocktail ($16.00), sliced tomatoes and onions ($6.00), and spinach salad ($7.50). For the main event, house specialties are the jumbo lobsters (four to five pounds and larger, market priced) and 36-ounce New York strip for two ($58.00). Other favorites include three double-cut lamb chops ($29.00), three single-cut pork chops ($19.00), prime rib ($29.00), and one mighty veal chop ($28.00). There's also veal scaloppine ($19.50) and a few pasta dishes ($14.00-$18.00). Grilled salmon ($23.00) and filet of sole ($21.00) are good choices among the seafood selections. Sides of crispy hash browns, onion rings, and cottage fries are served in portions enough for two or more. And desserts are steakhouse staples with creamy cheesecake usually the best bet.

The tab runs pretty high here, making the $19.97 prix fixe lunch a real steal.

PAMIR ★   Afghan
1065 First Avenue
(at 58th Street)
212/644-9258
Lunch - Tuesday through Friday Noon - 2:30 p.m.
Dinner - Daily 5:00 - 11:00 p.m.
All major cards

Hospitality abounds at this pleasant restaurant named for the mountainous region in Central Asia that includes part of Afghanistan. In keeping with the Afghan code of hospitality, the staff here treats you as they would treat a guest in their home. The food is also the kind that would be served in an Afghan home. It is all quite congenial and enjoyable.

I particularly like the appetizers—delightful things like turnovers stuffed with potato, onion, and spices, served with yogurt ($3.25), scallion-filled dumplings topped with yogurt and meat sauce, sprinkled with mint ($3.45), and the samosa-like deep-fried pastries of ground beef, chick peas, and spices, served with an Afghan sauce ($3.45). Mains are served with salad and Afghan bread—good choices include a traditional dish with chunks of lamb and eggplant, cooked with tomatoes, onions, and spices and served with white spiced rice ($11.75) and delicately seasoned diced chicken stew under a mound of brown rice, topped with almonds, pistachios, carrot strips, and raisins ($13.75). The house specialty is the Pamir Kabab, a combination of four kababs: marinated chunks of chicken, lamb, spiced ground beef, and tender lamb chops, served with vegetables and brown rice ($15.95). Popular vegetarian dishes are spiced sautéed pumpkin, topped with yogurt and served with spiced white rice ($10.95) and sautéed eggplant, also topped with yogurt and served with white rice ($10.95). For a sweet finish, there's baghlawa (paper-thin layers of syrup-soaked pastries with walnuts) ($3.25), Afghan pudding with almonds and pistachios ($3.25), and fried pastry, dusted with cardamon, pistachios, and confectioners sugar ($3.25).

PATROON ★★★   French/American
160 East 46th Street
(between Lexington and Third Aves.)
212/883-7373
Lunch - Monday through Friday Noon - 2:30 p.m.
Dinner - Monday through Saturday 5:30 - 10:30 p.m.
All major cards

This hot newcomer's name recalls the landed Dutch gentry in colonial New York and its ambience pays homage to the gentle manners of an earlier era. Since opening in the space that once housed Christ Cella, it has created a lot of favorable buzz, even winning three stars from *The New York Times* right out of the gate. Combining old school formality, a clubby setting, and a straightforward menu of delicious dishes, it has come up a winner.

The Caesar salad ($10.00) is a terrific starter. Other good selections include crabmeat salad ($18.00), duck sausage with sage polenta ($12.00), and shrimp cocktail ($16.00). Of the mains, the roast chicken with black truffles ($58.00 for two), seared salmon with a potato, artichoke, and black mushroom hash ($26.00), and prime sirloin ($35.00) are excellent choices. The potato and gorgonzola gratin ($9.00) is delicious and enough for two. Desserts ($9.00) are sensational with selections such as banana upside-down cake served with macadamia ice cream and caramel sauce, warm hazelnut tart, and coconut cake with lemon sherbet.

Pre-theater is a good time to sample this expensive restaurant. A three-course prix fixe menu is available with 5:30 and 6:00 p.m. reservations for $39.50. There are several choices in each category.

PEN & PENCIL ★★   Steakhouse
205 East 45th Street (between Second and Third Aves.)
212/682-8660
Lunch - Monday through Friday 11:45 a.m. - 3:00 p.m.
Dinner - Monday through Friday 3:00 - 10:00 p.m.;
Saturday 5:00 - 11:00 p.m.; Sunday 4:30 - 10:00 p.m.
All major cards

This gracious old-timer recalls the ambience of the steakhouses of an earlier New York. Named for the many authors, journalists, and artists who patronized it, Pen & Pencil opened as a neighborhood speakeasy in 1932 when the present owner's grandfather made bootleg gin upstairs and served great steaks downstairs. Over the years, such luminaries as Walter Cronkite, Ernest Hemingway, Ed Sullivan, Dorothy Kilgallen, and Clare Boothe Luce have tucked into its classic steakhouse fare. Today, dark wood panelling and spacious banquettes give it a warm, clubby feel. And while it may be short on pizazz, it offers a very genial comfort and good steaks.

To start, there's a nice, generous cold seafood sampler served with three sauces ($16.95), grilled asparagus with goat cheese and a balsamic vinaigrette ($9.75), onion soup ($5.95), smoked salmon ($12.95), and Maryland crab cake ($8.25). The main attraction of course is steak—big, juicy, and full of flavor. There's sirloin ($32.95), filet mignon with béarnaise sauce ($29.75), and chateaubriand for two ($59.50). Other satisfying mains include triple American lamb chops with fresh mint ($29.75), sea scallops ($17.25), Norwegian salmon ($17.95), Dover sole ($24.95), and chicken paillard ($16.95). In keeping with steakhouse tradition, cheesecake is the top dessert.

A pre-theater menu is offered until 6:30 p.m. with three courses for $29.75. You choose from a half-dozen appetizers (including penne arrabiata, Maryland crab cake, and top neck clams) and eight or so mains (filet mignon, roast pork tenderloin, lobster ravioli, rack of lamb for two). There's plenty of choice in desserts as well.

THE RAINBOW ROOM ★★★   Continental
30 Rockefeller Plaza, 65th Floor
(between 49th and 50th Sts.)
212/632-5000
Brunch - Sunday 11:00 a.m. - 2:30 p.m.
Dinner - Tuesday through Saturday 6:30 - 10:15 p.m.;
Supper - Tuesday through Saturday 10:30 p.m. - Midnight;
Dancing until 1:00 a.m.
All major cards

This stunning restaurant is a throwback to the elegance of yesteryear. Originally conceived as the crowning jewel of Rockefeller Center, it threw open its doors to New York cafe society in October 1934. Today, its unique ambience echoes that earlier, dressier time when women wore long white gloves and sassy hats and restaurants never had to post signs requesting that gentlemen wear jackets. It closed temporarily in 1985 for a $20 million modernization that restored it to its original art deco splendor. Since reopening in 1987, its movie credits include appearances in *Sleepless in Seattle*, *Prince of Tides*, and *Six Degrees of Separation*. In fact, you'll feel like you're in a movie yourself the moment you step off the special express elevator to the 65th floor into a long glass, ebony and rosewood hall. There, greeters wearing pastel tails show you the way to that magical land called The Rainbow Room. It's a place where the music never stops from 7:00 p.m. to 1:00 a.m. as two dance bands rotate and couples glide across the revolving dance floor while a crystal chandelier glitters overhead and sparkling lights flicker over the dramatic domed ceiling. Dining tables, covered in silver lamé, are set on three tiers and floor-to-ceiling windows offer stunning wraparound views spanning fifty miles in every direction.

This is definitely the stuff of celebration, but whether the food lives up to the experience depends on what you order. For the most part, its mainly retro menu delivers the goods. The shellfish extravaganza ($35.00 for two, $50.00 for three, $66.00 for four) ponies up with clams, mussels, and lobster on a mountain of crushed ice. Other good openers include Norwegian smoked salmon ($14.00), oysters Rockefeller ($17.00), a cake of wild mushrooms with watercress sauce ($11.50), and asparagus and leek soup ($8.50). For the main, good dishes with real tradition include lobster thermidor ($36.00), tournedos Rossini with a truffle sauce and pommes soufflés ($36.00), and roast rack of lamb with herb-roasted vegetables ($58.00 for two). Other good choices include pan-roasted red snapper with roasted pepper ratatouille ($28.00), New York sirloin grilled with mushrooms and onions ($32.00), and grilled double lamb chops with a plum tomato tart ($29.00). For a dramatic finale, opt for the flaming baked Alaska for two ($18.00).

There's a music surcharge of $20.00 per person—dining in wonderland does not come cheap. You can sample a bit of the heady atmosphere at a less lofty price (if you're willing to forego the cheek-to-cheek and whirling dervish part of the experience) with the **pre-theater dinner available from 5:00 to 7:30 p.m. It offers three courses for $42.00**, with at least a half-dozen choices in each category. Choose from starters like chilled shrimp with zucchini chutney, salmon tartare with crisped potatoes, and field greens with a mustard vinaigrette. The main course selections include: roasted salmon with a horseradish crust, braised fennel, and beet vinaigrette; wild mushroom ravioli with fresh tarragon and sun-dried tomatoes; roast chicken with rosemary sauce and a bouquet of vegetables; and filet of beef with herbed mashed potatoes, olives, and tomatoes. For dessert, there's Manjari chocolate profiteroles, blueberry tart with yogurt sorbet, or chocolate raspberry cake.

Sunday brunch has recently been launched. A large all-you-can-eat buffet table, featuring more than 100 items, occupies the slowly revolving dance floor as a kind of giant Lazy Susan. The buffet is $39.50 for adults, $19.50 for children under 12.

RESTAURANT RAPHAËL ★★★   French
33 West 54th Street (between Fifth and Sixth Aves.)
212/582-8993
Lunch - Monday through Friday Noon - 2:30 p.m.
Dinner - Monday through Friday 6:00 - 9:30 p.m.;
Saturday 5:45 - 10:00 p.m.
All major cards

You'll feel as though you've stepped into another time and place when you enter the romantic, old-fashioned atmosphere at Raphaël. Situated in a stunning turn-of-the-century townhouse, its château-like setting is picture perfect—with charms that include beautiful floral-stencilled beams, a glowing fireplace in winter, and a romantic little trellised garden bursting with freesia and ivy in summer.

The contemporary French cuisine is wonderful. Starter selections include an artfully-arranged and beautifully-prepared panache of baby vegetables tossed in a light vinaigrette ($10.50), an unusual and flavorful pea soup with shrimp ($8.00), herb-roasted oysters with a ragout of wild mushrooms ($12.50), and a

224

warm confit of duck and white bean salad with a sherry-shallot vinaigrette ($11.50). Good seafood specialties include Alaskan halibut steak with feta cheese and risotto in a tomato shrimp sauce ($25.00) and sautéed Maine salmon with a crispy skin, truffled mashed potatoes, and lamb juice ($24.00). Other recommended mains include wonderfully warming and delicious dishes like roasted free-range chicken with mashed potatoes and wild mushrooms ($21.00), roasted loin of veal with garlic mashed potatoes and asparagus with a balsamic vinegar sauce ($28.00), pan-seared sirloin with rosemary, sautéed bacon-roasted potatoes, and arugula, in a red wine sauce ($28.00), and roasted rack of lamb with fresh herbs and ratatouille ($35.00). The desserts are as beautiful to look at as they are to eat. My favorites are the warm caramelized apple tart with vanilla ice cream ($10.00) and crêpes filled with white chocolate mousse, crème anglaise, and chocolate sauce ($10.00). There's also a notable classic vanilla crème brûlée ($9.50).

A three-course pre-theater menu for $32.00 is available with 6:00 p.m. reservations.

SAN GIUSTO ★★★   Italian
935 Second Avenue
(between 49th and 50th Sts.)
212/319-0900
Lunch - Monday through Friday Noon - 3:00 p.m.
Dinner - Monday through Saturday 5:00 - 11:00 p.m.
All major cards

When I dine at San Giusto, I always have the feeling I'm at the right place at the right time. It's that kind of place. Yet, it seems largely an undiscovered neighborhood favorite. Many nice attributes combine to make it such a pleasing place and surprising sleeper. First, there's the staff—surely one of the sweetest in NYC. Also, it has such an appealing ambience—a nice blending of homespun charm and unfancy elegance. And the high-ceilinged space has an airy cheerfulness about it. Colorful decorative plates and delicate flowers in hand-painted pitchers on the tables hint at the genuinely sunny personality of the place.

The Northern Italian food is delicious and the menu is full of old standards with some innovative touches. Start with grilled asparagus and red pepper with cheese ($9.75), fried mozzarella with a tomato sauce ($7.00), clams casino ($9.75), rolled eggplant with ricotta ($8.75), or smoked trout with horseradish sauce ($8.50). Pastas and sauces are all delicious and may be

225

interchanged to produce your personal favorite combination. Good choices include angel hair with plum tomatoes and prosciutto ($16.00), spaghetti amatriciana ($16.00), gnocchi with a rich meat sauce or a light tomato basil sauce ($16.50), tortellini Bolognese ($16.50), fettuccine Alfredo ($16.00), and rigatoni with eggplant, ricotta, and a light tomato sauce ($17.00). Both the mushroom ($18.75) and seafood risotto ($19.75) are delicious as well. Other enticements on the lengthy menu include fresh poached salmon ($24.75), capon breast in white wine with asparagus tips ($17.75), medallions of veal with fontina cheese and a tomato topping ($19.75), and Italian sausage with dry porcini mushrooms and polenta ($18.75). Thin pancakes with chocolate or marmalade ($6.75) is a house specialty dessert.

SAN MARTIN ★   Mediterranean
143 East 49th Street
(between Lexington and Third Aves.)
212/832-0888
Lunch - Daily Noon - 3:00
Dinner - Daily 3:00 - Midnight
All major cards

While this Mediterranean bistro may not be exciting enough for a special evening, it does make for a nice one. A few sidewalk tables out front and a selection of foreign dailies give it a Eurocafe ambience. Inside, the long, narrow cream-colored dining room is bright with framed French posters and cheerful floral displays. It has a real feeling of conviviality about it, and its old-fashioned dark green booths and banquettes are the kind you can really sink into. It's pleasant dining here. Ask Anthony Quinn—he's been spotted inside wearing a very satisfied grin.

When you dine here, you can traverse the Med with a menu that embraces Spain, Greece, Italy, and France. You might start with polenta with sun-dried tomatoes, mushrooms, and a sweet tomato sauce ($4.75), addictively-good fried zucchini and eggplant with fresh tomato sauce ($5.75), deep-fried squid with marinara sauce ($6.75), fresh peeled shrimp in a garlic and olive oil sauce ($7.75), or Spanish sausage cooked in red wine with sweet red peppers ($5.75). And there are many good pastas to choose from—mushroom ravioli with a gorgonzola and walnut sauce ($12.75), crêpes with ricotta and spinach, served with a sun-dried tomato sauce ($11.75), penne with porcini mushrooms, sun-dried tomatoes, green peas, and a cream sauce ($12.75), and black pepper spaghetti with assorted seafood in a tomato sauce ($15.75). Meaty mains offer diversity and great choice as well with selections like roast suckling pig with apple sauce, black beans, and saffron rice ($19.75), rack of lamb for two ($45.00), sautéed sirloin with a pink pepper and Brandy sauce ($18.75), beef medallions in a porcini mushroom sauce ($19.75), sautéed veal with eggplant, prosciutto, and mozzarella ($15.75), and a terrific paella Valenciana with assorted seafood, meats, and vegetables ($38.00 for two). For dessert: tartufo, bread pudding, tiramisú, zabaglione, cheesecake, or sliced oranges in Grand Marnier (each $4.50).

A prix fixe three-course menu is offered for $21.00 ($16.00 at lunch) with three or four choices in each category. A very sweet deal.

SEAGRILL ★★★   Seafood
19 West 49th Street at Rockefeller Plaza
212/332-7610
Lunch - Monday through Friday 11:45 a.m. - 2:45 p.m.
Dinner - Monday through Saturday 5:00 - 9:45 p.m.
All major cards

Primely situated in the heart of Rockefeller Center, the SeaGrill's handsome setting is all the more appealing after a recent renovation. Its refined look is one of polished cherrywood and marble, beautiful linens, fresh flowers, and deep, comfortable armchairs, and virtually every table has a view of the ice rink. In winter, you can watch the skaters glide across the ice, and come warm weather, festive umbrella-topped tables, tubs of ficus and hibiscus trees, and hanging baskets transform the rink into a summer garden for the best in alfresco dining.

In years past, the food did not live up to its attractive setting. That changed with the arrival of talented executive chef Ed Brown, formerly of Tropica and JUdson Grill, who introduced a bold and innovative new menu. While much of it is dedicated to classic seafood dishes, it also offers many imaginative seafood dishes containing exotic ingredients from around the globe.

Wonderful starters include the SeaGrill chowder bursting with lobster, shrimp, and clams ($8.00), tuna tartare enlivened with Asian spices ($12.00), and chilled Malpeque oysters ($11.00). The superb crab cakes are the best you'll find anywhere in the city ($12.00 as a starter or $27.00 for a main course portion). Other notable main options include grilled swordfish with braised escarole and cannellini beans ($28.00), grilled Arctic char with a wild mushroom and radicchio risotto ($25.00), crispy-skin salmon with a dijon mustard and roasted shallot sauce, served with haystack potatoes ($25.00), pepper-seared tuna steak with grilled portobello mushrooms and olives ($27.00), and moist grilled Maine lobster served shelled with spaghetti vegetables (market priced). While true to its namesake—with seafood clearly the star attraction—you can still get a great steak with a Madeira demi-glaze and portobello fries ($29.00) or pan-seared guinea hen with spring onions, baby carrots, and fresh peas ($24.00). Desserts of distinction include warm chocolate steamed pudding with chocolate sauce and roasted orange ice cream ($10.00), Baileys caramel flan with bananas in phyllo pastry ($8.00), and warm apple crumb tart with caramel ice cream ($9.00).

A pre-theatre dinner menu is available from 5:00 to 6:30 p.m. with three courses for $39.00.

SHAAN ★★   Indian
57 West 48th Street
(between Fifth and Sixth Aves.)
212/977-8400
Lunch - Daily Noon - 3:00 p.m.
Dinner - Daily 5:30 - 11:00 p.m.
All major cards

Shaan has the kind of cool and elegant atmosphere that has raised the status of good Indian cooking to new heights. It occupies the space that once housed the elegant Raga and measures up with its own palatial look and easy elegance. The formal and graceful service and serene surroundings make dining here a relaxing oasis of calm.

When Shaan first opened, there were many dishes that just didn't work. Now when you dine here, there's little chance you'll be disappointed. The food is basically that of Northern India with many regional Indian specialties dotting the lengthy menu. Choices are great and the food is mostly wonderful. You might begin with sautéed shrimp with cumin seeds and fresh ginger ($10.95), puff pastry stuffed with delicately-spiced minced lamb ($6.95), potato patties stuffed with minced lamb ($6.95), flour puffs stuffed with potatoes, chickpeas, and bean sprouts topped with tamarind and mint sauces ($5.95), sweet corn soup with chicken and spices ($4.95), mulligatawny soup ($4.95), or an appetizer assortment ($9.95). You won't want to pass up the delicious breads—choices include garlic naan (freshly baked white bread topped with garlic and fresh butter) ($3.95), onion kulcha (a fluffy white bread topped with onions and bell peppers) ($4.95), and missi roti (unleavened wholewheat bread mixed with lentils, freshly baked in a clay oven) ($3.95). You can order a nice assortment for $9.95. The vegetarian specialties are numerous and delicious. Choices include baby eggplants stuffed with Indian spices and sautéed ($10.95), scooped potatoes stuffed with cashews and almonds and simmered in a tomato flavored sauce, a Kashmiri specialty ($10.95), baby corn and spinach cooked with a blend of fenugreek and spices ($10.95), skinless lentils cooked with ginger, onions, and whole chile peppers ($9.95), soft mixed vegetable croquettes stuffed with lotus roots and simmered in a creamy sauce ($10.95), and cauliflower, potatoes, and green peas in a blend of onions, ginger, and spices ($10.95). Other fine main choices are cubes of lamb sautéed with hot peppers ($16.95), gently fried lamb chops tossed in a spicy mint sauce and served with baby potatoes ($17.95), cubes of chicken cooked with freshly-ground peppercorn and spices, a South Indian preparation ($15.95), a fiery chicken vindaloo ($15.95), boneless chicken cooked with almonds and a lightly-spiced cream sauce, a Moglai specialty ($16.95), spiced lobster cooked in a wok ($24.95), and shrimp simmered in a tomato-flavored sauce with onions and peppers ($19.95). The good tandoori specialties include rack of lamb ($24.95), seekh kabab ($17.95), and marinated quail ($16.95). As with most Indian restaurants, desserts are nothing to shout about.

A pre-theater menu is offered from 5:30 to 7:00 p.m. with three courses for $21.95. A buffet luncheon is available daily at $13.95.

SMITH & WOLLENSKY ★★★   Steakhouse
797 Third Avenue
(at 49th St.)
212/753-1530
Monday through Friday 11:30 a.m. - 11:30 p.m.;
Saturday and Sunday 5:00 - 11:30 p.m.
All major cards

For those moments when a protein craving hits in a big way, this quintessential New York steakhouse is a good place to satisfy it. In a big way. Decked out in wood and brass, it has a decidedly macho air. Duck decoys, bird prints, and weather vanes add a pleasant touch of Americana to the restaurant's handsome setting in the turn-of-the-century building that houses it. An extraordinary wine list is another draw for those good boys who always cleaned their plates, did their homework, and can now afford to eat here.

Standbys like split pea soup ($5.00), shrimp cocktail ($13.75), and lobster cocktail ($14.50) are good openers. Among mains, classics are huge plate-filling steaks and chops (each $29.75) with choices that include sirloin, filet mignon, prime rib, triple lamb chops, and veal chops. Other popular options are the Maryland crab cakes ($24.50), sea scallops ($23.50), and lemon-pepper chicken ($19.50). Good sides for the table are delicious hash browns, onion rings, and fried zucchini (each $7.75). Of course, there is cheesecake for dessert ($6.75), creamy and good. Other favorites are homemade Austrian apple strudel ($7.75), hot deep-dish apple Betty with vanilla sauce ($7.00), and Bourbon pecan pie ($7.00).

SPARKS STEAK HOUSE ★★★   Steakhouse
210 East 46th Street (between Second and Third Aves.)
212/687-4855
Lunch - Monday through Friday Noon - 3:00 p.m.
Dinner - Monday through Thursday 5:00- 11:00 p.m.;
Friday and Saturday 5:00 - 11:30 p.m.
All major cards

If you like the clubby comfort and simplicity of menu found in an old-fashioned steakhouse, you'll appreciate all this Victorian cow palace has to offer. Known as much for its spectacular and well-priced wine list as for its great steaks, it is also remembered as the place where reputed mob-boss Big Paul Castellano had his last meal before being gunned down just outside. Today, things are quieter out front. Inside, bordello red, mahogany, and brass set the macho tone and fabulous steaks create the sizzle.

Some of the best starters include hot lump crabmeat and bay scallops ($13.95) and the combination baked clams and shrimp scampi ($11.95). Other popular choices include a good shrimp cocktail ($12.95), prosciutto with melon ($9.95), sliced tomato and onion ($6.95), and spinach salad ($8.95). Sparks is also the kind of steakhouse that does well by seafood with offerings such as fresh rainbow trout ($19.95), lemon sole ($22.95), striped bass ($26.95), and broiled bay scallops ($25.95). Lobster comes in three sizes—up to 5½ pounds. The meaty mains pretty much fill up a plate, too, with choices like an extra-thick veal loin chop ($29.95), three extra-thick rib lamb chops ($29.95), sliced steak with sautéed onions and peppers ($27.95), and a super prime sirloin ($29.95). Be sure to order the buttery hash browns ($4.50). For dessert, there's good New York cheesecake ($6.95), chocolate cheesecake ($6.95), walnut pecan pie ($6.95), fresh fruit ($7.50), and strawberries Romanoff ($10.50), among other caloric concoctions. And at this point, who's counting?

TATOU ★★   American/French
151 East 50th Street
(between Lexington and Third Aves.)
212/753-1144
Lunch - Monday through Friday Noon - 3:00 p.m.
Dinner - Monday through Saturday 5:30 - 11:00 p.m.
Late Nite Menu 11:00 p.m. - 2:00 a.m.
All major cards

Tatou looks a trifle grand with its thirty-foot high ceiling, massive chandelier, ornate balcony, and small curtained stage. In fact, the building that houses it was actually designed to be a small opera house in the late '20s, but the Depression made that impractical and the building sat idle for many years. In the late '30s, it opened as a supper club called Versailles, a rival of the famed Stork Club. In its glory days it featured top performers like Edith Piaf and Judy Garland, and in its early years Desi Arnaz was the house band leader. Today, its appealing atmosphere retains that snazzy '30s supper club feel along with a more contemporary look. Mustard yellow walls and French windows with flower boxes add a cheerful touch. The mood is mellow early in the day when a harpist plays during lunch. Then, in the evening, a jazz band livens things up, and later eclectic dance bands heat up the night.

The food is much better than you might expect from a place that appears so style-driven. The cooking is a "frenchified" American with some oriental touches. Good starters include house-smoked salmon ($14.00), open ravioli with a wild mushroom ragout ($14.00), scallop and lobster Napoleon with shiitake mushrooms and truffle juice ($16.00), and mixed seasonal greens ($9.00). For the main, try the chef's take on bouillabaisse with scallops, shrimp, sea bass, clams, red snapper, monkfish, mussels, and a saffron broth ($26.00) or striped sea bass Oriental served with jasmine rice—a house specialty ($27.00). Other notable mains include rack of lamb marinated and roasted in garlic and thyme and served with white beans and asparagus ($29.00), marinated roasted baby chicken with potato purée ($23.00), breast of chicken roasted with vegetables and served with herb risotto ($21.00), Pacific salmon with shallots and Zinfandel essence with Swiss chard gratin ($26.00), and Black Angus sirloin steak with potato galette and haricots verts ($29.00). Daily specials enlarge the menu with temptations like roasted pepper soup ($7.50) and pan-seared monkfish on truffled potato ravioli ($24.00). And do check on the daily desserts—they tend to be spectacular.

The pre-theater menu, offered from 5:30 to 6:45 p.m. with three courses for $19.97, makes dining here a less pricey affair.

TORRE DI PISA ★★   Italian
19 West 44th Street (between Fifth and Sixth Aves.)
212/398-4400
Lunch - Daily 11:45 a.m. - 3:00 p.m.
Dinner - Daily 5:30 p.m. - Midnight
All major cards

Playfully chic, Torre di Pisa's knockout style is yet another striking David Rockwell design triumph. A painting of the famous leaning Tower of Pisa depicting a tug-of-war between the devil (trying to pull the tower down) and an angel (struggling to keep it upright) is one of many elements that set a tone of devilish charm. Beautiful pottery, white Doric columns, and bold colors add to the lively scene. It has the feel of an Italian piazza and a definite wink in its eye. The small bar area also has a sweet touch in a wall adorned with Italian love letters from the owners' family.

This theater district newcomer is actually a spin-off of its namesake restaurant in Milan, known for its generous barter system whereby artists have traded their work for a Tuscan feast. Starter standouts at this branch include a watercress salad with Tuscan bread, gorgonzola cheese, and fresh grilled corn with a balsamic dressing ($9.50) and cold spinach soup topped with frizzled ginger, ricotta cheese, croutons, and grated parmesan ($7.00). Good pasta choices include rigatoni with a traditional meat sauce ($17.00), homemade ricotta and spinach gnocchi with fresh tomato and basil ($17.00), homemade wholewheat fettuccine with shiitake mushrooms, roasted garlic, and a touch of pesto ($18.00), spaghetti with fresh shrimp, garlic, and crushed red pepper ($17.50), and risotto with asparagus, saffron, and parmesan ($21.00). Other good mains include grilled spicy tuna, served with fresh tomato and red onion salad ($24.00), a skewered medley of marinated and grilled fish ($19.50), grilled red snapper in a citrus sauce, served with grilled zucchini ($22.00), roasted filet mignon infused with gorgonzola cheese and served with white truffle polenta ($26.00), New Zealand rack of lamb with a Chianti sauce ($25.00), calves liver with caramelized onions and soft polenta ($19.00), sautéed chicken breast with olives, tomato filet, roasted potatoes, and pesto ($21.00), and thinly-sliced beef tenderloin filled with mozzarella and served with artichokes and roasted potatoes ($24.00).

A pre-theater menu is available from 5:30 to 6:30 p.m. with three courses for $26.95. There are generally two choices in the starter and dessert courses and four choices in the main course.

TROPICA BAR & SEAFOOD HOUSE ★★   Seafood
200 Park Avenue (MetLife Bldg.)
(45th St. and Lexington Ave.)
212/867-6767
Lunch - Monday through Friday 11:30 a.m. - 3:00 p.m.
Dinner - Monday through Friday 5:00 - 10:00 p.m.
All major cards

This charming tropical hideaway is snugly perched above the main concourse of Grand Central Terminal in the MetLife Building. With such a commuter-driven location, its plantation house ambience is its first delightful surprise. Airy dimensions, pastel colors, rattan chairs, and lush tropical plants give the place a breezy, Caribbean feel. And while it's in full buzz at lunch, dinner is more relaxed and allows the mellow mood of the decor to transport you to an at-holiday frame of mind.

Chef Fred Sabo's seafood specialties with tropical and Asian influences are among the most innovative in town. His menu is creative, sophisticated, and geared to market availability of the best ingredients and freshest fish. A crowd favorite among starters is a sashimi and sushi combination ($14.00). Other top choices include a Dungeness crab spring roll with rosemary-ginger dipping sauce ($9.75), smoked trout with poached pears, goat cheese, endive, and a lemon-peanut vinaigrette ($8.50), crab cake with field greens ($13.50), conch chowder ($7.50), and a salad of butternut lettuce, roquefort cheese, and spicy cashew nuts ($7.50). Tropica's daily grilled whole fish selections might be yellowtail snapper or black sea bass served with grilled portobello mushrooms, polenta, roasted peppers, and a tomato caper olive sauce ($21.50). Other terrific main plates and house specialties include roasted breast of jerked chicken, quesadilla, and a red chile pepper sauce ($17.50), penne with baby shrimp, scallops, pesto, sun-dried tomatoes, and broccoli rabe ($18.00), crisp sautéed red snapper with a wild mushroom-corn risotto and a sherry sage sauce ($22.50), seared-marinated tuna with purple sticky rice, Chinese eggplant, and a red pepper sauce ($24.50), steak frites with a peppercorn sauce (12 oz. $24.00, 16 oz. $28.00), and Maine lobsters, char-grilled or steamed ($23-$32 according to size). Desserts are also good with choices like key lime pie ($7.50), coconut crème brûlée ($7.50), and Grand Marnier soufflé with vanilla ice cream and raspberry sauce ($9.50).

A three-course $29.00 prix fixe dinner is available, as well as a $39.00 three-course wine tasting dinner with wines selected by the sommelier to complement each course.

"21" CLUB ★★★   American
21 West 52nd Street (between Fifth and Sixth Aves.)
212/582-7200
Lunch - Monday through Friday Noon - 2:30 p.m.
Dinner - Monday through Friday 5:30 - 10:30 p.m.;
Saturday 5:30 - 11:30 p.m.
All major cards

There's an air of intrigue at this bastion of power and glamour that over the years has been one of the most famous restaurants in the world and a true New York institution. This is where, one rainy night, Robert Benchley wisecracked to a waiter, "Get me out of this wet coat and into a dry Martini." And where Ernest Hemingway would sometimes wave off a Papa Doble while announcing to the barman, "Since I'm not drinking, I'll just have tequila." You'll see a plaque at the bar that reads "Bogie's Corner" because Humphrey Bogart was such a regular, sipping Ramos Gin Fizzes while trailing cigarette smoke across the room. How steeped in nostalgia is this place? Plenty.

Once a private brownstone mansion, it opened as a speakeasy on New Year's Eve 1929. After Prohibition, it went on to become a sophisticated and convivial drinking and dining haven for the power elite. Hundreds of charming toys dangle from its ceiling—miniature cars, model planes and trains, and all sorts of sporting paraphernalia—with logos of companies who frequent "21." Even its exterior exudes an enchanting sense of whimsy with its colorful lineup of jockeys standing guard along its iron gate.

The first thing you notice about the menu may be its sky-high prices. Dining here is most enjoyable when someone else is paying. But if you can afford it, you won't mind a bit. The food is wonderful, the atmosphere still heady.

Start with a great Maryland crab cake with horseradish cream ($18.50), oysters or clams on the half shell ($15.00), roasted oysters with country bacon and brioche ($16.00), mushroom ragout with gorgonzola polenta ($15.00), or lobster-butternut squash bisque ($9.00). House specialties among the mains include pan-roasted Maine lobster with braised leeks ($39.00) and mixed game grill with a venison chop, roasted quail, boar bacon rumaki, and smoked rabbit sausage served with homefries and a berry relish ($36.00). Other notables include red snapper with chive potato lasagna ($37.00), chili-rubbed pork tenderloin with plantain fritters and roast poblano peppers ($34.00), Catskill Mountain rainbow trout with pine nut stuffing and sage butter ($37.00), and aged Black Angus cowboy T-bone, sirloin, or ribeye steak with mashed potatoes and onion rings ($39.00). There's also a daily game special ($38.00). And "21" still serves the priciest burger in town ($24.00) on buttered grilled sourdough. Another "21" tradition is the chicken hash with wild rice, sherry, and wilted spinach ($27.00). Desserts ($8.50) are nostalgic bliss: apple pie with maple-walnut ice cream, pecan pie with Bourbon crunch ice cream, baked banana bread pudding-ice cream split, and rice pudding with raisins and cream. A tasting plate of desserts for two ($14.00) is great for the undecided.

The good news is that you can sample both the atmosphere and food at this celebrated old classic for a relative pittance with its $29.00 prix fixe offered from 5:30 to 6:30 p.m. It consists of three courses with several choices in each category. Starter choices might be Caesar salad, the daily pasta, or spicy Cuban black bean soup; followed by herb-roasted young chicken with hash browns and seared spinach, grilled Canadian salmon with vegetable couscous and lemon caper butter, or four-peppercorn minute steak with mashed potatoes and chili rings. For dessert, perhaps a rich flourless chocolate torte, classic crème brûlée, or a lemon curd Napoleon with raspberry sauce.

VONG ★★   French-Thai

200 East 54th Street (Third Ave.)
212/486-9592
Lunch - Monday through Friday Noon - 2:30 p.m.
Dinner - Monday through Thursday 6:00 - 11:00 p.m.;
Friday 5:30 - 11:00 p.m.; Saturday 5:30 - 11:30 p.m.;
Sunday 5:30 - 10:00 p.m.
All major cards

Vong is the kind of showy restaurant you'll either like a lot or not like at all. Its dramatic interior is a dazzling sound and light show where a clamorous noise level and mind-bending decor of hot colors and odd angles embrace a chic clientele. Gold leaf abounds. A red and gold collage of Thai newspaper clippings covers one wall and a pagoda dominates the striking dining room, where colorful, silky banquettes provide comfortable people-watching perches.

Vong is the creation of Alsatian-born chef Jean-Georges Vongerichten (who also owns the much-loved East Side bistro Jo Jo). He spent two years in Thailand, as chef at one of the city's best French restaurants, where he acquired an affection for the spices and infusions of Southeast Asian cuisine. At Vong, he reinterprets the cuisine of Thailand by combining its spices, curry, and herbs with French cooking techniques. His light and innovative cuisine has won praise from restaurant critics and local foodies alike. Tops among starters is a crab spring roll with a tamarind dipping sauce ($11.00). Other good choices include a charred lamb salad with aromatic herbs ($12.00), marinated salmon with lime juice, green peppercorns, and scallion pancakes ($10.00), and seared tuna with Szechuan peppercorn and soy-mustard sauce ($9.00). Vongerichten's mains also combine bold flavors with a healthy lightness. Try the monkfish baked with special spices and seeds, potatoes, scallions, and asparagus ($22.00), steamed red snapper with cardamon sauce, cabbage, and watercress ($24.00), grilled beef and noodles in a ginger broth ($23.00), or duck breast roasted rare, with a spicy sesame sauce, duck egg roll, and tamarind glaze ($24.00). An ever-changing selection of exotic desserts will tempt you into a sweet finale. Opt for the white peppercorn ice cream with bananas, kiwi, and passion fruit.

A $35.00 three-course pre-theatre menu is available with 6:00 p.m. reservations. There's also a $65.00 tasting menu of signature dishes.

WOLLENSKY'S GRILL ★★   Steakhouse
205 East 49th Street
(between Second and Third Aves.)
212/753-0444
Daily 11:30 a.m. - 2:00 a.m.
All major cards

Kid brother to the venerable Smith & Wollensky next door, this amiable grill has a relaxed ambience and hours that allow for a midnight repast for the night owls among us. Its menu has much in common with its elder, but with more wallet-friendly prices. It also has a pleasant outdoor cafe/terrace from spring through summer.

You might start with Wollensky's famous pea soup ($4.75), fried zucchini and onion rings ($6.75), or a fresh lump crabmeat cocktail ($13.75). The red meat specials here are just as fine as those at big brother's—you might opt for the English-cut prime rib ($23.50) or the sliced filet mignon ($24.75). And you can also get a fabulous burger ($9.75). The veal piccata ($18.50), lemon-pepper chicken ($18.50), sea scallops ($16.75), and cobb salad ($16.75) are quite good as well. For dessert, tuck into the creamy cheesecake ($5.50), chocolate mousse cake ($6.50), apple Betty with vanilla sauce ($5.50), or Bourbon pecan pie ($6.50).

ZARELA ★★   Mexican
953 Second Avenue (between 50th and 51st Sts.)
212/644-6740
Lunch - Monday through Friday Noon - 3:00 p.m.
Dinner - Monday through Thursday 5:00 - 11:00 p.m.;
Friday and Saturday 5:00 - 11:30 p.m.; Sunday 5:00 - 10:00 p.m.
American Express and Diner's Club

Zarela is a lively, friendly party—a perfect place to unwind and chase away the blahs. Its high profile namesake, Zarela Martinez, was a social worker and part-time caterer when Paul Prudhomme (and later Craig Claiborne) discovered her. After dining here, you'll understand why they were so enthusiastic about her cooking and why the Reagans once snapped her up to cook for Queen Elizabeth at their California ranch. She opened this colorful piñata of a place in 1987, and its convivial atmosphere and her authentic, spirited Mexican food have created one long-running fiesta. Antique Mexican masks, vibrant fabrics, paper cutouts strung across the room spelling Zarela, and live mariachi music are part of its unrelentingly festive ambience. Be sure to ask for a table on the second floor (away from the raucous bar on the entrance level) where it is somewhat quieter and the atmosphere is quaint and colorful with print wallpaper, wood wainscotting, and a pretty wooden fireplace.

While Zarela's decor may give an impression of cheerful chaos, what appears on your plate shows that the kitchen has a more serious propensity. The menu features good homestyle regional Mexican food. Start out with a poblano chile stuffed with chicken and dried fruit picadillo, served with a roasted tomato sauce ($8.95), rolled chicken tacos, crisply fried and served with guacamole ($7.95), chicken and cheese enchiladas ($8.95), or snapper hash cooked with tomato, scallion, jalapeño, and aromatic spices ($8.95). Good mains include shrimp sautéed in a spicy jalapeño, onion, and cilantro sauce, garnished with fresh coconut ($13.95), salmon grilled and served at room temperature with chipotle mayonnaise and a cucumber relish ($15.95), grilled whole chicken breast seasoned with a peppery spice paste in a light chicken broth with habanero chile, grilled onion, and a roasted garlic head ($13.95), roasted marinated pork sautéed with roasted tomatoes, onions, chipotle chilies, and aromatic spices ($12.95), and fajitas served with salsa, guacamole, and flour tortillas ($16.95). Daily dessert selections are agreeably festive treats like coconut and raspberry frozen soufflé and dark chocolate fudge-pecan brownies with chocolate ice cream and Mexican chocolate sauce.

SOHO/TRIBECA

SoHo/TriBeCa

GREENWICH VILLAGE

Walker Park

E. Houston St.

W. Houston St.

MacDougal St.

Prince St.

King St.

Hudson St.

Varick St.

SOHO

Sullivan St.

Thompson St.

W. Broadway

Wooster St.

Greene St.

Mercer St.

Charlton St.

Vandam St.

Spring St.

Spring St.

Broadway

Crosby St.

Greenwich St.

Renwick St.

Dominick St.

Broome St.

Broome St.

Washington St.

Canal St.

Watts St.

Avenue of the Americas (6th Ave.)

Holland Tunnel

Grand St.

Watts St.

Howard St.

Desbrosses St.

Vestry St.

Lispenard St.

CHINATOWN/LOWER EAST SIDE/LITTLE ITALY

Laight St.

Callister St.

Church St.

Walker St.

Broadway

Cortlandt Alley

Lafayette St.

Hubert St.

Ericson Pl.

Varick St.

Beach St.

White St.

TRIBECA

Franklin St.

West St.

N. Moore St.

Franklin St.

Leonard St.

Catherine Ln.

Harrison St.

Worth St.

Jay St.

Staple St.

Hudson St.

W. Broadway

Thomas St.

Independence Plaza

Duane St.

Duane St.

Washington Market Park

Reade St.

Chambers St.

LOWER MANHATAN

New York City Courthouse

HUDSON RIVER

City Hall

ALISON ON DOMINICK STREET ★★★   French
38 Dominick Street
(between Varick and Hudson Sts.)
212/727-1188
Dinner - Monday through Thursday 5:30 - 10:30 p.m.;
Friday and Saturday 5:30 - 11:00 p.m.;
Sunday 5:30 - 9:30 p.m.
All major cards

When the occasion calls for romance, this is the place. Candlelight and soft music set a gentle tone and form a comfortable backdrop for the wonderful country French fare served here in a quietly chic brownstone setting. Decorated in soothing pastels with blue velvet banquettes, this is a luxury restaurant without pretension and attitude. And on nice evenings, sidewalk tables spring up outside for those willing to forego the romantic interior.

Excellent starters include a garlic soup, blanched and puréed, served with herb cream ($9.00), warm chevre and potato salad with arugula, niçoise olives, and chive oil ($10.00), a terrine of provençale vegetables, roasted and served with basil oil and tapenade ($10.00), lobster salad with yellow finn potatoes, fennel, wild greens, and lobster vinaigrette ($14.00), and roast sweetbread salad with arugula, crisped capers, and mustard vinaigrette ($11.00). Mains are equally delicious. Good seafood choices include a superb roast salmon with braised artichokes, lardons, creamer potatoes, and chives ($25.00) and pan-roasted scallops with potato purée, sautéed brussels sprouts, and a lemon coriander sauce ($28.00). Selections from the list of wonderful rustic, country French offerings include the ever-popular roast chicken with parsnip purée, roasted onions, and haricots verts ($25.00), roast rack of lamb with a Swiss chard and potato gratin, fava beans, and glazed baby vegetables ($33.00), and braised beef shin served on crispy polenta, with braised leeks, and a red wine sauce ($23.00). The desserts are elegant affairs, with a superb crème brûlée ($8.00) always a good choice. Its competition is stiff, though, with other offerings like caramelized apple and brioche Charlotte with sour cherries and vanilla ice cream ($10.00), sautéed pear with honey and spices served with pear bread and ginger ice cream ($9.00), a trio of chocolate mousses (dark, white, and milk) with fresh orange, sesame tuiles, and an almond-orange sauce ($12.00), and a warm chocolate timbale with red wine soaked strawberries, and pistachio ice cream ($12.00).

AQUAGRILL ★★   Seafood
210 Spring Street (at Ave. of the Americas)
212/274-0505
Lunch - Tuesday through Friday Noon - 3:00 p.m.
Brunch - Saturday and Sunday Noon - 4:00 p.m.
Dinner - Tuesday through Sunday 6:00 - 11:30 p.m.
All major cards

This relative newcomer to the hip SoHo dining scene radiates energy and vibrancy. An ice-covered raw bar at the front glistens with a variety of oysters and clams, and a friendly feel pervades the space. Its airy, minimalist decor has a lighthearted sophisticated look with pale yellow walls, blue banquettes with velvet pillows, vases of tulips, and shell-art lamps. Candlelight adds a nice blush to the pretty dining rooms at night. And there's also an inviting outdoor cafe (surrounded by bamboo trees) that seats 30.

It is owned and operated by husband and wife team Jeremy and Jennifer Marshall who have assembled a crackerjack staff, making dining here all the more enjoyable. Jennifer is one of New York City's few female sommeliers. And Jeremy prepares the exquisitely fresh seafood with true flair. He also bakes his own breads (onion focaccia and jalapeño cornbread) which come to the table warm. The starters are all winners, but the top popularity prize probably goes to the snail snaps—garlicky popovers containing a single snail ($8.00). Other terrific choices include a deliciously rich French mussel soup with saffron and potatoes ($5.50), peppered tuna carpaccio with avocado, lemon, and grilled Bermuda onions ($8.50), warm octopus salad with roasted peppers in a roasted onion vinaigrette ($7.50), and sautéed mussels and escargots served with a fabulous potato hash and garlic-chive oil ($8.00). Good, inventive mains include grilled Atlantic salmon with a falafel crust served with cucumbers, tomatoes, and a lemon coriander vinaigrette ($16.50), seared sea scallops with a wild mushroom and yellow Finnish potato hash with mushroom emulsion and chive oil ($18.00), grilled swordfish with sautéed broccoli rabe, bacon, and polenta ($18.50), and roasted cod with wilted spinach and artichokes in caper brown butter ($16.50). There's also a good bouillabaisse with poached snapper, shrimp, mussels, clams, scallops, and lobster in a garlic saffron tomato broth ($21.00). The menu also offers to try to accommodate special dietary needs and includes a list of à la carte options of fish (as well as chicken and steak) ($12.00-$16.50) that can be simply grilled, poached, or roasted with a choice of side offerings ($3.50 each). Desserts ($5.50 to $7.00) might be chocolate soufflé, pineapple skillet cake with caramel sauce and coconut milk sorbet, or apple tart with cinnamon ice cream and caramel sauce.

For a pre-theater oyster festival, arrive between 5:00 and 7:00 p.m. Tuesday through Friday when oysters are 75 cents each.

Brunch offers traditional selections such as eggs Benedict ($8.50), challah French toast with cinnamon apples, bacon or sausage, and pecan butter ($8.50), berry pancakes with maple syrup and bacon or sausage ($8.50), and Norwegian smoked salmon on a bagel with tomato, onion, and cream cheese ($10.50). Other choices might be warm grilled chicken salad with roasted potatoes, artichokes, and bacon in a thyme vinaigrette ($12.50), grilled tuna sandwich with avocado, arugula, and grilled onions ($9.75), Aquagrill burger with fries ($8.50), or fresh fettuccine with shrimp, tomato, toasted pine nuts, and pesto ($15.50).

CAPSOUTO FRERES ★★   French
451 Washington Street (Watts St.)
212/966-4900
Lunch - Tuesday through Friday Noon - 3:30 p.m.
Brunch - Saturday and Sunday Noon - 3:30 p.m.
Dinner - Monday through Friday 6:00 - 10:30 p.m.;
Saturday and Sunday 6:00 - 11:30 p.m.
All major cards

The only thing not to like about Capsouto Freres is its somewhat out of the way location. It's not the kind of place you might just happen on, but one you have to search out on a street of many huge warehouses. But, once inside, you'll be truly transported. For in a space of architectural distinction and high style, the Capsouto brothers have created a sophisticated and charming bistro and worthy destination. Housed in an 1891 landmark building, the multi-level dining room features red brick walls, wooden floors, ceiling fans, soaring columns, and floor to ceiling windows adorned with lace curtains. It is charmingly eclectic and dining here is truly delightful.

The contemporary French fare is nearly as pleasing as the surroundings. The house specialty among starters is the terrine provençale (layered eggplant, roasted peppers, and goat cheese ($7.50). Other good choices include country-style sausage with warm potatoes ($7.00), smoked salmon with caviar ($12.50), and onion soup gratinee ($4.25). Favorites among the mains: roast duckling with a ginger and black currant sauce ($17.50) and poached salmon with a warm fresh herb vinaigrette ($19.00). Other good bets include sole meuniere or almandine ($16.50), shrimp and scallops on fresh pasta ($17.00), homemade ravioli with scallops and mushrooms ($14.00), saddle of veal with a green

243

peppercorn sauce ($25.00), and, of course, a terrific steak frites ($24.00). Desserts are wonderful, particularly the profiteroles with chocolate sauce ($6.50), mousse of bitter chocolate ($6.50), hot French apple tart with crème fraîche ($6.00), and sensational fruit soufflés ($8.00).

This is also a popular place for weekend brunches with good choices like scrambled eggs with tomatoes, peppers, onions, and prosciutto ($8.50), eggs Benedict with Canadian bacon or salmon ($8.50), poached eggs with spinach and scallops ($9.50), French toast ($9.00), shrimp and scallop omelette ($11.00), and smoked salmon and leek egg white omelette with baby greens ($11.00).

CHANTERELLE ★★★★   French
2 Harrison Street
(between Greenwich and Hudson Sts.)
212/966-6960
Lunch - Tuesday through Saturday Noon - 2:30 p.m.
Dinner - Monday through Saturday 5:30 - 11:00 p.m.
All major cards

With an architecturally splendid interior, a superbly trained staff, and a brilliant chef, Chanterelle is the sort of place that spoils you outrageously, swiftly captures your affection, and always comes to mind when you think of a special place to dine. While the experience comes with a very serious price tag, it is the kind that memories are made of.

Owned by husband and wife team Karen and David Waltuck, it opened to immediate acclaim in 1979. Karen, the gregarious half of the duo, runs the front of the house with great warmth and is responsible for the glorious floral arrangements. David, one of the country's most gifted chefs, makes magic in the kitchen. He was only 24 when Chanterelle first opened. Then housed in a small storefront in SoHo, it quickly became a celebrity destination attracting the likes of Robert DeNiro, Robert Redford, Sandra Bernhard, and Frank and Barbara Sinatra. It was also a favorite of local artists.

In 1989, Chanterelle moved to its current location in the imposing 19th Century Mercantile Exchange Building in Tribeca. Here, the interior is spare and elegant. A study in quiet chic, the dining room is known for its lack of ornament other than the architectural details and spectacular flower arrangements. Yet, its soaring dimensions, custard colored walls, carved cherrywood pilasters, ornate tin ceiling with brass chandeliers, and mellow lighting give the place a quietly dramatic ambience. Still, the dining experience is the real focus. Its oversized tables are well spaced for a sense of privacy and beautifully set with classic white china, French silverplate flatware, and starched white napery. Servers are casually clad in bistro garb, but very serious about correct service. Some find it *too* serious and pretentious; most relax into the earnest pampering and enjoy it.

The menu changes monthly and as a salute to the artsy crowd that first adopted Chanterelle, menu covers change several times a year, featuring the work of different artists. As for the culinary creativity, David Waltuck combines the freshest and finest ingredients—culled from small sources all over the country—with his love for classic French cuisine and the flavors of the Far East. The results are dazzling.

At dinner, there is a choice of either a three-course prix fixe for $75.00 or the chef's six-course tasting menu which is $89.00. The constantly changing fare on the three-course prix fixe offers several choices in each category. One constant is the restaurant's signature appetizer, a superb grilled seafood sausage. Other recent selections among starters: gingered salmon and seaweed salad with wasabi; and mushroom consomme with wild mushroom ravioli. Mains entice with choices like breast of duck with fresh chilies; rib of beef with porcini and beef marrow; rack of lamb with mustard and thyme; and grilled turbot with peas and pancetta. Dessert might be warm rice pudding with rum-soaked currants and cream or crisp chocolate soufflé cake. There's also an extraordinary cheese board ($15.00).

A $35.00 three-course prix fixe lunch menu offers a nice opportunity to sample this special dining experience without breaking the bank. And what a nice mid-day treat.

COUNTRY CAFE ★★   French
69 Thompson Street (between Spring and Broome Sts.)
212/966-5417
Lunch - Monday through Friday 11:00 a.m. - 5:30 p.m.
Brunch - Saturday and Sunday 11:00 a.m. - 5:30 p.m.
Dinner - Monday through Thursday and Sunday 5:30 - 11:00 p.m.;
Friday and Saturday 5:30 p.m. - 12:30 a.m.
No credit cards

For authentic homestyle French cooking in a real country setting, Country Cafe is just the ticket. From the rooster sign outside that greets you to the decorative oxen yoke above the open-kitchen window, there's an air of friendly hospitality to the place. With illustrations of farm animals animating the pale yellow walls, an abundance of both fresh and dried flowers everywhere, and the fragrances of a thoroughly French kitchen wafting from the open window, this tiny cafe is a rustic charmer.

Of the starters, the wild mushroom casserole topped with triangles of polenta ($7.25) is a real standout. Other good choices include homemade pâté ($6.75), onion tart ($6.75), and a combination shrimp and crab cake ($8.00). Couscous royale ($15.75), the house specialty among the mains, has a border of cooked meats and a delicious broth with potatoes and other vegetables, and caramelized onions and chili sauce on the side. House-smoked salmon with lentils ($14.50) is another house specialty. You can't really go wrong with any of the mains. Other good choices include a traditional coq au vin ($15.75), braised lamb shank with barley risotto ($15.75), and steak au poivre ($16.75). You'll also want to save room for one of the daily desserts. And don't arrive with just plastic in your wallet—it's cash only here.

CUB ROOM ★★   Contemporary American
131 Sullivan Street (corner of Prince St.)
212/677-4100
Lunch - Tuesday through Friday Noon - 2:30 p.m.
Brunch - Sunday Noon - 3:30 p.m.
Dinner - Monday through Saturday 6:00 - Midnight;
Sunday 6:00 - 11:00 p.m.
American Express

The handsome Cub Room is a more casual retreat than the postwar oasis of glamour for which it is named—the swank back dining room of the Stork Club made memorable in Bette Davis' film classic, *All About Eve*. A still photograph of the film star as Margot Channing hangs near the entrance reminding film buffs of that inimitable voice saying things like, "Isn't it a lovely room! The Cub Room. What a lovely, clever name! Where the elite meet..." When you enter *this* Cub Room through the bar, you'll find a young, beautiful crowd creating a merry buzz at the in-spot of the moment. But beyond the busy bar scene, the dining room is rustically sophisticated and warm with rosy brick walls, beautiful lighting, cherrywood tables, and four back-to-back banquettes upholstered with kilim carpets.

When the Cub Room first opened in the summer of 1994, it was an immediate hit, but one in which style won over culinary achievement to a large

246

extent. Now, the kitchen seems to be turning that around and the well-conceived menu can hold its own with its stylish backdrop.

Chef/owner Henry Meer honed his skills early on in some very upscale kitchens. After five years at La Côte Basque, he spent ten years as sous-chef to the legendary Andre Soltner at Lutèce. Now, in his own restaurant, his seasonal contemporary American menu emphasizes farm-fresh, organically-grown produce, with very little use of cream and butter. Starters might be grilled asparagus with a Champagne tarragon vinaigrette ($9.00), beet salad with organic baby greens, candy cane beets, and goat cheese ($8.50), salad of sweetbreads with grilled portobello mushrooms, green beans, caramelized garlic, and shallots ($11.50), an elegant and artfully presented pressed vegetable terrine with leeks, zucchini, red and yellow peppers, fennel, and portobello mushrooms ($8.00), and a wonderful salmon Caesar ($9.00 or $17.50 as a main). There are daily pastas ($9.00 as a starter, $17.50 as a main), but so far they have represented the kitchen's weakest area. There's much to love on the list of mains, however, with offerings such as a superb cherrywood-smoked hanger steak with spoon polenta, wild mushrooms, and a hearty red wine sauce ($25.00), pan-roasted loin of veal with mashed potatoes, red wine onions, garlic chives, and a Madeira sauce ($28.00), grilled swordfish pierced with garlic slivers and whole parsley, with roasted sweet onion purée, wild mushrooms, and parsley coulis ($26.50), and grilled red snapper with baby bok choy and a sauce of fresh tomatoes and coriander ($22.00). Also delicious is the Cub steak (sautéed filet mignon with Cognac, raisins, and peppercorns, served with scalloped potatoes) ($28.00). One of the best-loved things to come out of the kitchen usually isn't on the menu, but is often a gift from the chef—out-of-this-world deep-fried curried onion curls. And for dessert, the soufflés (raspberry, Grand Marnier, pumpkin, or chocolate) ($8.00) are clear winners.

Next door to the Cub Room is the 36-seat **CUB ROOM CAFE** with its own kitchen. A pressed-tin ceiling, brick walls, and black and white marble flooring set the tone. Casual fare is served here all day long and weekend brunch is served from 11:00 a.m. to 4:00 p.m. The emphasis here is on salads, sandwiches, home-cooked favorites, and bakery items. Good choices include a delicious grilled bread salad with peasant bread, tomatoes, black olives, capers, mozzarella, and a balsamic vinaigrette ($6.95), Cobb salad ($9.95), meat loaf with red-skin mashed potatoes ($10.95), turkey pot pie ($7.95), and chicken fricassée with vegetable rice ($10.95). Sandwiches are delicious, especially grilled salmon with arugula, roasted tomatoes, and caper mayonnaise on rosemary focaccia ($10.95), honey-baked ham and brie with red onions and mustard mayonnaise on pumpernickel bread ($7.95), zucchini bread with cream cheese and Granny Smith apples ($3.95), and peanut butter and banana on seven-grain bread, drizzled with honey ($3.95). And desserts won't disappoint. There's a moist flourless chocolate cake served with vanilla ice cream, seasonal fruit crumble, and one of the best carrot cakes in town (each $5.00).

The third component in the Cub Room complex is a private dining room Meer calls his "chef's table" where twelve diners are seated at one large farmhouse table. This rustically charming space also has a fireplace, beautiful pottery, and a window looking into the kitchen. There's an eight-person minimum for the room. Robert Redford used it for a *Quiz Show* gathering.

DUANE PARK CAFE ★★   Contemporary American
157 Duane Street
(between W. Broadway and Hudson)
212/732-5555
Lunch - Monday through Friday Noon - 2:30 p.m.
Dinner - Monday through Saturday 5:30 - 10:00 p.m.
All major cards

Beautiful flower arrangements, a billowy ceiling, cherrywood accents, and tulip-shaped sconces give this very likeable cafe a look of casual grace. It manages to be both very smart and very comfortable at the same time.

The menu is truly eclectic with starters ranging from endive and pear salad with roquefort-pecan dressing ($8.00) to cornmeal crusted oysters with roasted tomatillo salsa ($10.00). There's also smoked trout with cornmeal blini and roasted pear syrup ($9.00) and frisée salad with goat cheese, bacon, and sweet garlic ($9.00). The very inventive mains include grilled herb chicken with rice noodles and Thai cucumber salad ($17.00), rack of lamb with goat cheese and eggplant terrine ($24.00), osso buco Milanese with mascarpone polenta ($20.00), seared coriander tuna with roasted corn salsa ($19.00), filet of tenderloin with smoked mushrooms, spinach, and fontina ($25.00), grilled lobster and scallops with risotto primavera ($23.00), angel hair pasta with scallops, roasted tomato, red pepper, and asiago ($15.00), and penne with asparagus, capers, and lemon ($14.00). Save room for dessert. The ever-changing selection is just as interesting as what has come before—perhaps a warm banana-pecan tartlet with banana-rum caramel or cherry fritters with vanilla ice cream and apricot caramel.

On Mondays a three-course prix fixe is offered all evening for $25.00. A three-course lunch is offered Monday through Friday for $19.97. Both offer exceptional value.

L'ECOLE ★★   French
462 Broadway (at Grand St.)
212/219-3300
Lunch - Monday through Friday Noon - 1:45 p.m.
Dinner - Monday through Thursday 6:00 - 9:30 p.m.;
Friday and Saturday 6:00 - 10:00 p.m.
All major cards

For a really unique dining experience, head for L'Ecole ("the school"), the restaurant of the French Culinary Institute where advanced students cook for the restaurant under the supervision of master chef instructors. The food is contemporary French, rooted in the basics, and spiced with other ethnic influences. While some finished dishes may lack the finesse their fledgling chefs will achieve over time, the food is generally delicious and attractively presented. Dining here is fun and a terrific bargain. The setting is delightful—spacious and airy, with tall windows, French country chairs, warm gold walls displaying colorful modern art, and softly rotating ceiling fans.

At lunch, there's a short menu plus a three-course prix fixe for $17.99 with two choices in each category. Dinner offers a four-course prix fixe from 6:00 to 8:00 p.m. for $24.95 with a number of choices. A five-course set menu is served after 8:00 p.m. for $24.95 which includes a starter, a fish course, a meat course, salad, and dessert. The set menu changes daily, but you can call in advance to find out what's cooking. Some recent enticements: leek and potato soup; provençale garlic soup; potato and mushroom cake; roquefort soufflé; cheese and chive stuffed ravioli; roasted salmon with an onion crust; lamb stew with spring vegetables; fish stew Marseille-style; mango and apple tart in puff pastry; crêpes flamed with Grand Marnier; warm nut cake with pistachio ice cream; and crème brûlée Le Cirque.

LAYLA ★★   Middle Eastern
211 West Broadway (at Franklin St.)
212/431-0700
Lunch - Monday through Friday Noon - 2:30 p.m.
Dinner - Monday through Thursday 6:00 - 11:00 p.m.;
Friday and Saturday 6:00 - 11:30 p.m.;
Sunday 5:30 - 10:00 p.m.
All major cards

The partnership of Robert DeNiro and Drew Nieporent has created yet another hipper-than-hip hot spot with a cool downtown crowd. Fabulously festive, it is an Arabian Nights fantasyland for foodies.   Designed by Christopher Chesnutt, its lively decor is a take on the 15th Century Topkapi Palace in Istanbul.   An eye-catching mural of broken mosaic tiles depicting snake charmers and belly dancers sets a whimsically exotic mood.   Dining in this funky oasis is fun—there's a jovial quality to the place that is contagious. And at 9 or so, a belly dancer sweeps into the room in a swirl of chiffon to stir things up a little.

The inventive menu puts a new spin on Middle Eastern classics with influences from Morocco, Greece, Turkey, Egypt, Israel, and Spain.   To start, there's a nice variety of hot and cold mezze ("small dishes meant to be shared").   Choices include familiars like hummus ($6.00) and tabbouleh ($8.00), along with specialties such as hot phyllo-wrapped sardines ($12.00), vine-ripened tomatoes stuffed with artichoke salad ($11.00), and lamb ravioli with mint yogurt sauce ($12.00). The house-made pita and grilled flatbread accompaniments are fabulous.   For the main, feast on the likes of shellfish "couscous royale" with lobster, shrimp, mussels, clams, and sausage in a spicy saffron broth ($26.00), spiced chicken with eggplant pancakes ($20.00), grilled salmon wrapped in grape leaves with a chick pea pancake and a red wine sauce ($23.00), apricot-glazed lamb kebob over curried bulgar ($24.00), and pan-seared veal chop with curried whipped potatoes and a vegetable tart ($27.00). Desserts are delicious.   Selections include sour cherry Napoleon ($7.00), fresh peach tart with honey coriander ice cream and spiced peach coulis ($7.00), and orange blossom crème brûlée ($7.00).

There's a $28.00 three-course prix fixe with a few choices in each category. Another option is "Layla's Feast" consisting of various selections of hot and cold mezze, chef's specials, and dessert (served family-style for the entire table only) at $42.00 per person.

LE PESCADOU ★★   French Seafood
18 King Street (at Sixth Avenue)
212/924-3434
Lunch - Daily Noon - 6:00 p.m. (Brunch menu on Sunday)
Dinner - Monday through Thursday 6:00 - 11:30 p.m.;
Friday and Saturday 6:00 p.m. - 12:30 a.m.;
Sunday 6:00 - 10:00 p.m.
All major cards

Le Pescadou ("The Fisherman") flaunts its charms in a breezy and intimate Parisian bistro setting with brick walls, a pressed tin ceiling, wood plank floors, and a sidewalk cafe. There's also a handsome French-style bar with wraparound windows and dining tables in front. Beyond the bar, a French glass door opens to the charming dining room where a pretty wood-framed fireplace is the focal point. It is a place oh-so-easy to love. Good looking young French waiters dart about, French tapes play softly in the background, and for a minute you might lose your head and think you're in Nice. Never mind, this is a nice compromise.

Provençale-style seafood reigns supreme here with daily specials listed on a huge blackboard. Everything is fresh and delicious. You might start with a traditional fish soup ($5.50), a grilled vegetable tart misted with basil oil ($7.25), salmon tartare and lime-marinated scallops drizzled with tomato and black olive infused oil ($9.00) or mussels steamed lightly in white wine with shallots and garlic ($6.75). There are also at least four types of oysters available daily. The bouillabaisse ($21.00) is unfailingly good and always a favorite. Other mains include filet of salmon with horseradish crust on a savoy cabbage and tapenade coulis ($17.25), roasted monkfish with steamed mussels in a light saffron sauce ($16.50), and grilled tuna sprinkled with pepper oil ($18.50). While seafood is the name of the game here, there are a couple well-prepared classic non-seafood options—steak frites ($16.50) and herb-encrusted roasted rack of lamb with French fries ($18.50). A daily selection of beautiful desserts is displayed near the entrance to tempt you right from the start. A late night menu is offered after 11:00 p.m., and during Sunday brunch there's solo jazz guitar.

LE STREGHE ★   Italian
331 West Broadway
(Grand Street)
212/343-2080
Lunch - Daily Noon - 5:00 p.m.
Dinner - Daily 5:00 p.m. - 4:00 a.m.
Visa, Diners, American Express

Creatively presented Northern Italian dishes are the hallmark of this bewitching SoHo trattoria. Its contemporary industrial look is highlighted by an aluminum bar and metal moon sculptures. Always amiable, it takes on a certain euro-club feel as the evening crowd disappears and the nightowls take over. Open till 4 a.m., this is the place to satisfy a late-night craving for a good bowl of pasta.

You might kick off with a salad of arugula, radicchio, endive, and parmesan ($7.50), smoked trout with a watercress salad ($9.50), calamari sautéed with wine, red pepper, and garlic ($7.50), or warm veal carpaccio with shavings of parmesan ($9.50). The house specialties are hand-made spaghetti with a lamb sauce and pecorino cheese ($13.75) and risotto with baby artichokes and fresh tomato ($14.50). Other good pasta choices are the spaghetti with imported clams ($14.75), vegetable ravioli with butter and sage ($13.75), pappardelle with asparagus tips, chicken, and fresh tomato ($14.25), gnocchi with a walnut sauce ($12.75), and penne with tomatoes, mozzarella, and basil ($11.50). Notable among the mains are Cornish hen grilled with vegetables ($17.75), sirloin steak grilled and sliced with arugula and parmesan ($20.50), breaded veal cutlet with a salad of tomatoes and basil ($18.75), salmon in a hazelnut sauce ($21.75), and a mixed grilled assortment of fish with lemon and olive oil ($21.75). For a sweet finale, there's tiramisú ($6.50), apple tart with raisins and cinnamon ($6.00), frozen white chocolate mousse with almonds ($7.00), and pears Napoleon with vanilla cream ($6.50).

MEZZOGIORNO ★★   Italian
195 Spring Street (at Sullivan)
212/334-2112
Lunch - Daily Noon - 3:00 p.m. (winter) 5:00 p.m. (summer)
Dinner - Daily 6:00 p.m. - 1:00 a.m.
No credit cards

With exuberance to burn, this lively scene restaurant features specialties of Florence in a space designed by Florentine architect, Robert Magries. It has a festive, playful, and very Italian air about it. Over 100 colorful dioramas decorate the walls, a large marble-topped bar presides over casual cafe tables and chairs, and jovial Italian waiters make it all a merry match. During warmer months, you may want to sit beneath the sprightly blue and white striped awning on the terrace and watch the SoHo parade pass by.

You'll find a great selection of starters with carpaccio a big favorite. Options include smoked goose carpaccio with parmesan and truffle oil ($13.00), salmon carpaccio with basil orange sauce ($12.00), fresh mozzarella with oven-roasted tomato, pepper, and basil ($9.50), assorted grilled vegetables ($10.00), shrimp and beans in a parsley and olive oil sauce ($10.50), polenta with a wild mushroom ragout and taleggio cheese ($10.00), eggplant croquettes with goat cheese and field salad ($10.00), and calamari sautéed with tomato and avocado ($10.00). The pastas are homemade and delicious. There's tagliolini with shrimp, squid, and oven-roasted tomatoes ($16.00), spaghetti with cherry tomatoes and four cheeses ($14.00), penne with fresh tomato, basil, and mozzarella ($13.00), and ravioli of the day ($14.00). There's also a daily preparation of risotto (minimum two persons $28.00). An outstanding crème tiramisú is the dessert of choice.

MONTRACHET ★★★   French
239 West Broadway (between White and Walker Sts.)
212/219-2777
Lunch - Friday only Noon - 3:00 p.m.
Dinner - Monday through Saturday 5:30 - 11:00 p.m.
American Express

Back in 1985 when Drew Nieporent opened this very personal restaurant, it was well off the fine dining map and was one of the first truly great restaurants in Lower Manhattan. Since then this TriBeCa neighborhood has become a treasury of terrific restaurants. And Mr. Nieporent is responsible for a number of them (Tribeca Grill, Nobu, Layla, Tribakery, and Zeppole). But Montrachet, his original venture (named after the Grand Cru white burgundy) remains his most endearing. Its decor at the outset was disarmingly plain. The fabulous fare coming out of its tiny kitchen, along with an outstanding wine list, was what dazzled. While that is still the case, the setting is no longer quite so stark. Arresting abstract art and decorative mirrors have brought a new liveliness to the decor.

Many fine chefs have manned the kitchen here, including David Bouley and Debra Ponzek. Now Chris Gesualdi upholds the tradition of providing the sort of dining experience that lingers in your mind long after the occasion. A memorable dinner here may start with lobster salad with asparagus and a passion fruit vinaigrette ($16.00), rabbit salad with roasted peppers, olives, and basil ($15.00), endive salad with pears, walnuts, and roquefort ($12.00), or warm bluepoint oysters with Champagne sauce and caviar ($14.00). From its ever-changing list of mains, you might select from such enticements as red snapper with oven-dried tomato eggplant ravioli ($27.00), Chilean sea bass with white beans and peppers in a saffron broth ($27.00), guinea hen with potatoes Anna and a vegetable ragout ($29.00), roasted chicken with potato purée and garlic sauce ($24.00), or rack of lamb with Yukon Gold mousseline and herb consommé ($30.00). Desserts are delightful: banana and chocolate gratin on linzer crust ($9.00), peach tart with blueberry sauce ($9.00), and crème brûlée ($8.00).

There are set three-course menus at $32.00 and $38.00 that allow you to sample the magic of this simple, yet elegant, restaurant at a very reasonable price. A $65.00 five-course tasting menu offers more pleasure. And the Friday prix fixe three-course lunch for $19.97 is quite a steal.

NOBU ★★★   Japanese
105 Hudson Street (Franklin St.)
212/219-0500
Lunch - Monday through Friday 11:45 a.m. - 2:15 p.m.
Dinner - Daily 5:45 - 10:15 p.m.
All major cards

Nobu's stunningly unique decor makes dining here as interesting a visual adventure as it is a culinary one. David Rockwell's splashy theatrical design transforms a former bank into a wholly original and chic destination for a bi-coastal celebrity crowd. Its beechwood floors are stencilled with cherry blossoms, tall birch tree columns rise into the ceiling, and the sushi bar stools have chopstick-inspired legs. There's also a curving wall of black river stones, copper-leaf archways, and a bank vault for a service bar. The highly successful partnership of actor Robert DeNiro and restaurant impresario Drew Nieporent lured Nobu Matsuhisa, one of America's greatest Japanese chefs, to preside over this fantasy forest. The setting is certainly one giant decorative leap from Matsuhisa's tiny, highly acclaimed storefront restaurant in Beverly Hills, long regarded as one of the finest Japanese restaurants in the country, but very short on ambience. This masterful matchup results in one terrific dining experience. Book well in advance.

The menu is one that will please not just those who love traditional Japanese food, but also the adventurous foodie and those with timid palates as well. Choices seem unlimited. Sushi and sashimi of superb quality is priced from $2.75 to $5.00 per piece; sushi rolls $3.80 to $8.00; tempura (2 pieces per order) is mostly in the $1-$4.50 range. Daily specials might include "Kumamoto" oyster with Maui onion salsa ($9.00), Chilean sea bass with black bean sauce ($12.50), shrimp and lobster with spicy lemon sauce ($23.00), and taro tartare with caviar ($27.00). House specialties include tender pasta cut from fresh squid and tossed with a garlic sauce ($16.00), black cod with miso ($13.50), and tuna tempura ($15.00). There's also a selection of dinner entrées served with miso soup and rice. Selections include filet of salmon with teriyaki sauce ($24.00), scallops with a pepper sauce ($23.50), a tempura dinner ($25.00), a sashimi dinner ($26.00), a sushi dinner ($26.00), and tenderloin of beef with teriyaki sauce ($24.50). Ginger crème brûlée makes a nice finish.

You might also just chuck the menu and opt for the omakase (chef's choice), a multi-course tasting assembled from the day's peak ingredients ($60.00 and up, $40 at lunch). There's also a 3-course $19.97 prix fixe lunch.

OMEN ★★   Japanese
113 Thompson Street
(between Prince and Spring Sts.)
212/925-8923
Dinner - Daily 5:30 - 10:30 p.m.
American Express only

A former parsonage serves as the setting for this outpost of serenity in the heart of SoHo. Omen's rustic interior and the genuine courtesy is reminiscent of a Japanese country inn. Natural brick walls, a timbered ceiling hung with Oriental paper lanterns, and arresting calligraphy on the walls give it a charming informal feel. Run by a family with three sister restaurants in Kyoto, it features specialties from various regions of Japan.

Omen, its signature dish ($9.50), is a must for those new to this cuisine. It's a hearty soup with a base made by steeping seaweed in chicken stock spiked with vibrant liquids like soy sauce and sake. Fresh vegetables, Japanese noodles, and sesame seeds complete the dish. Other good selections from the à la carte menu include the house salad with scallops, hijiki, cucumber, and watercress ($6.25), shrimp and avocado salad ($7.00), raw tuna with scallions ($6.50), fried soba noodles with seaweed ($7.50), salmon and endive teriyaki sautéed in sake ($16.00), seafood tempura ($16.00), mixed sashimi ($17.00), and cold somen noodles in broth with shrimp and vegetables ($9.25).

Several fixed price dinners are available, each at about $35.00.

PÃO! ★★   Portuguese
322 Spring Street
(at Greenwich St.)
212/334-5464
Dinner - Daily 5:30 - Midnight
All major cards

A delightful dining experience can be had at this still-undiscovered little slice of Lisbon where the food is a congenial mix of traditional and modern Portuguese dishes. And when a restaurant names itself after bread, it must be confident it offers something in that department worth shouting about. Pão's delicious bread comes from Newark's Portuguese bakeries and is indeed moniker-worthy.

The menu is one with many pleasant surprises. Several delicious soups head the list of starters. The caldo verde (a potato broth with shredded kale, bits of potato, and mild Portuguese sausage) ($4.00) is a house specialty. Also good is the stone soup with red beans, potatoes, cilantro, and smoked meats ($4.00). Other good openers include cod cakes ($3.50), shrimp turnovers ($4.00), and chicken empanadão ($5.50). House specialties among mains are grilled tiger shrimp served with a traditional lemon shellfish bread pudding ($13.95), cod and bananas with Portuguese cheese ($20.00 for two), and wild rabbit with chestnuts in a wine sauce ($12.95). Other popular choices include steak in a light Port cream sauce ($12.95) and sautéed cod with egg, onion, and straw potatoes ($11.95). Desserts are terrific. There's a creamy caramel rice pudding served with lime shavings ($3.50), soft poundcake with a lemon and creamy egg custard filling ($4.00), and chocolate mousse ($4.00).

PENANG ★★   Malaysian
109 Spring Street
(between Greene and Mercer Sts.)
212/274-8883
Lunch - Monday through Saturday 11:30 a.m. - 5:00 p.m.;
Sunday 1:00 - 5:00 p.m.
Dinner - Monday through Thursday 5:00 p.m. - Midnight;
Friday and Saturday 5:00 p.m. - 1:00 a.m.;
Sunday 5:00 - 11:00 p.m.
All major cards

Cozy and tropical, this offshoot of a storefront in Flushing introduces Malaysian home cooking to a cool SoHo clientele. Decked out in a rain forest motif, its rustic interior is one of tropical plants and exotic fragrances. There's even a cascading waterfall over a wall of stones and an open kitchen hut. Servers in sarongs complete the mood.

The kitchen successfully combines a variety of culinary influences in its style of cooking that includes curries, satays, chilies, and soy sauces. For a sensational start, try the roti canai ($3.60). This family recipe Indian-style pancake is grilled and served with a potato and chicken curry dipping sauce. Another winner is the roti telur ($5.50), the same Indian-style pancake filled with eggs and onions and served with the same sauce. Other good options include the wonton soup ($3.50), gado-gado (a combination of vegetables with homemade peanut sauce) ($5.50), and the Penang satay (marinated chicken or beef grilled on skewers and served with the same delicious peanut sauce) ($5.50). The noodle dishes are also admirable. Try the mee goreng (egg noodles pan-fried with tofu, potatoes, and bean sprouts, along with a shrimp pancake with squid sauce) ($7.95) or the Penang char keuh teow (flat rice noodles with shrimp, bean sprouts, eggs, and chives fried in a black and chili sauce) ($7.95). The Penang fried rice with basil leaves, mixed vegetables, and oyster sauce ($7.95) is also good. There's much to like among the mains as well. Choices include beef rendang (tender pieces of beef in a paste of ground onions, lemongrass, and chilies simmered in a rich coconut and curry sauce) ($10.50), kari ayam kering (chicken and potatoes cooked in red curry and coconut milk) ($9.95), butterflied jumbo shrimps in the shell fried with coconut batter ($17.95), and fried whole pompano with a black bean sauce ($16.95). Do have the delicious peanut pancake ($4.95) for dessert.

PROVENCE ★★★   French
38 MacDougal Street
(between Prince and Houston Sts.)
212/475-7500
Lunch - Daily Noon - 3:00 p.m.
Dinner - Daily 6:00 - 11:30 p.m.
American Express only

This delightful bistro has an intimate, spirited, and very French atmosphere. From its mustard yellow walls, green paint-chipped chairs, and iron chandeliers, to the plants and flowers in pots, crocks, and buckets, it exudes a rustic charm. And for summer dining, its intimate garden—sheltered under a blue and white striped tent—has a pretty flower-rimmed stone fountain and sets a very romantic mood.

With the scent of garlic in the air and the sound of French music in the background, dining here is like a quick getaway to the sunny side of France. And there is much on the menu to add to the pleasure. To start—a provençale onion and anchovy tart ($5.00), fried zucchini flowers ($8.00), and a tart of baby vegetables and goat cheese ($8.00). Notable mains include skate filet with citrus fondue and basil potato purée ($18.00), broiled filet of monkfish with artichokes and crawfish ($18.00), poached fish in an aïoli-thickened broth ($16.00), pan-roasted lamb with ratatouille (18.00), braised rabbit with olives, fava beans, and chick pea cakes ($18.00), and, of course, a very good steak frites ($19.00). Tops among desserts are the fruit tarts, chocolate terrine with coffee crème anglaise, and crème brûlée (each $6.00).

QUILTY'S ★★   American
177 Prince Street
(between Sullivan and Thompson Sts.)
212/254-1260
Lunch - Tuesday through Saturday Noon - 3:00 p.m.
Brunch - Sunday 11:00 a.m. - 3:00 p.m.
Dinner - Monday through Saturday 6:00 - 11:00 p.m.
All major cards

Quilty's decor is elegantly understated in pale cream on cream. Beautiful butterflies on the walls and sprigs of eucalyptus on each table add color. The real pizazz comes from the kitchen.

Chef Katy Sparks, whose resume includes Mesa Grill and Bolo, has a bold cooking style that is a nice counterpoint to the gracefully spare setting. Starter temptations include a country salad with grilled pears, Smithfield ham, and Maytag blue croutons in a sherry-walnut vinaigrette ($7.50), duck confit and walnut empanada with a red plum star anise sauce ($8.50), eggplant and goat cheese terrine ($8.50), and shrimp roasted over sea salt, served with baby greens and shiitake mushrooms ($10.00). Good mains include grilled pork tenderloin stuffed with cumin-roasted apples, served on braised red cabbage ($19.00), New York sirloin with a twice-baked potato, aged goat cheese, and crispy shallots ($25.00), roasted organic chicken in a caramelized shallot-chive jus with wild mushrooms and fennel gnocchi ($18.50), and grilled Atlantic salmon glazed with honey and green horseradish served with a roasted beet salad and garlicky white bean purée ($19.00). Desserts are wonderful—apple tart for two with whipped crème fraîche and black currant sauce ($12.00), warm berry gratin in a mascarpone chantilly cream and hazelnut praline ($7.50), chocolate and banana empanadas with a caramel-rum sauce ($7.00), and bittersweet chocolate cake with chestnut honey ice cream and a deep chocolate sauce ($7.00).

Come for Sunday brunch and you'll find terrific choices such as salmon hash with poached eggs and a green chile coriander hollandaise ($10.50), scrambled eggs on black olive bruschetta with sautéed spinach ($8.00), bread pudding-style French toast with a spiced mango butter and toasted almonds ($8.00), and a yummy macaroni and cheese in an herbed red chilies crust ($9.00).

RAOUL'S RESTAURANT ★★   French
180 Prince Street
(between Sullivan & Thompson Sts.)
212/966-3518
Dinner - Monday through Thursday 5:30 p.m. - Midnight;
Friday through Sunday 5:30 p.m. - 2:00 a.m.;
All major cards

Nostalgia prevails in this old-fashioned French bistro. Its friendly feel, genuine French atmosphere, and solid bistro cooking have kept it a SoHo favorite over the years. There's a funky bar area in front with a black tin ceiling, an art deco wood bar, colorful posters, and a collection of interesting wall decor. In back, a skylit room and pleasant dining area nicely round out this very amiable place.

Good starters include escargots with polenta ($9.00), house paté (6.50), and asparagus vinaigrette ($9.00). Favorites among the mains are the steak au poivre ($24.00), lamb medallions with gorgonzola ($22.00), and the sea bass papillote ($24.00). Desserts are standard: crème brûlée ($6.00), profiteroles au chocolat ($7.00), and chocolate gâteau ($6.00).

ROSEMARIE'S ★★   Italian
145 Duane Street
(between W. Broadway and Church St.)
212/285-2610
Lunch - Monday through Friday Noon - 2:30 p.m.
Dinner - Monday through Friday 5:30 - 10:00 p.m.;
Saturday 5:30 - 10:30 p.m.
All major cards

This wonderful place is cozy and charming. Though off the beaten path, it is well worth seeking out for its utterly delicious Northern Italian food and romantic ambience. At the entrance, there's a handsome dark wood bar that leads to a graceful brick-walled dining room with just sixteen tables. A huge Florentine photo mural of an Italian cloister covers one wall and attractive ceramics adorn the room. It is the kind of endearing place you almost want to keep as your own little secret, but in the end you just can't resist showing off your special find.

Good starters include wild mushrooms with polenta, pancetta, and sage ($10.00), quail with prosciutto and a potato cake ($10.00), shrimp with frisée, white bean salad, and cayenne vinaigrette ($9.00), and deep-fried calamari with anchovy lemon mayonnaise ($8.00). The standout pasta is the ravioli with a ricotta and spinach filling and fresh tomato ($15.00). Also delicious is a lusty rigatoni with broccoli rabe, pancetta, and pecorino cheese ($15.00), risotto with squash blossoms and white truffle oil ($17.00), tagliatelle with shrimp, sea scallops, and tomato ($16.00), and arugula gnocchi with parmesan and cream ($15.00). Half orders of pasta are $10.00. House specialties among mains are a crisp skate with greens, new potatoes, and balsamic brown butter ($18.00) and braised veal shank with vegetable risotto ($19.00). Other good choices include red snapper with artichoke, roast garlic, and lemon ($19.00), roast farm-raised chicken with whipped and shoestring potatoes ($18.00), sautéed veal chop with porcini mushrooms and polenta ($26.00), and roast loin of lamb with tomato mashed potatoes and black olives ($23.00). Of the desserts, the house specialty is an exceptional tiramisú ($7.00). Other sweet temptations include chocolate soufflé cake ($7.00), apple bread pudding with vanilla sauce ($7.00), and a strawberry and banana Napoleon ($7.50).

SAVORE ★★   Italian
200 Spring Street (Sullivan St.)
212/431-1212
Lunch - Daily Noon - 3:00 p.m.
Dinner - Daily 5:30 - Midnight
All major cards

Savore, with its pale yellow walls, gray slate floor, alabaster hanging lamps, white linen, and floor-to-ceiling windows, has a crisp, elegant simplicity. It's the sort of place you notice when you pass by, thinking how fresh and pleasant it looks. Once inside, you discover it's not the typical Tuscan trattoria you might have expected, for its menu draws inspiration from Tuscan Renaissance cooking and offers many unusual dishes. While not everyone will be tempted by the wild boar specialties, there's plenty to satisfy less adventurous palates as well.

To start, pappa al pomodoro ($8.00) is a simple and irresistible mix of tomatoes, bread, and olive oil. Other good choices include miniature eggplant pizzas with tomato, mozzarella, and capers ($8.00), grilled vegetables ($9.00), sautéed monkfish with artichoke hearts ($12.00), radicchio rolls with mozzarella, capers, and anchovies ($8.00), and a very good antipasto with prosciutto, salami, olives and crostini ($9.50). There's also a polenta-like corn mousse with wild boar sauce ($10.00) and stuffed calamari ($10.00). The pastas are all delicious. Choices include a ravioli of the day ($13.00), pasta rolled with crabmeat ($13.00), penne with sage, prosciutto, and tomato ($11.00), tagliolini with a lemon sauce ($11.00), and hand-cut spaghetti with roasted tomato and basil ($12.00). For the main, there's duck with raisins and pine nuts ($16.00), baby chicken slices with rosemary and black olives ($14.00), filet mignon in red wine ($19.00), and veal rolls with a daily preparation ($18.00). And there is wild boar ($17.00).

SAVOY ★★   Mediterranean
70 Prince Street (Crosby St.)
212/219-8570
Lunch - Monday through Saturday Noon - 3:00 p.m.
Dinner - Monday through Thursday 6:00 - 10:30 p.m.;
Friday and Saturday 6:00 - 11:00 p.m.;
Sunday 6:00 - 10:00 p.m.
Visa, Master

This unassuming and congenial eatery, favored by SoHo gallery owners and artists, has a friendly neighborhood feel. A working fireplace, fabric banquettes, and cozy cafe tables set the scene for its fresh and inventive Mediterranean cuisine.

Its seasonal menu changes often, drawing on the pick of the harvest. Recent enticements among starters included beet soup with jasmine rice and tarragon roasted peppers ($7.00), asparagus and potato salad with baked ricotta salata and chestnut honey vinaigrette ($8.50), house-smoked salmon with almond caper dressing and Jerusalem artichoke salad ($9.50), roasted lamb on garlic toast ($9.00), and grilled sea scallops with a fennel, rice bean, and green olive salad ($8.00). Mains have been equally imaginative with choices like spaghetti with grilled shrimp, leek purée, and sun-dried tomato gremolata ($17.00), roasted grouper in thyme broth with spinach ricotta gnocchi and baby clams ($19.50), asparagus risotto with black bass, shiitakes, and parsley ($17.00), sautéed calf's liver with spring peas, bacon, roasted shallots, and a yucca pancake ($19.00), roasted pork tenderloin with grilled polenta and braised escarole ($18.50), grilled lamb loin chops with tamarind spiced eggplant and saffron rice ($22.00), and soft shell crabs with beet gazpacho and garlicked spaghetti squash ($21.00).

In keeping with the personalized ambience here, a tiny upstairs bar and dining area has opened where from Tuesday to Saturday, chef Peter Hoffman prepares $48.00 four-course prix-fixe meals, all cooked in front of you in the fireplace on a special spit made in France.

TRIBECA GRILL ★★   Contemporary American
375 Greenwich Street
(corner of Franklin Street)
212/941-3900
Lunch - Monday through Friday 11:30 a.m. - 3:00 p.m.;
Brunch - Sunday 11:30 a.m. - 3:00 p.m.
Midday Menu - 3:00 - 5:00 p.m.
Dinner - Monday through Friday 5:30 - 10:45 p.m.;
Saturday 5:30 - 11:30 p.m.; Sunday 5:30 - 9:45 p.m.
All major cards

    Owned by Oscar-winning actor Robert DeNiro in partnership with celebrated restaurateur Drew Nieporent, it's not surprising that this is a place favored by a chic celebrity crowd. Situated in a converted coffee factory, the lofty brick restaurant space buzzes with an atmosphere of excitement and vivacity. The majestic old tiffany-styled bar that once graced Maxwell's Plum (New York's trendiest restaurant in the late '60s) stands centerstage and artwork by Mr. DeNiro's late father adorns the walls. The building also houses a film production center where major players like Steven Spielberg, Martin Scorsese, and Brian De Palma have offices. But this is not just a place to catch a glimpse of a movie producer, leading man, or cover girl. It holds its own as a restaurant where the food is very fine and you're made to feel welcome even if you've never made a magazine cover or been nominated for an Academy Award.

    Good starters on the contemporary American menu include crisp-fried oysters with garlic anchovy aïoli ($11.00), corn chowder with grilled shrimp and coriander ($8.00), smoked salmon with potato pancakes and a lemon-caper vinaigrette ($12.00), and a shrimp and vegetable spring roll with persimmon sweet and sour sauce ($12.00). Some standout mains are the angel hair pasta with seared sea scallops and Manilla clams ($22.00), crisp baby chicken with escarole and white beans with a lemon-thyme sauce ($21.00), grilled salmon with Japanese eggplant and wild greens with a sesame vinaigrette ($23.00), herb-crusted rack of lamb with roasted vegetables ($26.00), grilled ribeye steak with a goat cheese and onion tart ($26.00), and barbecued breast of duck with a carrot-ginger purée and spiced wild mushrooms ($23.00). The desserts are wonderful, too. Who could resist temptations like the banana tart with milk chocolate malt ice cream, warm pear fritters with pear sorbet, and chocolate cherry hazelnut tart with ice cream (each $7.00).

ZOË ★★★   Contemporary American
90 Prince Street
(between Broadway and Mercer St.)
212/966-6722
Lunch - Monday through Friday Noon - 3:00 p.m.
Brunch - Saturday and Sunday Noon - 3:00 p.m.
Dinner - Monday through Thursday 6:00 - 10:30 p.m.;
Friday and Saturday 6:00 - 11:00 p.m.;
Sunday 5:30 - 10:00 p.m.
All major cards

This very hip spot is much more than just a trendy SoHo destination of the moment. The food is so inventive and so good that after a first visit you'll be thinking about what to have on the next one. The setting is that of a SoHo loft with original vintage tiles and fourteen-foot columns. The huge space is warmed by lively colors and an exposed kitchen featuring a wood-burning oven, grill, and rotisserie. And there's a chef's counter overlooking the open kitchen for those wishing to watch the culinary magicians at work. During warm weather, folding doors in front open to add an alfresco feel.

You'll find a delightful Pacific Rim twist to some of the dishes on the contemporary American menu. Among starters, good choices include sautéed herbed gnocchi with wild mushrooms, pancetta, arugula, and pecorino romano ($9.00/$18.00 as a main), crispy calamari with a Vietnamese dipping sauce ($8.75), oak-smoked salmon with warm potato-goat cheese knishes with horseradish sour cream ($10.00), grilled vegetable gazpacho with a crab-basil salad ($7.75), and a delicious salad of grilled portobello mushrooms, mizuna, and gorgonzola with toasted almonds and a smoked red onion vinaigrette ($9.00). Terrific mains include a barbecued double-thick pork chop with jalapeño-cheddar cornbread and fire-roasted salsa ($18.50), oven-crisped chicken with buttermilk mashed potatoes, watercress slaw, and a roasted garlic sauce ($18.50), grilled ribeye steak with a baked potato with truffle butter and Kentucky Bourbon sauce ($25.00), smoke-roasted duck breast from the rotisserie with wild mushroom-hominy cakes and caramelized turnips ($24.00), and grilled salmon with Moroccan spices, basil mashed potatoes and charred tomato compote ($19.75). If desserts are your undoing, you'll be thoroughly undone here trying to decide between the likes of pear tarte Tatin with chamomile ice cream and berries, German chocolate cake with banana ice cream and chocolate sauce, and lemon-mascarpone tart with a strawberry and caramel sauce (each $7.00). Several alternative non-fat desserts are also offered—assorted fresh fruit and berries with housemade non-fat frozen yogurt

($8.00) and a lemon meringue sandwich concoction with a strawberry compote ($7.00).

The brunch menu is equally alluring with herb-scrambled eggs on smoked salmon potato cakes with cucumber-dill raita ($12.00), banana-stuffed almond French toast served with vanilla maple syrup with blueberries ($9.50), and veal and pork meatloaf with cheddar mashed potatoes, spinach, and crisp onions ($11.50). Some great sandwiches and pizzas round out the carte.

THEATER DISTRICT

Theater District

WEST SIDE

CENTRAL PARK

Columbus
Circle

Central Park South

W. 59th St.

W. 58th St. — W. 58th St.

W. 57th St. — W. 57th St.

W. 56th St. — W. 56th St.

W. 55th St. — W. 55th St.

W. 54th St. — W. 54th St.

De Witt Clinton Park

W. 53rd St. — W. 53rd St.

W. 52nd St. — W. 52nd St.

W. 51st St. — W. 51st St.

W. 50th St. — W. 50th St.

W. 49th St. — W. 49th St.

W. 48th St. — W. 48th St.

W. 47th St. — W. 47th St.

HUDSON RIVER

W. 46th St. — W. 46th St.

W. 45th St. — W. 45th St.

W. 44th St. — W. 44th St.

W. 43rd St. — W. 43rd St.

Times Square

W. 42nd St. — W. 42nd St.

W. 41st St.

Port Authority Bus Terminal

W. 40th St.

Lincoln Tunnel

W. 39th St.

W. 38th St.

Jacob K. Javits Convention Center

W. 37th St.

W. 36th St.

W. 35th St.

W. 34th St.

CHELSEA

10th Ave. · 9th Ave. · 8th Ave. · 7th Ave.

Broadway

Avenue of the Americas (6th Ave.)

MIDTOWN

11th Ave. · Galvin Ave. · Dyer Ave.

12th Ave.

Broadway

UNION SQUARE/GRAMERCY PARK/MURRAY HILL

Avenue of the Americas (6th Ave.)

B. SMITH'S ★★   International
771 Eighth Avenue (at 47th St.)
212/247-2222
Lunch - Daily Noon - 4:00 p.m.
Dinner - Sunday and Monday 4:00 - 11:00 p.m.;
Tuesday through Thursday 4:00 - 11:30 p.m.;
Friday and Saturday 4:00 p.m. - Midnight
All major cards

Owned by former model, Barbara Smith, this large, airy restaurant has a cool and attractive modern decor and a very popular deco-styled bar. Its stylish interior and sophisticated yet homey style of cooking—international eclectic with Southern accents—draws an attractive pre- and post-theater crowd.

You might begin with shrimp steeped in Chardonnay with garlic and herbs ($8.95), petite cassoulet of duck confit, sausage, and white beans ($9.95), classic Southern pea soup ($4.50), or low country crab and corn chowder ($6.95). Good mains include pan-fried cornmeal-dipped whiting with tartar sauce, coleslaw, and potato straws ($11.95), roast filet of fresh striped bass with a light tomato caper sauce ($19.95), breast of chicken filled with wild mushrooms and herbs, sautéed and served in a pool of braised fresh vegetables ($12.95), smothered pork chops with fried green apples ($13.95), Maine lobster ravioli with a tarragon shellfish bisque and warm mascarpone cheese ($17.95), and duckling sausage lasagna ($16.95). Several light plates are offered, too, such as grilled duck sausage with coarse mustard and warm potato salad ($8.75) and potato and leek pancakes with roast tomato, smoked salmon, crème fraîche, and caviar ($9.75). Most popular among desserts is Ms. Smith's grandmother's recipe for sweet potato pecan pie ($4.95). The coconut tuiles with white chocolate ice cream and macadamia nuts ($4.95) is another winner.

BARBETTA ★★   Italian
321 West 46th Street
(between Eighth and Ninth Aves.)
212/246-9171
Lunch - Monday through Saturday Noon - 2:00 p.m.
Dinner - Monday through Saturday 5:00 p.m. - Midnight
All major cards

A palatial atmosphere pervades this wonderful place, with its authentic 18th Century Piemontese furniture and glittering chandeliers. Established in

1906, it is a theater district institution as well as New York's oldest family-run Italian restaurant. Situated on the ground floors of what are actually several stately townhouses, it has the ambience of an Italian villa and one of the most pleasant gardens in town. Its stone terrace has a large, beautiful fountain at its center and is ringed with summery white tables and chairs. Pretty flowers surround the fountain and tiny flowering potted plants grace the tables. Century-old trees flowering with jasmine, magnolia blossoms, and gardenias add to its bucolic charm and create a fragrant oasis that seems a million miles away from Eighth Avenue.

The food is that of Northern Italy, particularly from Piemonte, Italy's northwestern most region. You might start with the house-smoked Atlantic salmon ($9.75), mozzarella and marinated eggplant ($9.00), or minestrone ($8.00). The pastas are delicious, but pricey. Served in half portions, offerings include linguine pesto ($15.00), handmade agnolotti ($16.00), cannelloni ($14.00), and the evening's special ($15.00). Pasta taken as a main course is $24.00. The risottos, particularly that with wild porcini mushrooms ($16.00 half portion), are also very good—and also pricey with full portions at $26.00. Mains vary daily and might include roasted organic and herb-fed rabbit in a white wine-lemon sauce with savoy cabbage ($28.00), beef braised in red wine ($26.00), charcoal-grilled rack of veal chop with a virgin olive oil herb sauce ($29.00), and roast rack of lamb with braising greens ($29.00). For dessert, the fruit tarts are particularly good ($9.00). Other good choices are the panna cotta, almond cake, and crème brûlée (each $9.00).

A special $39.00 six course pre-theater menu is available from 5:00 to 6:30 p.m. with a number of choices among appetizers, mains, and desserts—quite a bargain.

BECCO ★★   Italian
355 West 46th Street
(between Eighth and Ninth Aves.)
212/397-7597
Lunch - Monday through Saturday Noon - 3:00 p.m.
Dinner - Monday through Saturday 5:00 - Midnight;
Sunday Noon - 10:00 p.m.
All major cards

Becco, country cousin of the fabulous Felidia on East 58th Street, brims with its own brand of style and distinction. Its attractive two-story setting has an Italian country house feel and a variety of personalities. The appealing front dining room—dominated by a pewter and wood bar and wood-beamed ceiling—has a wine-cellar look and convivial, informal feel; the delightful back room has rough-textured and colorfully stencilled walls, a peaked skylight, and a sunny mood. The second level provides a more formal dining experience and has a small terrace overlooking Restaurant Row.

Wherever you land, you'll be greeted by a bowl of delicious warm country breads and breadsticks and a menu that, for my money, offers one of the best values in town. Part of it consists of a **prix fixe of $19.95**. This includes two courses—the first a delicious antipasto plate with grilled vegetables, roasted potatoes, and different types of seafood salads. The second course is three pastas (usually one a risotto) of the day that are served tableside from hot skillets. You're served a sampling of each and then an unlimited portion of any or all of the three. Each I've sampled has been perfectly delicious. (**At lunch, the price is $16.95.**) If you wish, you can add a third course with the price ranging from $27.95 to $37.95 depending on your entrée choice. Ordering à la carte (which includes a Caesar salad), choices include salmon in a mustard sauce served with garlic potatoes and escarole ($18.95), spicy, free-range chicken with onion mashed potatoes and mixed grilled vegetables ($18.95), braised veal shank with barley risotto and garden vegetables ($19.95), grilled rack of lamb with onion mashed potatoes, braised peas, scallions, and zucchini ($20.95), Italian peppers stuffed with beef, pork, veal, and rice served with onion mashed potatoes ($16.95), and porterhouse steak served with roasted garlic potatoes and spinach ($24.95). The wine list offers yet another bargain, with an extensive collection of selected Italian and American wines all priced at $15.00.

CAFE BOTANICA ★★   American
(Essex House)
160 Central Park South
(between Sixth and Seventh Aves.)
212/484-5120
Lunch - Monday through Saturday Noon - 2:30 p.m.
Brunch - Sunday 11:00 a.m. - 2:30 p.m.
Dinner - Daily 5:30 - 10:30 p.m.
All major cards

Just off the lobby in the Essex House, this delightful garden-themed cafe overlooks the lively street scene alongside Central Park. The sunny, flower-filled restaurant features a glass-enclosed atrium and fountain, colorful paintings, beautiful wicker armchairs, and nice big tables. It has just the right

269

mix of style and comfort, and is a particularly pleasant spot for lunch or brunch.

The eclectic dinner menu predominantly features a light Mediterranean-California style cuisine, with some favorite all-American starters like Maryland crab cakes with a roasted corn salad and cilantro cream ($12.50), poached jumbo shrimp cocktail ($14.50), sautéed artichoke and wild mushrooms ($9.00), and field greens with a lemon vinaigrette dressing ($12.50). Main course specialties include grilled chicken with field greens and tomato-olive salsa ($17.50), seared salmon scaloppine with roasted beets and horseradish cream ($21.00), grilled sea scallops ($21.50), seared tuna loin ($21.50), and grilled sirloin steak with herbed crushed potatoes, grilled zucchini, and tomato confit ($23.00). Desserts are spectacular. Daily selections might include excellent fruit tarts, chocolate truffle cake, and mango mousse.

A pre-theatre menu is served from 5:30 to 7:00 p.m., which offers three courses for $32.00. There are three or four choices in each category. Starters might include a selection of cold appetizers from the buffet, soup of the day, and orzo pasta sautéed with summer garden vegetables and fresh herbs. For the main, you might choose grilled breast of chicken with chicken sausage and whipped potatoes, roasted codfish with grilled endives, black olives, capers, and tomatoes, or grilled sirloin steak. Finish with a selection from the dessert buffet, along with coffee or tea.

The Sunday brunch is wonderful. It features a bountiful appetizer and dessert buffet and a menu choice of mains. The price is $42.00 per person and includes a glass of Champagne.

CARMINE'S ★   Italian
200 West 44th Street
(between Broadway and Eighth Ave.)
212/221-3800
Daily 11:30 a.m. - 11:00 p.m.
American Express

Garlicky aromas surround you from the moment you open the door to this immensely popular family-style Italian. While restaurant critics either ignore it completely or toss it off as mediocre to fair, it is clearly the people's choice. With its no-reservations policy for parties of less than six, the waits here are seldom under 45 minutes and more for before or after theatre dining. It is an old-fashioned red-sauce Italian place with a pleasant turn-of-the-century decor and a lot of convivial buzz. The Southern Italian offerings are served family-style with each platter enough to serve at least two people. You'll know you're close to Carmine's when you start seeing people on 44th Street carrying styrofoam containers of leftovers. It's that kind of place.

You might start with baked clams ($13.50), stuffed artichoke ($8.50), stuffed mushrooms ($7.50), or eggplant parmigiana ($8.00). The pastas, though mass-produced, are good and there's a lot of choice. Among them, you'll find rigatoni with broccoli and sausage ($19.00), pasta (your choice) with sausage ($16.00), ravioli ($16.00), manicotti ($19.00), and lasagna ($19.00). Other popular options include veal parmigiana ($19.00), veal Marsala ($17.00), porterhouse steak with peppers and onions ($39.50), chicken parmigiana ($17.00), lemon chicken ($15.00), shrimp marinara ($20.00), and shrimp parmigiana ($19.00).

CHEZ JOSEPHINE ★★   French
414 West 42nd Street (between Ninth and Tenth Aves.)
212/594-1925
Dinner - Monday through Saturday 5:00 p.m. - 1:00 a.m.
All major cards

The atmosphere is festive, theatrical, and very, very French at Jean-Claude Baker's bistro paying loving tribute to his mother, cabaret legend Josephine Baker. Evocative of Paris nightclubs of the '20s when she was all the rage, its ambience is one of playful decadence and *joie de vivre*. Shellacked brick walls, lush red draperies, lazy red ceiling fans, and antique wall sconces form the backdrop for images of the restaurant's seductive namesake in various stages of undress. An evening here is a delightful escape to a bygone era. Bluesy pianists and singers are featured and celebrity performers sometimes drop in for a guest stint. Open since 1986, its far west theater district location wasn't always so well-traveled, however. The endlessly entertaining Jean-Claude recalls times he would run to Holy Cross Church down the street to light candles and pray for a full house. His prayers have long been answered, so book well in advance for pre- or post-theater.

The appealing menu combines earthy French bistro fare with Southern American cooking, and it is all quite good. You might start with endive salad with roquefort and walnuts ($8.00), a Napoleon of warm asparagus with shiitake mushrooms ($8.00), Chinese ravioli with goat cheese and toasted pine nuts ($8.00), Maryland crab cake with tartar sauce and field greens ($9.50), crispy oysters on a bed of slivered fennel ($9.00), or chunky lobster bisque

($7.50). Lobster cassoulet with shrimp, scallops, seafood sausage, and black beans in a light shellfish broth ($23.00), Elvira's down-home fried chicken with sweet potato fries and red pepper cornbread ($16.50), and Black Angus steak au poivre ($24.50) are house specialties among mains. Other good main choices include angel hair pasta with wild mushrooms, basil, and sun-dried tomatoes ($17.00), scallops and shrimp risotto with collard greens ($19.50), sautéed chicken breast with portobello mushrooms and a Cognac sauce ($18.00), and double lamb chops with provençale vegetables and whipped potatoes ($26.50). Desserts are delicious: black and white chocolate mousse ($6.50), warm apple and rhubarb crêpe cake ($6.50), and crème brûlée ($7.00).

CHRISTER'S ★★   Scandinavian
145 West 55th Street (between Sixth and Seventh Aves.)
212/974-7224
Lunch - Daily Noon - 3:00 p.m.
Dinner - Daily 5:30 - 11:00 p.m.
All major cards

Christer's charming interior, designed by David Rockwell, mixes whimsy and humor with colorful, rustic appointments to create the ambience of an alpine mountain lodge. A narrow 40-foot passage, which Rockwell calls "the covered bridge," connects the bar to the dining areas. Copper fish scales on the bar's ceiling, fanciful blown-glass fish sconces, and fish sculptures throughout signal the restaurant's affectionate leaning to the treasures of the sea. Fish paintings and old sepia photos of catches line the walls. Even the floor recalls the sea with colorful stencils of fish, seaweed, and other ocean life. Within this aquatic oasis, a huge stone fireplace, red and white checkered banquettes, and wooden chairs painted in bright colors set a cheerful tone and give the place the feel of a snug Alpine harbor.

Swedish-born chef/owner Christer Larsson (who made a name for himself at Aquavit over a period of six years) presents a Scandinavian-inspired menu—with a specialty of salmon—that integrates contemporary and ethnic influences with the classical. A good way to start a meal here is with the smorgasbord bar (an assortment of delicious Scandinavian appetizers) ($12.50; $21.00 as a main). Other popular openers include smoked salmon with toasted brioche and herb cheese ($12.50), oysters on half shells with Absolut horseradish sauce ($9.50), grilled tomato with mozzarella, basil, and roasted peppers ($8.00), mushroom soup with a potato and bacon dumpling ($7.00), and field green salad with a goat cheese spring roll ($7.50). Top choices among the mains are the salmon specials: house-smoked salmon with black beans, corn, avocado, and tomatillo salsa ($24.00); ginger-glazed salmon with fried wild rice, cabbage, and mushrooms ($24.00); baked salmon with bacon, sweet potato purée, and vegetable slaw ($24.00); and tandoori salmon with fresh mango chutney, vegetable curry, and a tamarind sauce ($24.00). Fish from the grille includes swordfish ($23.50), monk fish ($19.00), and North Atlantic halibut ($21.50) served with stir-fried vegetables. Also nice is sautéed red snapper with roasted plum tomato sauce and rosemary mashed potatoes ($24.00). Non-seafood offerings also entice with choices like tenderloin of beef with garlic potatoes and creamed spinach ($26.00), grilled chicken with polenta and sun-dried tomato sauce ($18.50), veal fricadelles with mashed potatoes and plum compote sauce ($17.50), and venison loin with juniper sauce and lingonberries ($27.00). And for a pleasant finale, there's blueberry and brioche pudding with lemon sabayon and cardamom ($7.50), apple leaf with vanilla ice cream and caramel ($8.00), and chocolate mud pie with pecan crumble and vanilla ice cream ($8.50).

A pre-theater prix fixe is available from 5:30 to 7:00 p.m. with two courses for $27.00 or three courses for $34.00. There are several choices in each category; some are specials, others from the main menu.

CITÉ ★★   Continental
120 West 51st Street
(between Sixth and Seventh Aves.)
212/956-7100
Lunch - Monday through Friday Noon - 5:00 p.m.
Dinner - Daily 5:00 - 11:30 p.m.
All major cards

The character and charm of a Parisian brasserie is recreated in this delightful cafe/steakhouse. The stunning creamy multi-level quarters are filled with colorful Parisian artifacts and art deco details taken from the original Au Bon Marché department store in Paris. The atmosphere is one of casual sophistication.

The eclectic American/Continental menu features a nice variety of starters with choices that include grilled corn chowder ($6.75), shrimp cocktail ($13.75), chilled spicy tomato and fennel soup ($6.50), and pan-seared crab cake with summer salsa ($10.75). Terrific main selections include baby rack of lamb with polenta and rosemary ($25.50), spit-roasted lemon pepper chicken with golden couscous and fennel ($19.75), filet mignon and fries ($22.50), and swordfish steak with black bean and corn salsa ($26.50). But the grilled classics

($25.50) seem to be the most popular choices: sliced steak, roast prime rib, sirloin prime, filet au poivre, and veal chop. Sides include great fries ($6.50), creamy mashed potatoes ($6.25), and okay creamed spinach ($6.50). Of the desserts, my vote goes to the profiteroles with vanilla ice cream in a nice big puddle of warm deep chocolate sauce. Also good are the shortcake with seasonal fruit, a chocolate cake duo with pistachio ice cream, and crème brûlée rice pudding (each $7.75).

A prix fixe dinner with three courses and coffee is $39.50; but the real steal is Cité's wine dinners where four superior wines are served freely with an after 8:00 p.m. prix fixe three-course dinner ($49.95).

COCO PAZZO TEATRO ★★   Italian
235 West 46th Street
(between Broadway and Eighth Ave.)
212/827-4222
Lunch - Monday through Saturday 11:30 a.m. - 3:00 p.m.;
Sunday 11:00 a.m. - 3:00 p.m.
Dinner - Monday through Saturday 5:30 p.m. - Midnight;
Sunday 5:00 - 10:00 p.m.
All major cards

A snazzy setting, snappy service, terrific pastas, and fab desserts combine to create one happy dining experience at Pino Luongo's Broadway baby. This welcome newcomer is stylish, but informal, with an attractive dining room that boasts a recessed wood ceiling, maple wood floors, and gray and white marble columns. Colorful frescoes of wine bottles echo those on the walls of its Upper East Side sibling and add to its casually chic ambience. Its convenient location—smack-dab in the heart of the theater district—and the good buzz it has been generating since its opening makes for a lively full house both pre- and post-theater.

The menu offers dishes from Mr. Luongo's native Tuscany, including some recipes from his mother. But this is not essentially a Tuscan restaurant. While the menu features some rustic Tuscan fare, it is also spiked with an American accent. For starters, a house specialty is the jicama salad with oranges and onion ($6.75). Other refreshing choices include cured swordfish layered with tomato and cucumber ($8.50) and calamari in a lemon-mustard dressing ($8.00). And there's always a good homemade soup of the day ($6.00). Pasta choices might be oversized meat ravioli in butter and sage ($12.50), spaghetti with bay scallops browned in beer ($13.50), or Mrs.

Luongo's rigatoni with calamari and baby artichokes ($13.50). Signature dishes among mains include a giant Florentine steak for two ($42.00) and lobster in two acts—grilled and in pasta ($32.00). Other notable choices include seared tuna with curry-fried potatoes ($18.00), braised lamb with orange zest, fava beans, and olives ($16.00), double-cut pork chops served with apple-bacon chutney ($15.50), and roasted veal with artichoke relish ($17.50). The menu is rounded out with some good pizzas ($9.50-$12.50). The changing parade of desserts ($6.00) feature irresistible and gorgeous goodies like Baked Alaska, peach cobbler, old-fashioned banana splits, and the house specialty watermelon parfait.

FANTINO ★★★   Italian
Ritz Carlton Hotel
112 Central Park South
(between Sixth and Seventh Aves.)
212/664-7700
Brunch - Saturday and Sunday 11:00 a.m. - 2:00 p.m.
Lunch - Monday through Friday Noon - 2:00 p.m.
Dinner - Tuesday through Saturday 5:30 - 11:00 p.m.
All major cards

Two working fireplaces, crystal chandeliers, and china designed by Gianni Versace set an elegant tone at this gracious dining room nestled in the Ritz Carlton Hotel. Decorated in warm peach and mauve tones with beautiful tapestry armchairs, fresh flowers, and French and Italian oil paintings, it has the kind of easy elegance that seems in perfect harmony with the impeccable service. It is a restaurant so steeped in luxury you immediately sense you're going to spend a lot of money here and that you might not even regret it.

The contemporary Italian fare is as appealing as the room in which it is served. To start, you might opt for the grilled vegetable goat cheese tian ($11.00), vine-ripened tomatoes with mozzarella and fresh basil ($11.00), tomato basil risotto with artichokes, carrots, peppers, fennel, and shaved reggiano ($9.00), or porcini mushroom soup ($10.00). The outstanding pastas can be taken as either a starter or main course. Choices include pappardelle with grilled shrimp, plum tomatoes, asparagus, and fresh basil ($12.00/$24.00), white and black tagliatelle with fresh Maine lobster and tender fava beans ($18.00/$26.00), and penne with string beans, artichokes, roasted yellow peppers, and aged ricotta ($10.00/$18.00). Good choices among mains include roasted rack of lamb with grilled vegetables and mint couscous ($28.00), grilled beef tenderloin with foie gras, portobello chanterelle mushrooms, and truffle béarnaise ($30.00), and roasted veal chop with a white bean lentil ragout, broccoli rabe, and grilled polenta ($30.00).

A good way to sample the luxury of dining here without breaking the budget is with the pre-theater dinner menu served between 5:30 and 7:00 p.m., which offers three courses for $29.00. You might start with smoked salmon, a Caesar salad, or lamb Tuscany white bean soup with fresh mint. For the main: baby red snapper with roma tomatoes, capers, and saffron risotto croquettes; roasted baby free-range chicken with broccoli rabe, whipped potatoes, and truffle jus; or pepper-crusted New York sirloin with wild mushrooms, rosemary potatoes, and Merlot sauce. Finish with a classic tiramisú, Tahitian vanilla crème brûlée, or flourless chocolate cake with cinnamon ice cream.

FIREBIRD ★★   Russian
365 West 46th Street
(between Eighth and Ninth Aves.)
212/586-0244
Lunch - Wednesday and Saturday 11:45 a.m. - 2:15 p.m.
Dinner - Sunday through Thursday 5:00 - 10:30 p.m.;
Friday and Saturday 5:00 - 11:30 p.m.
All major cards

A posh atmosphere sets the stage for the pre-Revolutionary Russian cuisine that has recently come to Restaurant Row. Two brownstones have been renovated to resemble a turn-of-the-century St. Petersburg mansion with eight ornately decorated rooms. The polished waitstaff has been outfitted by Oleg Cassini and the dining rooms are lavish with antiques and Russian bric-a-brac. Dining in this old-fashioned charmer is in itself a theatrical experience with tableside service that can be quite a show as well. The setting seems perfect for Champagne and caviar. While many restaurants aim to transport you to another time and place, FireBird—for a time—really can.

The changing menu's recent starter offerings have included smoked salmon with a cucumber salad and five-grain bread ($10.50), Georgian baby eggplant stuffed with peppers, walnuts, and tomatoes with a scallion sauce ($8.50), and crab and rice croquettes ($9.75). Good selections among mains include grilled marinated sturgeon with roasted potatoes ($22.00) and seared beef filet with wild mushrooms and a potato/apple casserole ($23.50). The crisp roast chicken with apricots, a bulgar-okra salad and spinach with yogurt and spices ($23.50) is also good, but the chicken can sometimes be dry. There are specials for each night of the week. If good chicken Kiev ($19.75) is your fancy, you'll have to come on Saturday. Desserts tend to be disappointing, except for the appealing plump cheese-filled crêpes served with caramel sauce.

A pre-theater menu is offered every day from 5:00 to 7:30 p.m. with three courses for $19.50.

FRANKIE AND JOHNNIE'S ★★   Steakhouse
269 West 45th Street
(between Broadway and Eighth Ave.)
212/997-9494
Dinner - Monday through Saturday 4:00 - 11:30 p.m.
All major cards

There's nothing trendy about this old theater district standby. It's been around since the Roaring Twenties when it operated as a speakeasy. Later, its prime location and reputation for great steaks made it somewhat of a celebrity hangout. Today, it's the kind of place with no surprises—everything you expect to find on a chophouse menu, you'll find here. The steaks are terrific, the portions enormous, and in spite of close quarters, high prices, and a hectic feel, its popularity endures. And you still might spot a celeb (like longtime customer Tony Roberts) after a show.

Among starters, choices include Blue Point oysters ($7.50), shrimp cocktail ($11.50), fresh lump crabmeat ($12.75), and tomatoes and Bermuda onions ($4.75). For the main attraction: sirloin ($24.95), filet mignon with mushroom caps ($24.95), double loin lamb chops ($24.95), broiled filet of sole ($18.50), and surf & turf ($29.50). Good sides include hash browns ($3.50), cottage fries ($3.50), potato pancakes ($4.00), au gratin potatoes ($3.50), broiled mushrooms ($3.75), onion rings ($3.75), and fresh asparagus ($5.50). Dessert might be marble or plain cheesecake ($5.00), fresh strawberries with cream ($5.00), or blueberry pie with whipped cream ($4.50).

FRICO BAR ★★   Italian
402 West 43rd Street
(Southwest corner of 43rd St. and Ninth Ave.)
212/564-7272
Lunch - Monday through Saturday Noon - 3:00 p.m.;
Dinner - Monday through Saturday 4:30 p.m. - Midnight;
Sunday 11:00 a.m. - 11:00 p.m.
All major cards

This lively spot gets high marks all around—no surprise since it comes from the Bastianich family (of Becco and Felidia fame). The most casual of the trio and patterned after the informal osterias of Italy, it has a colorful and warm atmosphere. Its moon motif—carried through on the wall posters, cornice, and wooden tables—along with an exhibition kitchen and breezy bar area give it a trendy edge of its own. A large, seasonal veranda is another of its many delights.

Its namesake—a specialty of the province of Friuli in northeastern Italy—is a thin, lacy, crisp disk made entirely of melted Montasio cheese. It is sautéed to a golden brown and stuffed with potatoes and onions ($7.25). There's also a frico of the day with different fillings ($7.75). Fabulous! The individual thin crust pizzas are also delicious with combinations like eggplant, fresh ricotta, and basil ($8.25), homemade sausage ($8.25), and chopped clams, garlic, and olive oil ($8.25). Other good offerings include spaghetti with tomato and basil ($6.75), linguine with clams, garlic, and olive oil ($7.75), rigatoni with oven-dried tomatoes, basil, and spinach ($7.50), baked ziti with tomato, chunky eggplant, and fresh ricotta ($7.50), grilled salmon with mustard sauce ($12.25), chicken, mushrooms, and peppers in a light tomato sauce with polenta ($9.75), braised lamb shank with barley risotto ($12.95), veal chop stuffed with spinach and mozzarella in a light porcini carrot sauce ($15.95), and ribeye steak with garlic French fries and caramelized onions ($15.50). And just as in the Friulian countryside, inexpensive wines are served from the cask. There's a good selection of beer on tap as well. And for dessert: good gelati (vanilla, chocolate, hazelnut, or black cherry) ($4.50), tartufo ($5.00), bread pudding ($4.50), and tiramisú ($5.00).

Brunch is served on Sunday until 3:00 p.m. All mains are $14.95 and include the freshly squeezed juice of the day and coffee or tea. Selections include NY strip steak with spicy homefries and two eggs, lemon ricotta pancakes with fresh strawberries, the omelet of the day, and panetone with warm maple syrup.

GALLAGHER'S STEAK HOUSE ★★   Steakhouse
228 West 52nd Street
(between Broadway and Eighth Ave.)
212/245-5336
Lunch - Daily Noon - 3:00 p.m.
Dinner - Daily 3:00 p.m. - Midnight
All major cards

Gallagher's, a real New York tradition, dates back to the Roaring Twenties. It opened in 1927—the year the Yankees took the Pirates in the World Series, Al Jolson starred in the first talkie, and Fred and Adele Astaire were wowing Broadway crowds in "Funny Face" at the Alvin Theater next door. The Alvin Theater is now the Neil Simon Theater and over the years has housed an ever-changing variety of hit shows, while Gallagher's remains the longest running hit on the block. Originally a speakeasy owned by ex-Ziegfield Girl Helen Gallagher and Ed Gallagher (half of the vaudeville comedy team of Gallagher and Shean), it drew a clientele of gamblers, show biz celebs, and big-name jocks. Then in 1933—the watershed year that saw the Depression bottom out and FDR deliver on his promise to end Prohibition—the Gallaghers conceived a new kind of dining salon. A real departure from the plush European-style restaurants then in favor, Gallagher's sported a virile and convivial ambience with a grand old mahogany bar, red checkered tablecloths, hardwood floors, and dark panelled walls. Those walls are now hung with photographs and plaques recording the political, theatrical, and sporting life of NYC since the early '20s. Its vast lineup of photographic memorabilia shows off some of its famous customers over the years—Mae West, Jack Dempsey, Irving Berlin, Richard Burton, Jackie O, Spencer Tracy, Babe Ruth, Ethel Merman, Sylvester Stallone, Paul Newman, Katharine Hepburn, George C. Scott, Jimmy Breslin, T. Boone Pickens, Bill Clinton, and Joe DiMaggio (who called Gallagher's a "real eating restaurant"). Like the setting, the waiters are vintage New York, and the place has the nostalgic feel of an earlier era.

Eating here, and eating well, means steak. You'll see it, whether you want to or not, hanging in its virgin state in the glass-enclosed cold storage locker at the front where it is air-dried for 21 days to achieve its distinctive tenderness and flavor.

The oxtail soup ($4.50) is a long-time favorite among the starters. Other predictable choices include jumbo shrimp ($10.95), chopped chicken livers ($7.75), and Caesar salad ($6.25). For the main, go for either the sirloin ($29.75) or the filet mignon ($28.75) for a taste of what Gallagher's does best. Other good choices are the double rib lamb chops ($26.75) and the roast prime rib ($27.75). Seafood is not a high note here, except for the Maine lobster (3 pounds $44.00 or half that for $24.00). Other choices from the sea include fried shrimp in beer batter ($26.95) and salmon steak ($26.50). Spuds are extra, but a must to accompany the steaks. Forget the baked, and go for the hash browns, cottage fried, O'Briens, or Gallagher's own concoction (each $4.95). The onion rings ($5.50) are also a popular accompaniment here. If you're up to dessert, the best are the cheesecake and the apple pie (each $5.50). In season, the strawberry shortcake ($5.75) is also a winner.

HALCYON ★★   American
(Rihga Royal Hotel)
151 West 54th Street
(between Sixth and Seventh Aves.)
212/468-8888
Lunch - Daily 11:30 a.m. - 2:30 p.m.
Dinner - Daily 5:30 - 10:30 p.m.
All major cards

The tranquil atmosphere at Halcyon is faithful to its name, which refers to the poetic phrase "the Halcyon days," as well as to a mythical bird which calms the waves as it nests at sea. Its extravagant hand-painted trompe l'oeil ceiling features harlequin figures, peacocks, and a tent of striped teal and beige fabric. The room it crowns is in total harmony with peacock green banquettes along the perimeter with striped green and beige wall coverings and mirrors lining the walls. Flickering oil lamps and the soft sound of show tunes wafting in from the adjacent lounge add to its relaxed ambience.

Award-winning chef John Halligan's approach to cooking pays homage to classical cuisine while reflecting a real dedication to today's healthier ways. He characterizes his style as American contemporary, but his cooking has also been described as "nouvelle down home." It is eclectic, imaginative, unrestricted by ethnic boundaries, and always expanding. The menus change about eight times a year with absolute freshness of ingredients a constant. You might start with lobster bisque ($7.50), a salad or arugula, candied pecans, corn, roasted peppers, and sherry wine vinaigrette ($8.50), sweetbread and morel mushroom cassoulet with fresh tarragon and navy beans ($11.50), or applewood-smoked lobster chili with white beans and Virginia ham ($11.50). The wonderful pastas are offered either as a starter or main course and include wholewheat pasta with rock shrimp, sun-dried tomatoes, arugula, and grilled scallions ($12.00/$17.50), rigatoni with grilled chicken, andouille sausage, morel mushrooms, and spinach in a Cajun cream sauce ($11.50/$16.50), and orecchiette with plum tomatoes, olives, buffalo mozzarella, and basil ($11.00/$16.50). Among the mains, Halligan's signature dish of lightly-smoked and roasted rack of lamb with rosemary mascarpone risotto ($25.00) is a menu constant. Another delicious house specialty is New York sirloin, marinated in dark beer for 24 hours, and served with basil mashed potatoes and crisp onions ($24.00). Other options might include a vegetable gâteau of wild mushroom couscous and grilled vegetable hash with curried yogurt ($21.50) and grilled medallions of veal with zucchini, olives, tomato, and smoked mozzarella ($23.50). Specialties from the grill (served with roasted rosemary new potatoes and assorted vegetables) include herb-crusted double breast of chicken ($19.00), double lamb chops ($25.00), and swordfish ($22.00).

A pre-theatre menu offers three courses for $29.97 between 5:30 and 6:30 p.m. on Monday through Thursday; on Friday and Saturday the price goes up to $31.97.

HARD ROCK CAFE ★   American
221 West 57th Street
(between Broadway and Seventh Ave.)
212/489-6565
Daily 11:30 a.m. - 2:00 a.m.
All major cards

The music is hot and loud, and the burgers are big and juicy at this rock n' roll teen mecca. Its popularity hasn't waned over the years, so there always seems to be a line waiting to get in. When you do, you'll be surrounded by nostalgic memorabilia that includes a collection of guitars belonging to various legendary musicians, dozens of gold records, and even the purple jacket worn by the artist formerly known as Prince. From its guitar-shaped bar to the tail end of its mascot '58 Cadillac marquee, its atmosphere is colorful and its conviviality contagious.

The fare of choice on the all-American menu are the decent burgers and decadent desserts. Burgers come with various toppings, along with fresh handcut fries and salad (starting at $7.50 up to $9.95 for a double-the-meat and double-the-cheese burger). Other popular choices include chili ($4.95), South of the Border salad overflowing in a giant tortilla shell with sour cream, pico de gallo, guacamole, and salsa vinaigrette, with spicy ground beef, peppers, and onions or marinated grilled chicken ($9.95), New York strip steak served with salad and a choice of baked potato or fries ($17.95), pork barbecue served with fries and a choice of coleslaw or ranch beans ($8.95), and a California club sandwich with grilled marinated chicken breast with Swiss cheese, crisp bacon, lettuce, tomato, and low-fat watercress mayonnaise, served on a honey-wheat roll with fries and salad ($8.95). There's also a good gardenburger—a meatless patty made from fresh mushrooms, fresh onions, grains, low-fat cheese, seasonings, and spices—served with coleslaw and fries ($7.95). The irresistibly gooey desserts include a mountain of vanilla ice cream and hot fudge on a fresh homemade brownie topped with chopped brazil nuts and fresh whipped cream ($5.95), homemade strawberry shortcake with fresh whipped cream ($5.95), a towering banana split ($5.95), and Etta B's homemade apple pie with ice cream and fresh whipped cream or melted cheese ($4.95).

HARLEY-DAVIDSON CAFE ★   American
1370 Avenue of the Americas (at 56th St.)
212/245-6000
Lunch - Daily 11:30 a.m. - 5:00 p.m.
Dinner - Monday through Thursday and Sunday 5:00 p.m. - Midnight;
Friday and Saturday 5:00 p.m. - 1:00 a.m.
All major cards

This high-energy eatery revved into town in October 1993 and has been packed ever since. Its hog theme celebrates 90+ years of Harley-Davidson history with over 30 motorcycles on display—among them, the 1903 original Harley-Davidson, the Captain America model from the movie *Easy Rider*, and bikes owned by Billy Joel, Mickey Rourke, and Malcomb Forbes. Other eye-catching details include a 38-foot Sheetrock American flag with illuminated stars and a map of Route 66 carved and painted into the floor on the lower level. On some nights, you might catch Elvis impersonators, magicians, or jugglers adding to the fun of the place. And, in the cigarette girl tradition of years gone by, a woman works the main floor offering skin tattoos and face paintings. Loud rock music and one of the biggest sidewalk cafes in town are other draws for a lively crowd. This is also the site of many celebrity bashes. Kathleen Turner belted out a few songs with great gusto at a party here. And while you may not see a star turn yourself, there's plenty of action and good American road food.

The lengthy menu features everything from bar snacks, soups and sandwiches, and homey mains to yummy desserts. Good bar snacks and starters include chicken wings with hot sauce and blue cheese dressing ($6.50), beer-batter onion rings ($4.50), terrific fried shoestring potatoes topped with chili ($4.75), six steamed shrimp pot stickers with hoisin sauce ($4.95), roquefort and field greens with toasted walnuts ($5.95), and both meaty and vegetarian chili (each $4.95). Sandwich specialties include a giant vegetarian hand roll (soft unleavened bread rolled with eggplant, squash, tomato, spinach, herbs, and toasted pine nuts, served with bean sprouts, greens, and corn mayonnaise) ($7.95), an old-time sloppy Joe ($7.75), sliced steak on an onion roll with fried onions and shoestring potatoes ($11.75), and fried fish filet with cole slaw, shoestring potatoes, and classic tartar sauce ($9.25). The best of the mains are Harley roast chicken (half chicken marinated in lemon juice, garlic, and barbecue spices, served with mashed potatoes and creamed corn) ($13.95), homestyle meatloaf with mashed potatoes and brown gravy ($9.75), crunchy shrimp with cucumber salad and onion rings ($16.50), and a chicken and ribs combo (one-half rack of barbecued ribs and two pieces of maple barbecued chicken with cole slaw and baked beans) ($14.95). The burgers are good, too ($7.50). For dessert, throw caution to the wind and indulge in childhood fantasies with Reeses chocolate peanut butter pie with a scoop of chocolate ice cream ($5.95), warm chocolate chip toll house cookie pie with Ben & Jerry's English toffee crunch ice cream ($5.95), or the big Snickers blitz pie with vanilla ice cream ($5.95). Share it with a friend and you'll feel downright virtuous.

ISLAND SPICE ★   Jamaican
402 West 44th Street
(between Ninth and Tenth Aves.)
212/765-1737
Lunch - Monday through Saturday 11:00 a.m. - 4:00 p.m.
Dinner - Monday through Thursday 5:00 - 11:00 p.m.;
Friday and Saturday 5:00 p.m. - Midnight
All major cards

A prerequisite for a restaurant calling itself Island Spice is its ability to pony up with a potent jerk sauce. Chef Basil Jones delivers the goods at this sunny evocation of a Jamaican cafe. Its location—on the perimeter of the theater district beyond Ninth Avenue—makes it easy to miss, since it's not an area you're likely to be browsing. But if you make a bee-line here, you'll be rewarded with a tropical atmosphere, some terrific dishes, and all-around good value. The pretty dining room is small and cozy, with lazy ceiling fans, sponged sea-green walls, baskets of fruits and vegetables, and a blackboard menu.

With reggae music playing in the background, you can escape to the tropics with starters like Calypso shrimp ($12.50), miniature beef patties gently spiced and encased in half-moons of flaky dough ($3.75), and jerk chicken wings ($4.50). Mains are served with steamed vegetables, rice, or turned cornmeal (the house specialty which is similar to spoonbread or polenta). Lively options include jerk pork ($7.50), jerk chicken (Jamaica's most popular dish—tender chicken in a spicy brown sauce) ($7.50), and jumbo shrimp in a rich curry sauce ($12.50). Other good choices might be fricasséed chicken ($6.50), ginger lime chicken ($8.50), and steamed calaloo (a vegetarian delight of fresh spinach, or calaloo in season, steamed with onions, tomatoes, peppers, and island spices ($7.50). For dessert: Mom's bread pudding with a rum raisin sauce ($4.50), an excellent carrot cake with nutty cream cheese frosting ($3.50), and sunshine cake (poundcake topped with cinnamon and walnuts) ($3.50).

JOE ALLEN ★   American
326 West 46th Street
(between Eighth and Ninth Aves.)
212/581-6464
Lunch - Daily Noon - 4:00 p.m.
Dinner - Daily 4:00 - 11:45 p.m.
Master and Visa only

This animated theatre district bar-restaurant began as the dream of a bartender at P. J. Clarke's who wanted to own a place where theater performers and crew could get a good meal and drink at an affordable price. Now, 20-some years later and with branches in London and Paris, Joe Allen's dream is long fulfilled and his restaurant is a theater district mainstay. Its walls are lined with Broadway posters of failed shows, a playful reminder that for every Broadway hit there are many misses. Along with an amiable bar scene, celeb-watching has long been a draw here—you never know who might pop in. And if your waiter looks familiar, he may be a young actor between jobs.

Black bean soup ($4.00) is a favorite starter. Other popular options include cucumber salad with feta cheese, chopped tomato, black olives, and mint ($6.00), and smoked salmon with a corn-leek pancake and sour cream ($7.25). Good main choices include grilled sirloin with fries ($19.50), Cajun Andouille sausage with rice and beans ($12.75), pot roast with vegetables and mashed potatoes ($15.75), and a dynamite meatloaf with mashed potatoes and gravy ($12.75). And it's hard to say no to the homey desserts. The gooey goodies include tollhouse cookies with vanilla ice cream ($5.00) and hot fudge pudding cake with vanilla ice cream and chocolate sauce ($5.50). My favorites, though, are the fruity temptations: peach and blueberry cobbler, banana cream pie, and warm apple crumb pie (each $5.00).

JUDSON GRILL ★★   Contemporary American
152 West 52nd Street
(between Sixth and Seventh Aves.)
212/582-5252
Lunch - Monday through Friday Noon - 2:30 p.m.
Dinner - Monday through Thursday 5:30 - 11:00 p.m.;
Friday and Saturday 5:30 - 11:30 p.m.
All major cards

Warm-hued woods, lipstick red velvet banquettes, soaring ceilings, vast copper-leaf vases, massive brass chandeliers, huge sprays of forsythia, arresting John Parks murals, and a large brass-and-mahogany bar make for a stunning setting at this grand American brasserie. Named after the telephone exchange of the '40s and '50s, JUdson Grill sports the easy glamour of that era in its big, lofty space.

The eclectic contemporary American menu embraces Pacific Rim and Mediterranean flavors and is the kind that makes you want to return to explore more fully. Among starters, house specialties include a Vietnamese shrimp roll with a spicy dipping sauce and pickled cucumbers ($11.00) and seared sesame tuna with a savory red pepper relish and a jicama orange salad ($11.50). Also worth a try is the unusual salt cod and potato gnocchi with niçoise olives, caramelized fennel, and oven-dried tomatoes ($9.50). The innovative nature of chef John Villa's cooking is evident in the mains as well. Seasonal offerings include such fare as saddle of rabbit with wild mushrooms, asparagus, and a pommery potato cake ($26.00), roasted organic chicken with Moroccan eggplant, couscous, cilantro, and a lemon-scented consomme ($19.50), whole crispy Florida red snapper with sticky rice and a coconut-peanut sauce ($24.50), a double-cut pork chop with creamy polenta with broccoli rabe and a tomato-asparagus salsa ($21.50), and sun-dried tomato and goat cheese ravioli with basil pesto, roasted red peppers, and pignoli ($19.00). Desserts are good, too. There's a Judson chocolate sampler ($8.50), warm chocolate bread pudding with cinnamon-cherry parfait in a chocolate cup ($8.00), lemon ricotta cheesecake with blueberry compote ($8.00), and a cobbler of the day ($7.00).

A pre-theater menu is available (with departure by 8:00 p.m.) with three courses for $32.97. There are three or four choices of specialties from the regular menu in each category.

JULIAN'S ★   Mediterranean
802 Ninth Avenue (between 53rd and 54th Sts.)
212/262-4288
Lunch - Monday through Saturday Noon - 3:30 p.m.
Brunch - Sunday 11:30 a.m. - 3:30 p.m.
Dinner - Daily 4:00 p.m. - Midnight
All major cards

Julian's is a likeable place both for its cozy candlelit, brick-walled ambience and satisfying Mediterranean fare. Modest prices and convenience to theaters add to its appeal. And in nice weather, there's a delightful alley garden for dining.

You might start with minestrone ($4.50), a medley of shrimp, calamari, and scallops lightly-seasoned and deep-fried, served with a spicy marinara sauce ($7.50), grilled vegetables ($6.50), or an antipasto plate of prosciutto, mozzarella, salami, provolone, and caponata ($9.95). Pasta specialties include a very good gnocchi with fresh mozzarella and a pomodoro sauce ($10.25), rigatoni with eggplant, ricotta cheese, and tomato sauce ($9.95), and spaghetti Bolognese ($9.95). Good main course selections include tuna steaks grilled and served over white bean salad ($15.95), stuffed shrimp ($16.95), sautéed chicken breasts with shiitake mushrooms in a smooth mascarpone cheese and Brandy sauce ($14.95), sautéed veal in a light sauce of lemon and capers ($16.96), twin filet mignon medallions topped with bel paese cheese and served with a porcini mushroom sauce ($21.95), and tender baby lamb chops grilled and served with a red wine and porcini mushroom sauce ($21.95).

The Sunday buffet brunch is an unbeatable bargain at $13.95. The price includes a Bloody Mary or Mimosa.

LANGAN'S ★   American
150 West 47th Street
(between Sixth and Seventh Aves.)
212/869-5482
Lunch - Monday through Friday 11:30 a.m. - 4:00 p.m.
Brunch - Saturday and Sunday 11:30 a.m. - 4:00 p.m.
Dinner - Daily 4:00 p.m. - Midnight
All major cards

Black and white pictures of famous past and present stage and screen stars and framed theatre posters line the walls at Langan's. Show tunes play softly in the background adding to the cheerful, theatrical feel of the place that is in keeping with its location in the heart of the theater district. The bright and spacious dining room is appealing and comfortable with fresh white walls, crisp white linen, and affable service. And it's much more sedate than the busy and convivial bar at the front would indicate. You can even spot a celeb or two supping here from time to time—sightings have included Aidan Quinn, Dana Delaney, Jean Stapleton, and Lisa Niemi and Patrick Swayze.

The cuisine is contemporary American with a hint of traditional American popping up here and there. Some good choices on the menu include starters like oak-smoked Irish salmon with diced capers and onion salsa ($11.95), crab-stuffed jumbo shrimp in casino butter with pepper confetti ($9.25), tomato, mozzarella, and onion in black vinegar with fresh basil ($7.95), and French onion soup ($5.25). There are at least a half-dozen entrée salads to choose from. Lemon pepper-crusted chicken over seasonal greens with mustard herb dressing ($16.95) is the house salad specialty. Also good is the grilled shrimp Caesar ($17.95) and Langan's classic chef salad ($14.95). Those who like their pasta not too spicy might enjoy the rigatoni with oven-roasted tomato, brie, and fresh basil ($15.95), though I found it much too tame. Of the mains, the house specialty is Maryland crab cakes with a tomato and mustard coulis ($21.95). Other good choices include baked crab-stuffed trout in a citrus glaze over potato and almond hash ($18.95), onion-crusted salmon over creamy seafood polenta ($18.95), garlic-crusted aged sirloin with caramelized onion, potato, and spinach coulis ($20.95), and roast rack of lamb ($22.95). Ask about the daily dessert selections.

A three-course pre-theatre dinner for $22.95 (with three or four choices in each category) is offered from 4:00 to 7:30 p.m. and is quite a good deal. As a matter of fact, the *Daily News* has named Langan's one of the top ten restaurants in value for pre-theatre dining.

LE BERNARDIN ★★★★   French Seafood
155 West 51st Street
(between Sixth and Seventh Aves.)
212/489-1515
Lunch - Monday through Friday Noon - 2:30 p.m.
Dinner - Monday through Saturday 5:30 - 10:30 p.m.
All major cards

One of the top seafood restaurants in the country and worth every one of its four stars, Le Bernardin shines on every level. It was opened in 1986 by brother/sister team Gilbert and Maguy Le Coze who had already established a highly acclaimed restaurant of the same name in Paris (named after a folk song their father sang to them as children, "Les Moines de St. Bernardin," about monks who loved life). The New York offshoot proved so successful—earning four stars within three months of opening—that they sold the Paris restaurant to devote themselves to the New York operation. The imaginative and dazzling seafood creations of Gilbert Le Coze took the city by storm and inspired a whole new wave of sophisticated seafood-dedicated restaurants and influenced a new generation of chefs. Sadly, in the summer of 1994, Mr. Le Coze died suddenly at the age of 49 while working out in a health club. The restaurant world was stunned and wondered if Le Bernardin could retain its status without him. Today, it is still winning rave reviews thanks to the charming ways of Maguy in running the house and chef Eric Ripert's brilliance in the kitchen. Its wondrous selection of fish is infallibly fresh and beautifully prepared—Le Bernardin remains a seafood lover's nirvana. The room itself is elegantly clubby, with high ceilings, an abundance of beautiful flowers, oil paintings of fishermen and their catch, and roomy, widely-spaced tables. The crowd looks well-heeled and often includes famous faces like Dustin Hoffman, Mick Jagger, Warren Beatty and Annette Benning. The atmosphere is heady, the prices high, and reservations sometimes hard to come by. But for seafood aficionados, it's well worth the trouble.

Both lunch and dinner are prix fixe; with lunch $42.00 and dinner $68.00. Each menu changes with the catch and the market's bounty. The dinner prix fixe offers choices like an assortment of oysters, tuna tartare with Asian seasoning in a crispy potato nest, lightly-smoked salmon gravlax and brioche toasts with a salad of baby arugula and horseradish vinaigrette, herbed crabmeat in saffron ravioli, and a pizza-like dish with tender shrimp and tomato compote on a phyllo crust. Main course offerings might be roast skate spiced and served in a sage-perfumed broth with a potato-onion cake, coconut-marinated grilled swordfish in a light curry sauce with basmati fried rice, roast grouper with a spicy confit of zucchini, onions and red bell pepper, and Atlantic salmon seared on seasonal vegetables with coriander grains and herbs. For companions not enticed by the incredible gifts from the sea to be had here, there's roast free-range chicken stuffed with wild mushrooms, pan-sautéed lamb chops, or a roast medley of vegetables. Desserts are delectable. Choose from the likes of caramelized apricot tarte with almond ice cream, glazed bananas on pillows of passion fruit and blankets of tuiles, and warm chocolate orange tart in a light hazelnut crust with shaved chocolate.

A set $90.00 six-course tasting menu and a set $120.00 seven-course tasting menu are other options in the evenings.

LE BOUCHON ★★   French
319 West 51st Street (between Eighth and Ninth Aves.)
212/765-6463
Lunch - Monday through Saturday 11:30 - 2:30 p.m.
Dinner - Monday through Thursday and Sunday 5:00 - 11:00 p.m.;
Friday and Saturday 5:00-11:30 p.m.
All major cards

If you're weary of the fashionable designer food and decor so much in vogue these days, Le Bouchon is the perfect antidote with its simple, homey French fare and warm hospitality.

Good country French cooking is its hallmark. To start, there's onion soup ($5.00), country-style paté ($5.00), crab cake with tartar sauce ($9.00), mixed green salad with goat cheese ($6.00), and frisée with croutons and bacon ($7.00). The well-prepared main course choices include trout almandine ($14.00), grilled salmon with a mustard dill sauce ($15.00), shrimp provençale ($16.00), potato gnocchi with a pesto cream sauce ($12.00), linguine with bay scallops and shrimp ($16.00), magret of duck with an orange-ginger sauce ($18.00), veal scaloppine with lemon butter ($16.00), grilled ribeye steak ($18.00), and roast rack of lamb ($21.00). For dessert: homemade cheesecake ($5.00), lemon mousse ($5.00), créme caramel ($5.00), and chocolate mousse ($5.00).

The $20.50 four-course prix fixe is popular with theatergoers and is also available all day. This menu offers starter choices that include the soup of the day, onion soup, and mussels marinières. A salad follows, then the main with choices like boneless trout almandine, breast of chicken tarragon, roasted half duck with black current sauce, minute steak with fries, and pasta of the day. Dessert selections are from the regular menu.

LE MADELEINE ★★   French
403 West 43rd Street
(between 9th and 10th Aves.)
212/246-2993
Lunch - Daily Noon - 4:00 p.m.
Dinner - Daily 5:00 - 11:00 p.m.
All major cards

You'll find a country rustic feel and good French bistro dishes at this very popular spot for theatergoers. Skylights, mural-covered brick walls, and a glass enclosed garden (open year round) are part of its charm. Modest prices and watchful service add to its appeal.

Its menu of classic French bistro fare includes starters of French vegetable soup with a dollop of garlic and basil ($5.50), garlic sausage baked in pastry crust, sliced, then grilled ($7.00), grilled gulf shrimp with cucumber and aged balsamic vinegar ($7.50), and warm goat cheese salad (fresh mixed greens with bacon, mustard vinaigrette, and rounds of toasted baguette) ($6.50). Popular mains include duck l'orange roasted in a classic fresh orange sauce and served with vegetables ($16.50), grilled salmon on a bed of ratatouille ($16.50), roasted leg of lamb au jus ($18.00), grilled free-range chicken breast with a pommery mustard sauce and vegetables ($14.00), grilled pork medallions (marinated in olive oil, garlic, and white wine and served with mashed potatoes, braised apple sauce, and black currants) ($16.50), and classic steak frites ($20.00).

A pre-theater menu is offered between 5:00 and 8:00 p.m. with two courses for $24.00.

LE RIVAGE ★★   French
340 West 46th Street (between Eighth and Ninth Aves.)
212/765-7374
Lunch - Monday through Saturday 11:30 a.m. - 2:30 p.m.
Dinner - Monday through Saturday 5:00 - 9:30 p.m.
All major cards

This cozy, old-fashioned French bistro, conveniently perched on Restaurant Row, has long been a reliable choice for theatergoers. Generous portions of consistently good bistro fare at bargain prices, along with caring service and charming surroundings, combine to create one heck of a deal.

The price of the main also includes a starter, soup, salad, dessert, and coffee. Your starter might be antipasto French-style, duck terrine, artichoke hearts with house dressing, mussels with garlic, egg with Russian dressing, or snails in garlic butter. And there's much choice among mains, with options that include filet of sole baked in a white wine sauce ($23.75), shrimp with onions, mushrooms, and a wine sauce ($25.75), frog legs with garlic sauce ($26.75), grilled red snapper with tarragon and lemon ($26.75), chicken cooked in red wine with herbs, garlic, and onions ($23.75), duck with an orange sauce ($25.75), pot roast braised with wine, herbs, and mushrooms ($23.75), mignonette of beef in a peppercorn sauce ($26.25), and pork chop with apple sauce ($23.75). Desserts are just as no-nonsense and just as appealing, with choices like apple tart, caramel custard, peach melba, and chocolate mousse.

LES CÉLÉBRITÉS ★★★★   French
Essex House
155 West 58th Street (between Sixth and Seventh Aves.)
212/484-5113
Dinner - Tuesday through Thursday 6:00 - 10:00 p.m.;
Friday and Saturday 6:00 - 10:30 p.m.
All major cards

Dining in this small, exceptional restaurant is a luxurious experience that begins in a chic red-walled art deco anteroom—a seductive little parlor for sipping a martini and taking a look at some of the celebrity artwork that gives the restaurant its name. The changing display of original art that lights up the walls is by international celebrities such as Elke Sommer, Gene Hackman, Peggy Lee, Pierce Brosnan, and Tennessee Williams. The exquisite dining room is unabashedly lavish—its tables are set with Limoges plates, Christofle silver, and glittering crystal. Massive ebony columns, ornate moldings, rich red carpets, and burnished mahogany walls create a dramatic backdrop for the colorful artwork. The setting is formal, the service as polished as it gets. This is a place for special occasions.

Executive chef Christian Delouvrier's versatility is evident in the rich variety that composes the menu. He can be seen at work from time to time during the evening when his glassed-in kitchen (discretely covered by a painting) is revealed. Starters from an ever-changing (and always expensive) selection might include a salad of sea scallops and haricots verts with truffle vinaigrette, tomatoes, chives, and prosciutto ($23.00) and Maine lobster salad gazpacho-style ($26.00). The main course might offer poached filet of salmon with angel hair pasta ($37.00), veal tenderloin filled with foie gras, truffles, wild mushrooms, and potatoes ($39.00), spit-roasted free-range chicken with black truffles, a purée of cauliflower and sautéed spinach leaves ($42.00), and braised Hawaiian snapper cooked in a bouillon of mussels, clams, bay scallops, shrimp, and baby vegetables served with tomato risotto ($39.00). Desserts are sumptuous. Choices might be lime cream Napoleon with red berries ($14.00), sautéed apples with caramel, almond, raisin, and vanilla ice cream ($13.00), and crêpes Suzette with confit orange peel and chocolate sherbet ($14.00).

If money is burning a hole in your pocket and you need an extravagant treat, come for the six-course tasting menu ($95.00 or $155.00 with wines).

LES PYRÉNÉES ★★   French
251 West 51st Street
(between Broadway and Eighth Ave.)
212/246-0044
Lunch - Monday through Saturday Noon - 3:00 p.m.
Dinner - Monday through Saturday 5:00 p.m. - Midnight;
Sunday 4:00 - 10:00 p.m.
All major cards

This informal French country-style restaurant has a comfortable charm, and in winter is made all the cozier by its working fireplace. Mirrors, old brick, country copper decorations, and a stately antique French grandfather clock enhance its homey feel.

While its convenient location attracts theatergoers, its good country cooking is what keeps them coming back. You might start with Norwegian smoked salmon ($8.00), warm goat cheese over French chicory ($8.00), lobster ravioli ($9.00), or onion soup ($5.50). House specialties among the mains include broiled salmon béarnaise ($20.50), cassoulet ($19.75), and breast of duck with a green peppercorn sauce ($22.50). Other good mains include Maryland crab cakes with shrimp ($23.00), veal chop with stuffed vegetables ($24.00), pan-fried steak with bone marrow and red wine ($24.00), and rack of lamb for two ($65.00). Desserts are made on the premises (each $6.00). You'll find good renditions of crème brûlée, chocolate mousse, and fruit tarts.

A prix fixe three-course dinner menu offers many choices in each category and is an excellent value at $27.00.

LES SANS CULOTTES SPORTS ★   French
329 West 51st Street (between Eighth and Ninth Aves.)
212/581-1283

LES SANS CULOTTES WEST ★
347 West 46th Street (between Eighth and Ninth Aves.)
212/247-4284
Lunch - Daily Noon to 3:00 p.m.
Dinner - Daily 5:00 - Midnight
All major cards

All decked out in red, white, and blue, this sprightly bistro (at each of its three locations) has a French Revolution decor and such a thoroughly cheerful air about it, chances are good you'll find it easy on the spirit and good for a hearty, unpretentious bistro meal. You will definitely leave stuffed and amazed at how little you've spent in the process.

The complete dinner offer at $19.95 starts you off with a bountiful basket of whole vegetables, a rack of sausages to hack off to your heart's content, rolls, and a crock of pâté. Main choices are bistro standbys like grilled salmon in a basil sauce, crisp duck with an orange sauce, grilled chicken with a tarragon sauce, grilled shell steak, and grilled baby rack of lamb with a garlic sauce. Chocolate mousse, ice cream with chestnuts, or crème brûlée might be your dessert choice. If you don't want the complete dinner option, other main choices to consider include veal piccata ($11.95), coq au vin ($11.95), sea scallops provençale ($13.95), grilled pork chops ($11.95), and minute steak with shallots ($15.95). While the food may not be memorable, it's hard not to like a place that treats you so generously and has such a merry personality.

LOTFI'S MOROCCAN RESTAURANT ★★   Moroccan
358 West 46th Street (between Eighth and Ninth Aves.)
212/582-5850
Dinner - Monday through Saturday 4:30 - 11:00 p.m.
All major cards

For a deliciously different dining experience, try this Restaurant Row charmer. You'll be truly transported by the colorful decor and the heady aroma of exotic spices that surround you the moment you walk in the door. Its ambience is at once cozy, a long room glowing with rich-colored hangings and beautiful Moroccan pottery. Here chef-owner Abdel Rebbaj and his family serve his lovingly-prepared classic Moroccan fare. The restaurant's namesake, Mr. Rebbaj's son Lotfi, helps with the serving while Mrs. Rebbaj welcomes diners. It is the kind of family-run restaurant that is fast disappearing in this era of celebrity chefs and picture-perfect model hostesses. It is a breath of sweet Moroccan air and its handy location is a wonderful gift to theatergoers.

Start with a plate of breewats (flaky pastry stuffed with either seafood, chicken, spinach and cheese, fish, lamb, chicken liver, vegetables, or homemade Moroccan sausage) ($3.25) and you won't be sorry. Other good openers include spicy Moroccan sausage grilled and served with a green pepper and tomato salad ($3.50), a mixed salad sampler with eggplant salad, hommous, and green pepper and tomato salad ($5.25), and harira, a rich homemade vegetable soup with chickpeas and lentils ($3.50). Couscous, the steamed semolina grain that is the Moroccan national dish, gets fine treatment here. Surrounded by steamed vegetables, it comes with a choice of lamb, chicken, fish, or sausage ($13.95-$14.95) or you can opt for Lotfi's special couscous with shrimp, calamari, fish, and vegetables ($16.95). Other popular options include the gently cooked Moroccan stews called tajines—lemon chicken with olives and preserved lemons ($13.95), hot and spicy chicken with mixed vegetables and olives ($13.95), lamb and vegetables ($13.95), fish with olives, herbs, and vegetables ($14.95), and mixed vegetables with olives and chickpeas ($12.95). The grilled kababs ($13.95) are excellent. And the chicken b'stilla ($14.95)—a concoction of chicken cooked to falling-apart tenderness in spices and then layered between phyllo pastry with chopped roasted almonds, eggs, cinnamon, lemon, and ginger and dusted with powdered sugar—is the kind that reminds you why this is one of Morocco's best-loved dishes. End with the ever-so-fragrant mint tea and one of the flaky pastries. The almond breewats ($2.75), similar to baklava, are a popular choice. Other good options include apricot strudel ($2.75), crescent-shaped orange blossom-flavored pastry stuffed with almond paste ($2.75), and Moroccan butter cookies ($2.75).

MANHATTAN CHILI CO. ★   Southwest
1500 Broadway (entrance on 43rd St.)
212/730-8666
Daily 11:30 a.m. - Midnight
Brunch - Saturday and Sunday 11:30 a.m. - 3:30 p.m.
All major cards

This casual eatery was a Greenwich Village favorite for ten years before moving uptown to its colorful new quarters at Times Square, within shouting distance of dozens of Broadway theatres. Animated chili peppers set the tone of the light-hearted decor featuring three-dimensional murals of Manhattan depicted as if it were chili-hattan. If you're a chili fan, this is the place for you. This is also a nice choice for families. Child-friendly, there's a special kids menu and booster seats and high chairs are readily available.

There are ten different kinds of chili, ranging from mild to hot-hot, and to wash it down there are freshly brewed batches of Catamount Gold, Amber, and Porter nal from the Catamount Brewing Company of White River Junction, Vermont. Bowls of chili are served with rice and your choice of two toppings from a list that includes sour cream, cheese, red onions, white onions, jalapeños, diced tomatoes, cilantro, and scallions. Popular choices among the various chili offerings include the Numero Uno with coarse ground beef, beans, tomato sauce, cumin, cocoa, and cinnamon (medium hot) ($7.50), Texas Chain Gang with coarse ground beef, beans, tomatoes, fresh and smoked jalapeños (hot-hot) ($7.50), High Plains Turkey with ground turkey, tomatoes, carrots, peppers, hominy, corn, roasted cumin, basil, and oregano (medium hot) ($7.50), Totally Vegetable with beans, corn, celery, tomatoes, bulgar, orange juice, cumin, and thyme (mild) ($6.95), and the Tierra Del Fuego 3-Bean with black beans, kidney beans, garbanzo beans, green peppers, celery, and smoked jalapeños (spiked with rum and served flaming, hot) ($7.50). You can also get just a cup if you like ($3.95). And there's also a chili sampler with a choice of three chilies with three toppings and rice ($7.50). Beyond the namesake specialties, the menu offers quesadillas with sautéed poblano peppers, onions, jalapeños, and smoked cheese ($3.95/$7.50), spicy black bean soup ($2.25/$3.00), grilled steak or chicken nachos with guacamole ($5.95/$10.95), and sizzling fajitas (vegetable $9.95, chicken $10.95, or steak $11.95). Other house specialties include drunken peanut chicken in a roasted peanut chipotle chili sauce spiked with tequila and dark ale, served with rice, vegetables, and corn tortillas ($8.95), soft tacos with a choice of grilled vegetables, chicken, or steak with lettuce, cheese, and pico de gallo in a four tortilla ($3.95 each), and chicken burritos ($8.50). There are also burgers ($7.50 to $8.95) and grilled chili dawgs (two all-beef franks with chili and chopped onions) ($7.95). All this and homemade desserts, too—gooey goodies like chocolate banana flour tortilla cake with chocolate sauce ($3.75), apple raisin walnut bread pudding served warm with butterscotch sauce ($3.75), and Margarita pudding spiked with gold tequila and triple sec ($3.50).

Saturday and Sunday brunch is prix fixe at $8.95 with specialties like scrambled egg nachos, omelettes, and sourdough French toast.

MOTOWN CAFE ★   Regional American
104 West 57th Street
(between Sixth and Seventh Aves.)
212/581-8030
Daily 11:00 a.m. - 1:00 a.m.
All major cards

This lively spot celebrates the legendary music label Motown with life-sized sculptures of Motown artists, memorabilia from the era, and homestyle regional American food, along with the sounds of such legends as The Supremes, The Temptations, The Four Tops, Stevie Wonder, Marvin Gaye, and Martha and the Vandellas. Its ceiling is a giant, revolving 45 rpm of the Supremes' "Stop, in the Name of Love!" and video screens everywhere flash photos and clips from variety shows that featured Motown artists. And there's live entertainment every hour—either a gorgeous Supremes-style girl group in big hair and lots of glitter or a boy group with all the right Motown moves and metallic dinner jackets. Music is the thing here, and if you have fond memories of the period and the music, it's hard not to have a good time at Motown.

Southern-accented homestyle fare makes up the menu, and the food can be pretty good. Both the chicken fingers ($6.50) and catfish fingers ($6.50) are popular starters. And the Buffalo wings prepared with a sweet and tangy red pepper sauce and served with homemade blue cheese dressing ($6.95) carry a nice zing. Of the sandwiches, the BBQ brisket served on an onion roll with sweet potato fries ($8.95) and the Sloppy Joe also served with good sweet potato fries and corn salsa ($8.50) are clear winners. Other main choices include old-fashioned chicken pot pie ($11.25), Maryland crab cakes with rice pilaf and corn salsa ($16.95), fried chicken served with yummy macaroni and cheese ($11.95), and braised short ribs with mashed potatoes and gravy ($16.95). But the best course here is dessert, so unless the cholesterol doctor is at the next table, don't skip it. The chocolate cake is three-layered decadence with creamy chocolate frosting and deep chocolate shavings ($5.95). The brownie sundae ($5.95) is another crowd pleaser. But for down-home eating, opt for the strawberry shortcake with homemade biscuits and freshly whipped cream ($5.95), a seasonal fruit cobbler ($5.95), or the sweet potato pecan pie ($5.95).

NEW WORLD GRILL ★   Eclectic
329 West 49th Street
(between Eighth and Ninth Aves.)
212/957-4745
Lunch - Monday through Saturday Noon - 4:00 p.m.
Dinner - Monday through Saturday 4:00 - 10:30 p.m.
All major cards

This tiny gazebo-like restaurant features a snappy looking bar area surrounded by small tables. While pleasant, the diminutive space is not for the claustrophobic. But its wonderful sidewalk terrace can't be beat on a pretty spring or summer day. Situated in World Wide Plaza, a relatively unknown and delightful oasis between Eighth and Ninth Avenues, it has an atmosphere far removed from the clamorous, untidy avenues that border it.

The fusion cuisine of its talented chef, Katie Keck, has a strong Asian and Southwestern slant. The menu contains many sophisticated twists and some dishes work better than others. The best of the starter temptations include grilled pears with field greens, stilton cheese, and crunchy walnuts ($6.25), crispy Cajun chicken with creole salsa ($6.00), squash pancakes with chipotle pepper sauce ($5.75), and roasted wild mushrooms with grilled polenta ($6.25). Good mains include rigatoni with kalamatas, oyster mushrooms, and basil in a smoked tomato sauce ($12.00), barbecued chicken with roasted corn-on-the-cob, and a grilled sweet potato ($12.75), grilled salmon with blood orange citrus sauce, roasted potatoes, and asparagus ($14.00), and grilled steak with a Merlot glaze, shallots, and braised vegetables ($14.50).

OFFICIAL ALL STAR CAFE ★   American
1540 Broadway (at West 45th St.)
212/840-8326
Daily 11:00 a.m. - 2:00 a.m.
All major cards

If you've got a super-fan kid with you—or in you—you'll probably enjoy this testosterone temple celebrating sports. Restaurateur Robert Earl, with his lineup of superstar partners (Andre Agassi, Wayne Gretzky, Ken Griffey, Jr., Joe Montana, Shaquille O'Neal, and Monica Seles) launched this massive 650-seat homage to professional sports in December 1995. The 30,000-foot space with 40-foot ceilings—in the heart of Times Square—features mezzanine skybox booths, a center court arena-sized scoreboard, bars on both the upper and lower "decks," and booths shaped like huge baseball mitts. Superstar memorabilia on display includes Andre Agassi's Wimbledon uniform, Wayne Gretzky's hockey stick, Ken Griffey Jr.'s Louisville Slugger, Joe Montana's helmet, Monica Seles' U.S. Open trophy, and the backboard Shaquille O'Neal smashed on his way to becoming one of the NBA's leading scorers. Over 100 video monitors are positioned around the restaurant to allow everyone a front row view of the greatest plays in sports history, orchestrated by DJ's. There's a lot going on here and the noise level is high; it's a kick when you're in the mood for this sort of audio-visual overload and have a hankering for ballpark/road food.

You might lead off with Louisiana crab dip served with crisp Cajun garlic bread ($8.95), chicken quesadillas ($5.95), Buffalo wings ($6.95), chili topped with cheese, sour cream, and scallions ($4.95), or chili and cheese nachos served with jalapeños and salsa ($6.95). There are burgers galore: chili and cheddar ($9.50), bacon, cheddar, and barbecue sauce ($9.95), Mexican with onions, cheeses, red salsa, avocado, sour, cream, and jalapeños ($10.95), and tomato, mozzarella, and parmesan ($9.95). But to conjure up a happy ballpark memory, go for the all star hot dog with chili and cheese ($8.95) or the all

American dog topped with ketchup, relish, mustard, and onions ($8.50). Other choices include rotisserie chicken with creamed corn and garlic mashed potatoes ($11.95) and meatloaf with mashed potatoes, beef gravy, and green beans ($10.95). Dessert choices are caloric temptations like Heath Bar Cake (a moist cake laced with Health Bar ice cream, chocolate sauce, caramel sauce, and chunks of Heath Bar candy) ($6.25) and Chocolate Chip Cookie Supreme (a large warm white chocolate chip cookie topped with white chocolate-chocolate chip caramel swirl ice cream, whipped cream, and chocolate and caramel sauces ($5.95).

ORSO ★★   Italian
322 West 46th Street
(between Eighth and Ninth Aves.)
212/489-7212
Daily Noon - 11:45 p.m.
All major cards

Orso draws a very pretty crowd. A hit with both celebrities and theatergoers, this split-level trattoria is one of the most popular spots on Restaurant Row. The decor is invitingly casual with an open kitchen, skylit ceiling, and mottled ochre walls covered with photos of celebrities, peasants, and village scenes. If you want a quiet meal, come after the 8:00 curtain. But part of the fun of dining here is the after-theater buzz of activity and star-gazing. Owned by Joe Allen—whose namesake restaurant is just next door—it is named after a dog (who wandered near the Gritti Palace in Venice) that he befriended many years ago. You'll see a picture of this affectionately immortalized pooch near the entrance.

This breezy trattoria is more than just a convenient theatrical hangout. The country Italian fare here is also delightful. The same menu is served all day long. Starter choices might be artichoke salad with roasted peppers and onion ($8.00), warm spinach salad with mushrooms, white beans, and onions ($8.00), and roasted eggplant stuffed with goat cheese ($8.00). The delicious thin-crusted pizzas ($12.00) come in various combinations and are also nice starters. Pasta choices might include ravioli stuffed with wild mushrooms, walnuts, and spinach with a cream sauce ($15.00), penne with a rustic meat sauce ($15.00), and fettuccine with wine-roasted chicken breast, onions, green peas, and tomato sauce ($16.00). Also good is a risotto with sea scallops and asparagus ($16.00). Other pleasing mains are grilled salmon with roasted garlic potatoes and a basil sauce ($18.00), grilled spicy sausage with lentils, roasted onions, spinach, and polenta ($18.00), and grilled marinated chicken breast with portobello mushroom and tomato sauce ($18.00). A nice way to end a meal here is with pistachio biscuits and dessert wine ($5.50). There's also a nice light tiramisú ($5.50), chocolate walnut cake ($6.00), and rice pudding with raspberry sauce ($5.50).

OSTERIA AL DOGE ★★   Italian
142 West 44th Street
(between Sixth Ave. and Broadway)
212/944-3643
Monday through Thursday Noon - 11:30 p.m.;
Friday and Saturday Noon - Midnight;
Sunday 4:00 - 10:30 p.m.
All major cards

A lively atmosphere and well-prepared Northern Italian specialties make this delightful restaurant a theater district favorite. Its two-level interior is charming. Pale yellow walls, high ceilings, metal chandeliers, and soaring columns combine to give it a look that is striking and somewhat grand, yet at the same time projects a rustic and very warm feel. While its location makes it tremendously convenient for before or after the theater, it is buzzing with activity at any time.

Grilled vegetables with extra virgin olive oil ($8.50) make a terrific starter. Other good choices include minestrone with rice ($6.50), Venetian-style fried calamari and shrimp ($11.50), or a selection from the fresh antipasto bar ($12.50). The inventive pizzas are delicious and come in a variety of interesting combos (from $11.50 to $14.50). The pasta dishes are also good. Choices include spinach and ricotta green ravioli with a butter and sage sauce ($13.50), penne with bacon, onion, and a spicy tomato sauce ($13.50), and risotto with fresh lobster meat ($17.00). Other good mains include sautéed salmon with shrimp and mushrooms, served with mashed potatoes ($19.50), seafood and shellfish stew in a light tomato broth with garlic bread ($17.50), lightly-pounded aged sirloin steak, grilled and served with roasted potatoes ($22.00), and grilled breast of chicken with sautéed vegetables ($16.50). You'll also find a delectable assortment of desserts which change from day to day.

A $22.95 pre-theater menu is offered from 5:00 to 7:00 p.m. with a choice of salad or soup of the day, a choice from three mains, and tiramisú and coffee or tea.

OSTERIA DEL CIRCO ★★   Italian
120 West 55th Street (between Sixth and Seventh Aves.)
212/265-3636
Lunch - Monday through Saturday 11:30 a.m. - 2:45 p.m.
Dinner - Sunday through Thursday 5:30 - 11:00 p.m.;
Friday and Saturday 5:30 - 11:30 p.m.
All major cards

A circus theme sets a lively tone at this whimsically chic restaurant of the moment. It is the offspring of brilliant restaurateur Sirio Maccioni (owner of Le Cirque), his wife Egidiana, and their three sons, Mario, Marco, and Mauro. Despite its chic parentage, it has a personality very much its own—cheeky, stylish, and high-spirited. Festively designed by Adam Tihany, its under-the-big-top theme is carried out in flying panels of red and yellow stripes descending tent-like from the ceiling with bronze monkeys cavorting around a huge pole. Overseeing this sophisticated sideshow are the three personable Maccioni sons who have had the good sense to make their mother's traditional home cooking the focus of the menu. As executive consulting chef, anything on the menu bearing her name is a sure winner.

While the decor is abundantly light-hearted, the kitchen takes a serious turn with offerings both sophisticated and rustic. An indulgent starter is the Tuscan fish soup laden with lobster, fresh prawns, calamari, monkfish, clams, and mussels ($26.00). Another expensive opener is a wonderful Maine lobster salad with baby lettuce, roasted peppers and fresh cucumbers in a yellow pepper vinaigrette ($26.50). Other starters have prices more palatable. Good choices include grilled rare yellowfin tuna with cannellini beans, sweet red onions, and basil-infused extra virgin olive oil ($13.25) and mesclun salad with balsamic vinaigrette, shaved goat cheese, and focaccia ($8.50). And the thin-crusted pizzas ($13.25) are delightful. Of the pastas, Mrs. Maccioni's ravioli with fresh spinach, bitter greens, and ricotta with either butter-sage or fresh tomato sauce ($15.50) is the standout. Also good—tagliatelle with duck ragu ($15.75), tortelloni filled with wild mushrooms and parmesan ($15.75), and gnocchi with morel mushrooms, shallots, and parmesan ($16.50). The risotto with shrimp and asparagus ($16.50) is another winner. Good main choices include a sliced T-bone steak with cannellini beans, seasonal mushrooms, and oven-baked tomatoes ($53.50 for two), polenta-dusted cod with baby artichokes, tomato compote, asparagus, and black olives ($24.00), and roast rack of lamb with a ragout of fresh peas, onions, baby carrots, and braised potatoes ($26.75). There are also excellent rotisserie offerings, such as herb-roasted free-range chicken with polenta gratin, grilled baby eggplant, and green onions ($18.75). And like the circus, the big festive desserts will send you off with a smile. Daily offerings might include ricotta tart with lemon custard and fresh berries and chocolate polenta cake—both delicious. But it's hard to beat the irresistible bomboloncini, a trio of doughnuts filled with chocolate, vanilla, and raspberry cream, garnished with chocolate swirls and a candy clown.

PALIO ★★★   Italian
151 West 51st Street
(between Sixth and Seventh Aves.)
212/245-4850
Lunch - Monday through Friday Noon - 2:30 p.m.
Dinner - Monday through Saturday 5:30 - 10:45 p.m.
All major cards

This is a strikingly smart restaurant, both in decor and cuisine. As you enter through the main level bar, you'll be dazzled by the stunning Sandro Chia wraparound mural of the famous horse-racing festival in Siena, Italy, that gives the restaurant its name. From there, you'll be taken by elevator to the second level dining room, where style and sophistication also abound. The room is spacious and quietly elegant with a high coffered ceiling, walls covered with flags from the Palio competition, trellised woodwork, bold floral bouquets, plush banquettes, and tables set with glittering brass plates and bowls of dried flowers.

You'll be welcomed with a basket of fabulous homemade breadsticks. Go easy—if you can—because there are some good starters to consider, such as the marinated smoked salmon with orange dressing ($14.50), tuna tartare with marinated eggplant ($14.00), prosciutto and fresh mozzarella with marinated vegetables ($16.50), and lobster salad with cannellini beans and a roasted pepper sauce ($16.50). The pastas are all homemade and completely delectable with choices that include gnocchi with sausage ($22.00) and spaghettini with seafood ($22.00). Other good main choices include lamb chops with a potato herb crust ($29.50), filet of Dover sole in a black olive sauce with brussels sprouts ($29.50), rosemary flavored roasted baby Cornish hen with new potatoes ($24.00), filet of rabbit with prosciutto and roasted peppers ($29.50), and veal scaloppine with prosciutto and mushrooms ($28.00). Desserts are wonderful—Capri-style chocolate almond cake, warm lemon soufflé with red and black currants, orange crème brûlée tart with ice cream, and tiramisú (each $10.00).

Various tasting menus are offered, as well as a three-course pre-theatre menu for $45.00 between 5:30 and 6:30 p.m.

RACHEL'S ★★   American
608 Ninth Avenue
(between 43rd and 44th Sts.)
212/957-9050
Monday Noon - 11:00 p.m.;
Tuesday and Thursday Noon - Midnight;
Wednesday 11:30 a.m. - Midnight;
Friday Noon - 12:30 a.m.;
Saturday 11:30 a.m. - 12:30 a.m.;
Sunday 11:30 a.m. - 11:00 p.m.
All major cards

This American Bistro is a delightful surprise. You might easily walk past its unassuming front never guessing at the many pleasures just inside. It is a cozy place where candlelight gives the tiny room a romantic feel and a highly congenial staff makes you feel pampered. And the prices—so modest for the quality of the cuisine—make this animated and homey bistro a real find.

Stars among starters include a Napoleon with smoked salmon, spinach and brie ($6.00), grilled portobello in vinaigrette on a bed or arugula ($5.50), and grilled shrimp served with citrus soy sauce ($5.95). There are several good homemade pastas—linguine tossed with fresh plum tomatoes, basil, and cubes of homemade mozzarella ($8.95), basil fettuccine with seasonal vegetables, and a touch of pesto ($8.95), and lobster ravioli in its own stock ($10.95). Other good mains include an excellent lamb shank, braised in a Cabernet sauce ($12.00), chicken breast coated with pecans in a honey mustard sauce ($10.95), chicken pot pie ($9.95), veal scaloppine sautéed with portobello mushrooms, red wine, veal stock, and a touch of tomato ($11.95), and sea scallops sautéed with fresh lemon juice, white wine, fresh tarragon, and black beans ($10.95). Vegetables accompany the mains, and the freshly made bread is the kind made to remember. The homemade desserts include apple-sour cream pie, chocolate peanut butter pie, and cherries jubilee cheesecake (each $4.50).

This is also a great place to know about for brunch, served Wednesday, Saturday, and Sunday from 11:30 a.m. until 3:00 p.m. Its $8.95 set price includes a cocktail, wine, or beverage. Favorites on the menu: pancakes with bananas and walnuts; French toast prepared from the so-good homemade bread brushed with cinnamon-sugar and topped with plantains; spinach omelette with cheddar and mozzarella; smoked salmon and brie omelette; and a chili omelette with red onions and sour cream.

REMI ★★★   Italian
145 West 53rd Street
(between Sixth and Seventh Aves.)
212/581-4242
Lunch - Monday through Friday 11:45 a.m. - 2:30 p.m.
Dinner - Monday through Saturday 5:30 - 11:30 p.m.;
Sunday 5:30 - 10:00 p.m.
All major cards

Remi emanates a polished smartness with soaring twenty-five foot ceilings, gothic detailing, and a spectacular wraparound fantasy mural of Venice. A delightful skylit open-air atrium, seating about 65, is another appealing feature of this chic trattoria.

Starters on the Venetian-inspired menu include artichokes with pecorino cheese in a parsley garlic sauce ($10.50), crabmeat and shrimp cakes with warm barley salad ($13.00), pan-seared sea scallops with braised fennel ($12.50), and soft yellow polenta with porcini mushrooms ($11.00). Pasta choices include fusilli with radicchio and smoked bacon in a light tomato sauce ($17.00), tortelloni filled with ricotta cheese and spinach in a light red pepper sauce ($17.00), and spaghetti served with oven-dried tomatoes and roasted garlic in extra virgin olive oil ($15.00). Good main course offerings include roasted rack of lamb with garlic ($26.00), seared tuna served with spinach and capers in a shallot sauce ($25.00), and braised veal shank served with potatoes and zucchini ($26.00). Desserts might include apple mascarpone cheesecake, warm chocolate soufflé cake with a cappuccino parfait, or caramelized banana tart with toasted almond ice cream and a caramel glaze.

RENÉ PUJOL ★★   French
321 West 51st Street
(between Eighth and Ninth Aves.)
212/246-3023
Lunch - Monday through Saturday Noon - 3:00 p.m.
Dinner - Monday through Thursday 5:00 - 10:30 p.m.;
Friday and Saturday 5:00 - 11:30 p.m.
All major cards

With its decidedly old-fashioned ambience and French country inn setting, you'll feel a long way from Broadway when you dine at this charming family-run bistro. Colorful pottery, hand-painted plates, and whimsical lamps and shades enliven the two cream-toned dining rooms—one graced with a brick fireplace, the other with a handsome antique chiming grandfather clock. This wonderful place has been a favorite of theatergoers for a quarter of a century.

The food is elegant and sophisticated and has a lightness that is new to a cuisine that has traditionally featured heavy sauces and much butter. **The nightly $36.00 prix fixe is a wonderful value.** In addition to the many choices among its three courses, chef/owner Claude Franques offers four or five specials each day. Longtime favorites among starters are the small onion tart in phyllo dough and the broiled sliced giant sea scallops on a bed of provençale vegetables. The lobster bisque and onion soup are also fine openers. For the main, good choices include: pan-seared tuna with red onions, leeks, a ginger compote, and roasted red pepper jus; roasted chicken breast with an herb crust and tomato compote; pan-seared beef mignonettes with roasted shallots; and lobster fricassée in a light ginger sauce with angel hair pasta (supplement according to market). Everything is fresh and delicious, and the desserts are just as enticing as what has come before. Choose from a selection that includes caramelized coconut custard, pear tart, and chocolate mousse.

RESTAURANT CHARLOTTE ★★   American
145 West 44th Street (between Sixth Ave. and Broadway)
212/789-7508
Lunch - Daily 11:30 a.m. - 3:00 p.m.
Dinner - Daily 5:15 - 11:30 p.m.
All major cards

This oasis of tranquility off Times Square has a cool, sophisticated look. Its postmodern design in black and white is accented with handsome marble and African mahogany, with a striking floral arrangement at its center providing a dash of color. Well-spaced tables, tall ceilings, and indirect lighting add to the relaxed ambience of the room.

You might start with roasted corn chowder ($6.00), rock shrimp and white bean soup with jalapeño pesto ($7.00), or carrot risotto with grilled shrimp ($10.00). Mains might include (if you're lucky) a lobster and cheese quesadilla with avocado salsa ($21.00), marinated leg of lamb with niçoise bread salad ($19.00), grilled salmon with salsa ($22.00), roast chicken with spaghetti squash and peas ($19.00), seared tuna on a bed of grilled corn salad ($22.00), penne with tomato and spring vegetables ($17.00), or sirloin with mashed potatoes ($25.00). Desserts are nostalgic and delicious.

A daily prix-fixe menu is offered with three courses for $32.50.

SAM'S ★   Italian/American
263 West 45th Street
(between Broadway and Eighth Ave.)
212/719-5416
Lunch - Daily Noon - 4:00 p.m.
Dinner - Daily 4:00 - 12:45 a.m.
All major cards

Cheerful and theatrical, Sam's is a Broadway institution. At over 70 years old, it has long been a popular watering hole for theater people, particularly the chorus gypsies. But its conviviality appeals to those whose names are on the marquis and cabaret stars as well. Nathan Lane recently told *Where* magazine that if he comes here any more often "they might start calling it Nathan's." The casual interior with red brick walls, low lighting, and theater posters evokes a homey feel. And while the early prix fixe offer is a real bargain, the after-theater scene is the most fun. Wednesday through Saturday at 10:30 p.m. Ken Lundie (from Broadway's "Crazy for You") entertains at the keyboard and your theatrically-inclined waiter may belt out a showstopper or two.

The American/Italian fare is served in plentiful portions, so come hungry. You might start with baked clams oreganata ($6.95), hot brie ($6.50), hummus with pita ($6.75), or potato skins with cheddar ($6.50). Most mains are served with a vegetable and potato or rice, some with salad. The selection includes grilled tuna ($14.95), broiled bay scallops ($13.95), linguine Sinatra (linguine with shrimp and scallops in a red clam sauce) ($14.95), cheese ravioli with a tomato basil sauce ($10.95), homemade lasagna ($10.95), fettuccine carbonara ($11.95), broiled flank steak ($13.95), veal parmesan with pasta ($17.95), and broiled lamb chops ($15.95).

The prix fixe menu is offered Monday through Saturday from 4:00 to 6:15 p.m. and on Sunday from 3:30 to 6:45 p.m. It includes three courses for $17.95. There's a choice of four starters (soup of the day, house salad, mozzarella and tomatoes, or clams oreganata). There are eight mains to choose from including linguine with red or white clam sauce, the chicken special of the day, eggplant parmesan with pasta, and the fish catch of the day. Homemade dessert choices include carrot cake, tiramisú, frozen key lime pie, and cheesecake.

SAN DOMENICO ★★★★   Italian
240 Central Park South
(between Broadway and Seventh Ave.)
212/265-5959
Lunch - Daily Noon - 2:45 p.m.
Dinner - Daily 5:30 - 11:00 p.m.
All major cards

With a look both contemporary and provocative, San Domenico provides a warm, inviting backdrop for dining on exquisite Bolognese cuisine. Vibrant Italian paintings, burnt orange leather chairs, ocher-tinted stucco walls, and a terra-cotta floor imported from Florence recall its famous namesake in Imola, Italy. Look around and you'll see the crowd is as smart-looking as the surroundings. You might even spot a few very famous faces, or overhear Isabella Rossellini ordering in Italian.

This is a luxurious and expensive place where you will indeed be pampered and very well fed. You might start with warm lobster salad with artichokes and potatoes ($17.50), grilled Mediterranean baby octopus with cucumbers and cherry tomatoes ($14.95), or chilled fava bean soup with soft goat cheese and truffle oil ($9.50). The pasta dishes are sensational. Homemade spaghetti with tomato and basil ($18.50) is a good example of how memorable the simplest of dishes can be. But of the many good pasta dishes, the most remarkable is a single large ravioli containing ricotta, spinach, and a soft-cooked egg in a sauce of browned butter and truffle oil ($21.50)—a very rich trick. Other terrific pasta choices are the handmade pasta quills with chives, caviar, and asparagus ($22.50), ricotta-filled ravioli with marinated tomatoes and black olives ($19.95), and risotto with asparagus, herbs, and extra virgin olive oil ($21.00). The mains reflect the same sophisticated flair with choices like Australian loin of lamb with fava beans and broccoli rabe ($29.95), Dover sole sautéed in herbs and flavored with extra virgin olive oil ($35.00), grilled Norwegian salmon with caviar and sour cream ($30.95), roasted veal loin with braised radicchio, pearl onions, and a bacon cream sauce ($32.50), grilled prime rib marinated with herbs and served with mushrooms ($32.50), and breast of duck with an olive sauce and caramelized endive ($29.95). For dessert: white chocolate mousse in a chocolate wafer cone on flourless chocolate cake ($11.25), chilled lemon and pistachio soufflé cake ($9.50), chocolate and cherries in a crisp shell with ricotta ice cream ($9.50), and tropical fruit Napoleon with coconut ice cream in a mango coulis ($11.95).

A $65.00 four-course tasting menu, which includes three wines, is available all evening every evening (to entire table only). Selections change every two weeks.

A $29.50 prix fixe three-course menu is available from 5:30 to 6:45 p.m. (departure by 8:00 p.m.) Monday through Saturday and from 5:30 to 10:00 p.m. on Sundays. There are only a few choices in each category, but it's an outstanding value and an inexpensive way to sample the superb cooking of gifted chef Odette Fada.

SARDI'S ★   Continental
234 West 44th Street
(between Broadway and Eighth Ave.)
212/221-8440
Lunch - Monday through Saturday 11:30 a.m. - 3:30 p.m.
Dinner - Monday through Saturday 3:30 - 8:30 p.m.
Supper - Monday through Saturday 8:30 p.m. - 12:30 a.m.
All major cards

What a rich, theatrical history this place has! Founded in 1921 by Vincent (Sr.) and Eugenia Sardi, it was for many years the unrivalled toast of Broadway. At its inception, an agreement was made with an unemployed caricaturist named Alex Gard to draw caricatures of Sardi's famous patrons in exchange for two meals a day. These caricatures became Sardi's trademark. Plays have been written and financed at Sardi's. And decades of hit shows have celebrated openings at Sardi's while awaiting delivery of the first edition reviews. For me, there was a time when a theater spree in New York invariably meant an after-theater supper at Sardi's. While the service was sometimes of the "whatdaya want" school, the welcome at the door was always gracious and we were often lucky enough to get the same sweet little waiter, who would eagerly tell us where the celebs were seated that night. But, while I've had many memorable evenings at Sardi's (including literally bumping into John Travolta), I've never had a memorable meal there.

In 1985, Vincent Sardi, Jr., sold the restaurant, which had already seen the celebrity scene shift, and it went through troubled times. Then in 1990, he returned and the place received a much-needed facelift. Now, with a new chef on hand, there's talk it may return to its glory days. I'm rooting for it.

Good first course mainstays include sautéed shrimp with a garlic sauce ($15.00), spinach cannelloni au gratin ($10.00), homemade mozzarella and vine-ripened tomatoes with basil and a balsamic vinegar dressing ($8.00), and chilled vichyssoise with chives ($5.00). Traditional house specialties include supreme of chicken Sardi (sliced breast of chicken, asparagus tips, and duchess potatoes with a cream sauce au gratin ($27.00), cannelloni with a combination of beef, chicken, and spinach with a tomato cream meat sauce ($23.00), and veal cutlet Vincent (sautéed veal dusted with flour, topped with diced ham and mozzarella cheese and served with zucchini and new potatoes) ($29.00). Other good choices include prime rib served with seasonal vegetables and a baked potato ($27.00) and grilled pork chops with apple fritters, served with whipped potatoes ($23.00). For dessert, choose the baked Alaska for two ($16.00), the old-fashioned snowball with vanilla ice cream topped with shredded coconut and chocolate sauce ($6.00), or the imported cheese plate for two served with grapes and crackers ($9.00). The supper menu supplements the dinner offerings with a selection of nice salads—Sardi's salad with grilled chicken, roast beef, ham, Swiss cheese, mixed greens, hard-boiled egg, tomato, and olives ($20.00) and grilled chicken breast on a bed of California greens with vine-ripened tomatoes, Bermuda onion, and crisp potatoes ($19.00).

A prix fixe dinner menu, available from 3:30 to 8:30 p.m., offers three courses (with many choices in each category) for $39.00.

TAPIKA ★★   Southwest
950 Eighth Avenue (at W. 56th St.)
212/397-3737
Lunch - Monday through Friday Noon - 2:30 p.m.
Brunch - Sunday 11:00 a.m. - 2:30 p.m.
Dinner - Monday through Thursday 5:30 - 11:00 p.m.; Friday 5:30 - 11:30;
Saturday 5:00 - 11:30 p.m.; Sunday 5:00 - 10:30 p.m.
All major cards

This cowboy fantasyland replaces the staid old Symphony Cafe where the food was very fine but the lobby-like setting lacked personality. Owners Penny and Peter Glazier sensed that "Symphony Cafe was too uptight, and it was time for a change." So architect David Rockwell was called upon to weave his magic and the colorful, kitschy Tapika was born. Comfortably casual, it is full of fanciful details and has a rugged warmth. Rough-hewn woods with simulated cattle brands, large disc-shaped lighting fixtures with Native American symbols, and a stylized picket fence set the scene. Pony skin barstools, hand-stencilled wood floors, and a corral-shaped, fenced-in chef's table add to its personality.

Rising star chef David Walzog (who made a name for himself at Red Sage in Washington, D.C., then later at Manhattan's Arizona 206) came on board as Executive Chef and things were off to a dandy start. Combining whimsy with serious cooking, his Southwest-inspired creations are primarily American-rooted with just traces of Mexican and Latin influence. Starters are deliciously inventive with choices like spicy black bean purée with ground chorizo, crumbled goat cheese, and roasted garlic flatbread ($9.50) and a wild mushroom tamale with red mole, toasted pecans, and an herb salad ($8.00). The good tequila-cured salmon comes with a green chile corncake and an icy shot of El Tesoro Plata tequila on the side to wash it down ($14.00). Tapika's Caesar-like house salad with tender romaine, taleggio cheese, and a spicy green chile dressing ($8.00) is fabulous. Barbecued short ribs with warm potato salad and buttermilk slaw ($8.50) is another good starter. Among the most popular mains: a delicious ground vegetable chile relleno with smoked tomato salsa and crumbled cheese ($17.00); roasted farm-raised chicken breast with wild mushroom barley risotto and bitter greens ($18.00); sliced Long Island duck with a braised duck spring roll, organic peanut sauce, and black bean salsa ($23.00); chili-rubbed salmon with smoked trout mashed potatoes and blackened tomato smoked chili sauce ($21.00); and chili-rubbed beef filet with an oxtail-jalapeño quesadilla, asparagus, and roasted tomatillo sauce ($26.50). Good dessert choices include bittersweet chocolate cake with cinnamon ice cream and a pair of cherry-apricot empanadas ($8.00), Southwestern profiteroles with coffee ice cream and warm chocolate sauce ($7.00), and warm apple cobbler for two, served in an iron skillet with individual plates of ice cream and tiny candied caramel apples ($11.00). For a real downhome finale, you can order a plate of assorted homemade cookies and a shot of ice cold milk ($6.00).

There's a nice pre-theater menu available from 5:30 to 6:30 p.m. on weekdays and from 5:00 to 6:30 p.m. on weekends with three courses for $31.00 (offering three choices in each category). You might start with the Tapika salad, chicken tortilla soup, or aged goat cheese ravioli in a smokey pinto bean sauce. Main choices might be roasted chicken breast with mushroom risotto; roasted red snapper with green chile sauce and garlic mashed potatoes; or New York strip steak with crisp corn fries, grilled vegetable salsa, and chili sauce. For dessert: lime tart; double chocolate pudding with fresh raspberries and whipped cream; or assorted ice creams and sorbets.

On Sundays, brunch is $16.50. It includes selections from a buffet table and either a main course or cocktail.

TOUT VA BIEN ★   French
311 West 51st Street (between Eighth and Ninth Aves.)
212/265-0190
Lunch - Daily Noon - 3:00 p.m.
Dinner - Daily 5:00 - 11:30 p.m.
All major cards

This cozy, old-fashioned French restaurant is like a page from the past. Not at all trendy, it has been serving a loyal clientele the same kind of hearty country French homestyle cooking for decades. Its small courtyard with umbrella-shaded tables is a pleasant, relaxed place to dine in nice weather. The interior—cramped and now looking a bit timeworn—is cheerful and unpretentious, with colorful posters and checkered tablecloths. In spite of some shortcomings, the place is warm and likeable and makes you feel—at least for the evening—that style and ambience are highly overrated.

The prices are quite pleasing as well. You might start with an excellent house pâté ($4.00). Other popular choices include shrimp cocktail ($5.00), hearts of palm ($4.00), and onion soup gratiné ($4.00). Bouillabaisse ($18.00) is a favorite main here, but is only served on Fridays. Other good mains include shrimp with garlic and tomatoes ($16.00), grilled lobster ($18.00), coq au vin ($13.00), beef bourguignon ($13.00), chicken cordon bleu ($14.00), Cornish game hen ($14.00), and chateaubriand for two ($44.00). Desserts are old standards like peach melba, pears Helene, and chocolate mousse (each $5.00).

A three-course prix-fixe is offered all evening for $20.00.

TRATTORIA DOPO TEATRO ★   Italian
125 West 44th Street (between Sixth Ave. and Broadway)
212/869-2849
Lunch - Daily Noon - 5:00 p.m.
Dinner - Daily 5:00 p.m. - Midnight
All major cards

From the handsome long antique mahogany bar with its original brass railing and mirrors at the entrance to the open brick oven in the rear, Trattoria Dopo Teatro ("Trattoria After the Theater") projects warmth and has a decidedly friendly feel. Soft orange-toned sponged walls, antique crystal lamps, an enticing antipasto display, and a collection of original, early Italian movie posters complete the pleasant atmosphere.

Chef Franco Migliorini's menu offers the Northern Italian dishes of his homeland near Portofino where his cooking career began at the age of fourteen in the area's resort hotels. In New York, he has manned the kitchens at Felidia and Campagnola, and most recently, at a private club in the West Village. His thin-crusted pizzas, focaccia, and peasant-style breads fired in the open brick oven are fabulous. To start, try a generous selection from the antipasto table ($11.50) or the Tuscan-style bean soup ($6.50). Other popular choices include grilled portobello mushrooms ($8.00), crêpes stuffed with wild mushrooms and topped with melted cheese ($7.50), grilled vegetables ($8.50), and hearts of lettuce with walnuts and dried goat cheese ($7.50). Of the pastas, I like the simplicity of the penne with spicy tomato sauce ($9.50). Other good choices might be penne with melted fontina cheese and a ragu of wild mushrooms ($14.00), tagliatelle with lamb ragu ($12.50), gnocchi with pesto sauce ($12.00), risotto with cream of asparagus ($15.00), cappellini with lobster sauce ($16.50), and homemade Italian dumplings with pesto sauce ($14.00). For the main, choices include skewered chicken with polenta ($14.50), grilled baby lamb chops ($21.00), pan-fried veal chop, Milanese-style ($19.50), sautéed calamari ($21.00), and grilled swordfish ($19.50). The delicious pizzas come in all varieties ($10.50 to $15.00). Desserts ($6.00) change daily.

A great value prix fixe is offered all evening for $22.50. It includes four courses plus an after-dinner cordial.

UNION SQUARE
GRAMERCY PARK
MURRAY HILL

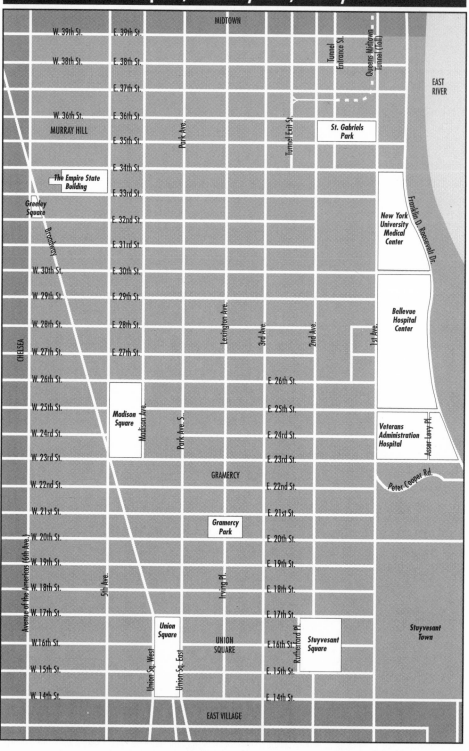

ALVA ★★   American
36 East 22nd Street
(between Park Ave. So. and Broadway)
212/228-4399
Lunch - Monday through Friday Noon - 3:00 p.m.
Dinner - Daily 5:30 p.m. - Midnight
All major cards

Places with elbow to elbow seating and a bustling noisy atmosphere can have an appealing vitality and energy when you're in the mood for that sort of thing. This sophisticated retro-fitted American bistro is such a place—best enjoyed when the spirit moves you in a convivial kind of way. With a whimsical salute to Thomas Edison, the bare light bulb is the theme here. Tiny ones line the walls amongst an arty collection of black and white photographs; a giant one rests in a glass case. Yet, the lighting here is low and the tables for two are romantically lit with candles. In many ways this is the consummate neighborhood restaurant. It is small and friendly with comforting things like mashed potatoes and roasted chicken and desserts like Mom used to make from scratch. Many of the dishes, though, have an interesting twist that keeps the menu interesting and fresh.

There's much to like on the list of starters. Particularly good is the warm goat cheese and beet salad ($8.00) and the crispy shrimp cocktail—a nice variation with breadcrumb-fried shrimp served in a stemmed glass with cocktail sauce ($9.00). Other options include grilled polenta and portobello mushrooms with shaved parmesan ($9.00) and salmon gravlax with grilled brioche ($9.00). Good mains (served with vegetables) include a dynamite juicy double-garlic roast chicken ($17.00), grilled salmon in a grain mustard Riesling sauce ($18.00), Alva veal stew ($16.00), and grilled sirloin au poivre ($24.00). The best is saved for last. Desserts are glorious American classics: apple pie, pineapple upside down cake, and yummy chocolate pudding (each $6.00).

AN AMERICAN PLACE ★★★   American
2 Park Avenue (on 32nd St.)
212/684-2122
Lunch - Monday through Friday 11:45 a.m. - 3:00 p.m.
Dinner - Monday through Saturday 5:30 - 9:30 p.m.
All major cards

This warm and appealing restaurant offers some of the most innovative all-American dishes in town. Although celebrated chef/owner Larry Forgione's career began in England at London's Connaught Hotel, he is generally regarded by insiders as the godfather of the New American cuisine movement. He opened An American Place in 1983 on the Upper East Side, but relocated to this landmark art deco building in 1989 where the setting seems in perfect harmony with the food. The large high-ceilinged postmodern dining room has sponged yellow walls, mahogany-sheathed columns, wood floors, scattered rugs, and art deco lamps. Pretty flowers and well-spaced tables add to its appeal.

Selected as one of America's 25 great restaurants by *Playboy* magazine, An American Place was also featured as one of the World's Best Restaurants by *Lifestyles of the Rich and Famous*. Dine here and you'll understand why. The classical, regional-styled American dishes are prepared using only fresh American products and the seasonal menu is the kind that makes selection difficult when everything sounds so interesting, so good. For instance, choices among starters include temptations such as crisp cornmeal-coated sweet Maine clams done Ipswich-style with a fresh tomato-tartar sauce ($9.50), fresh Maine deviled crab spring roll with a Charleston vegetable slaw and smoked onion remoulade ($10.50), and warm Hudson Valley camembert crisp with sautéed pears, field greens, and gooseberry conserve ($9.50). It's not any easier to select a main with choices such as roast breast of free-range chicken with sautéed fresh artichoke hearts, golden tomatoes, tarragon, and roast garlic with whipped potatoes ($25.00), roast medallions of milk-fed organic spring lamb from the Hudson Valley with a gratin of yellowfin potatoes, spring vegetables, and a roast lamb jus ($29.00), and Black Angus New York sirloin with twice-baked potatoes and creamy barbecued sweet onions ($29.50). Desserts are delicious and pure Americana—old-fashioned devil's food chocolate cake with sweetened cream ($6.00), strawberry-rhubarb deep dish pie with honey ice cream ($6.00), fresh berry shortcake with sweetened cream ($6.50), and warm New England banana Betty with a ginger-snap topping ($6.00).

BOLO ★★★   Spanish
23 East 22nd Street
(between Broadway and Park Ave. So.)
212/228-2200
Lunch - Monday through Friday Noon - 2:15 p.m.
Dinner - Daily 5:30 p.m. - Midnight
All major cards

Star chef Bobby Flay and partner Laurence Kretchmer, the dynamic duo behind Mesa Grill fame, conceived Bolo after kicking ideas around for a venture that would bring something new to the local dining scene. Since there

316

seemed to be a lack of contemporary Spanish restaurants in New York, Flay went to Spain to sample the true flavors and accents of its cuisine. "Authentic Spanish food, with its heavy use of pork and animal fats, does not reflect the health conscious way New Yorkers want to eat," explains the dashing redhead. "By using American ingredients, I've modified my dishes to suit the way people eat today without losing the distinct flavors of Spain." At Bolo, you can sample his bold and innovative Spanish-inspired creations. "Inspired" is the operative word here, for Flay's interpretation of Spanish cooking includes an added measure of spicing and pizazz with dazzling results.

As for its ambience, Bolo's interior has a playful edge in keeping with Flay's concept that it should have a sense of humor. Architect James Biber, who also designed Mesa Grill, combined Braquian and Matisse-like colors and images to create a festive mood. A large free-form wall mural recalls outdoor billboards, evoking New York's vibrant street life. Columns are cleverly covered with oversized sections of Spanish newspapers and red, gold, and cobalt blue hues comprise the color scheme in fabrics, dishes, and even custom designed light fixtures.

You'll be off to a good start here with any of the inventive openers. You might opt for the sensational oven-baked flatbread with roasted vegetables, spicy hummus, and robiola cheese ($10.75), oven-roasted baby shrimp with toasted garlic and fresh thyme ($9.50), or oven-roasted wild mushrooms with goat cheese and chilies ($9.50). And when it comes to the mains, Flay really displays his talents, pulling out all the stops with creations such as a curried shellfish and chicken paella ($27.00), wild mushroom rice with roasted chicken, roasted garlic sauce, and white truffle oil ($22.00), oven-roasted lamb shank with toasted orzo and house-dried tomatoes ($25.50), grilled pork chop with charred peppers and onions and a caramelized date sauce ($22.50), grilled Black Angus steak rubbed with fresh garlic and hot peppers ($27.00), and grilled grouper with preserved lemon sauce, crispy capers, and garlic mashed potatoes ($25.00). Daily desserts provided by Mesa Grill's pastry chef tend to be fantastic as well.

CAFE BEULAH ★★   Southern
39 East 19th Street
(between Broadway and Park Ave. So.)
212/777-9700
Lunch - Monday through Friday Noon - 2:30 p.m.
Sunday Brunch 11:00 a.m. - 3:30 p.m.
Dinner - Monday through Wednesday 5:30 - 11:00 p.m.;
Thursday through Saturday 5:30 p.m. - Midnight
All major cards

Cafe Beulah's setting is pleasant and homey. Its owner, Alexander Smalls, is a former operatic baritone who once sang the role of Jake in the Houston Grand Opera's production of "Porgy and Bess." The enjoyable fare here is the food of his childhood in Charleston, South Carolina, and the restaurant is affectionately named after an aunt. Nostalgic Smalls family photos adorn the walls, tiny lamps illuminate the room, and ceiling fans hum softly overhead. When a yearning for Southern comfort food hits, you'll do well to head here.

Its Southern revival cooking is based on the low country cooking of South Carolina, with some dishes showing a sophisticated twist. For starters, there's grilled barbecued shrimp with okra ($10.00), Carolina crab croquettes with roasted yellow pepper corn sauce ($12.00), warm chicken liver salad with crispy bacon and barbecued mustard dressing ($8.00), and spicy Southern-fried chicken wings ($6.50). Good mains include shrimp macaroni and cheese casserole ($14.00), baked ham in a praline Bourbon sauce with lemon yams and stewed collard greens ($16.00), grilled pork chops with sweet potato fries and apple fennel chutney ($21.00), Alexander's gumbo plate (a deep dish plate of spicy jumbo shrimp, fresh lump crabmeat, farm-raised duck, and spicy duck sausage simmered in a creole sauce) ($26.00), and grilled spiced filet mignon with brown oyster gravy and baby green beans ($26.00). Cobblers, pies, and cakes on the dessert carte will remind you of Sunday dinner at Grandma's.

Sunday brunch Southern-style includes offerings such as poached eggs on toasted cornbread with smothered chicken livers in a Bourbon brown gravy ($12.00), free-range Southern-fried chicken with pecan waffles and seasonal fruit ($12.00), sweet potato buttermilk pancakes, sage sausage, and seasonal fruit ($10.00), eggs, baked ham, hominy grits, and a buttermilk biscuit ($10.00), as well as creole steak au poivre with French fries ($14.00).

CAFFE BONDÍ RISTORANTE ★★   Italian
7 West 20th Street (between Fifth and Sixth Aves.)
212/691-8136
Lunch - Monday through Saturday 11:00 a.m. - 5:00 p.m.
Dinner - Monday through Saturday 5:00 - 11:00 p.m.
All major cards

This is a family operation with a lot of pride. When Salvatore and Filippa Settepani arrived in New York twenty-some years ago, their twin sons, Nino and Biagio, were 13 years old. Anticipating their arrival, the twins' aunts (the Bondí sisters) arranged work for the boys in a local bakery and pastry shop. Some years later, while in college, they decided to open a pastry shop, and in 1981 purchased Bruno Bakery in Greenwich Village. Later, the profusion of Northern Italian restaurants that opened in the '80s piqued their interest and they joined forces with their cousin, Salvatore, in learning about the restaurant business. Nino enrolled at the French Culinary Institute and Salvatore at the NY Restaurant School. Wishing to establish that Italian food was regional, they enlisted help from a food historian to help them research authentic Sicilian recipes. This was the inception of Caffe Bondí. Today it is the kind of restaurant that makes you long to be a regular. Sleek and attractive, it has a cheerful air about it. Its changing photographic exhibits add to the casually sophisticated look of the place, and in warm weather, a romantic Mediterranean-style garden—sheltered by an arbor of vines—adds to its other delights.

The authentic Sicilian fare served here will introduce you to another kind of Italian cooking. Its seasonal menu starter offerings include braised artichokes served with almond sauce ($8.50), mushrooms stuffed with almonds, then sautéed and grilled ($10.00), and grilled seasonal vegetables ($10.00). Pastas are particularly good. The house specialty is the perciatelli with fresh sardines, fennel, pine nuts, and currant sauce ($15.00). There's also fresh tagliatelle with mushrooms, fennel, tomato, and vermouth sauce, delicately flavored with anchovies ($13.00) and homemade tortelli filled with chestnuts, ricotta, and rabbit ($15.00). Swordfish steak sautéed in a vegetable sauce with pine nuts and raisins ($19.00) is another house specialty. Other mains include a brioche filled with lobster, shrimp, clams, mussels and rice, flavored with curry ($19.00), almond-breaded veal cutlet ($19.00), and steak marinated in rosemary, garlic, and olive oil ($20.00). There's a nice selection of wines by the glass, and, of course, desserts are delicious.

A three-course prix fixe lunch is offered at $19.97 and a five-course prix fixe dinner at $39.00.

319

CAL'S ★★   Continental
55 West 21st Street
(between Fifth and Sixth Aves.)
212/929-0740
Lunch - Monday through Friday 11:30 a.m. - 5:00 p.m.
Dinner - Daily 5:00 p.m. - Midnight
All major cards

Inventive cooking, genuinely friendly service, and a cheerful ambience combine to make this turn-of-the-century bistro a really likeable place. Situated in a renovated warehouse, its loft-like setting is handsome and warm. A long antique mahogany bar, high pressed-tin ceiling, globe lights, and soaring columns create a striking backdrop. Vivid artwork by the owner and fresh flowers add bold punctuations of color and give the casually elegant space personality and style.

The food is delicious—a rather wide-ranging continental with much Mediterranean influence. To start, you'll be tempted by the likes of grilled portobello and arugula salad ($7.50), roasted mussels ($8.00), and lobster ravioli on a bed of fresh spinach ($8.50). Mains might be spinach fettuccine carbonara ($16.50), linguine with shrimp ($17.00), shrimp couscous ($16.50), grilled filet of salmon in a soy ginger sauce over basmati rice with snow peas and carrots ($19.50), crisp-roasted Cornish hen with roasted potatoes ($17.50), duck à l'orange with potato pancakes and braised red cabbage ($21.50), and grilled Australian lamb chops with string beans and a side of mashed potatoes ($24.00). And Cal's aged sirloin burger with fries ($12.00) is considered one of the best in town. The changing variety of desserts usually look too good to resist. The brownie ice cream sandwich even made the cover of *Chocolatier Magazine*.

CAMPAGNA ★★★   Italian
24 East 21st Street
(between Broadway and Park Ave. So.)
212/460-0900
Lunch - Monday through Friday Noon - 3:00 p.m.
Dinner - Monday through Saturday 6:00 - Midnight;
Sunday 5:30 - 10:00 p.m.
All major cards

In a setting that is casually chic, Campagna radiates generous hospitality and substantial charm. Its Tuscan farmhouse setting is framed in soft shades of green and cream. Rustic Italian curios, abstract paintings, a huge terra-cotta urn bursting with beautiful blooms, and a bountiful antipasto display all combine to create a colorful backdrop for the fabulous food served at this likeable trattoria.

Chef/owner Mark Strausman describes his food as Italian but not "textbook" Italian, preferring to give each dish his own interpretation. Judging by the satisfied looks on the faces of those dining here, it appears his interpretations are coming out just fine. And the robust, irresistible creations are served in copious portions. You might start with a generous selection from the antipasto table ($9.50) which changes from day to day. Other possibilities include grilled portobello mushrooms ($10.00), grilled jumbo shrimp with warm white beans and arugula ($12.50), tartare of fresh smoked salmon with warm potato pancakes ($8.50), and Roman gnocchi with assorted mushrooms and truffle oil ($9.50). As for pasta mains, Grandma's lasagna ($16.00) is a definite crowd pleaser. Also delicious—penne with a ragout of spicy seafood ($17.00), rigatoni with chunks of lobster, garlic, and artichokes ($19.00), and spaghetti with a spicy, garlicky tomato sauce ($15.00). There's also a risotto of the day ($18.00). House specialties among mains are the couscous with steamed fish in a spicy broth flavored with lemon and oregano ($24.00) and a smashing Florentine ribeye steak with spinach and Yukon gold mashed potatoes ($29.00). Other good choices would be the whole roasted baby chicken with rosemary, garlic, lemon, sage, and roasted potatoes ($20.00), veal Milanese ($29.50), and braised rabbit in red wine served with soft polenta and brussels sprouts ($24.00). The changing selection of desserts are in the $5.00 to $6.50 range. Plum tart with vanilla ice cream is a top contender.

DA CIRO ★   Italian
229 Lexington Avenue (between 33rd and 34th Sts.)
212/532-1636
Lunch - Daily Noon - 3:00 p.m.
Dinner - Sunday through Thursday 5:30 - 11:00 p.m.;
Friday and Saturday 5:30 p.m. - 12:30 a.m.
All major cards

Pleasant and appealing, Da Ciro has an unpretentious feel, offers a warm welcome, and serves good Italian specialties from a wood-burning oven. Its atmosphere is attractive and inviting, with a polished wood floor, marble tables, and black and white photographs of Italy setting a casual tone. Service here is also nice—thoroughly professional and genial at the same time.

Chef/owner Ciro Verdi turns out some terrific appetizers, particularly those from the wood-burning oven such as a casserole of wild mushrooms baked in a crock with arugula, goat cheese, olives, diced tomatoes, and mozzarella ($6.50) and a casserole of baked mozzarella wrapped in prosciutto and served over a bed of tomato sauce. Other good openers include fried calamari ($8.95), toasted bread with prosciutto and mozzarella ($7.95), polenta with wild mushrooms ($7.95), arugula with gorgonzola and walnuts ($7.95), and a warm salad prepared with shrimp and zucchini ($8.95). The pizzas are excellent and come in a multitude of variations ($10.50 to $13.50). Pastas are pleasing as well with choices like bucatini alla matriciana ($14.00), spaghetti with broccoli rabe and spicy sausage ($14.00), rigatoni with eggplant, tomatoes, ricotta, homemade mozzarella, and basil ($14.00), and fettuccine with wild mushrooms ($14.95). And each day brings a different preparation of both ravioli and risotto (p/a). Other popular main courses are the veal chop served with spinach and mashed potatoes ($23.95) and roasted baby chicken with spinach and roasted potatoes ($16.95). Dessert might be a good bitter chocolate mousse cake ($6.00) or a refreshing sorbet ($5.50).

DA VITTORIO ★★   Italian
43 East 20th Street
(between Park Ave. So. and Broadway)
212/979-6532
Lunch - Monday through Friday Noon - 3:00 p.m.
Dinner - Monday through Thursday 5:30 - 11:00 p.m.;
Friday and Saturday 5:30 - 11:30 p.m.
All major cards

From its rustic Tuscan-style dining room and very Italian waiters to its authentic homestyle Florentine cooking, Da Vittorio offers the best of old-world charm. The setting is a pleasing mix of brick and autumn colors. And an arched open kitchen window relays wonderful aromas into the small dining room. Its namesake owner is an ebullient 26-year old, Vittorio Assante, son of Umberto Assante, owner of the fabulous Da Umberto in Chelsea.

As at Da Umberto, there's an antipasto table at the front that is so colorful and so laden with irresistible temptations that many diners know before they're seated—let alone before they glance at the menu—what they'll start with. If you decide not to try the antipasto sampling ($9.00), other good choices include sliced Tuscan bread toasted with various toppings ($7.50), arugula and taleggio cheese with truffle oil ($8.50), and Tuscan-style tomato and bread soup with fresh basil and a touch of extra virgin olive oil ($7.00).

Good pasta choices include a light potato gnocchi with gorgonzola and fresh rosemary ($16.00), fettuccine in a light cream sauce with shrimp, zucchini, and saffron ($19.00), and linguine with a purée of sun-dried tomatoes, garlic, black olives, and crushed red pepper ($15.50). Notable mains include rack of veal chop in a white wine truffle sauce served on a bed of asparagus with freshly shaved black truffles ($35.00), tender pieces of lamb braised with fresh rosemary, diced potatoes, extra virgin olive oil, and a touch of garlic ($22.00), marinated Cornish hen, flattened and char-grilled ($18.00), and chunks of chicken sautéed with fresh rosemary, garlic, sausages, and red and yellow sweet peppers in a balsamic vinegar sauce ($18.00). Daily dessert selections ($6.00 to $8.00) might include apple tart, tiramisú, panna cotta, and chocolate cake.

F.STOP ★   Eclectic
28 West 20th Street (between Fifth and Sixth Aves.)
212/627-7867
Lunch - Monday through Saturday 11:00 a.m. - 4:00 p.m.
Dinner - Monday through Saturday 4:00 - 11:30 p.m.
All major cards

This affectionate homage to photography is pretty as a picture. Situated in the heart of the photography district in what was formerly an umbrella factory, the soaring space has a casual elegance. Banquettes in lively African-inspired prints, striped cushioned chairs, burnished wood floors, and a fireplace off in a corner make it a visual treat. Striking photos by world-famous photographers line its walls and are available for sale with proceeds going to charity.

This is the sort of place you want to be great because at first sight you're already a little bit in love with it. And when the food is served and you see that it is as pretty as everything else about the place, your expectations soar. But the eclectic fare covers a lot of culinary territory and while much of it is quite good, there are disappointments along the way.

To start, try the black bean soup with jalapeño Jack cheese and crisp tortilla chips ($6.00), soft taco of smoked salmon served with jicama salad and tomato salsa ($8.50), or risotto with grilled asparagus, aged parmesan, and prosciutto ($8.50). Good choices among mains include grilled swordfish with crispy shoestring yams ($19.00), penne tossed with grilled chicken in a Vodka sauce ($15.00), grilled rack of lamb with barbecued fire-roasted onions ($21.00), and Cabernet-braised short ribs of beef on a sweet potato risotto ($17.00). Desserts ($6.00) are baked on the premises and end the meal on a sweet note with choices like individually baked apple pie a la mode, banana crêpes in a caramel sauce with cinnamon ice cream, and individual warm lemon pie.

FLOWERS RESTAURANT ★★   American
21 West 17th Street
(between Fifth and Sixth Aves.)
212/691-8888
Lunch - Daily Noon - 3:00 p.m.
Dinner - Daily 6:00 p.m. - Midnight
All major cards

You'll find a romantic atmosphere in this picture-pretty restaurant, known for its celebrity clientele as much as its inventive new American cuisine. Each of its three distinctive dining areas has a personality all its own. First, there's the street level restaurant with golden ochre-washed walls, rough-hewn ceiling beams, and lovely tapestry banquettes. A semi-circular bar handcrafted in wood, stained glass, and zinc divides the space. The back dining area has a stained wood beamed ceiling and wide plank floors, soft lighting from lanterns, and abundant baskets of dried flowers and herbs. While the front dining area has a casually sophisticated light look, this one has a decided country warmth. And the rooftop garden has a charm all its own, with planters of ivy and geraniums, a bubbling fountain, and jewel-colored mosaic glass sculptures that add to the glitter of the Manhattan skyscape.

Style isn't everything here, no matter how pretty the setting and the crowd. Chef and co-owner Marc Salonsky has won raves for his creative style of cooking and intense sense of flavor. Striving for a balance of flavor and lightness, he prefers cooking with natural juices and vinaigrettes, instead of butter and cream. A nice selection of starters provides a good introduction to his talents. Choices include grilled five-spice quail with papaya salad, bean sprouts, and Thai vinaigrette ($10.00), tuna tartare timbale with vine-ripened tomatoes, avocado salsa and chips ($10.00), wild mushroom salad with arugula, aged pecorino, and truffle vinaigrette ($9.00), and crispy calamari with charred tomato-jalapeño dipping sauce ($9.00). Good pasta selections include rigatoni with grilled vegetables, roast garlic, and parmesan ($17.00), risotto with chorizo, shrimp, jalapeño, and fresh thyme ($18.00), and capellini with roast tomato, garlic, basil, and olive oil ($17.00). For the main, there's pan-seared striped bass with Manila clams, Napa cabbage, and sweet curry ($23.00), crispy roast chicken with Yukon gold mashed potatoes, crispy onions, and lemongrass broth ($18.00), roast baby lamb chops with grilled onions, orzo salad, and Moroccan

324

spices ($23.00), grilled sirloin steak with sweet potato fries, sautéed greens, and balsamic glaze ($25.00), and roast game hen with creamy polenta, grilled scallions, and cranberry sauce ($24.00). Hopefully, you'll save room for dessert. Planning ahead, think about the warm individual flourless chocolate cake ($6.00), raspberry brown butter tart with a walnut crust and vanilla bean ice cream ($5.50), warm apple-cranberry crumble with coconut gelato ($5.50), pecan chocolate torte with deep dark chocolate ice cream ($6.00), and black and white bread pudding with blood orange soup ($6.00).

FOLLONICO ★★   Italian
6 West 24th Street (between Fifth and Sixth Aves.)
212/691-6359
Lunch - Monday through Friday Noon - 3:00 p.m.
Dinner - Monday through Thursday 6:00 - 10:30 p.m.;
Friday and Saturday 6:00 - 11:00 p.m.
Sunday 5:30 - 9:30 p.m.
All major cards

A real find, Follonico is truly transporting. It has such a warmth and simplicity about it that you may find yourself lapsing into memories of Tuscan nights and trattorias with names you recorded to pass on to friends. Golden stucco walls, turn-of-the-century terra-cotta tiles, tapestry banquettes, and a wood-burning oven covered with sand-toned tiles all combine to create a dining room so comfortable and inviting you'll want to linger over each course. A very sweet staff rounds out its appeal.

Chef-owner Alan Tardi's cooking emphasizes fresh, seasonal ingredients, and pure, straightforward flavors. House specialties include game in season, superb fresh pastas, irresistible focaccia, and a variety of items roasted in the wood-burning oven. A typical meal here might start with house-smoked trout with endive and arugula salad and salsa verde ($9.00), warm goat cheese with roasted beets and string beans ($7.00), wood-roasted calamari with garlic, lemon, and crushed red pepper ($7.50), or bread soup ($6.50). The wonderful pastas are available as starters or mains. Choices include spaghetti alla puttanesca ($10.50/$16.75), cannelloni of wild mushrooms with white truffle oil ($12.00/$19.00), orecchiette with sweet sausage and bitter broccoli ($11.00/$16.75), and chestnut fettuccine with venison stew ($11.50/$18.25). The flavors of a true trattoria, along with a sophisticated twist or two, are evident in the mains as well. Winter signals offerings such as poached turbot with braised fennel, oysters, leeks, and cream ($23.50), roast lobster with julienned root vegetables and twice-baked potato ($24.00), wood-roasted loin veal chop with roasted potatoes, wild mushrooms, and white truffle oil ($25.00), braised lamb shank with white beans, rosemary, garlic, and tomato ($24.00), and roast whole baby chicken with wood-cooked winter vegetables ($18.50). The menu also offers a few knockout dishes for two: whole fish roasted in a rock salt crust with herb pesto, tomato coulis, roasted potatoes, and sautéed spinach ($44.00) and grilled rib steak "alla Fiorentina" with spinach and mashed potatoes ($48.00). The changing parade of desserts might include apple tart cooked in the wood-burning oven and sparkling granitas.

GRAMERCY TAVERN ★★★   New American
42 East 20th Street
(between Broadway and Park Ave. So.)
212/477-0777
Lunch - Monday through Friday Noon - 2:00 p.m.
Dinner - Monday through Thursday 5:30 - 10:00 p.m.;
Friday and Saturday 5:30 - 11:00 p.m.; Sunday 5:00 - 10:00 p.m.
All major cards

Gramercy Tavern exudes a friendliness not usually identified with luxury restaurants. This is just what principal owners Danny Meyer and Tom Colicchio had in mind with their aim to "reinvent the four-star restaurant" and recreate the classic American tavern. In a space that was once an army-medal factory, Gramercy Tavern emerged from its multi-million dollar renovation with the look of a combination tavern and graceful country inn. White plaster walls contrast dramatically with dark heavy beams. Copper trim, tapestry upholstery, a wood-burning oven, and country antiques add to its handsomely rustic appeal. The ambience is one of casual elegance.

The contemporary American menu created by Tom Colicchio, the much acclaimed chef, has French and Italian influences. **The dinner menu is a three-course prix fixe at $56.00.** Starter choices might be tuna tartare; lobster and artichoke salad (+$5.00); mussel, fennel, and celery root soup; or a ragout of sea urchin and crab with shallot butter, purée potato, and curry essence. For the main: roasted monkfish with pancetta, sage, roasted tomatoes, and braised mustard greens; seared pepper-crusted tuna with wilted arugula, white beans, and lemon confit (a house specialty); saddle of rabbit with olives, roasted garlic, shallots, and rosemary; or roasted farm chicken with risotto. Desserts here are always special—temptations include warm chocolate tart with expresso pot au crème and mocha sorbet; buttermilk panna cotta with a fig Napoleon and concord grape sorbet; and lemon soufflé. The pastry chef does not serve out-of-season ingredients, so you'll have to be lucky and dining at the right time of year to opt for her lovely peach tarte Tatin. **Another option is a six-course tasting menu for $72.00.**

In addition to the main dining room, the Tavern offers its own menu daily from noon to 11:00 p.m. that features an excellent selection of dishes at very reasonable prices. Here you might start with tomato-garlic bread soup ($6.50), roasted beet, red onion, and parsley salad ($6.50), or marinated goat cheese with roasted red peppers, black olives, and baby greens ($8.00). For the main, choose from a selection that includes filet mignon with mashed potatoes and a balsamic-onion relish ($17.00), braised beef short ribs with creamy polenta and hot peppers ($16.00), and baby chicken with broccoli rabe and pancetta ($13.00). Desserts ($5.00) are terrific, with choices that include blueberry shortcake, pumpkin flan with gingersnaps, and chocolate devil's food cake with vanilla ice cream.

I TRULLI ★★   Italian
122 East 27th Street
(between Lexington and Park Ave. So.)
212/481-7372
Lunch - Monday through Friday Noon - 3:00 p.m.
Dinner - Monday through Thursday 5:30 - 11:00 p.m.;
Friday and Saturday 5:30 p.m. - Midnight
All major cards

At i Trulli, owner Nicola Marzovilla aims to recreate the rustic specialties of his childhood in Apulia, one of the lower regions of Italy. In fact, if you've ever travelled through the Southern Italian countryside, the food here is the sort of hearty, peasant fare that brings to mind memories of simple Italian inns with names you've long forgotten but meals you still recall. When you dine here, you'll find Mr. Marzovilla moving about from table to table—every inch the genial and welcoming host you're sure you've met before. There's a friendly feel to the place that you notice as soon as you walk in. Both the greeting and service have the kind of warmth that makes you think it might be the real thing. By the time you leave, you're sure of it.

The understated pale yellow stuccoed dining rooms at i Trulli have a spare elegance with wooden chairs and tables set with snowy white cloths. A glass-enclosed fireplace divides the space and blue hydrangeas displayed on a sideboard add a dash of color. A beehive-shaped brick oven flanks the attractive wine bar at the entrance and adds both warmth and enticing aromas to the room. And in warm weather a gracious Mediterranean shaded and semi-covered courtyard with whitewashed walls, terra-cotta toned frescoes, and a wall of shrubbery provides a delightful alfresco alternative.

The earthy—and often unfamiliar—dishes of Apulia dominate the menu. An early treat is a small plate of blended ricotta and ewe cheeses that accompanies the enticing bread basket. Good choices among starters include a traditional Sicilian eggplant relish with artichokes ($8.00), baked mushrooms, potatoes, and herbs ($9.00), grilled homemade game sausages with beans ($9.00), asparagus wrapped in prosciutto with parmesan ($9.00), and grilled imported prawns ($10.00). The hearty pasta choices include appealing dishes like asparagus lasagna ($15.00), linguine in a lobster sauce tossed with clams ($16.00), ricotta dumplings with fresh tomatoes and arugula ($15.00), penne with asparagus, fresh tomatoes, and pecorino ($14.00), and baked macaroni stuffed with veal and baked in a casserole ($14.00). For the main, choose from assorted seafood Apulian-style ($22.00), one-half free-range chicken with sausages and potatoes ($19.00), venison chops with artichokes ($23.00), and veal chop with a Sicilian wine sauce ($24.00). Desserts ($6.00-$9.00) might include cannolis, pine nut tart, flourless chocolate cake, and pears baked in red wine—pleasant enough but nothing special.

LA COLOMBE D'OR ★★   French
134 East 26th Street
(between Lexington and Third Aves.)
212/689-0666
Dinner - Monday through Thursday 6:00 - 10:30 p.m.;
Friday and Saturday 6:00 - 11:00 p.m.;
All major cards

Situated in a charming townhouse, La Colombe d'Or's country French decor is a delightful blending of lace curtains, rough walls, terra-cotta floors, an original tin ceiling, and lovely fresh flowers. It has an air of intimacy and romance about it, and is the kind of place that will make you want to return—again and again.

It features the lusty, flavorful cuisine of Provence with influence drawn from other Mediterranean cuisines as well. Starters are hearty and satisfying. House specialties include an excellent fish soup with aïoli slathered croutons floating on top ($5.50) and socca roulade (the traditional chickpea flour pancake served with fresh goat cheese and provençale vegetable stew) ($7.50). Another fine beginning is a dish of whole baby artichokes braised with garlic, lemon, thyme, and coriander seed and served with aïoli and roasted tomatoes

($8.00). A favorite among mains is the cassoulet ($18.00), made from plump, moist white beans cooked slowly in duck stock with tomato, onion, and bacon. The beans are then layered in an individual crock with confits of duck, pork, lamb sausage and braised duck. A top crust of duck cracklings and sourdough bread crumbs is its crowning glory. Pasta also has its place here—offerings include angel hair with shrimp and salmon (half $8.00/full $16.00), ravioli filled with ricotta cheese and Swiss chard (half $7.00/full $14.00), and cannelloni de daube (fresh pasta filled with stewing beef first marinated in, then simmered in, white wine, Cognac, olive oil, onions, carrots, parsley, thyme, bay leaf, bacon, tomato, black olives, garlic, orange peel, and veal stock) (half $7.50/full $15.00). Other good choices include a large skinless breast of chicken filled with black olive butter and served with garlic mashed potatoes and sautéed spinach ($16.50) and steak frites maison (hanger steak with a shallot and balsamic vinegar sauce, served with ribbons of deep-fried potatoes, parsnips, and sweet potatoes) ($18.00).

LA PETITE AUBERGE ★★   French
116 Lexington Avenue
(between 27th and 28th Sts.)
212/689-5003
Lunch - Monday through Friday Noon - 3:00 p.m.
Dinner - Monday through Saturday 5:00 - 11:00 p.m.;
Sunday 4:30 - 10:00 p.m.
All major cards

La Petite Auberge has all the warmth and romance of a rural French country inn. Charmingly decorated with dark woods, Quimper plates, posters of Brittany, checkered tablecloths, and exposed wooden beams, it is atmospheric and homey all at once.

Pierre Landet, formerly sous chef at Taillevent in Paris, is spinning his magic here these days. Don't miss his delicious Coquille Saint Jacques ($5.75) or the coarsely textured pâté du chef ($5.00) to start. Other good choices include onion soup ($4.75) clams casino ($7.75), and smoked salmon ($7.75). Top choices among mains include roast duckling in orange sauce ($16.75), filet mignon béarnaise ($19.95), roasted rack of lamb for two ($48.00), broiled salmon ($16.75), and frog legs with garlic ($16.75). The signature dessert, chocolate soufflé for two ($13.00), is outstanding.

A four-course prix fixe is available at $21.95 with five or six choices in each category.

MARCHI'S ★★   Italian
251 East 31st Street (between Second and Third Aves.)
212/679-2494
Dinner - Monday through Saturday 5:00 - 10:00 p.m.
All major cards

This family-run restaurant has been around since 1930 when the Marchi family turned a nice ivy-covered brownstone townhouse into the kind of dining establishment New Yorkers immediately embraced as their own. And not much has changed over the years. Marchi's set menu never went fancy. It continues to reflect an affection for and sensitivity to the simplicity that produces the kind of homestyle cooking Italian mothers serve their families. My Italian grandmother never made anything fancy. Yet, some of the best meals I've ever had came out of her kitchen. She would have liked Marchi's. Dining here is like going to Sunday dinner at a favorite Italian relative's house. There's no menu—the food just keeps coming.

The set price is $33.75. First, there's an antipasto platter. This is the time to start pacing yourself. Next comes homemade lasagna, followed by crispy deep-fried fish served with string beans and cold beets. Hold on—there's more. The main course is roast chicken and roast veal with fresh mushrooms and a tossed salad. Then comes fresh fruit and cheese, then a lemon fritter. After coffee and crostoli (crisp-fried twists with powdered sugar), the meal is over, and you can stagger off into the night to loosen your belt.

MESA GRILL ★★★   Southwest
102 Fifth Avenue
(between 15th and 16th Sts.)
212/807-7400
Lunch - Monday through Friday Noon - 2:30 p.m.
Brunch - Saturday and Sunday 11:30 a.m. - 3:30 p.m.
Dinner - Sunday through Thursday 5:30 - 10:30 p.m.;
Friday and Saturday 5:30 - 11:00 p.m.
All major cards

Large, noisy, and great fun, Mesa Grill is immensely popular with a chic young crowd appreciative of rising-star chef Bobby Flay's sensational Southwest-inspired American cuisine. His hot and sassy creations are served in a curiously zany setting—one of columns, bold colors, big black and white photos, and huge industrial strength fans. The banquette lining the front room is upholstered in red vinyl with a wild west cowboy pattern reminiscent of my second grade lunch box.

Flay's talents are evident right up front, with terrific starters like corn-zucchini quesadillas with smoked tomato salsa and avocado relish ($10.50), cornmeal-coated oysters with green chile coconut sauce and salmon caviar ($12.00), shrimp and roasted garlic corn tamale ($10.50), cornmeal-coated chile relleno filled with goat cheese and served with a spicy black bean sauce ($11.00), and blue corn pancakes filled with barbecued duck ($10.50). Mains are equally tantalizing and so delicious. Try to choose from choices that include smoked pork tenderloin with dried apricot-Serrano chile sauce and a corn-goat cheese taco ($22.50), barbecued salmon filet with salsa and black pepper spoonbread ($23.00), Black Angus steak with house-made Mesa steak sauce with a potato-corn taco and smoked red pepper grilled onion relish ($24.50), red pepper-crusted tuna steak with shellfish mole sauce and cilantro rice ($24.50), grilled porterhouse lamb chops with jalapeño preserves, asparagus, and sweet potato gratin—a house specialty ($23.00), and blue corn skillet-fried chicken served with red chili Southwestern fries ($19.50). The changing selection of desserts might include a gingerbread ice cream sandwich, deep-fried dough with vanilla ice cream and chocolate sauce, bittersweet chocolate cake, and pumpkin cheesecake with cranberries. Let the good times roll!

NOVITÁ ★★★   Italian
102 East 22nd Street (between Lexington and Park Ave. So.)
212/677-2222
Lunch - Monday through Friday Noon - 3:00 p.m.
Dinner - Monday through Thursday 6:00 - 11:00 p.m.;
Friday and Saturday 6:00 p.m. - Midnight
All major cards

Novitá has a spare elegance and warmth that is very inviting. Golden yellow Sienna walls, richly polished floors, beautiful Murano glass sconces, Etro paisley upholstery, and colorful Italian vases combine to create an ambience that is so appealing in its artful simplicity you immediately settle in with a feeling of pleasure and anticipation. Owned by Marco Fregonese (the talented chef), his wife, Elizabeth, and her sister, Gina Yoshida, it is a family affair that glows with hospitality.

Mr. Fregonese's modern regional Italian cooking is inventive and delicious. The wonderful house-made breadsticks that greet you set a standard

331

for what is to follow. The pastas are all wonderful, with ravioli as good as it gets. There's much diversity among starters with choices that include grilled salmon salad with steamed string beans, potatoes, and a balsamic vinaigrette ($10.00), frisée salad with pear, gorgonzola, and walnut dressing ($8.00), tart of eggplant, tomato, and mozzarella with a pesto sauce ($8.00), and chilled asparagus with shavings of parmesan and a hazelnut vinaigrette ($9.00). Pasta choices might be spaghettini with a spicy red pepper and tomato sauce ($11.00), orecchiette with spicy sausage and broccoli rabe ($13.00), linguine with mixed seafood in a light tomato sauce ($14.00), and the not-to-be-missed ravioli of the day (market price). The risotto of the day is invariably superb as well. There are also many good choices among mains—grilled salmon with crisp potato carpaccio, sweet onions, and black olives ($18.00), seared tuna with tomato, capers, and black olive concasse ($19.00), roasted red snapper with a spicy red pepper crust and shrimp ($20.00), roasted duck with Barolo sauce, pomegranate, and pine nuts ($18.00), herb-roasted baby chicken served with truffle potato purée ($17.00), sliced sirloin on a warm mixed bean salad with aged balsamic vinegar ($19.00), and pan-sautéed veal medallions with porcini ragu ($20.00). Desserts ($6.00) include a nice tiramisú, individual warm chocolate tart with pistachio sauce and white chocolate ice cream, and a refreshing baked peach with amaretto cookies, homemade vanilla gelato, and raspberry coulis.

A three-course prix fixe lunch is pleasantly priced at $19.97.

OLD TOWN BAR & RESTAURANT ★   Tavern
45 East 18th Street
(between Broadway and Park Ave. So.)
212/529-6732
Lunch - Daily 11:30 a.m. - 3:00 p.m.
Dinner - Daily 5:00 - 11:00 p.m.
All major cards

For a quintessential New York pub experience, try this 19th Century American tavern. It's not a trendy singles spot and it's not a juke joint—it's a neighborhood bar. You'll see both blue suits and blue jeans bending elbows at its massive, long mahogany bar. The space across from the bar is outfitted with cozy wooden booths separated by tall wood and glass dividers topped by inverted tulip-type lamps. It's comfortable at the Old Town Bar; it feels like it could be your neighborhood hangout. It is also highly photogenic—in an old-fashioned saloon kind of way—appearing in ad campaigns for both Miller Lite and Chivas Regal.

The menu contains the usual pub grub and it's pretty good. There's Old Town chili with cheddar, diced onions, and sour cream ($2.25 cup, $4.75 bowl), crispy spuds that are baked, sliced, and then deep-fried and served with a horseradish-cheddar dip ($3.75 small, $6.75 large), fried calamari with cocktail sauce ($4.25 small, $7.25 large), club salad ($7.75), steak salad (marinated flank steak, grilled medium-rare and thinly-sliced, served on mixed greens with grated Swiss cheese, red onions, and tomatoes, with pita bread) ($8.25), good burgers with a variety of toppings ($6.00 and up), hot ham and Swiss on rye with grainy mustard ($6.50), and sliced steak on toast with sautéed mushrooms and a red wine sauce ($8.50). Or how about a chili dog?—all the way with chopped onions and grated cheddar ($6.25).

PATRIA ★★★   Latin
250 Park Avenue So. (20th St.)
212/777-6211
Lunch - Monday through Friday Noon - 3:00 p.m.
Dinner - Daily 5:30 - 11:30 p.m.
All major cards

When Patria breezed into town a few years ago with its lively Latin fare, it created quite a stir of excitement among local foodies. And it is still one hot ticket. Set over three levels, Latin-spirited mosaics splash across the floors and walls. Decorated in striking earth colors with handsome displays of dried flowers and a lively bar at the front, the ambience is at once exuberant and animated.

Chef Douglas Rodriguez's spirited nuevo Latino cuisine is full of innovation and takes all sorts of interesting ethnic twists and turns. His bold style does result in some disappointing dishes from time to time. But for the most part, dining here is an exciting culinary trip that doesn't require a passport. And the menu is the kind that leaves you with a desire to keep coming back to work your way through it. To start, any of the empanadas would be a good choice: Cabrales with Spanish blue cheese with mixed greens and a walnut pear vinaigrette ($10.00), shredded beef, wild mushroom ceviche, and shaved manchego cheese ($13.00), white arepa dough with black beans, roasted corn, and tomato salsa ($9.00), or roasted eggplant and goat cheese with asparagus and a smoked morel sauce ($11.00). One of my favorite starters is the cured beef roll, plantain filled with tasajo, and white bean salad ($10.00). Another winner is ceviche of tuna with chilies, ginger, and coconut milk ($13.00). When it comes to the main, top choices include sugarcane-pierced tuna, coconut-glazed with malanga purée, chayote, and dried shrimp salsa

($24.00), Nicaraguan-style beef tenderloin ($25.00), crispy red snapper with coconut conch rice and Dominican-style coleslaw ($27.00), and loin of rabbit wrapped in Spanish ham ($25.00). The ever-changing selection of tempting desserts (around $9.00) might include chocolate soufflé, a chocolate cream-filled cigar cookie with white mocha ice cream, sweet banana cake, and cashew-crusted flans.

PAUL & JIMMY'S RESTAURANT ★★   Italian
123 East 18th Street
(Irving Place and Park Ave. So.)
212/475-9540
Lunch - Daily Noon - 4:00 p.m.
Dinner - Daily 4:00 - 11:00 p.m.
All major cards

This is a comfortable kind of place. Soft lighting, a warm atmosphere, reliably good food, and a cordial staff have kept it a long-time Gramercy neighborhood favorite.

You might start with stuffed mushroom caps ($5.75), assorted seafood marinated in olive oil, garlic, and lemon ($7.75), steamed shrimp served with cocktail sauce and greens ($7.50), an assortment of cold appetizers ($6.00), or an assortment of hot appetizers ($7.00). The kitchen's wise ways with pasta make it a sure bet here. Choose from fettuccine with onions, prosciutto, and plum tomatoes ($8.75), gnocchi with ricotta cheese and tomato sauce ($9.50), rigatoni with a rich meat sauce ($9.50), fettuccine carbonara ($9.50), penne with artichokes, shrimp, and sun-dried tomatoes ($10.75), and homemade cheese-filled ravioli or manicotti ($9.50). All pasta dishes are served with a salad. Other entrées are served with a choice of house salad or pasta. Options include veal scaloppine ($11.75), chicken cacciatore ($10.75), rolled veal with provolone and prosciutto, sautéed with garlic, lemon, and white wine ($11.75), chicken and sausage sautéed with peppers and mushrooms ($10.75), and sliced beef with mushrooms and marinara sauce ($15.50). Good seafood choices include shrimp broiled with garlic, wine, lemon, and butter (served with rice) ($12.50) and filet of sole poached with garlic, onion, white wine, and a dash of tomato ($12.00). For dessert, there's cannoli ($3.00), zabaglione ($4.50), and assorted pies and cakes ($3.50 each).

A three-course pre-theater menu is offered from 5:00 to 6:30 p.m. for $21.50. There's also a prix fixe lunch menu with three courses for $16.50.

PERIYALI ★★★   Greek
35 West 20th Street
(between Fifth and Sixth Aves.)
212/463-7890
Lunch - Monday through Friday Noon - 3:00 p.m.
Dinner - Monday through Saturday 5:30 - 11:30 p.m.
All major cards

Periyali offers authentic Greek cuisine in a sophisticated taverna setting. Its enchanting ambience easily induces a holiday frame of mind. Whitewashed walls, colorful banquettes, tiled floors, dark beams, and a tent-like ceiling of billowing white cloth combine to create a cool Aegean oasis that will remind you of seaside places you've been where the sun almost always shines.

The kitchen turns out delicious authentic Greek specialties and in keeping with its "seashore" moniker serves some of the best grilled fish dishes in the city. Starters include things that are fun to share, such as the assorted Greek appetizers you will see on display ($9.50) and the sensational spinach and cheese pies ($8.50). Other top choices include crisp calamari with tossed salad greens and a caviar mousse dip ($9.00) and octopus in a red wine marinade grilled over charcoal ($10.50). The avgolemono soup (a rich chicken soup finished with egg and lemon) ($7.00) is outstanding. Mains are equally enticing with delicious choices that include grilled shrimp with olive oil, herbs, and lemon ($21.00), filet of snapper baked with tomato, onion, and garlic ($22.00), filet of salmon baked in phyllo with spinach and feta cheese ($22.50), charcoal-grilled filet mignon with brown butter garlic sauce ($23.00), lamb chops grilled over charcoal with fresh rosemary ($25.00), and grilled escallops of veal with oregano and olive oil ($19.50). And, of course, there's a good moussaka ($17.00). The changing selection of desserts includes a wonderful baklava as well as a heavenly lemony rice pudding.

PITCHOUNE ★★   French
226 Third Avenue (at 19th St.)
212/614-8641
Brunch - Saturday and Sunday 11:30 a.m. - 3:00 p.m.
Dinner - Daily 6:00 - 11:30 p.m.
Visa, Master

This tiny restaurant, whose name translates to "any little cute thing," was quickly adopted by its neighborhood. Though low on frills, it is pleasant and cozy. Sunny yellow walls, plaid banquettes, a toy fire truck, and dried flowers give the casual room a cheerful feel and aromas drifting from the kitchen hint of Provence.

The food is wonderful. While the surroundings may be casual, the kitchen turns out affordable French food that is both creative and beautifully presented. You might start with a cool asparagus and chive soup ($5.00), spicy salmon tartare ($6.00), garlic-roasted squid salad with celery and roasted peppers ($6.00), or roasted sweetbreads with toasted almonds and arugula (a house specialty) ($7.00). Among mains, the house specialty is a delicious seared crisp codfish with black olive-mashed potatoes and a Madeira-onion marmalade ($15.00). Other terrific choices include grilled free-range chicken with barley fricassée and snow pea pods ($14.00), filet mignon with braised spinach ($16.00), and roast leg of lamb with Italian lentils and succotash ($15.00). Desserts ($6.00) are delicious, too, with choices like molten chocolate cake with hazelnut ice cream, warm, flaky apple tart with caramel sauce and vanilla ice cream, and vanilla fruit custard with madeleines and a sugar crust.

Brunch ($10.50) includes a main dish, a Mimosa, and coffee. Selections include omelette provençale, blinis with caramelized apples and almonds, poached eggs with cured salmon and toast, and hamburger with potato gratin and grilled corn-on-the-cob.

TURKISH KITCHEN ★   Turkish
386 Third Avenue
(between 27th and 28th Sts.)
212/679-1810
Lunch - Daily Noon - 3:00 p.m.
Dinner - Daily 5:30 - 11:00 p.m.
All major cards

Deep red-painted walls with colorful hanging kilim rugs and copperware provide a pleasantly exotic backdrop to the many Turkish delights offered here. The popularity of this highly personal duplex restaurant is largely due to a kitchen that produces many good Turkish specialties, along with a very relaxed atmosphere.

A good way to enjoy this flavorful cuisine is to make a meal of appetizers. It's certainly tempting with choices like phyllo scrolls stuffed with feta and pan-fried until golden brown ($5.50), chargrilled eggplant salad ($6.50), homemade stuffed vine leaves ($6.50), crunchy fried calamari with garlic sauce ($7.50), bulgur wheat patties stuffed with ground lamb, pine nuts,

336

currants, and walnuts ($7.50), and Circassian chicken in a paprika-laced walnut sauce ($6.50). But there are many good mains to choose from as well, with selections that include delicious baby lamb chargrilled on skewers and served with rice ($15.00), baked lamb shank wrapped with eggplant slices and served with rice ($15.50), steamed beef dumplings served with a garlic yogurt sauce ($11.50), cabbage stuffed with ground beef, rice, and fresh herbs ($13.50), cubes of chicken breast and fresh mushrooms chargrilled on skewers and served with rice ($14.50), boneless Cornish hen stuffed with a traditional Turkish rice and served with zucchini pancakes and slices of baked potato ($14.50), a casserole of baked shrimp with mushrooms and tomatoes, topped with kasar cheese and served with rice ($15.50), fresh grilled brook trout with a lemon and parsley sauce ($13.50), and fresh swordfish chargrilled on skewers ($16.50).

A four-course set lunch is offered for $13.95. It includes a choice from among four appetizers and four mains, along with a fresh cucumber, tomato, and onion salad, and the dessert special of the day.

UNION SQUARE CAFE ★★★   American
21 East 16th Street (between Fifth Ave. and Union Sq. W.)
212/243-4020
Lunch - Monday through Saturday Noon - 2:30 p.m.
Dinner - Monday through Thursday 6:00 - 10:15 p.m.;
Friday and Saturday 6:00 - 11:15 p.m.; Sunday 5:30 - 9:45 p.m.
All major cards

Since opening in 1985, Union Square Cafe has become one of New York's most critically acclaimed restaurants. Consistently voted one of the top ten favorites by New Yorkers in the *Zagat Survey*, it earned the number one spot in 1997. This art-filled, stylishly appointed American bistro has a very special appeal. It combines the innovation of a gifted chef, excellent value, and a jaunty setting totalling lacking in pretension. Dining here is such a satisfying experience, its popularity comes as no surprise. The multi-leveled dining room spaces are all pleasant and airy, each with a style of its own. The convivial dining area past the long mahogany bar at the entrance has a soaring ceiling and playful wall murals. Overhead is a small balcony dining area. The main dining room—a step-down to sidewalk level—has an easy, casual elegance with hunter-green wainscotting, polished cherrywood floors, off-white walls, Milan-style furnishings, dark pillars, and colorful artwork.

Much of Chef Michael Romano's robustly flavored Italian-inspired American fare changes with the seasons, but many now-classic favorites remain available all year long. For starters, the black bean soup with lemon and a shot of Australian sherry ($6.50) is a long-standing favorite, along with the addictive hot garlic potato chips ($4.50).   The fried calamari with spicy anchovy mayonnaise ($9.50) is another standout. Pasta choices might be a lively porcini gnocchi in a parmesan cream sauce ($11.00) or red pepper fettuccine with artichokes and romano cheese ($8.75). And there's an international spin to many of the main course specialties. Choices include marinated filet mignon of tuna with eggplant, sticky rice, and beans ($27.00), cornmeal and sage fried rabbit with creamy polenta and vegetable hash ($19.75), grilled smoked Black Angus shell steak with creamy mashed potatoes and frizzled leeks ($25.50), roasted free-range chicken with a pepper-mustard sauce, root vegetables, and mashed potatoes ($21.50), spicy sizzled shrimp with coconut chutney and Indian-style sautéed vegetables ($23.50), and crispy orange-pepper duck with almond-rice pilaf, and spiced spinach purée ($23.00). Desserts are wonderful. Selections (each $7.50) include pineapple crème brûlée with coconut macaroons, apple streusel pie with lemon ice cream, and maple bread pudding with buttermilk ice cream. The signature dessert is a warm banana tart with honey-vanilla ice cream and macadamia nut brittle.

VERBENA ★★★   American
54 Irving Place (between 17th and 18th Sts.)
212/260-5454
Lunch - May through September Noon - 2:45 p.m.
Brunch - Sunday Noon - 3:00 p.m.
Dinner - Sunday through Thursday 5:30 - 10:30 p.m.;
Friday and Saturday 5:30 - 11:00 p.m.
All major cards

This starkly elegant restaurant, with delicate lighting and a very soothing atmosphere, occupies the ground floor of a charming 19th Century townhouse near Gramercy Park. In keeping with its herbal moniker, a glass wall in the entryway displays embedded botanical samples of irises, daffodils, eggplant, and calla lilies. And beyond, its dining room has a quiet, graceful look with light wood, a soft muted color scheme, and candlelight. Here, it is the bold, imaginative cooking of chef/owner Diane Forley that supplies the glitz. And when she comes out of the kitchen to say hello, you notice that she has the same soft prettiness as her restaurant. Perhaps her brother's hand in its design accounts for the nice match.

In good weather, the courtyard garden in back is a surprising urban delight—a true garden where you'll dine amidst rows of lettuce, tomatoes on vines, and beans strung up on poles. Pressed flower screens divide the space and four huge canvas market umbrellas ripple overhead and shade the tables.

Ms. Forley's Mediterranean-influenced American cuisine is wonderful. The standout among starters is the butternut squash ravioli flavored with roasted oranges and sage ($9.00). Other excellent openers include a fricassée of wild mushrooms with angel hair pasta, spinach, and truffled broth ($11.00), bow tie pasta with a ragout of baby artichokes, escarole, and veal meatballs ($12.00), and a chopped endive salad with pickled beets, watercress, and melted taleggio cheese ($8.00). Mains display the same innovation with choices such as seared sea scallops with cauliflower soufflé and saffron-scented oyster stew ($24.00), beer-braised ribs of beef with horseradish dumplings and root vegetables ($23.00), grilled sirloin steak with sherry wine onions and herbed potato croquettes ($25.00), and Scottish red venison with sweet potato compote, chestnuts, and huckleberries ($26.00). Desserts ($7.00) such as a rum-soaked savarin cake with chocolate chip ice cream or a dreamy crème brûlée provide a sweet finale.

A chef's tasting menu with five courses is available each evening for $55.00-$58.00.

VILLA BERULIA ★★   Italian
107 East 34th Street (between Lexington and Park Aves.)
212/689-1970
Lunch - Monday through Friday 11:30 a.m. - 4:30 p.m.
Dinner - Monday through Saturday 4:30 - 10:30 p.m.
All major cards

This pretty place seems romantically inclined. It offers room after room of intimate dining areas and has the kind of courteous and attentive service that is a throwback to old-world charm. White linen tablecloths, lush floral arrangements, good Northern Italian food, and a villa-like setting make this largely undiscovered treasure a terrific find.

Supplementing the menu are delicious daily specials, including homemade pastas, wild game dishes, and Dalmatian coast delicacies. Starters include house antipasto ($8.50), clams oregano ($8.00), roasted portobello mushrooms ($8.00), and minestrone ($4.50). Pasta selections include gnocchi Bolognese ($12.95), rigatoni amatriciana ($12.95), cannelloni ($13.95), linguine with red or white clam sauce ($14.95), and the lasagna of the day ($13.95). Of the mains, good choices include fried calamari ($15.50), veal scaloppine ($14.95), veal paillard ($17.50), broiled lamb chops ($18.95), and osso buco with gnocchi ($20.00). For dessert: Italian pastry, cheesecake, or tiramisú (each $5.00).

WATER CLUB ★★   American
500 East 30th Street (at East River)
212/683-3333
Lunch - Monday through Friday Noon - 2:30 p.m.
Brunch - Sunday 11:15 a.m. - 3:00 p.m.
Dinner - Sunday through Thursday 5:30 - 10:30 p.m.;
Friday and Saturday 5:30 - 11:00 p.m.
All major cards

The Water Club dazzles with one of the best views in town. Built on a secured platform 40 feet into the East River, this glass-enclosed barge has the feel of a Newport yacht club. And at night when the city skyscape glitters and the 59th Street Bridge glows in emerald suspension, it is truly transporting. Ship-racing flags strung across the skylit ceiling, wicker chairs, and green-and-white striped canopies add to its festive, holiday feel. If the setting and dramatic food presentation are more wonderful than the service, no one seems to mind too much for this magical instant-vacation is much too intoxicating.

Seafood takes center stage in fine starters such as applewood-smoked salmon with caviar and warm rye blini with honey mustard ($11.00), shellfish gumbo in a kettle with tiny clams, shrimp, blue crab, and andouille sausage ($9.00), and shrimp cocktail with a marinated cucumber salad ($12.00). There are many delicious main choices as well—sautéed red snapper with lobster dumplings ($26.00) and seared salmon basted with lemon and tarragon with garden peas, a potato pillow, and grain mustard sauce ($24.00). Other good choices include roasted rack of lamb with sweet garlic, baked macaroni and porcini mushroom gratin, and broccoli rabe ($28.00), wood-grilled filet mignon with scalloped potato strudel and horseradish cream ($28.00), and herb-grilled chicken with a sweet corn risotto cake, Jack cheese confit quesadilla, and a smoky pepper vinaigrette ($20.00). For dessert, warm apple tart provides a pleasing finale.

A set three-course dinner prix fixe menu is $28.00. At lunch, there's a $19.95 prix fixe that includes a choice of appetizer, a main course, the house specialty mashed potatoes, and dessert. On Sundays, a buffet brunch is served from 11:15 to 3:00 p.m. for $29.00.

UPPER EAST SIDE

Upper East Side

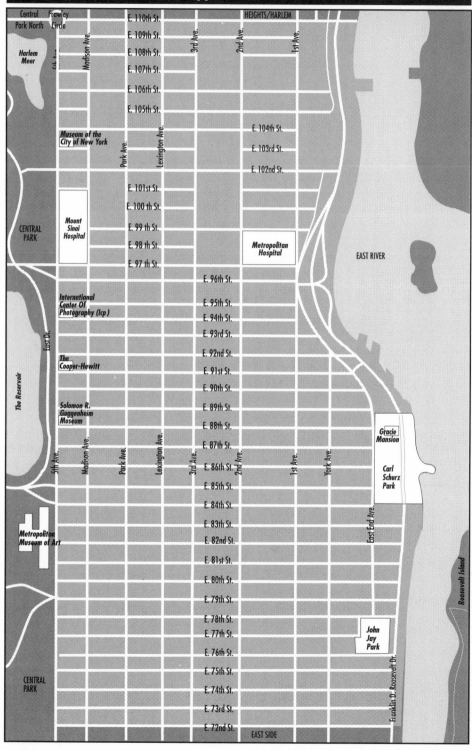

Central Park North · Frawley Circle

Harlem Meer

HEIGHTS/HARLEM

E. 110th St.
E. 109th St.
E. 108th St.
E. 107th St.
E. 106th St.
E. 105th St.
E. 104th St.
E. 103rd St.
E. 102nd St.
E. 101st St.
E. 100th St.
E. 99th St.
E. 98th St.
E. 97th St.
E. 96th St.
E. 95th St.
E. 94th St.
E. 93rd St.
E. 92nd St.
E. 91st St.
E. 90th St.
E. 89th St.
E. 88th St.
E. 87th St.
E. 86th St.
E. 85th St.
E. 84th St.
E. 83rd St.
E. 82nd St.
E. 81st St.
E. 80th St.
E. 79th St.
E. 78th St.
E. 77th St.
E. 76th St.
E. 75th St.
E. 74th St.
E. 73rd St.
E. 72nd St.

EAST SIDE

Madison Ave.
3rd Ave.
2nd Ave.
1st Ave.
Park Ave.
Lexington Ave.
5th Ave.
York Ave.
East End Ave.
Franklin D. Roosevelt Dr.

Museum of the City of New York

CENTRAL PARK

Mount Sinai Hospital

Metropolitan Hospital

EAST RIVER

First Dr.

International Center Of Photography (Icp)

The Cooper-Hewitt

The Reservoir

Solomon R. Guggenheim Museum

Gracie Mansion

Carl Schurz Park

Metropolitan Museum of Art

John Jay Park

CENTRAL PARK

Roosevelt Island

BARKING DOG LUNCHEONETTE ★   American
1678 Third Avenue (94th St.)
212/831-1800
Daily 8:00 a.m. - Midnight
No credit cards

The cutesy-poo Barking Dog dishes up a much more interesting culinary experience than its name suggests. A doggy drinking fountain out front and homey canine decor inside set the light-hearted tone of this very likeable eatery. Cheerfully decorated in buttery yellows and warm browns with stuffed dogs perched on shelves, it is the kind of casual retreat welcome in any neighborhood and one that was instantly adopted by this one.

The food combines hearty home cooking with dishes drawn from a variety of cuisines and with some surprisingly sophisticated twists. Good starters include grilled marinated chicken and shrimp saté served with Thai peanut sauce ($5.95), crispy cornmeal-crusted calamari ($5.75), pan-fried Maryland crab and corn cake with spicy mustard-scallion remoulade ($6.95), and grilled portobello mushrooms with sun-dried tomatoes, garlic confit, arugula and balsamic vinaigrette ($8.95). Comfort food classics head the list of mains: meatloaf with mushroom and tarragon gravy and terrific garlic mashed potatoes ($10.50); fresh roast breast of turkey with apple-pecan stuffing, mashed potatoes, cranberry chutney, and homemade gravy like Mom used to make ($11.95); and fried chicken with a buttermilk and herb crust, mashed potatoes, and a biscuit ($10.95). Other good choices include horseradish-crusted filet of Atlantic salmon with a red wine glaze and braised green lentils and shallots ($13.95), Louisiana jambalaya with shrimp, scallops, clams, calamari, Andouille sausage, and ham in a spicy tomato sauce with steamed rice ($14.50), and a satisfying cobb salad ($7.75). Daily blue plate specials are offered, as well as sandwiches, burgers, salads, and great breakfasts. Top dessert choices are the daily pies ($3.75), chocolate peanut butter gâteau ($4.50), dark rum, banana, and raisin bread pudding ($3.50), and a low-cal angel fruit sandwich with fat-free raspberry ice cream, angel food cake, and strawberry sauce ($4.95). For the kid in you, or with you—ice cream sodas ($2.95), milkshakes and malts ($2.95), egg creams ($1.95), Barking Dog sundaes ($2.95), and a Barking Dog banana split ($4.95).

From 5:00 to 7:00 p.m. Monday through Friday, the price of the main includes soup or salad and dessert.

CAFFE GRAZIE ★★   Italian
26 East 84th Street (between Madison and Fifth Aves.)
212/717-4407
Lunch - Daily 11:30 a.m. - 3:30 p.m.
Dinner - Daily 4:30 - 11:00 p.m.
American Express

This sunny, authentic Italian cafe is the kind of warm, informal place that fits so well into any neighborhood. You might pop in for a bite before or after visiting the nearby Metropolitan Museum of Art, before or after theatre, or maybe after a run in Central Park. Its well conceived menu and cozy ambience serves many moods, from a quick sandwich or cappuccino and dessert, to a satisfying three-course meal with wine.

The cooking style is contemporary, confident, and full of lively flavors. A bruschetta assortment topped with artichokes and marinated tomatoes with basil and served with a small salad ($8.00) is a terrific starter. Other winners include a goat cheese salad served over arugula with walnuts and raisins ($8.00), a warm white bean salad served over prosciutto with shaved parmesan ($8.00), and a hearty cold antipasto with Genoa salami, provolone, marinated artichoke hearts, tomatoes, olives, prosciutto, and arugula ($8.50) that's big enough to share. The pastas are fresh and delicious, with choices that include penne with tomato sauce and fresh basil and topped with mozzarella ($10.50), linguine pesto ($11.50), gnocchi with tomato sauce and fresh mozzarella ($11.50), and grilled chicken lasagna ($15.00). Other good main choices are the chicken breast with shiitake mushrooms and lemon sauce served with roasted potatoes ($16.50), veal stuffed with prosciutto and spinach, served with roasted potatoes ($18.00), and cold poached salmon served over arugula with a raspberry vinaigrette ($15.50). For dessert, choose one of the delicious Italian ice creams.

CHEF HO'S ★   Chinese
1720 Second Avenue
(between 89th and 90th Sts.)
212/348-9444
Daily Noon - 11:00 p.m.
All major cards

This pleasant family restaurant has a comfortable setting and modest prices. I think you will find its popularity is well justified by the terrific dumplings it is famous for.

For a firepowered starter, try the Hunan dumplings with red hot oil ($3.95). But if you'd like a less palate-startling beginning, opt for the home-style fried dumplings ($3.95), six steamed shrimp dumplings ($4.75), or the boiled vegetable dumplings ($3.95). Other popular starters are the minced chicken with a spicy sauce and lettuce ($3.95), seafood soup for two ($5.95), and honey spareribs ($6.95). Of the mains, specialties of the house include crispy prawns smothered in a vegetarian spicy sauce ($12.95), Ho's beef (marinated beef tenderloin slices, pan-seared with diced orange peels and flecked with garlic and ginger) ($11.95), Peacock Fantasy (shredded chicken and bean sprout stems sautéed in a light rice wine sauce along with shredded chicken and young ginger roots sautéed in a spicy Hunan sauce) ($10.95), filet of lamb sautéed with Hunan hot peppers, minced ginger, scallion stalks, and watercress on the side ($8.95), and banana chicken ($8.95). Other good mains include sliced beef with oyster sauce ($7.95), moo shu pork with three pancakes ($7.50), hot spicy baby shrimp ($8.50), cashew chicken ($7.95), Grand Marnier shrimp ($13.95), and ginger duck ($11.95).

COCO PAZZO ★★★   Italian
23 East 74th Street
(between Fifth and Madison Aves.)
212/794-0205
Lunch - Daily Noon - 3:00 p.m.
Dinner - Monday through Friday 6:00 - 11:45 p.m.;
Saturday 5:45 - 11:45 p.m.; Sunday 5:30 - 11:00 p.m.
All major cards

Coco Pazzo (crazy chef) has a comfortably elegant feel with soft colors, fresh flowers, beautiful moldings, and Morandi-inspired murals. Owned by sage restaurateur Pino Luongo—who knows how to deliver the goods when it comes to Italian restaurants with both style and wonderful food—its casually glamorous ambience and Tuscan specialties have made it a culinary haven for a well-heeled crowd of local hotshots and show biz celebs. Sightings have included a sampling of smooth crooners—Frank Sinatra, Vic Damone, and Julio Iglesias. Kate Capshaw has also been spotted here, as well as Rod Stewart on several occasions.

The chef, Cesare Casella, formerly of a much acclaimed restaurant in Lucca, Italy, puts his own magic spin on rustic Tuscan country cooking. His menu changes twice each season. Of the starters, a house specialty is a wilted salad of baby lettuces with herbs, a scrambled egg, and pancetta ($8.00). Other choices might include mussels in a tomato and white wine broth with a garlic crouton ($8.50), antipasto of prosciutto and salami, grilled bread, and homemade pâté ($9.00), and portobello mushroom caps grilled with rosemary ($9.00). A simple and delicious pasta choice is the maccheroncini al pepolino (rectangles of fresh egg pasta with a rich tomato sauce and grated aged pecorino cheese) ($16.50). Other good options include spaghetti with crumbled hot and sweet sausage and tomato sauce ($17.00), and pappardelle with assorted mushrooms ($17.00). And the lasagna, sometimes a special, is simply divine. Of the mains, the bistecca fiorentina is a clear favorite—a huge ribeye steak grilled on the bone with herb-infused olive oil ($32.00). Other notable offerings might include sautéed shrimp lightly-flavored with chestnut honey and served with deep-fried asparagus ($27.00), oven-roasted filet of salmon with a potato crust ($24.00), half a grilled free-range organic chicken with a peppery tomato sauce on the side ($23.00), and grilled pork tenderloin slices with mixed grilled mushrooms ($24.00). The changing assortment of sweet indulgences are well worth consideration, especially the apple cake and the warm chocolate and cinnamon cake with milk chocolate sauce.

DANIEL ★★★★   French
20 East 76th Street (Fifth and Madison Aves.)
212/288-0033
Lunch - Tuesday through Saturday Noon - 3:00 p.m.
Dinner - Monday through Saturday 5:45 - 11:30 p.m.
All major cards

Daniel delivers the kind of fabulous dining experience that truly memorable meals are made of. The setting itself is very understated in its mellow yellow, honey-toned simplicity. But the soft—almost bland—look of the room is enlivened by spectacular floral arrays that add a warm note and a touch of drama. And quietly elegant taste is also reflected in the Limoges china, splendid antique mirrors, and graceful arches. Yet what sets this expensive and rather formal restaurant apart is its friendliness, its total lack of pretense or attitude. It is posh, but without a trace of snobbery.

On pleasant days, you may be drawn to the sidewalk tables charmingly nestled alongside tomato plants and hibiscus, creating the kind of harmony that seems to go so well with this wonderful place.

Superlatives abound for the culinary gifts of its namesake, Daniel Boulud, the master chef who performed culinary magic and displayed extraordinary range at Le Cirque for six years before opening his own restaurant. Now classical French dishes, hearty homestyle fare, and regional delicacies all have a place on his menus here, influenced by market availability of the best products from around the world. The menu evolves with the seasons. Recent winning combinations among starters have been chilled eggplant and artichoke soup with black olives, tomato, and cumin ($13.00), curried tuna tartare with pink radishes and a celery coulis ($18.00), rillettes of duck, squab, quail, rabbit, and foie gras with cherries and hazelnuts ($21.00), ravioli of nine herbs and spring greens with chanterelles, ricotta, and a tomato coulis ($17.00), and whole roasted asparagus with rosemary, garlic, aged balsamic vinegar, and parmesan shavings ($16.00). Mains reflect the same innovation in signature dishes such as roasted black sea bass in a crisp potato shell on a bed of leeks with a red wine sauce ($35.00), roasted rack of lamb flavored with fennel, coriander and anise seeds, served with artichokes, zucchini, fresh fennel, and tomato confit ($72.00 for two), and a smashing duo of braised short ribs in red wine and roasted beef tenderloin with spring root vegetables and scallion mashed potatoes ($35.00). Other notable selections include roasted cod with basil on a bed of crushed potatoes with lobster, tomato, fennel, and a lobster jus ($34.00) and roasted veal chop with a wild mushroom sauce and stuffed spring vegetables ($36.00). François Payard's desserts are wonders as well. Coconut sorbet on a bed of pineapple with a star-anise sabayon is a current triumph.

In addition to the seasonal à la carte menu, there are daily market specials and a selection of prix fixe tasting menus: at lunch $35.00 for three courses and at dinner $70.00, $85.00, and $110.00 for four courses, six courses, and eight courses, respectively. After-theater reservations are taken from 10:30 to 11:30 p.m.

HEIDELBERG RESTAURANT ★   German
1648 Second Avenue (between 85th and 86th Sts.)
212/650-1385
Lunch - Daily 11:30 a.m. - 3:00 p.m.
Dinner - Daily 3:00 - 11:00 p.m.
All major cards

This beergarden restaurant is appealingly old-fashioned, both in its ambience and its old-world homestyle cooking. In addition to moderate prices and pleasant Bavarian food, it boasts a great selection of German beer on tap and oompah-pah bands on weekends.

This is the kind of hearty fare that seems particularly comforting on a cold winter day. Start with baked camembert cheese with cranberry and pear ($7.95), asparagus rolled in Westphalian ham ($7.95), liver dumpling soup

($3.95), or a mixed salad composed of potatoes, cucumber, beets, string beans, greens, and carrots ($4.95). As for the main, wursts ($9.95) are popular choices, served with potato salad and sauerkraut. Other good options include roulade (sliced beef, stuffed with pickle, onion, and bacon) ($13.95), sauerbraten with red cabbage and potato dumpling ($15.25), roast pork with bread dumpling, sauerkraut, and applesauce ($15.25), paprika chicken with spätzle ($13.95), wiener schnitzel with homefries ($15.25), veal shank off the bone with roasted potatoes and vegetables ($17.95), and roast Long Island duckling with potato dumpling and red cabbage ($16.95). A "little guests" portion of the menu has kid-friendly foods like potato pancakes and applesauce ($5.95) and chicken fingers with potato chips ($6.95). For dessert, tuck into homemade apple strudel with fresh whipped cream ($4.75), apple fritters ($5.75), Black Forest cherry torte ($4.75), or hot raspberries on vanilla ice cream ($5.95).

J. G. MELON ★   Pub
1291 Third Avenue (74th St.)
212/744-0585
Daily 11:30 a.m. - 4:00 a.m.
No credit cards

J. G. Melon is a casual, congenial neighborhood pub where any shortcomings in the cuisine are made up for by the endearing personality of the place. The melon in the name derives from a limited startup decorating budget and the availability of some bargain melon prints, rather than from any particular affection for the fruit itself. Indeed, there's no sign of a melon anywhere on its no-nonsense saloon menu. Favored by an eclectic uptown crowd, this likeable place buzzes with activity and conviviality day and night.

As for the food, the typical saloon offerings are really quite good. You can certainly get a great bacon burger ($5.75) and good chili bowl ($4.50). There's also a turkey burger ($5.95) for the health-conscious among us and a good club sandwich ($7.50) for the rest of us. Other sound choices include omelettes ($6.75) and a terrific salad niçoise ($8.75). Dessert choices might be chocolate chip cake ($4.50), apple sour cream walnut pie ($3.95), or lemon mousse pie ($3.95).

348

KING'S CARRIAGE HOUSE ★★   Continental
251 East 82nd Street (Second Ave.)
212/734-5490
Lunch - Daily Noon - 4:00 p.m.
Afternoon Tea - Daily 3:00 - 5:00 p.m.
Dinner - Daily 6:00 - 11:00 p.m.
All major cards

It's difficult to imagine a more attractive backdrop for a special meal than this lovely place. Housed in a charming original two-story carriage house, the restaurant is comprised of a sitting room and three dining rooms, each with an individual look.   In this romantic space, genuine decorating flair and needlepoint pillows combine to create an atmosphere both sophisticated and cozy. You'll feel as though you're dining in a gracious private home.

The continental fare is quite appealing and nicely prepared. **A three-course prix fixe is offered all evening ($34.00).** This can quickly add up, however, since many of the dishes bear an asterisk indicating a $4.00 supplement. Good starters include shrimp bisque, endive salad with stilton vinaigrette and toasted walnuts, grilled shrimp and quail over greens with a cranberry vinaigrette, and oak-smoked Irish salmon (*).   There's a nice selection of inventive mains like the wild salmon with pistachio nut crust and lemon-scented basmati rice and the grilled loin of lamb with quince and walnut and rosemary-scented mashed potatoes (*). Other enticements include grilled filet mignon with stilton cheese sauce and horseradish potato gratin (*) and roasted chicken breast with a red pepper coulis and creamy polenta. Typical desserts include temptations like rhubarb tart, chocolate banana bread pudding, pecan carrot cake, and dark chocolate truffle cake.

THE KIOSK ★   European/American
1007 Lexington Ave.
(between 72nd and 73rd Sts.)
212/535-6000
Breakfast Daily 8:00 - 11:00 a.m.
Lunch - Monday through Friday 11:30 a.m. - 3:30 p.m.
Brunch - Saturday and Sunday 11:00 a.m. - 3:00 p.m.
Dinner - Daily 5:30 p.m. - Midnight
All major cards

Panelling foraged from an old church, ancient tilted mirrors, golden-glazed walls, and French country windows add a nice dash of character to this tiny new bistro/dinette. Co-owner Nell Campbell (of Nell's nightclub fame locally) first earned recognition in London as a star of the original Off-Off West End production "The Rocky Horror Picture Show." The chic Ms. Campbell (an Australian) eventually came to New York to model in a fashion show for British designer Zandra Rhodes. Celebrated for her considerable personal élan, it's still a tossup as to whether the kitchen of her charming sliver of a bistro will be able to deliver the goods and keep the crowds coming when the initial hype dies down. I hope so. Its delightful ambience and convenient hours certainly make it the kind of place that is appealing at any time of day and is nice to have around.

The short menu, while somewhat limited, offers good daily specials and has enough diversity to please most diners. You might start with tuna carpaccio ($9.00), grilled portobello mushrooms with arugula ($8.00), house-smoked salmon with cucumber and toasted brioche ($11.00), or roast pumpkin soup ($7.00). For the main, choices include good steak frites ($22.00), grilled organic chicken with spinach and mashed potatoes ($17.50), mustard-crusted salmon ($21.00), and balsamic marinated tuna served rare with pesto wontons ($22.00). You won't be missing anything if you skip dessert.

A three-course pre-theater dinner is offered from 5:30 to 7:00 p.m. for $18.50.

LA FOLIE ★★   French
1422 Third Avenue
(between 80th and 81st Sts.)
212/744-6327
Brunch - Saturday and Sunday 11:00 a.m. - 4:00 p.m.
Dinner - Sunday through Thursday 5:00- 11:00 p.m.;
Friday and Saturday 5:00 p.m. - Midnight
All major cards

Corinthian columns soar toward a high navy blue ceiling, dark polished floors gleam, and French antiques pepper the room. This very stylish bistro is indeed a dramatic and beautiful space, but in a friendly fashion. Once you settle in, you realize how comfortable the room is—not at all stuffy in spite of the ornate marbleized pillars, antique tapestries, fringed damask curtains, and grand piano.

The food is quite good, too—more a "frenchified" American than classic French. You might start with chilled gazpacho with cucumber and Louisiana

350

shrimp ($7.50), warm grilled vegetable tart with roasted goat cheese ($7.50), or a chilled stuffed artichoke with shrimp, grilled endive, and aged wine vinegar ($8.50). There are also some good pastas to choose from—notably, homemade cappellini with rock shrimp, lobster, and white asparagus ($16.50), penne with a smoked tomato sauce, baked ricotta, and roasted eggplant ($15.00), and homemade spaghetti with baby clams and roasted garlic ($15.50). Favorites among mains are the pan-roasted free-range chicken with basil mashed potatoes and crispy onions ($18.00), braised lamb with grilled vegetables ($22.00), and grilled ribeye steak with frites ($23.00). There are some nice fish dishes, too, like a pan-roasted halibut with summer squashes and tomato coulis ($20.00). Check the daily desserts and hope there's pot de crème. Another delight is a luscious caramelized banana enclosed in phyllo with coconut ice cream.

A five-course prix fixe menu is available all evening for $19.75—one spectacular buy.

LE REFUGE ★★   French
166 East 82nd Street (between Lexington and Third Aves.)
212/861-4505
Lunch - Monday through Friday Noon - 3:00 p.m.
Brunch - Saturday Noon - 3:00 p.m.; Sunday Noon - 4:00 p.m.
Dinner - Monday through Saturday 5:00 - 11:00 p.m.;
Sunday 5:00 - 9:30 p.m.
American Express only

A romantic 1868 townhouse serves as the setting for this wonderful old-fashioned French restaurant. Three charming rooms comprise the restaurant and give it the look and feel of a rustic French country inn. Each of the dining rooms has an appealing character—one in the rear overlooks a small garden, another has a fireplace. Pretty 17th Century tapestries, wainscotting, country tiles, timber beams, provincial armoires, abundant flowers, and well-worn wooden tables with kitchen towels for napkins combine to create an ambience throughout that will transport you to the Normandy countryside. Candlelight in the evening heightens its romantic appeal. And the back garden, open in summer, has a few tables for hand-holding Mediterranean-style alfresco dining.

Chef/owner Pierre Saint-Denis, a Normandy native, opened Le Refuge in 1977. His delicious traditional French homestyle cooking has made it a longstanding neighborhood favorite. Cured Norwegian salmon with a dill vinaigrette ($9.50), snails in puff pastry ($10.50), a crab cake with basil sauce

($11.50), and lobster ravioli ($11.50) are all terrific starters. Among mains, the house specialties are shrimp with couscous ($23.50), bouillabaisse ($24.50), and roasted duck with fresh fruit ($21.50). Other appealing mains include linguine with seafood ($19.50), salmon with shallots and red wine ($21.50), grilled chicken with bacon ($19.50), loin of lamb with spinach ($23.50), and filet mignon with peppercorns ($24.50). Daily dessert selections might include a delicious strawberry tart, profiteroles, and chocolate soufflé cake. Most notable is what Pierre labels Vivaldi's Sweet Revenge, a medley of chocolate soufflé cake, a puffed profiterole, white chocolate mousse with raspberries and almonds, and a black current sorbet. All that along with a CD of Vivaldi's *Four Seasons*, a recording with the violins replaced by a synthesizer and Pierre's flute artistry. Who could resist?

For pre-theater dining, between 5:00 and 6:00 p.m., the price of the main includes soup or salad and dessert.

LETIZIA RISTORANTE ★★   Italian
1352 First Avenue
(between 72nd and 73rd Sts.)
212/517-2244
Lunch - Daily 11:45 a.m. - 4:00 p.m.
Dinner - Daily 5:00 - 11:30 p.m.
All major cards

Once you've been here, you'll understand why most of Letizia's clientele are regulars. Lace curtains, pale golden walls, and delicate floral arrangements combine to create a warm, relaxed atmosphere. But it is the warmth of the staff that gives dining here such a special feel. It may be just a simple neighborhood Italian among many on this stretch of real estate, but when you dine here, the delicious food and caring service will leave you with the feeling that you've chosen very, very well. This congenial spot is also appreciated by such diverse personalities as Harry Connick, Jr., Andy Rooney, Tony LoBianco, Chuck Scarborough, and Beverly Sills.

Among starters, good choices include pan-fried artichokes with garlic basil, parsley, and olive oil ($9.75), antipasto fantasia (an assortment of roasted sweet peppers, asparagus, sun-dried tomato, portobello mushroom, and mozzarella) ($9.75), snails with melted polenta, garlic, and an herb sauce ($9.00), homemade mozzarella with roasted peppers, tomato, and basil ($8.25), a chopped salad of zucchini, tomato, and olives ($6.75), and antipasto Letizia for two (asparagus, parmesan, shrimp wrapped in prosciutto, portobello mushrooms, fried mozzarella, and baked clams) ($25.00).   The kitchen consistently displays an innovative way with pasta. Try the penne in a light spicy tomato and Vodka sauce ($13.75), malfatti filled with ricotta, spinach, and tomato ($14.25), half-moon shaped pasta filled with chopped broccoli rabe and shrimp, garlic, and rosemary ($14.75), linguine in red or white clam sauce ($15.75), angel hair with tomato, ricotta, and pesto ($13.75), or pappardelle with portobello mushrooms, asparagus, sun-dried tomatoes, pine nuts, and a touch of pesto ($15.75). Notable mains include grilled Cornish hen with herbs, garlic, and lemon ($16.50), boneless breast of chicken filled with apple and mozzarella ($17.75), veal scaloppine topped with mozzarella, sun-dried tomatoes, and asparagus ($18.75), veal chop filled with prosciutto, fontina, and black truffles in a white wine sauce ($22.75), Milanese-style veal shank stew ($20.25), roast rack of lamb with shallot and garlic confit and braised radicchio ($21.75), beef medallions with portobello mushrooms ($21.75), red snapper baked in parchment with vegetables ($21.75), and pan-seared filet of salmon with mustard and Cognac ($19.75). The daily desserts are homemade.

THE LOBSTER CLUB ★★   American
24 East 80th Street
(between Fifth and Madison Aves.)
212/249-6500
Lunch - Monday through Saturday 11:30 a.m. - 3:00 p.m.
Dinner - Monday through Saturday 5:30 - 11:00 p.m.
All major cards

If you've ever had the pleasure of dining at Arcadia, Anne Rosenzweig's lovely townhouse restaurant on East 62nd Street, you probably have some idea how special her newborn Lobster Club might be.   More casual and less expensive than its fancy-face sibling, it has its own appealing character. Situated in a townhouse duplex with handmade tiles and fireplaces on each floor, it has a casual elegance and is altogether inviting.

The innovative and eclectic American fare Ms. Rosenzweig creates here is sophisticated comfort food. The originality that is her hallmark and her work-in-progress menu can sometimes result in dishes that just don't work. But for the most part, the food here is wonderful. For starters, there's terrific crispy rock shrimp with jalapeño tartar sauce ($11.75), crab and couscous cake with arugula vinaigrette ($12.00), pumpkin soup with curry spices ($7.50), mashed potato cakes filled with duck confit, pine nuts, and roasted garlic with greens in a sherry vinaigrette ($11.50), and smoked trout salad with endive and tangerines ($10.50). Pastas comes in both starter and main course portions with enticing choices like pumpkin papardelle with roasted garlic, bacon, and brussels sprouts ($8.00/$16.00), mussels with pasta, garlic, and white beans ($8.50/$17.00), and wild buckwheat penne with wild mushrooms ($9.00/$18.00). Heading the list of mains is the namesake lobster club sandwich, deliciously rich with bacon and mayo ($23.00). Other winning mains include grilled short ribs with horseradish gnocchi ($21.50), lemon and herb roasted chicken with dynamite provençale fries tossed with parsley and garlic ($20.50), fish and chips of the day (p/a), and a homey Mom's meatloaf—delicious and with a different preparation each day ($18.50). The changing parade of desserts (like rice pudding with a burnt sugar topping, almond-crusted banana split with a hidden malted milk ball in the ice cream, pear cobbler, angel food Baked Alaska, and caramel-chocolate tart) will bring out the happy child in you.

MARK'S ★★★   French
(The Mark Hotel)
25 East 77th Street (Madison Ave.)
212/879-1864
Lunch - Daily 11:30 a.m. - 2:30 p.m.
Afternoon Tea - Daily 2:30 - 5:30 p.m.
Brunch - Sunday 11:30 a.m. - 2:30 p.m.
Dinner - Daily 6:30 - 10:30 p.m.
All major cards

Exquisite decor, gracious service, and splendid French cooking can be expected at this elegant restaurant perched in The Mark Hotel. Two terraced levels comprise the restaurant, enhanced by striking columns, Italian marble borders, ebony and gold leaf edged moldings, and a seductive color scheme of burgundy, rose, and teal. A large faux-skylight casts a soft illumination over richly panelled walls, magnificent mahogany furniture, beautiful antique prints, and luxurious fabrics. And with its refined Neo-Classical decor and English-style tufted banquettes, Mark's is somewhat reminiscent of a private English club, and has the nice quality of being perfectly lovely and completely comfortable at the same time. Harp music in the background and leafy potted palms and orchids further enhance its truly romantic ambience.

With tables sumptuously set with Villeroy & Boch china and engraved silver, dining here is certainly one lavish and pleasurable experience. **Afternoon Tea (with a selection of sandwiches, pastries, and scones for $16.50) seems right on the mark in such a setting.** At dinner, you might start with a mélange of baby salads with sherry vinaigrette ($8.50), Pacific Northwest oysters in a Champagne vinaigrette ($14.00), house apple-smoked salmon with artichoke and fennel salad in a citrus vinaigrette ($13.00), or Maine jumbo sea scallops in a lemon broth ($15.50). Beautifully prepared mains include pan-seared red snapper with rosemary potatoes and a black olive tapenade ($29.00), lobster shepherds pie with chanterelle mushrooms and salad ($31.00), roasted free-range chicken for two with potato skin and sautéed endives ($48.00), and roasted Colorado rack of lamb with potato gratin ($34.00). Simple grilled specialties served with fresh market vegetables include salmon ($27.00), sirloin ($31.00), and lamb chops ($32.00). Good dessert choices are the chocolate soufflé ($11.00), caramelized pear Napoleon with honey-pine nut ice cream ($9.00), and orange-chocolate crêpes ($8.50).

Sunday brunch is also lovely here with choices like Hawaiian pancakes ($8.50), brioche French toast with cinnamon honey ($8.00), house apple-smoked salmon with cream cheese and red onions ($12.50), eggs Benedict with Canadian bacon or spinach ($14.50), goat cheese and mushroom frittata ($15.50), scrambled eggs, ranchero style, with tequila shrimp, guacamole, and fresh tomato salsa ($13.50), roasted free-range chicken with tomato salad and shoestring potatoes ($19.00), and roast prime rib with Yorkshire pudding, seasonal vegetables, and a Cabernet sauce ($22.00). **A three-course prix fixe brunch with a complimentary brunch cocktail and coffee is $32.00. During the week a three-course prix fixe lunch is $19.97.**

A pre-theater menu is available for orders prior to 7:00 p.m. with three courses for $29.00.

MOCCA HUNGARIAN ★   Hungarian
1588 Second Avenue (between 82nd and 83rd Sts.)
212/734-6470
Lunch - Daily 11:30 a.m. - 4:00 p.m.
Dinner - Daily 4:00 - 10:30 p.m.
No credit cards

Its interior is unremarkable—small, not at all smart—with a comfortably worn, old country feel. The service is brisk—so brisk that courses sometimes come one on top of another making it possible to down a three-course meal in not much more than half an hour. With my fondness for leisurely meals, that makes Mocca Hungarian not my kind of place. Yet I like it here. It's hard not to like a place that presents you with such a tiny bill for authentic Hungarian food that is as homey and warming as it might be around a simple kitchen table in the Hungarian countryside.

Zsa Zsa Gabor has dined here. So has Anthony Quinn and Governor George Pataki. But mostly the clientele is a neighborhood crowd of regulars who eat here many times a week. The specials are bargains in the truest sense. **The dinner prix fixe is available all evening with three courses for $13.95.** You might start with breaded cauliflower with tartar sauce, marinated herring, spare ribs, homemade noodle soup, or cold cherry soup in season. There's a nice choice among mains, including house specialties such as chicken paprikash with dumplings, stuffed cabbage on a bed of sauerkraut, and beef goulash. Other options include wiener schnitzel, paprika schnitzel, roast loin of pork with sauerkraut, roast veal, and the catch of the day. Homemade strudels (apple, cherry, or cheese) and palacsinta (crêpe-like desserts filled with either walnuts, apricot, or cheese) are the desserts of choice. **The $6.45 lunch special is one of the biggest bargains around.** It offers a choice of soup or juice, a main course from a list that includes all the house specialties, and palacsinta and coffee.

ORIENTA ★★   Southeast Asian
205 East 75th Street (between Second and Third Aves.)
212/517-7509
Lunch - Daily Noon - 3:00 p.m.
Dinner - Daily 6:00 p.m. - Midnight
All major cards

When this stylish newcomer breezed onto the restaurant scene, it caused quite a stir of excitement. Its owners already had a loyal uptown following with chic Euro-bistros like Le Comptoir, Le Colonial, Le Relais, and L'Absinthe on their plates. And judging by the throng of pretty people crowding in here nightly, this looks like another winner. Sponged ocher walls, tall greenery, and Chinese straw hats as light sconces form the pretty backdrop, and a cool clientele adds to the hip feel of the place.

House specialties among starters are the classic Vietnamese spring rolls with shrimp, minced pork, vermicelli, and ear mushrooms wrapped in rice paper ($6.00), tuna sashimi ($8.00), and scallion-sautéed noodles with duck ($8.00). Other good openers include Malaysian chicken satays with peanut dip ($5.50) and steamed leak and pork dumplings with sesame soy ($6.00). Bouillabaisse d'Orienta (filet of red snapper, sea scallops, and tiger prawns in a fish broth with ginger and lime leaves) ($17.00) is another house specialty. Other good mains include large sea scallops seared in red curry with fresh chilies and aromatic herbs ($16.00), chicken curry with tamarind ($13.00), filet mignon seared with masala spice and fresh mint leaves ($17.00), and Saigon caramelized chicken (a classic southern dish of Vietnam with breast of chicken hot wok-sautéed with chilies in a caramelized lemongrass sauce) ($13.00). The spicing of some dishes is on the tame side, but diners are encouraged to indicate the level of spiciness they would like. For dessert ($6.00), try one of the refreshing fruit sorbets (pink grapefruit, mango, or raspberry). The fruit tart and coconut crème brûlée are also nice.

PARIOLI ROMANISSIMO ★★★   Italian
24 East 81st Street (between Fifth and Madison Aves.)
212/288-2391
Dinner - Monday through Saturday 5:30 - 11:00 p.m.
All major cards

Recapturing the formality and elegance of an earlier time, Parioli Romanissimo is one of the East Side's most seductive restaurants. Its setting is a gracious townhouse with beautiful architectural details, elaborate moldings, and soaring ceilings. A lovely fireplace, tables spaced for privacy, and gentle lighting are other elements that combine to create a romantic mood. And in back, there's another appealing and intimate dining room overlooking a striking skylit garden. The regular clientele here has the same easy elegance as the setting and appear to have achieved a certain stature and time in life when price is no object. This is a place where the spending is easy and there's no room for penny-pinching. Reservations are required, as are jacket and tie.

Dining here is a luxurious experience and the contemporary Italian food is wonderful. Seasonal menus combine American and European ingredients culled from small producers and local farmers. The stunning cheese cart—boasting at least 50 cheeses from around the world—is one of the finest in town. The starters are both pricey and delicious. Choices might be baby artichokes filled with minced vegetables topped with bacon ($14.75), pepper-crusted yellowfin tuna served rare over grilled shiitake mushrooms ($16.75), and grilled scampi with a garlic and herb marinade ($15.75). The pastas are fabulous with selections that include spinach tagliatelle with tomatoes, olives, sweet garlic, and marjoram ($22.75), tagliolini with baby clams and sweet garlic ($24.75), and goat cheese ravioli with basil butter and a tomato coulis ($23.75). For the main, choices include seared sea scallops with morel mushrooms drizzled with a citrus butter sauce ($31.50), roasted baby chicken with sweet garlic and rosemary, served with risotto ($32.50), roasted rack of veal scented with rosemary and juniper and served with broccoli purée ($68.00 for two), and grilled ribeye steak with potatoes ($33.00). Daily desserts or a selection from the impressive cheese cart will add another $12.00 to your bill.

PETALUMA ★★   Italian
1356 First Avenue (73rd St.)
212/772-8800
Lunch - Daily Noon - 3:00 p.m.
Dinner - Daily 5:30 - 11:30 p.m.
All major cards

In recent years, Petaluma has made a graceful transition from a trendy hot-spot-of-the-moment to a congenial neighborhood favorite. While the look of its clientele may have changed, the restaurant remains as popular as ever. Its pastel color scheme and postmodern decor provides a winsome setting for good homemade pastas, brick-oven pizzas, and grilled fish and meats.

Your first taste of the place will be the good fluffy Tuscan bread. Then, for starters, choices include creamy buffalo mozzarella with tomatoes and basil ($8.50), baked goat cheese salad ($8.50), home-smoked salmon with rugola ($9.00), fried mozzarella with a julienne of fried zucchini ($9.00), grilled chicken on skewers with rugola salad ($9.00), and an antipasto sampler ($9.00). You might also start by sharing one of the delicious pizzas with prosciutto, artichokes, olives, and mushrooms or ham, leeks, tomato sauce, rugola, and mozzarella (each $13.00). The bianca pizza with four cheeses ($13.00) is also delicious. Of the pastas, the spinach gnocchi with tomato, basil, and a touch of cream ($14.00) is a favorite. Other good choices include penne in a spicy tomato sauce with olive purée, capers, and garlic ($13.50) and fusilli with sausage, tomatoes, and garlic ($14.50). The simple spaghetti with tomato sauce and basil ($12.50) is nice and light. For the main, good choices include fried calamari and shrimp ($18.50), chicken sautéed with Marsala, shallots, mushrooms, prosciutto, and fontina cheese ($15.00), and veal Milanese with tomato, basil, and rugola and onion salad ($21.50). Tops among the grills are the lamb chops with a fresh mint sauce, chunks of garlic, and roasted potatoes ($23.00) and salmon with steamed vegetables ($20.00). For dessert: Belgian chocolate cake, a light tiramisú, or vanilla bean cheesecake (each $5.50).

PRIMAVERA ★★   Italian
1578 First Avenue (at 82nd St.)
212/861-8608
Dinner - Daily 5:30 p.m. - Midnight
All major cards

This is an old-fashioned, genteel "coat and tie" kind of place. Its wood-panelled dining room is clubby and warm with marbled columns, brick walls, oil paintings, and tulip sconces that cast a gentle light. The pampered regulars look well tended and aristocratic; waiters in formal attire exude patrician grace. And while this expensive sometimes-great restaurant can disappoint, most often it soars.

Good, though pricey, starters include assorted cold antipasto ($14.50), sturgeon with baby shrimp ($16.50), scallops sautéed with shallots ($16.50), mozzarella with bread, fried and served with anchovy sauce ($14.50), and baked artichokes ($14.50). It's the fabulous pastas, though, that highlight the comprehensive menu. Choices include capelli Primavera ($22.50), meat ravioli with sage ($21.50), tortellini with peas and prosciutto ($21.50), penne with a spicy red sauce ($19.75), and linguine with clam sauce ($22.50). Mains reflect the diversity of this cuisine, with choices such as filet of sole with fresh tomatoes and herbs ($26.50), grilled swordfish with lemon, oil, and oregano ($29.50), breast of chicken stuffed with prosciutto and spinach ($26.50), veal chop stuffed with cheese, prosciutto, and truffles ($31.50), rolled veal stuffed with prosciutto and spinach ($28.50), and sirloin sautéed with mushrooms and red wine ($32.00). The longtime house specialty is roasted baby goat ($32.00). Among desserts (around $11.00), the terrific ricotta cheesecake is a standout.

A pre- and post-theater menu is offered between 5:30 and 6:30 p.m. and after 10:00 p.m. with three courses for $39.50.

QUISISANA ★★   Italian
1319 Third Avenue (between 75th and 76th Sts.)
212/879-5000
Lunch - Monday through Saturday Noon - 3:00 p.m.
Dinner - Monday through Saturday 5:30 - 11:30 p.m.
All major cards

A rustically elegant and warm ambience, delicious food, and a very genial staff make this a wonderful place to dine. The kitchen takes its inspiration from the cuisine of the Isle of Capri where simplicity and natural flavors rule. This is mainly an Italian seafood restaurant and chef/owner Beppe Desiderio specializes in roasted dishes prepared in the wood-burning oven that is the dining room's centerpiece.

House specialties among starters are calamari grilled with lemon ($9.00) and warm spinach salad with goat cheese and red onions ($9.00). Also good is the striped bass salad with black olives, russet potatoes, and a vinaigrette dressing ($9.00) and a salad of cucumbers, tomatoes, and onions ($7.00). The homemade pastas are terrific, with choices like ricotta ravioli in a tomato sauce ($16.00), spinach fettucini with a sauce of tomato, basil, and sweet peppers ($15.00), and linguine with shrimp, scallops, mussels, and clams ($17.00). Other good choices include penne with mozzarella and eggplant in a tomato sauce ($15.00) and rigatoni with a veal meat sauce ($16.00). Orata (sea bream) and branzino (striped bass) are house specialties, and one or the other is offered nightly (market price). Specialties from the wood-burning oven include roasted scallops with fresh herbs and arugula ($21.00), marinated roasted baby chicken with garlic and rosemary ($19.00), and John Dory baked in a potato crust with tomato, shallots, and black olives ($20.00). Other popular mains are fresh cod with basil, onions, capers, and pine nuts ($20.00) and red snapper grilled with tarragon, lemon, and white wine ($21.00).

TABLE D'HOTE ★★   French/New American
44 East 92nd Street (between Madison and Park Aves.)
212/348-8125
Lunch - Monday through Friday Noon - 4:30 p.m.
Brunch - Sunday 10:30 - 4:30 p.m.
Dinner - Daily 5:00 - 10:30 p.m.
All major cards

A cozy, romantic setting, warm service, and delicious food make this tiny jewel box a winning ticket. The charmingly old-fashioned French country dining room—fetchingly decorated with antiques and hand-painted plates—has just nine tables. But the kitchen has big ambitions and turns out consistently good French/New American fare with flair.

Your starter might be watercress salad with apples, walnuts, and goat cheese ($9.00), seared lamb sausages with curried chick peas ($9.00), or seared shrimp with mango salsa ($11.00). Mains include roasted free-range chicken with new potatoes and green beans ($18.00), pan-roasted veal chop with a wild mushroom sauce ($25.00), black sesame Atlantic salmon with Japanese rice and ginger-soy ($21.00), and bistro-style hangar steak with frites ($20.00).

Sunday Brunch features framed eggs (eggs in a bread pocket with provolone cheese and Black Forest ham) ($9.50), lamb sausages with polenta and spinach ($10.00), eggs Benedict with warm potato salad ($9.50), and French toast with whipped cream and fresh fruit ($8.50).

A pre-theater three-course dinner is available from 5:00 to 7:00 p.m. for $19.95.

TWINS ★   American
1712 Second Avenue (at 89th St.)
212/987-1111
Brunch - Sunday 11:00 a.m. - 3:30 p.m.
Dinner - Daily 5:00 p.m. - Midnight; Bar open until 3:00 a.m.
All major cards

This delightful place is the smallest and most original of the theme restaurants that keep popping up around town. Owned by actor Tom Berenger and twin sisters Lisa and Debbie Ganz, Twins—as its name implies—is a lighthearted tribute to doubles. Staffed entirely by 37 sets of identical twins, you'll start seeing double the minute you enter through the amiable bar and lounge area. And chances are you'll see twin diners as well. Debbie and Lisa say they get from ten to twenty sets of twin customers each evening for dinner.

Multicolored banquettes and twin paraphernalia add to the fanciful ambience in the dining room and a pleasant outdoor garden doubles the pleasure of dining here in spring and summer. The menu offers an eclectic blend of fun food and tastes of various cuisines. To start, a house specialty is the spicy lobster and cappellini crab cakes with a black sesame dijon sauce, topped with guacamole ($8.95). For the young, as well as the young-at-heart, there's a playful double cheese fondue made with gorgonzola and fontina cheeses and served with tiny hot dogs, assorted bread chunks, curly Cajun fries, Granny Smith apples, and broccoli ($12.95). Other choices include a good Caesar salad ($8.95 or $9.95 with chicken) and vegetarian quesadillas ($6.95). Pizza offerings include some unusual combos such as the Pacifico which is topped with grilled sirloin, garlic mashed potatoes, jalapeños, and wild mushrooms ($12.95). For the main, good choices include rigatoni tossed with smoked mozzarella and sun-dried tomatoes in a pink Vodka sauce ($10.95), spit-roasted half chicken with seasonal vegetables and crispy shoestring fries ($11.95), grilled Atlantic salmon on a roasted corn and black bean salsa topped with a garlic-lime-dill butter and grilled green apples ($16.95), maple and soy marinated pork chops chargrilled and served with roasted garlic mashed potatoes and sesame grilled asparagus ($15.95), and chili-seared beef tenderloin accompanied by a cool tomato and pepper relish and corn-crusted jalapeño Jack polenta ($18.95). For dessert: cake soup (flourless chocolate cake in warmed chocolate fondue with ice cream) ($10.95); caramel pecan fudge pie ($6.95); and white chocolate raspberry cheesecake ($6.95). And what would a theme restaurant be without T-shirts and hats ($15.00).

Sunday brunch ($9.95) includes a choice of Bloody Mary, Mimosa, Champagne, or juice. Selections include a two-fold omelette with your choice

361

of two fillings, served with potatoes, sausage, or bacon; buttermilk pancakes served with sausage or bacon; sunflower and pumpkin seed double waffles served with house-made Amaretto syrup and strawberry butter; and toasted almond and Amaretto French toast served with bacon or sausage and strawberry butter. There are salads, sandwiches, and breakfast pizzas as well.

VIVOLO ★★   Italian
140 East 74th Street (between Lexington and Park Aves.)
212/737-3533
Lunch - Monday through Friday Noon - 3:00 p.m.
Dinner - Monday through Saturday 5:00 - 11:30 p.m.
All major cards

Vivolo's many charms and moderate prices make it a neighborhood favorite. Situated on two floors of an 1886 townhouse with redwood panelling and two working fireplaces, it is warm and romantic. The downstairs dining room has a clubby atmosphere; the upstairs is prettier with high ceilings, mirrors, and lovely flower arrangements.

Good value early and late dinners make dining here a terrific bargain as well as a genuine pleasure. Its regular menu features good starter choices such as rolled eggplant with cheese and tomato ($5.95), fresh mozzarella stuffed with prosciutto, then rolled in parmesan and fried ($5.95), and a classic antipasto sampling ($7.95). Good pasta choices include rigatoni with a sauce of tomato, pancetta, and onion ($11.95), penne with tomato and basil ($11.95), and linguine with clam sauce ($11.95). Other notable mains are boneless chicken prepared with garlic and white wine ($13.75), veal Milanese ($18.95), shrimp with mussels in a spicy tomato sauce served with a twist of linguine ($17.50), and sliced seared sirloin with roasted potatoes, rucola, and tomato ($18.95).

The early pre-theater menu (available from 5:00 to 6:30 p.m.) offers wonderful choice and great value with three courses for $18.95. There's a choice of eight starters, including mussels in a light tomato sauce; baked Long Island little neck clams with seasoned breadcrumbs; soup of the day; and the pasta special of the day. Mains (with over a dozen choices) might be angel hair pasta primavera; rigatoni with Bolognese sauce, green peas, and a touch of cream; filet of sole in a white wine sauce; the fish special of the day; breast of chicken with roasted peppers, mushrooms, and tomato; and a combination plate of the veal and chicken specialties of the day. Then there's a choice of ricotta cheesecake, cannoli, or one of the desserts of the day.

The late night dinner menu (offered after 9:00 p.m.) is another great buy with three courses for $13.95. There's much choice in this menu as well. The ten starter choices include options such as a Caesar-like salad with romaine, radichio, and polenta croutons; a salad of endive, chopped tomato, and bacon; and a salad of fresh mozzarella, tomato, and basil. Then there are about two dozen mains to select from. Choices include farfalle with broccoli and sweet sausage; rigatoni with tomato, onion, and pancetta; linguine with clam sauce; scaloppine of veal rolled with mozzarella and prosciutto and prepared with a mushroom Marsala wine sauce; chicken Milanese; bucatini with veal, onion, carrots, celery, fresh sage, mushrooms, peas, and tomato; and fresh taglierini with salmon in a light cream sauce. End with one of the specialty desserts of the day.

There's also an adjacent cafe (and takeout) called Vivolo Cucina at 138 East 74th Street that serves delicious sandwiches, pastas, and simple salads.

VOULEZ-VOUS ★★   French
1462 First Avenue (76th St.)
212/249-1776
Lunch - Monday through Saturday 11:30 a.m. - 3:00 p.m.
Brunch - Sunday 11:30 a.m. - 3:00 p.m.
Dinner - Sunday through Thursday 5:15 - 11:00 p.m.;
Friday and Saturday 5:15 p.m. - Midnight
All major cards

Voulez-Vous's simple setting and delicious food may remind you of a Paris bistro that still plays on your mind when you catch the scent of a simmering cassoulet. Neighborly in the truest sense, this pleasant place is comfortably family-oriented. Glass-fronted with tinted mirrored walls and a handsome bar, it has a rather split personality with its sleek, contemporary look and hearty, rustic fare.

The food here is wonderfully satisfying, particularly on a cold winter's day. For starters, choices include a rich onion soup ($6.25), tomato and goat cheese flan ($7.50), and leeks vinaigrette ($6.25). House specialties include choucroute ($21.50) and cassoulet ($19.50). Other good mains include filet mignon au poivre ($23.95), lamb chops with a garlic sauce and vegetables ($23.50), and shrimp with couscous ($18.50). There are daily specials as well—on Fridays and Saturdays it's bouillabaisse ($21.50). Desserts are always delicious. Selections include profiteroles au chocolate ($6.50) and wonderful fruit tarts ($6.95). The crème brûlée ($6.50) is also a treat.

A terrific way to dine here is to opt for the regional menu ($39.50) featuring the dishes of a different part of France every week, along with unlimited wine from the same region. The choices are limited to two or three in each category, but it's a wonderful value and the food is all so good.

There is also a nice prix fixe Sunday brunch for $15.25. It includes a brunch cocktail, a selection of breads or fresh bagels, a starter, and a main course.

WILLOW ★★   French/New American
1022 Lexington Avenue (at 73rd St.)
212/717-0703
Lunch - Monday through Saturday Noon - 3:00 p.m.
Brunch - Sunday 11:30 a.m. - 3:00 p.m.
Dinner - Daily 5:30 - 11:00 p.m.
All major cards

Housed on the first two floors of a townhouse that was once a small hotel, Willow is compact and pleasant. Nineteenth Century oil paintings line its pale walls. Windows on two sides give it a light-filled prettiness by day and a golden glow at night. A clubby bar and several tables comprise the main level; the larger upstairs dining room has floor-to-ceiling windows and a light, airy feel. And on nice days, there are sidewalk tables along 73rd Street, a beautiful tree-lined block of historic townhouses.

Its contemporary and health-conscious menu is delightful. For starters, there's a watercress, strawberry, and cantaloupe salad ($7.00), seared sea scallops with scallion pancakes and a light curry sauce ($11.00), and fried baby artichokes with garlic aïoli ($9.00). Good mains include penne with grilled vegetables ($16.50), roasted organic chicken with garlic mashed potatoes and spinach ($18.00), salmon with a grilled sweet potato and tropical salsa ($20.00), and grilled loin veal chop with a potato-corn fritter, portobello mushroom, and asparagus ($25.00). Desserts ($5.50) are wonderful—lemon meringue tart, blueberry brioche pudding, and warm chocolate cake with chocolate ice cream.

A three-course prix fixe is offered from 5:30 to 7:30 p.m. for $19.97.

Sunday brunch is also nice here with such morning delights as a goat cheese omelette with a haricots verts salad ($10.50), French toast with fresh fruit and warm Vermont maple syrup ($9.50), eggs provençale with a tomato-olive sauce ($10.00), and eggs Benedict with warm potato salad ($9.50).

UPPER WEST SIDE

Upper West Side

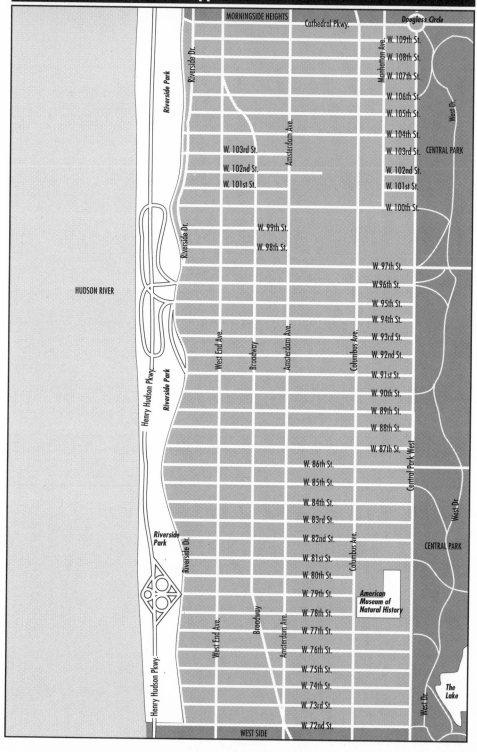

MORNINGSIDE HEIGHTS

Cathedral Pkwy.

Douglass Circle

CENTRAL PARK

HUDSON RIVER

Riverside Park

Riverside Dr.

Henry Hudson Pkwy.

Riverside Park

Riverside Dr.

Riverside Park

Riverside Dr.

Henry Hudson Pkwy.

Amsterdam Ave.

West End Ave.

Broadway

Amsterdam Ave.

Columbus Ave.

Central Park West

West Dr.

West Dr.

American Museum of Natural History

CENTRAL PARK

The Lake

W. 109th St.
W. 108th St.
W. 107th St.
W. 106th St.
W. 105th St.
W. 104th St.
W. 103rd St.
W. 102nd St.
W. 101st St.
W. 100th St.
W. 99th St.
W. 98th St.
W. 97th St.
W. 96th St.
W. 95th St.
W. 94th St.
W. 93rd St.
W. 92nd St.
W. 91st St.
W. 90th St.
W. 89th St.
W. 88th St.
W. 87th St.
W. 86th St.
W. 85th St.
W. 84th St.
W. 83rd St.
W. 82nd St.
W. 81st St.
W. 80th St.
W. 79th St.
W. 78th St.
W. 77th St.
W. 76th St.
W. 75th St.
W. 74th St.
W. 73rd St.
W. 72nd St.

W. 103rd St.
W. 102nd St.
W. 101st St.

Manhattan Ave.

Amsterdam Ave.

WEST SIDE

DELPHINI ★★★   Mediterranean
519 Columbus Avenue (corner of 85th St.)
212/579-1145
Brunch - Saturday and Sunday 11:30 a.m. - 3:30 p.m.
Dinner - Sunday and Monday 5:30 - 11:00 p.m.;
Tuesday and Wednesday 5:30 - Midnight;
Thursday through Saturday 5:30 p.m. - 1:00 a.m.
American Express only

Burnt red walls, an ocean blue ceiling, and immense candle-festooned wrought-iron chandeliers create a lush atmosphere at this delightful newcomer. The charming room—illuminated only by flickering candles—is romantic and warm. But Delphini is much more than just a lovely face. The menu combines Greek, Italian, Spanish, and Moroccan specialties for a taste of Mediterranean heaven.

When you dine here, you have the feeling that owner Liza Slaman (who played Krystle Carrington's cousin Virginia on *Dynasty* for a season) and Turkish partner, Turgut Balikci, are in for a long run. The food is terrific. A *mezze* menu offers a tasting of three choices for $14.00 or individual dishes at $7.00 per item. Choices are tempters such as the bastilla (Moroccan-spiced pastry with squab and chicken), wild mushroom polenta cake, and crispy Greek pastry stuffed with feta cheese and fresh dill. If you move on to the list of appetizers and salads you'll find delightful choices such as lamb dumplings with yogurt and fresh mint ($8.00), braised duck and wild mushroom rigatoni ($16.00), lamb sausage risotto ($16.00), and spicy Caesar salad with toasted sweet croutons ($7.00). Main offerings include Moroccan roasted chicken ($15.00), whole oven-roasted red snapper with salsa and saffron rice ($22.00), spicy grilled marinated steak with roasted garlic and herb potato gratiné ($19.00), and crispy roasted duck with sweet potato cake, dates, ginger, and almonds ($18.00). Dessert might be rice pudding laced with rose water or apricots served with whipped cream inside a pastry basket.

The brunch menu offers a $12.00 prix fixe that includes a glass of Champagne, wine, or a Bloody Mary, along with a main course. The $17.00 prix fixe includes all of the above, plus a starter. Good starter options include a savory tart of the day with fresh greens ($7.00), a Mediterranean mixed salad with sun-dried tomatoes, crumbled feta, calamata olives, avocado, and watercress ($8.00), and fresh seasonal fruit salad with honey-sweetened yogurt ($8.00). Main choices include apple cinnamon sweet potato pancakes ($9.00), Spanish potato and onion torta with fresh greens ($9.00), and poached eggs over spinach purée wrapped in puff pastry ($10.00).

DOCKS OYSTER BAR AND SEAFOOD GRILL ★★   Seafood
2427 Broadway (89th St.)
212/724-5588
Lunch - Daily 11:30 a.m. - 3:00 p.m.
Dinner - Sunday through Thursday 3:00 - 11:00 p.m.
Friday and Saturday 3:00 p.m. - Midnight
All major cards

This amiable, old-fashioned seafood house has a casually handsome setting with posters and prints, black and white tile, lots of gleaming brass and wood, and waiters in long white aprons darting about. It has a comfy, neighborhood feel and a busy buzz that attests to its immense popularity.

The fresh seafood is served in a no-nonsense kind of way, nothing fancy but awfully good. Among favored starters: chowder ($4.75), steamers in beer broth ($9.00), fried calamari ($7.50), Maryland crab cake ($8.75), mussels in tomato and garlic ($8.00), and Caesar salad ($6.50). Grilled seafood—with choices of Norwegian salmon ($18.50), swordfish ($19.50), tuna ($19.50), and red snapper ($19.50)—is served with Docks crunchy slaw and a choice of potato or rice. The fried seafood offers the same accompaniments and is nicely done here—choices include sole ($17.00), scallops ($18.00), shrimp ($18.00), Ipswich clams ($18.00), and a mixed platter ($19.00). For those in a land-locked mindset, there's grilled New York shell steak ($22.00), grilled chicken ($14.50), or a Docks burger with bacon and/or cheese ($8.75). Desserts include a nice homemade key lime pie ($4.00), rich chocolate mud cake ($5.00), and gooey hot fudge sundaes ($5.50).

Sunday and Monday are New England clambake nights with a choice of twin one-pound lobsters ($24.00) or a two-pound lobster ($29.00) with salad, mussels, clams, new potatoes, corn-on-the-cob, and key lime pie or ice cream.

JOSIE'S ★★   Eclectic/Organic
300 Amsterdam Avenue (at 74th St.)
212/769-1212
Dinner - Monday 5:30 - 11:00 p.m.;
Tuesday through Saturday 5:30 - Midnight;
Sunday 5:00 - 11:00 p.m.
All major cards

This breezy spot adds an exciting flair to healthy dining. It's sleek, retro-funky setting has vinyl booths, potted plants, ceiling fans, and an undulating zinc bar with a very cool clientele. And (part-owner/actor) Rob Morrow's *Northern Exposure* doc character would have to approve of its health-conscious cuisine. If you've ever wondered whether really healthy fare could also be really good, the answer is certainly yes when you eat at Josie's.

All appetizers, mains, and pastas are prepared dairy free. You'll be off to a good start with the carrot, sweet potato, and onion dip that arrives with a platter of good onion focaccia and jalapeño cornbread to nibble while you decide on a starter. Great choices are the steamed three-potato dumplings in a lively tomato and white truffle oil coulis spiked with chipotle pepper ($5.50) and ginger grilled calamari with a pineapple red pepper salsa ($6.50). Other good selections include roasted butternut squash-sweet potato soup with toasted pumpkin seeds ($4.75) and Cuban black bean-corn soup ($4.75). Good seafood choices include grilled Atlantic salmon ($15.00) and seared cornmeal-coated Mississippi catfish ($13.75). Free-range poultry choices include teriyaki chicken breast with stir-fried seasonal vegetables ($12.75) and chicken fajitas with tomato-avocado salsa, cilantro pesto, and wholewheat tortillas ($12.75). Good pasta choices include sweet potato ravioli with Gulf shrimp, sweet corn, and roasted peppers in a white wine-leek sauce ($13.75) and spinach, basil, and walnut ravioli with a roasted vegetable marinara ($11.75). Vegetarian specialties include vegetable meatloaf with brown rice, red beans, and mashed potatoes ($10.75) and marinated portobello mushroom fajitas with tomato-avocado salsa and wholewheat tortillas ($11.75). All seafood, poultry, and meat entrées come with your choice of a side: barbecued baked beans with brown rice, three-potato mash, steamed vegetables, brown rice, mashed sweet potatoes, or the daily soft polenta. Desserts ($5.00) include both dairy-free choices and dairy delights like the luscious triple-chocolate mousse.

LE SELECT ★★   French
507 Columbus Avenue (between 84th and 85th Sts.)
212/875-1993
Lunch - Monday through Friday Noon - 4:00 p.m.
Brunch - Saturday and Sunday 11:30 a.m. - 4:00 p.m.
Dinner - Tuesday through Saturday 5:30 - Midnight;
Sunday and Monday 5:30 - 11:00 p.m.
All major cards

Le Select is an affectionate tip of the beret to the famed Montparnasse cafe where expatriate Americans gathered in the 1920s and 1930s. Its spirited atmosphere and moderate prices have already earned it a nice following here. The interior is a comfortable mix of art deco and provincial with a long oak bar, fanciful over-sized wall sconces, old brick walls, homey green banquettes, and restless ceiling fans.

The eclectic menu embraces classic French bistro favorites, Thai specialties, and a touch of Italian. Starters include a delicious onion soup ($5.25) and an exemplary Caesar salad ($6.50). Other good choices include warm goat cheese with mesclun salad ($7.00), leeks vinaigrette ($5.75), Thai spring roll with plum sauce ($6.50), marinated chicken brochette with curry, peanuts, lemon, and coconut milk ($6.50), and crab cake ($7.25). Mains show the same diversity with offerings like grilled Norwegian salmon with ratatouille ($16.25), red snapper with ginger and lemon sauce ($16.75), roast chicken and mashed potatoes ($14.50), roasted rack of lamb with potatoes gratin ($16.75), grilled ribeye steak with mesclun, fries, and béarnaise sauce ($18.50), penne with fresh basil and tomatoes confit ($12.25), spaghetti Bolognese ($13.50), roasted black sea bass with a spicy Thai sauce ($16.00), sautéed chicken with a red curry coconut milk sauce ($14.50), and sliced sautéed ginger pork with a soy sauce ($14.50). A changing assortment of desserts usually includes a nice variety of fruit tarts.

A two-course prix fixe is available until 7:30 p.m. for $19.95.

MISS ELLE'S HOMESICK BAR & GRILL ★   American
226 West 79th Street
(between Broadway and Amsterdam Ave.)
212/595-4350
Lunch - Monday through Friday 11:30 a.m. - 4:00 p.m.
Brunch - Saturday and Sunday Noon - 4:00 p.m.
Dinner - Daily 4:00 p.m. - Midnight
All major cards

When your dining budget is on the wane, or when you just have a craving for unfancy real home cooking, head for Miss Elle's. Housed in a charming landmark brownstone duplex, its interior is cheerful and inviting with soft colors and a pretty enclosed garden atrium. There's also an upstairs terrace with just one table. The Elle who now produces this home cooking—alongside fellow chef Jimmy Lam—is Elle Parrino, a former Playboy Bunny. You'll see pictures out front revealing this earlier Elle.

This very sweet place has friendly servers and a menu designed to accommodate just about any mood. If you grew up in an Italian family, you are no doubt familiar with the expression, "I'm not really hungry, I think I'll just pick." Well, Miss Elle even accommodates that kind of mood with an "I'll just pick..." section to the menu. And you know you've found a home-away-from-home when you can order a sandwich of leftovers and milk and cookies. While American homestyle dishes dominate the menu, it has a decided Italian accent with many old-fashioned Italian favorites from recipes handed down from Elle's mom. You might start with fried calamari ($4.95), escarole soup ($3.50), or tomatoes and mozzarella ($4.50). Main dishes are served with your choice of one side dish from a list that includes fried cauliflower, mashed potatoes, sweet or white fries, sautéed mushrooms, macaroni and cheese, pasta, Italian potato salad, and baked potatoes. Popular choices among mains include meatloaf ($8.95), pot roast with carrots ($9.95), roast turkey with stuffing ($10.50), and prime rib ($14.50). The homey Italian offerings include spaghetti with either meatballs or sausages ($8.95), rigatoni with meat sauce ($8.95), penne with fresh mozzarella, tomato, and basil ($9.95), and baked ziti ($8.95). Save room for dessert—they're homemade daily and include temptations like banana cream pie and chocolate fudge cake. You'll be homesick no more.

Every day an early bird dinner is served from 4:30 to 6:30 with your choice of soup of the day or salad, a main (from a selection of four or five), and dessert and coffee or tea ($12.95).

PHOEBE'S ★   American
380A Columbus Avenue (78th St.)
212/724-5145
Lunch - Monday through Friday Noon - 3:00 p.m.;
Brunch - Saturday 11:00 a.m. - 3:30 p.m.;
Sunday 10:00 a.m. - 3:30 p.m.
Dinner - Sunday through Thursday 5:30 - 11:00 p.m.;
Friday and Saturday 5:30 p.m. - Midnight
All major cards

This laid-back saloon has the feel of a neighborhood hangout. Its popular bar is particularly cozy on cold days when the fireplace—surrounded by couches—crackles with the warmth of a blazing fire. Exposed brick, terra-cotta-colored walls, and clouds painted on the ceiling add to its homey appeal. And in warm weather, sidewalk tables allow you to take in this pleasant neighborhood's street life.

The menu is a mix of American comfort food and contemporary American dishes with Far East and European influence. Satisfying starters include New England clam chowder ($3.75 cup; $4.50 bowl), grilled eggplant, tomato, arugula, and ricotta with a balsamic glaze ($6.50), and steamed Prince Edward Island mussels with white wine, lemon, and garlic ($6.50). For a light main, opt for the charred rare tuna with sesame noodles in a soy dipping sauce ($9.95), Thai chicken salad with cilantro vegetables, chilies, and crispy noodles ($10.95), or linguine with shrimp, scallops, clams, fennel, and roasted tomatoes in a marinara fish broth ($13.95). Other good pasta mains include black lobster ravioli with grilled zucchini and a pepper Vodka cream sauce ($12.95) and penne with fresh plum tomatoes, basil, and ricotta ($10.95). For more substantial fare, options include a marinated grilled pork chop with apple-ginger compote and caramelized onion mashed potatoes ($12.50), roasted chicken with spinach and caramelized onion mashed potatoes ($11.95), chicken pot pie ($11.95), grilled flank steak with portobello mushrooms and crispy onions ($13.95), and grilled sirloin burger with red onion and tomato salad and sweet potato fries ($8.95). When available, cobblers are the dessert of choice.

A prix fixe is available Monday through Friday from 5:30 to 7:00 p.m. with soup, salad, and a main for $14.95 ($11.95 for non-seafood, non-meat mains).

RAIN ★★   Pan-Asian
100 West 82nd Street (off Columbus Ave.)
212/501-0776
Lunch - Monday through Friday Noon - 3:00 p.m.;
Saturday and Sunday Noon - 4:00 p.m.
Dinner - Monday through Thursday 6:00 - 11:00 p.m.;
Friday 6:00 p.m. - Midnight; Saturday 5:00 - Midnight;
Sunday 5:00 - 10:00 p.m.
All major cards

Rain swept into this Upper West Side neighborhood in the spring of '95 and took it by storm. Situated in a beautiful old building that once housed an historic hotel, its ambience now evokes a tropical plantation house. You'll feel like a character in a Somerset Maugham novel sipping a tropical drink in its veranda-like lounge with leafy palms, tasseled lanterns, and rattan sofas and chairs. Beyond the lounge, the expansive, high-ceilinged dining room is handsome and spare with stenciled floors, columns, ceiling fans, classical wood accents, exposed brick, and large shuttered bay windows. Coveted fabric-enclosed booths provide a cozy oasis for a romantic rendezvous.

Bangkok-native chef Taweewat Hurapan presents an eclectic mix of good Thai, Vietnamese, and Malaysian dishes. Meals begin with a basket of fresh shrimp chips with a delicious peanut dipping sauce. One of the best starters is a charred beef salad with lemongrass, basil, and chilies in a lime vinaigrette ($9.50). Other top choices are the Vietnamese spring rolls with shrimp, vegetables, glass noodle filling, and plum sauce ($5.50) and Vietnamese steamed ravioli with lump crab, bean sprouts, and chili-soy sauce ($8.50). Other good choices include a nice, spicy green papaya salad ($6.50), a Malaysian-style mixed green salad with warm peanut dressing ($5.50), Thai-style crab cakes with toasted coconut sauce ($8.50), shrimp and chicken parcels with a tamarind sauce ($7.50), Malaysian chicken satay with cucumber salad and peanut sauce ($6.50), and chicken and coconut soup ($5.00). There's also the traditional Phad Thai with noodles, chicken, shrimp, bean sprouts, and egg ($8.00). The best of the mains include stir-fried beef in a Malaysian peanut curry sauce ($13.00), fresh green curry chicken ($13.00), stir-fried prawns and pineapple in a red curry stew ($14.50), and peppery grilled roasted salmon with garlic served in a banana leaf ($15.50). Other good choices include sautéed chicken with cashews and assorted vegetables ($12.00), and stir-fried spicy jumbo shrimp with bamboo shoots, fresh chilies, basil, and lemongrass ($16.50). Of the daily dessert specials, the rich chocolate cake ($5.00) outshines its more exotic sidekicks.

RESTAURANT TWO TWO TWO ★★★   American
222 West 79th Street
(between Amsterdam Ave. and Broadway)
212/799-0400
Dinner - Daily 5:00 - 11:00 p.m.
All major cards

A lovely turn-of-the-century skylit townhouse with ornate chandeliers, oak panelling, and an enclosed garden provides an intimate setting at this romantic restaurant. Velvet drapes and gold-framed mirrors recall 19th Century elegance and add to the special occasion feel of the place.

The food is American with French and Italian overtones. It is utterly delicious and beautifully presented. Dazzling first courses include house-cured gravlax with a warm potato cake, horseradish, mascarpone, and black and red caviar ($13.00), a green salad with grilled tomato and parmesan cheese melt in a shallot vinaigrette ($9.00), and seared peppered tuna with Asian mixed greens, ginger, wasabi vinaigrette, and chopped scallions ($14.00). Superb main choices include oak-fired sirloin with creamy horseradish whipped potatoes, caramelized carrots, shallots, and a wild mushroom ragu ($36.00), filet of Canadian salmon pan-seared and served on a potato scallion cake with grilled vegetables and a Cabernet wine reduction ($27.00), and penne in a porcini cream sauce encircled with wild seasonal mushrooms ($20.00). Desserts are delicious. Choices include warm chocolate cake with a molten chocolate center served with homemade vanilla bean ice cream ($8.50), Granny Smith baked apple in phyllo with cinnamon honey ice cream and caramel sauce ($8.75), and a light maple crème brûlée with a crisp raw sugar crackling crust ($8.50).

A pre-theater menu is available from 5:00 to 6:30 p.m. with three courses for $36.00.

SAVANNAH CLUB ★★   Southern/Soul
2420 Broadway
(corner of W. 89th St.)
212/496-1066
Lunch - Daily Noon - 4:00 p.m.
Dinner - Daily 5:00 p.m. - 1:00 a.m.
All major cards

Soaring ceilings, fabric-covered walls, white tile floors, and whirring ceilings fans create a pleasant backdrop for the terrific soul food dished up at this bright and welcome Savannah-styled newcomer to the Upper West Side dining scene.

Chef Sarah Bonner hails from Opelika, Alabama, and her only professional experience was cooking for a few years at a soul food restaurant—Fred's Kitchen in Brooklyn—owned by her brother. Maybe that's why her food is so unjaded, so unsophisticated, so downhome, and so good. When you dine here, you'll be greeted with a bread basket of biscuits and cornbread with sweet-potato butter and onion jam that offers the first glimmer of comfort-food heaven. You'll be well under way with starters like catfish fritters with homemade okra pickles ($6.95) Southern-fried oysters with green onion tartar sauce ($6.95), and lump crab and green onion griddle cakes ($7.95). You can also get a good BBQ on a bun ($7.95) or a Po'Boy (chicken $7.95, catfish $8.95). But the real reason to come here is for Mama's fried chicken served with cream gravy, mashed potatoes, and collards ($11.95). Tuck into this juicy treat, and you'll understand why owner John Valenti pursued Mrs. Bonner for his kitchen. Another Savannah Club specialty is chicken and dumplings ($10.95). Other pleasures on the list of mains include homestyle meatloaf with onion gravy, mashed potatoes, and succotash ($10.95), griddle-fried hamsteak with ginger gravy and candied yams ($12.95), smothered pork chops with candied yams and corn-on-the-cob ($11.95), and pan-roasted salmon on a bed of spinach ($12.95). Desserts are good, too. Choose from temptations like sweet potato pie ($4.95), fresh fruit cobblers ($4.95), bananas Foster with ice cream ($5.95), and dark chocolate pie with whipped sweet cream ($4.95).

An early bird special (which changes daily) is available from 4:00 to 7:30 p.m. with three courses for $9.95.

SCALETTA ★★   Italian
50 West 77th Street
(between Central Park West and Columbus Ave.)
212/769-9191
Dinner - Daily 5:00 - 11:00 p.m.
All major cards

Scaletta's dining room is light and lovely. The spacious room—bathed in soft, soothing shades of peach, green, rose, and blue—has arches, pillars, and frosted windows. Roomy, well-spaced tables add to its comfortably elegant feel. You wonder why it's not more crowded.

The Northern Italian menu offers a terrific selection of starters: baby artichokes and mushrooms sautéed with olive oil and garlic ($7.50), scampi on a bed of tomatoes and leeks ($9.95), lightly-breaded baked clams ($7.75), fresh buffalo mozzarella with tomatoes and roasted peppers ($7.25), and grilled vegetables ($7.25). Pasta choices include goat cheese ravioli with sun-dried tomatoes in a porcini cream sauce ($14.50), lasagna Bolognese ($13.95), angel hair with fresh vegetables ($14.25), rigatoni with broccoli, garlic, and olive oil ($12.95), and spaghetti Bolognese ($13.25). Half portions are $7.75. Good choices among mains include grilled Atlantic salmon with a mustard sauce ($18.95), Louisiana shrimp in a marinara sauce with Bombay rice ($19.25), breast of chicken served with braised wild mushrooms ($15.25), chicken breast stuffed with cheese and wild mushrooms ($15.25), veal with eggplant, prosciutto, and mozzarella in a white wine sauce ($17.25), grilled veal chop ($22.95), and grilled sirloin ($20.95). A changing selection of rich Italian desserts and good expresso round out this pleasant dining experience.

WEST SIDE
LINCOLN CENTER

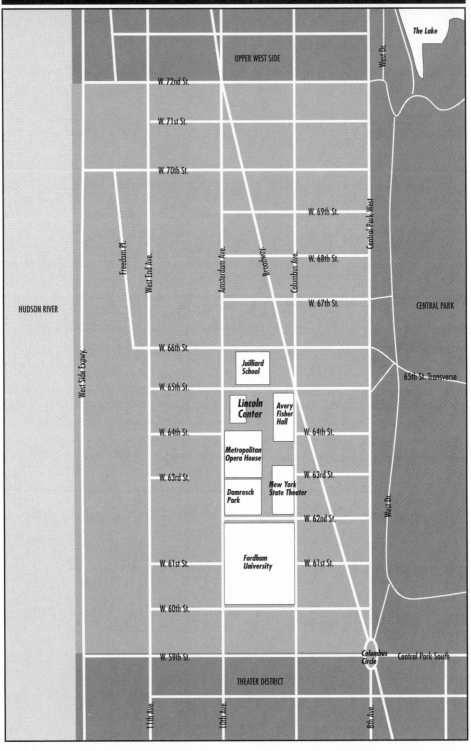

THE LAKE

UPPER WEST SIDE

W. 72nd St.

W. 71st St.

W. 70th St.

W. 69th St.

Central Park West

W. 68th St.

Freedom Pl.

West End Ave.

Amsterdam Ave.

Broadway

Columbus Ave.

W. 67th St.

CENTRAL PARK

HUDSON RIVER

West Side Expwy.

W. 66th St.

Juilliard School

W. 65th St.

65th St. Transverse

Lincoln Center

Avery Fisher Hall

W. 64th St.

W. 64th St.

Metropolitan Opera House

W. 63rd St.

W. 63rd St.

New York State Theater

Damrosch Park

W. 62nd St.

West Dr.

Fordham University

W. 61st St.

W. 61st St.

W. 60th St.

W. 59th St.

Columbus Circle

Central Park South

THEATER DISTRICT

11th Ave.

10th Ave.

8th Ave.

CAFÉ DES ARTISTES ★★★   French
1 West 67th Street
(between Columbus Ave. and Central Park West)
212/877-3500
Lunch - Monday through Friday Noon - 3:00 p.m.
Brunch - Saturday 11:00 a.m. - 3:00 p.m.;
Sunday 10:00 a.m. - 3:00 p.m.
Dinner - Daily 5:30 - Midnight
All major cards

With its leaded glass windows, ornate mirrors, luxurious floral arrangements, and Howard Chandler Christy's effervescent murals of frolicking nude wood nymphs, this is one of the West Side's most enchanting restaurants. Its saucy and romantic setting lures a loyal following of television personalities and celebrities such as Barbara Walters, Peter Jennings, Paul Newman, and Kathleen Turner. It was also the choice of President Clinton on his one free night during the United Nations' 50th Anniversary celebrations. A celebrity in its own right, Café des Artistes was the setting of *My Dinner with Andre* as well as where Anjelica Houston and Woody Allen lunched in *Manhattan Murder Mystery*.

Its location, as well as its many charms, makes this a perfect spot for before or after a Lincoln Center performance. It is housed in the gracious Hotel des Artistes apartment building, built in 1918, which provided studios for artists such as Norman Rockwell and Christy. Other famous residents included Rudolf Valentino, Isadora Duncan, and Noel Coward. Entering off the lobby, you'll find the main dining room dominated by an old-fashioned three-tiered buffet table boasting a sensuous display of desserts amidst a profusion of flowers and greenery. The atmosphere in the back dining room is more intimate, with cozy booths around a beautiful mahogany bar gently illuminated by old-fashioned glass fixtures suspended from the ceiling. In keeping with its old-world European atmosphere, **men must wear jackets after 5:00 p.m.**

The French and European bourgeois menu is wide-ranging. You might start with black bean soup ($9.00), salmon four ways—smoked, poached, dill-marinated, and tartare ($16.00 for one, $30.00 for two), sliced short ribs of beef vinaigrette ($11.00), shrimp, scallop, and squid salad with a spicy lemon-cilantro dressing ($12.00), or with a charcuterie assortment with walnut pâté, prosciutto, and smoked pork loin ($16.00 for one, $22.00 for two). For the main, notable choices include poached or grilled salmon ($28.00), sturgeon schnitzel with sauce remoulade and a cucumber salad ($27.00), free-range chicken with roasted potatoes ($27.00), breast of veal stuffed with homemade sausage and chestnuts ($29.00), grilled loin of lamb with ratatouille ($29.00), penne with spinach-basil pesto ($19.00), and steak au poivre ($29.00). Desserts are spectacular. Choices include key lime pie ($7.00), banana coconut cake ($7.00), lemon crumb cake ($7.00), chocolate peanut butter candy bar mousse cake ($7.00), old-fashioned baking powder biscuit strawberry shortcake ($7.50), and a terrific hot fudge sundae ($8.00). There are also a couple real extravaganzas: "chocolatissimo" for two—a platter of chocolate-based treats to make chocolate lovers swoon ($19.50) and "the great dessert plate" with a bit of everything (also $19.50).

A three-course prix fixe dinner menu is offered at $35.00 ($22.00 at lunch). Each changes daily.

FISHIN EDDIE ★★   Seafood
73 West 71st Street
(Columbus Ave.)
212/874-3474
Dinner Only - Daily 5:00 p.m. - Midnight
All major cards

Its atrium-like setting, warm colors, faux-antique farmhouse tables, painted furniture, and tiny brass table lamps lend a sunny atmosphere to this very pleasant fish house. Comforting as a port in a storm, its weather-beaten, nautical ambience will give you that old Cape Cod feeling.

The seafood is invariably fresh, and the menu is varied, inventive, and quite pleasing. Among starters, you'll find good fresh fried oysters with fennel slaw and cilantro-lime sauce ($8.95), wonderful Chesapeake Bay crab cakes with corn relish ($11.95), steamed Maine mussels with herbed broth ($8.50), Maine fish and smoked ham chowder ($6.25), and a delightful salad of endive leaves stuffed with julienned apples, roquefort, and walnut chunks in a Champagne vinaigrette ($8.95). For the main, try the New England cod with laced potatoes and sauce Veronique ($17.95), swordfish Oscar with a watercress garnish ($20.95), tuna steak au poivre with fries ($19.95), butterflied shrimp and garden tomatoes with penne pasta ($17.50), or homemade Maine lobster ravioli ($20.95). There's also pan-roasted chicken with great garlic mashed potatoes ($16.50) and chargrilled New York strip steak with homemade fries ($19.95). Dessert might be something as warming as a berry cobbler or as refreshing as a cool pear sorbet.

GABRIEL'S ★★   Italian
11 West 60th Street
(between Broadway and Columbus)
212/956-4600
Lunch - Monday through Friday Noon - 3:00 p.m.
Dinner - Monday through Thursday 5:30 - 11:00 p.m.;
Friday and Saturday 5:30 p.m. - Midnight
All major cards

This terrific restaurant is a top choice for dining near Lincoln Center. But it is not just theatergoers and people from the neighborhood who flock here, it is also a favorite of performers and media types. And while neighboring tables might have faces more well-known than yours, owner Gabriel Aiello is the kind of doting host that makes everyone feel special.

The rectangular dining room has a long mahogany bar up front and high ceilings. Comfortable and convivial, the decor would be rather dull were it not for the huge modern paintings by Gabriel's wife Christine Keefe.

The food is wonderful with a seasonal menu that often strays from the traditional with delicious surprises. While billed as Tuscan, the food has such a strong American influence that portions of the menu are as much American with Italian orientation as Italian with American influence. But, never mind! It is all immensely satisfying. Starter choices might include roasted beets and onions with green beans and goat cheese with basil-flavored olive oil ($7.50), wood-grilled portobello mushrooms topped with raddichio and smoked mozzarella served with a sweet and sour balsamic sauce ($10.00), wood-grilled pork short ribs over polenta with roasted cabbage and whole grain mustard ($10.00), spicy mussel soup ($9.00), and roasted and marinated fresh shrimp served over a white bean and tomato salad ($12.00). Pastas are sensational. A big favorite is the light, homemade gnocchi with tomato and basil ($16.00). Other fine choices include mushroom lasagna ($18.00), fettuccine with sweet sausage and hot and sweet peppers ($17.50), potato ravioli mixed with meat sauce ($17.00), and tagliatelle with garlic, olive oil, white wine, hot peppers, and baby clams ($17.00). Mains are delightful as well. Choose from a tempting array that includes rabbit cacciatore over polenta with peppers, onions, and wild mushrooms ($25.00) and roasted mackerel filet over couscous with red onions and radicchio braised with balsamic vinegar ($24.00). The wood-grilled specialties are wonderful: chicken marinated with buttermilk and rosemary and served with mashed potatoes, onions, and hot peppers ($23.00); strip steak with garlic-flavored olive oil, parsley, and black pepper, served with mashed potatoes and broccoli rabe ($27.00); and brook trout wrapped in prosciutto and topped with lemon, capers, and olive oil and served with roasted potatoes and spinach ($25.00). Desserts are nice, too. Choose from the likes of toasted lemon-blueberry pound cake with walnut gelato ($8.00), dark and white flourless chocolate cake with raspberry coulis ($8.00), and baked rice pudding served with an orange caramel sauce ($8.00). Gelatos and sorbets ($7.00) are other good options.

LA BOÎTE EN BOIS ★★   French
75 West 68th Street
(between Columbus Ave. and Central Park West)
212/874-2705
Lunch - Monday through Saturday Noon - 2:00 p.m.
Brunch - Sunday 11:30 a.m. - 2:30 p.m.
Dinner - Daily 5:00 - 11:00 p.m.
No Credit Cards

Old farm implements and pastoral paintings adorn the plank wood walls in this tiny bistro on the ground floor of a townhouse near Lincoln Center. Copper pots and pans and pretty floral arrangements in big ceramic vases add to its homey charm. True to its name ("wooden box"), it is snug and romantic. With its lack of pretension, simple classic bistro fare, and nostalgic setting, it is a Lincoln Center favorite. And with only 15 tables, booking is essential for pre-theater.

The well-prepared bistro fare has the taste of the French countryside in starters such as warm sausage with lentils ($6.00) and a salad of French string beans and wild mushrooms ($6.50). Other popular starters include home-cured smoked salmon with a chive sauce ($8.00) and seafood crêpes with a tomato coulis ($6.50). House specialties among mains are the grilled salmon with black olives and anchovy butter ($19.00), fish stew ($20.00), pan-roasted chicken with herbs ($17.00), and entrecôte au poivre ($21.00). Crème brûlée is the star dessert.

Sunday brunch is $17.00 prix fixe. It includes a choice of assorted juices, soup or mesclun salad, a main course, and dessert with coffee or tea. Main choices include chicken hash, goat cheese and herb omelette, poached eggs Benedict or Florentine, and a ragout of escargots with roquefort and angel hair pasta. For dessert: lemon sorbet, fresh fruit salad, chocolate mouse, or ricotta cheesecake.

A pre-theater menu is offered between 5:30 and 6:30 p.m. with three courses for $29.00. There are many choices in each category. Starter selections include soup of the day, leeks vinaigrette, smoked trout with a chive sauce, and mussels Marseillaise. For the main, you might choose scallops and shrimp with ginger, cod with roasted onions, pan-roasted chicken, or braised duck in red wine.

O'NEALS ★   American
49 West 64th Street
(between Broadway and Central Park West)
212/787-4663
Lunch - Monday through Friday 11:15 a.m. - 4:30 p.m.;
Saturday and Sunday 10:00 a.m. - 4:00 p.m.
Dinner - Sunday through Thursday 4:30 - 11:00 p.m.;
Friday and Saturday 4:30 - Midnight or so
All major cards

O'Neal's is a good example of the casual and laidback attitude of this neighborhood. The pretty art-filled restaurant space—once a warehouse—is colorful and inviting. It has a nice relaxed feel and a particularly charming bar. Situated directly opposite Lincoln Center, it is a very popular destination for theatergoers.

The menu offers straightforward American fare that is reliably good. To start, there's onion soup with melted gruyere and croutons ($5.95), mushroom pie (sautéed wild mushrooms with diced potatoes and frizzled leeks in a pastry shell) ($6.95), and avocado, hearts of palm, and red onion salad with a coriander vinaigrette ($6.95). Most popular among mains are the chicken pot pie ($14.95) and BBQ baby back ribs with cornbread and mashed potatoes ($15.95). Other good choices include broiled shrimp curry with basmati rice ($17.95) and sirloin steak with garlic mashed potatoes and fresh vegetables ($23.95). You can also get a good burger here with homemade fries ($12.95).

The Sunday brunch menu offers eggs Norwegian (poached eggs atop an English muffin with smoked salmon and hollandaise sauce ($7.95), six different styles of omelettes ($7.95-$8.50), seared rare tuna served on Caesar salad ($10.95), and grilled chicken breast and eggplant on country bread with arugula, mild jalapeño cheese, and herbed aïoli ($8.95).

PICHOLINE ★★★   Mediterranean
35 West 64th Street
(between Broadway and Central Park West)
212/724-8585
Lunch - Tuesday through Saturday Noon - 2:30 p.m.
Dinner - Daily 5:30 - 11:30 p.m.
All major cards

This enjoyable place—named after a Mediterranean olive—has a warm, French country ambience and is just a stone's throw from Lincoln Center. Green and white checkered fabric wallcoverings, sprays of dried flowers, Italian pottery, and French country antiques set the scene. Though the dining areas are quite pleasant and comfortable, the wonderful food and extraordinary cheese cellar are what have earned Picholine its reputation as one of the top restaurants in the Lincoln Center area. Theatergoers flock here both before and after the curtain.

Chef/owner Terrance Brennan's innovative approach to cooking is evident right up front in starters such as his signature grilled octopus with fennel, potato, and lemon-pepper vinaigrette ($11.50) and sheeps milk ricotta gnocchi with wild mushrooms, Swiss chard, and butternut squash ($12.75). Other good starters include the house salad with grilled vegetables, feta cheese, olives, and pine nuts ($10.50) and crabmeat salad with avocado and a citrus vinaigrette ($13.00). One of the best-loved mains is wild mushroom and duck risotto ($23.00). Other outstanding selections include salmon in a horseradish crust served with cucumbers and salmon caviar ($25.50), daube of beef short ribs with caramelized root vegetables and potato purée ($26.50), poached halibut with eggplant pancakes and tomato confit ($25.00), and Moroccan-spiced loin of lamb with vegetable couscous and minted yogurt ($26.50). If you opt for dessert instead of selections from the amazing cheese tray, you'll find many great choices—coconut tuile cannoli with chocolate mousse and roast banana sauce, maple pumpkin bread pudding, lemon curd Napoleon, and Valrhona chocolate cake with pistachio ice cream and two sauces.

There's a five-course signature tasting menu for $68.00 and an $80.00 seven-course tasting menu which changes daily.

THE SALOON ★   Eclectic
1920 Broadway (64th St.)
212/874-1500
All day menu Monday through Friday 11:30 a.m. - Midnight;
Brunch Saturday and Sunday 11:00 a.m. - 3:00 p.m.
and regular menu 3:00 p.m. - Midnight
All major cards

The Saloon is known locally for its jovial atmosphere, huge menu, and sensational sidewalk cafe where all seats face the street and provide the ultimate vantage point for watching this West Side neighborhood in action. With a location just opposite Lincoln Center, its cavernous, funky interior has a decidedly busy buzz near curtain time. And with some of the waitstaff zipping around on roller skates, the frenzied feel of the place intensifies. But if you don't feel the press of time, this can be an enjoyable spot for a casual meal at a good price.

Its enormous menu scans the globe with no ethnic commitment whatsoever. Starters might be grilled asparagus and smoked salmon ($7.50), Chinatown shrimp dumplings with an oriental stir-fry in a ginger sesame dressing ($7.95), crispy fried calamari with a spicy plum tomato sauce ($6.95), guacamole Pueblo-style with salsa, tortillas, and chili-dusted potato chips ($6.50), or fennel and onion soup ($4.50). A tempting variety of wafer thin pizzas with all sorts of interesting topping combos range from $6.50 to $7.95. Sandwich selections include sliced roast sirloin on a semolina roll with fresh horseradish, grilled onions, and melted provolone ($9.50), salmon club on 7-grain bread ($9.50), ciabatta with fresh mozzarella, roasted red and yellow peppers, roma tomatoes, red onion, and basil with extra virgin olive oil ($8.50), and a sirloin burger on a grilled tomcat roll with crisp fries ($7.50). Satisfying pasta choices include rigatoni with roasted eggplant in a plum tomato sauce with pancetta, sliced red onion, and hard ricotta ($12.95), wild asparagus ravioli with fresh tomato sauce ($13.95), and penne with grilled salmon tossed with roasted bell peppers, fresh asparagus, and sweet onions ($13.95). Of the mains, top choices are pan-roasted chicken breast with a fricassée of wild mushrooms, smoked bacon, roasted potatoes, and pearl onions ($13.95) and pan-fried pork tenderloin with whipped sweet potatoes, braised red cabbage, and a Port wine shallot compote ($14.95). Other options include grilled sirloin and fries with fire-roasted onion gravy ($17.95), grilled Atlantic salmon on tomato mashed potatoes with crisp arugula and a roasted red pepper sauce ($16.95), and pan-roasted Florida red snapper filet with saffron couscous, grilled vegetables, and fresh tomato-basil vinaigrette ($16.95). Dessert choices include Mississippi mud cake with lots of whipped cream and chocolate sauce ($4.50), pecan pie with vanilla bean ice cream ($4.75), and flourless chocolate cake with warm chocolate sauce ($4.75).

The Sunday prix fixe brunch is $12.95. It includes a Bloody Mary, Mimosa, Champagne, wine, or juice, along with mains like traditional eggs Benedict; smoked salmon Benedict with tomato; Santa Fe egg scramble with poblano chilies, Monterey Jack cheese, tomato, and onions, rolled in flour tortillas; and sliced sirloin with eggs. All egg dishes are served with hash browns and sautéed vegetables. Other choices might be a salmon platter with onion, tomato, cream cheese, and a bagel or New Orleans-style French toast with maple Bourbon syrup. Coffee and tea, too.

TAVERN ON THE GREEN ★★   American
Central Park at West 67th Street
212/873-3200
Lunch - Monday through Friday 11:30 a.m. - 3:45 p.m.
Brunch - Saturday and Sunday 10:00 a.m. - 3:30 p.m.
Dinner - Monday through Thursday 5:00 - 10:30 p.m.;
Friday and Saturday 5:00 - 11:30 p.m.
Sunday 5:00 - 10:30 p.m.
All major cards

The glittery fantasy world that is Tavern on the Green was originally a sheepfold for a flock of Southdown sheep that grazed in Central Park's Sheep Meadow in the late 19th Century. Today, it is out-of-town visitors who flock here. It is the city's top-grossing and most famous restaurant, renowned for a setting that is one of the prettiest and most festive in town. Situated in the heart of Central Park, its interior is one of dazzling theatrical ostentation. Outside, it is pure magic. Its famous tiny, twinkling tree lights (500,000 of them) hug the trees in fall and winter; in spring and summer they are replaced by a thousand colorful chintz-covered lanterns.

The over-the-top interior—comprised of a souvenir shop, halls-a-plenty, and six spectacular dining rooms overlooking three beautiful gardens—is a celebration of excess and eye-popping flamboyance. Each dining room has its own distinctive, lavish decor. Grandiose chandeliers, elaborate mirrors, lovely floral displays, and garden views are common themes. The most sought-after tables are in the Crystal Room where shimmering crystal chandeliers create a glittering oasis of light. Its walls of glass allow fabulous vistas of Central Park where the twinkling snow-covered trees of winter create a frosty fantasyland and in summer its fabulous topiary display provides a backdrop both bucolic and festive. The Chestnut Room, a rustic contrast, is a baroque vision of brass, copper, and carved mirrors overlooking the Chestnut Garden. Performances by jazz and pop musicians are featured here. And from May to October (weather permitting), the charming Crystal Garden is (for me) the most stunning space and my absolute first choice for where to dine here. It is also a terrific spot for brunch. With Lincoln Center a pleasant two-and-a-half block stroll away, combining the two makes a great outing. While many New Yorkers dismiss this flashy park palace as a tourist haven, I suspect that they, too, find it a celebratory kind of place every now and again.

The food here used to play second fiddle to the setting and was mediocre at best. Since award-winning chef Patrick Clark came on board as Executive Chef there's been a culinary reawakening in the kitchen. For starters, there are lively choices such as portobello mushroom "pizza" with onions, poblano chilies, and eggplant ($10.50), crab and corn tart with a toasted corn sauce ($12.00), goat cheese and artichoke tortelloni with spring peas and tomatoes ($12.00), seared potato gnocchi with artichokes and grilled shrimp ($12.50), and Maytag blue cheese strudel with mixed greens, roasted pear, and grilled portobello mushrooms ($11.50). For the main, the grilled pork porterhouse with pancetta mashed potatoes, caraway-scented cabbage, and tomato and sage jus ($27.00) is terrific. Other delicious choices include mustard-glazed salmon on spinach with old-fashioned mashed potatoes ($27.00), grilled Atlantic swordfish with roasted eggplant, marinated peppers, and basil-garlic broth ($28.00), lemon-glazed rotisserie chicken with garlic mashed potatoes and haricots verts ($26.00), roast rack of lamb with a pine nut herb crust, eggplant pudding, and Swiss chard ($31.00), and Black Angus sirloin with red potatoes, balsamic onions, and Zinfandel sauce ($33.00). Desserts (around $7.00) include a good crème brûlée and cheesecake. But the towering banana split is the top choice.

A seasonal pre-theater menu is offered Monday through Friday from 5:00 to 6:45 p.m. The price of the main includes a starter and dessert. Your starter choice might be the soup of the day, penne with plum tomatoes and crushed red pepper, or Caesar salad. Mustard-glazed roast salmon ($28.50) and rotisserie chicken ($27.00) from the regular menu are offered as mains, as well as specials like grilled lamb steak with zucchini, pearl onions, and a fresh thyme red wine sauce ($27.50) and fettuccine with shrimp, mushrooms, and zucchini ($25.50). For dessert, choose from a selection that includes crème brûlée with praline wafers, New York cheesecake, and chocolate layer cake with malted milk ice cream.

VINCE & EDDIE'S ★★   American
70 West 68th Street
(between Columbus Ave. and Central Park West)
212/721-0068
Lunch - Monday through Saturday Noon - 3:00 p.m.
Brunch - Sunday 11:00 a.m. - 3:00 p.m.
Dinner - Daily 5:00 p.m. - Midnight
All major cards

This Lincoln Center neighbor is like a breath of New England. Loaded with charm, it has the ambience of a country cottage. Low ceilings, bare wooden floors, old tools on the walls, mismatched chairs, and country antiques give the place a wonderfully rustic feel. And while it can be considered cozy or cramped—depending on your outlook—its romantic appeal is undeniable. In winter, its fireplace crackles with warmth and in summer its delightful back garden beckons diners to sup under its sheltering maple tree.

In keeping with its homey setting, the food is old-fashioned hearty American fare, but with contemporary overtones. The menu changes often and Executive Chef Scott Campbell (formerly of Le Cirque and Union Square Cafe) keeps it interesting. Openers might include Scottish lamb and barley soup ($6.50), endive salad with roquefort and walnuts ($8.95), crisp calamari with cilantro lime sauce ($8.50), Chesapeake crab cakes with sauce Diablo ($11.95), or Finnan Haddie and new potatoes chowder ($10.25). Current mains include grilled filet of salmon with broccoli and mushrooms ($19.95), roast Yankee leg of lamb with whole grains ($17.95), pan-roasted chicken with spinach and lentils ($16.50), chargrilled sirloin and steak fries ($20.95), and braised lamb shank and mashed turnips with Michigan cherry sauce ($17.95). Spring for a side of whipped potatoes ($4.95) and you'll have a delicious treat. For dessert ($6.25), fruit cobblers and caramelized apple tart are winners.

On Sundays, the brunch menu entices with offerings like Austrian apple pancakes ($9.75), Georgian pecan waffles ($9.50), wholewheat wild rice flapjacks with maple syrup ($9.95), Virginia country-style eggs Benedict ($10.50), corned beef hash and poached eggs with cheddar cheese grits ($11.75), and griddle corncakes with apple butter ($9.25).

INDEX

RESTAURANTS BY AREA AND CUISINE

CHELSEA

EAST SIDE

EAST VILLAGE

(GREENWICH VILLAGE continued)

MIDTOWN

(MIDTOWN continued)

THEATER DISTRICT

(THEATER DISTRICT continued)

UNION SQUARE
GRAMERCY PARK
MURRAY HILL

UPPER EAST SIDE

WEST SIDE
LINCOLN CENTER

OPEN ON SATURDAY
FOR LUNCH

OPEN ON SUNDAY

RESTAURANT INDEX

GENERAL INDEX

ORDER FORM

ON AND OFF BROADWAY
A Theater/Dining/Lodging Guide to New York City

If you borrowed this book and would like to buy one of your own, or would like to give a copy as a gift to a fellow theater lover, please check with your local bookstore. If it is unavailable, you may order directly from the publisher.

Name _____

Street _____

City _____

State _____ Zip Code _____

Each book is $17.95. Please add $4.00 for the first book and $1.00 for each additional book to cover postage and packaging. Maryland residents add 5 percent sales tax ($.90). Send this form with your check to:

Britain Books
P. O. Box 66005
Department BNY
Washington, DC 20035-6005

Please inquire about bulk discounts.

F R E E

ON AND OFF BROADWAY
A Monthly Theater/Dining Guide to New York City

This monthly guide contains the latest information on restaurants near both Broadway and Off-Broadway theaters, with details on cuisine, ambience, current menus, and prices. It also features up-to-date information on Broadway and Off-Broadway productions.

To receive a free two-month subscription, please mail a copy of this form to Britain Books.

To Britain Books
Newsletter Office
P.O. Box 66005
Washington, DC 20035-6005

Please enter a free two-month subscription to *On and Off Broadway* to the following:

Name _____

Street _____

City _____

State _____ Zip Code _____

For information on yearly subscriptions (which include a free book), please contact Britain Books at the above address or telephone 301/858-6213.